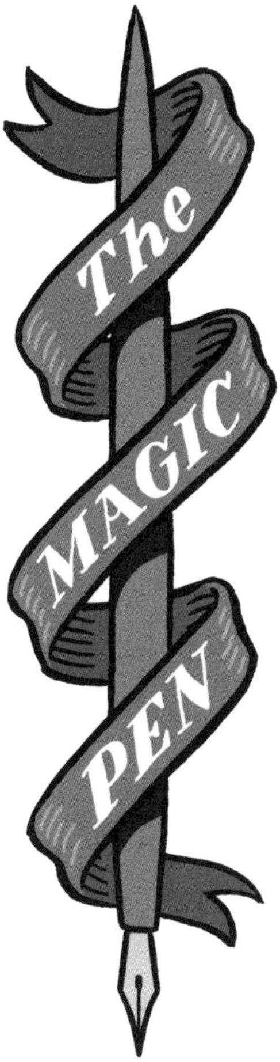
The
MAGIC
PEN

SAM ZABEL AND THE MAGIC PEN

DYLAN HORROCKS

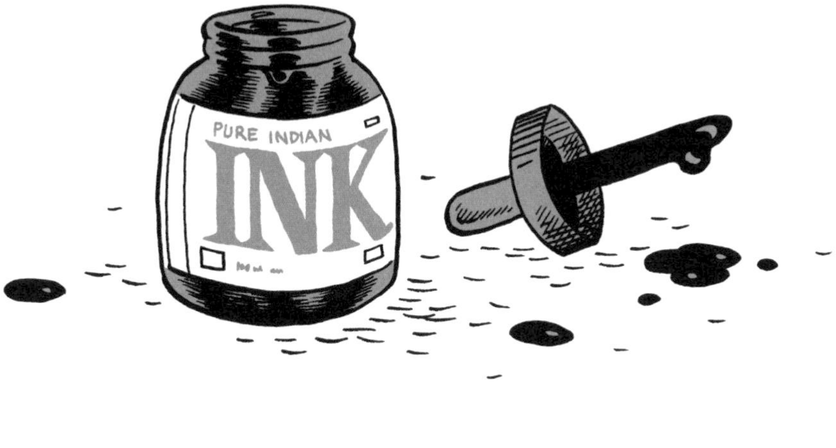
PURE INDIAN
INK

FANTAGRAPHICS BOOKS INC.

FANTAGRAPHICS BOOKS, INC.
Seattle, Washington, USA
www.fantagraphics.com

Coloring assistance: Sophie Dumas, Jonathan King, and Abe Horrocks
Production assistance: Paul Baresh
Editor and Associate Publisher: Eric Reynolds
Publisher: Gary Groth

First Fantagraphics Books printing: December 2014
Printed in Singapore

ISBN 978-1-60699-790-1

For...

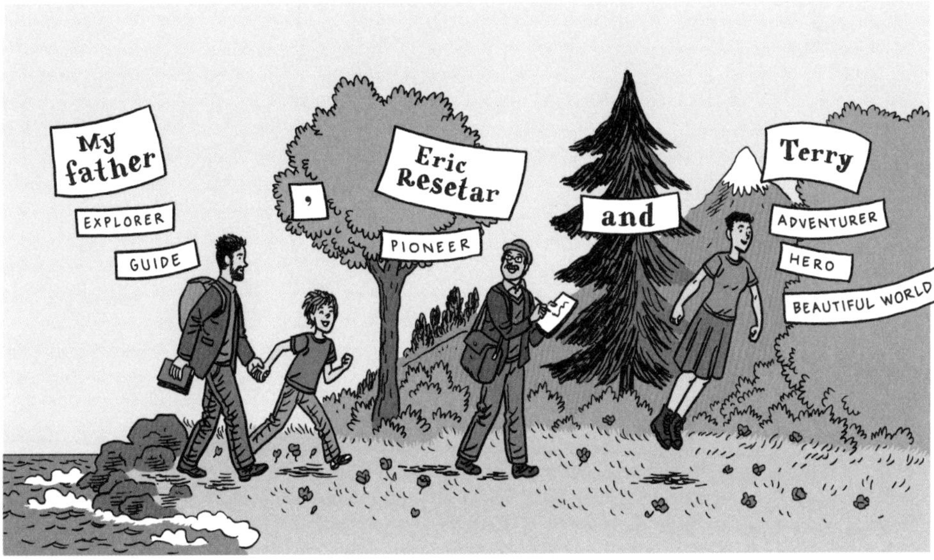
My father
EXPLORER
GUIDE
,
Eric Resetar
PIONEER
and
Terry
ADVENTURER
HERO
BEAUTIFUL WORLD

"IN DREAMS BEGINS RESPONSIBILITY."
William Butler Yeats

" DESIRE HAS NO MORALITY."
Nina Hartley

CHAPTER ONE

ANHEDONIA

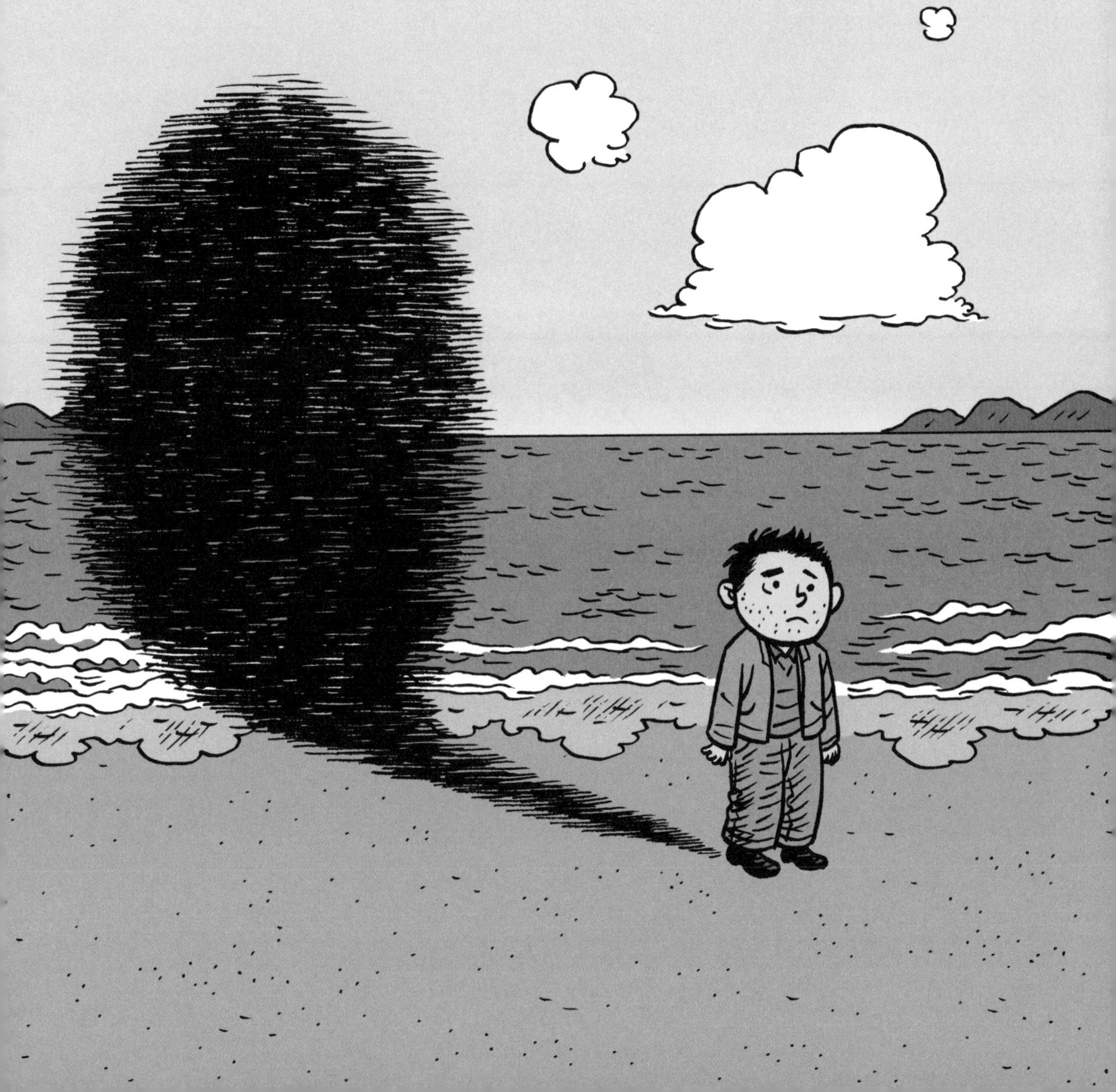

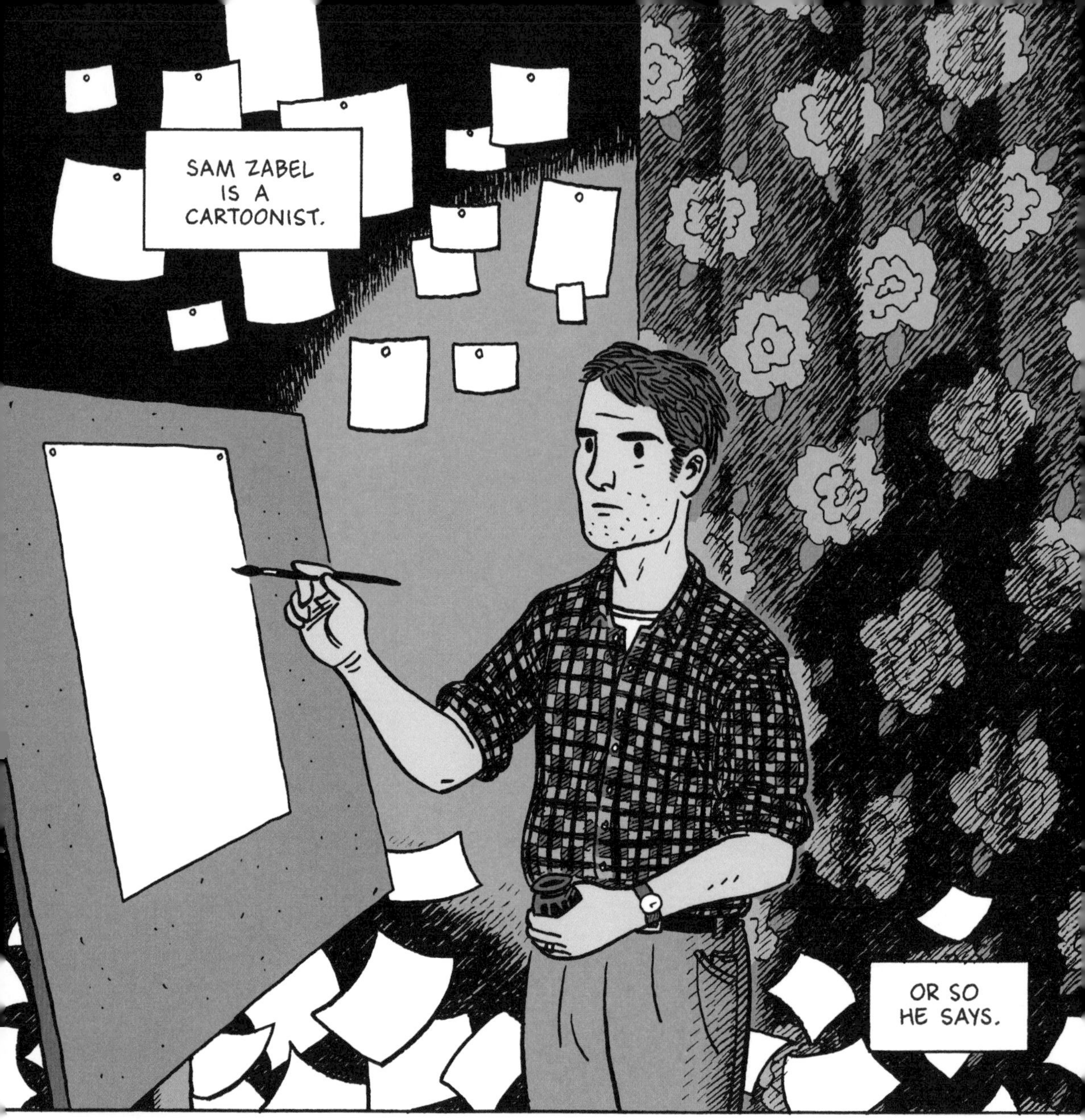
SAM ZABEL
IS A
CARTOONIST.
OR SO
HE SAYS.

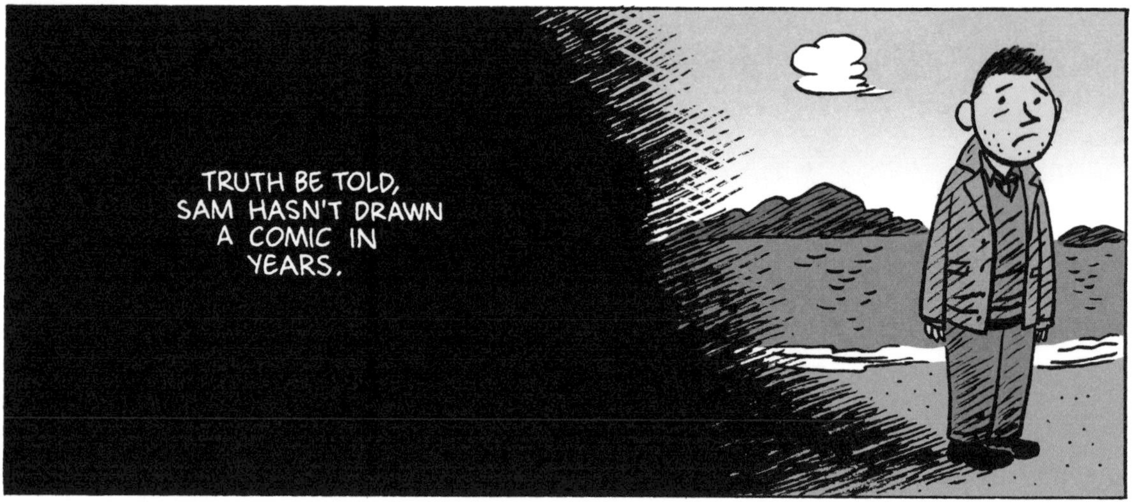
TRUTH BE TOLD,
SAM HASN'T DRAWN
A COMIC IN
YEARS.

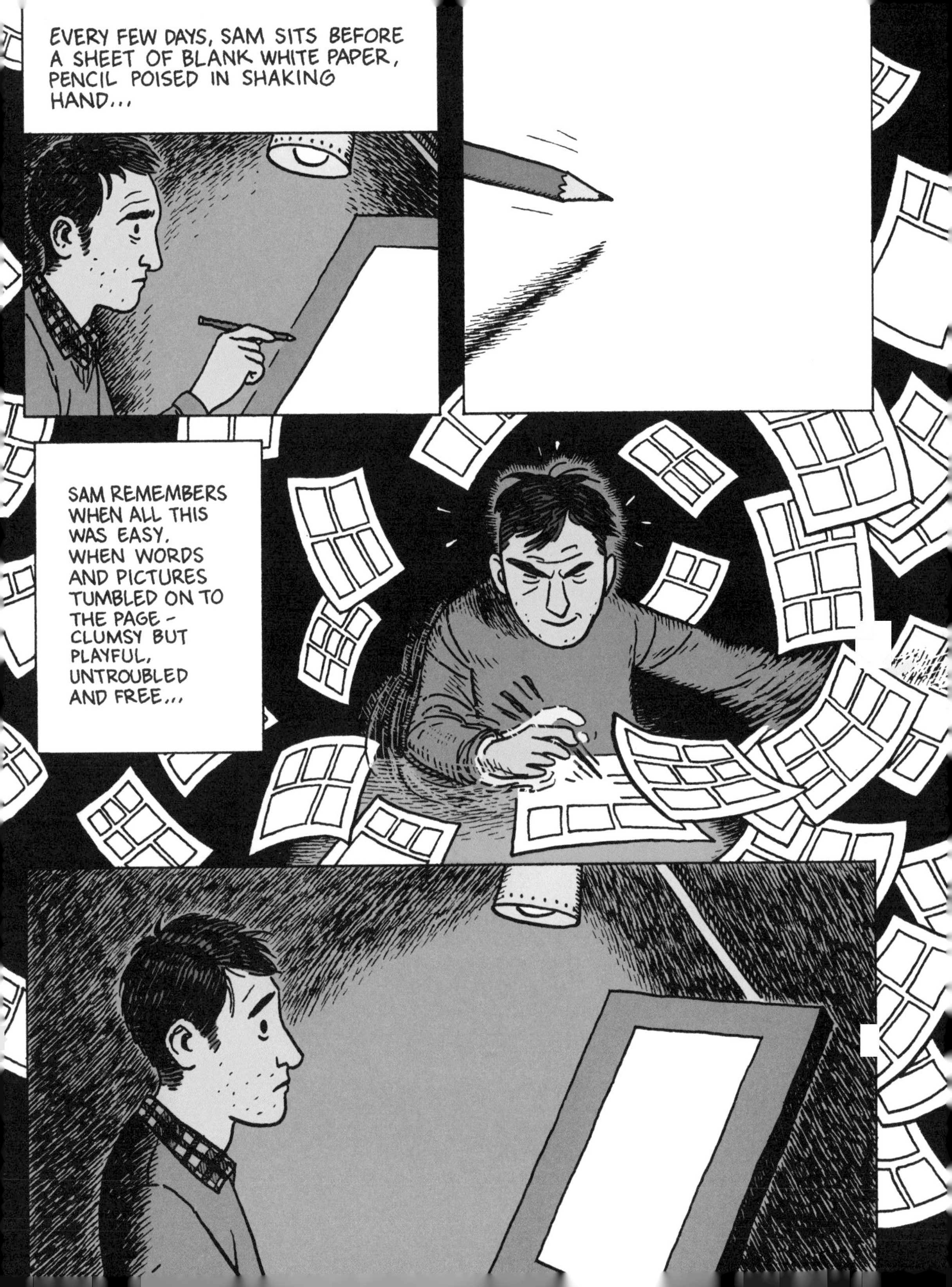
EVERY FEW DAYS, SAM SITS BEFORE A SHEET OF BLANK WHITE PAPER, PENCIL POISED IN SHAKING HAND...
SAM REMEMBERS WHEN ALL THIS WAS EASY. WHEN WORDS AND PICTURES TUMBLED ON TO THE PAGE - CLUMSY BUT PLAYFUL, UNTROUBLED AND FREE...

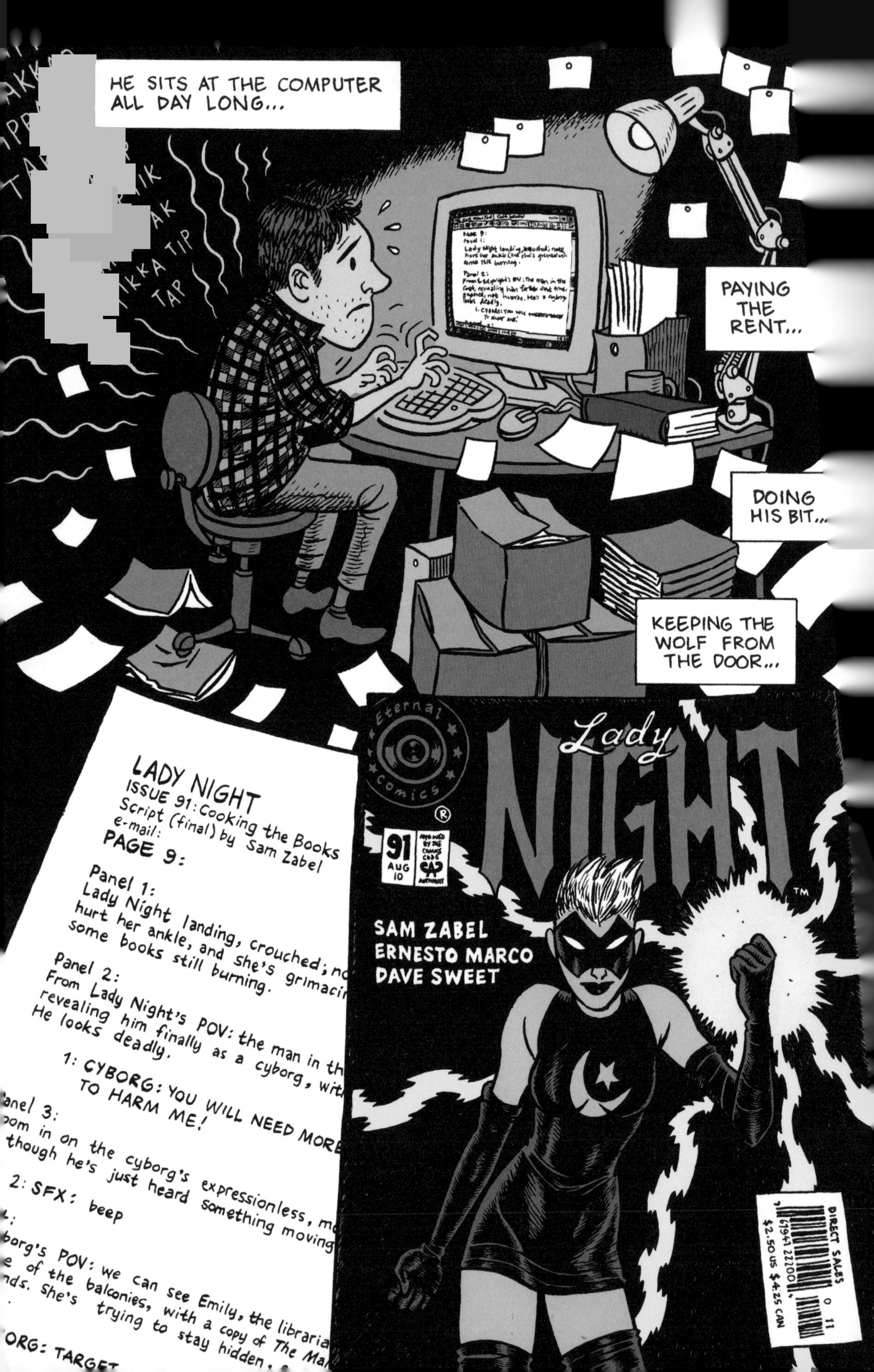

HE SITS AT THE COMPUTER ALL DAY LONG...
TIKKA TIP
TAP
PAYING THE RENT...
DOING HIS BIT...
KEEPING THE WOLF FROM THE DOOR...
LADY NIGHT
ISSUE 91: Cooking the Books
Script (final) by Sam Zabel
e-mail:
PAGE 9:
Panel 1:
Lady Night landing, crouched;
hurt her ankle, and she's
some books still burning.
Panel 2:
From Lady Night's POV: the man in
revealing him finally as a cyborg,
He looks deadly.
1: CYBORG: YOU WILL NEED MORE
TO HARM ME!
Panel 3:
on the cyborg's expressionless,
though he's just heard something moving
2: SFX: beep
borg's POV: we can see Emily, the libraria
of the balconies, with a copy of The
She's trying to stay hidden.
ORG: TARGET
Eternal Comics
Lady NIGHT
91
AUG
10
SAM ZABEL
ERNESTO MARCO
DAVE SWEET
DIRECT SALES
$2.50 US $4.25 CAN

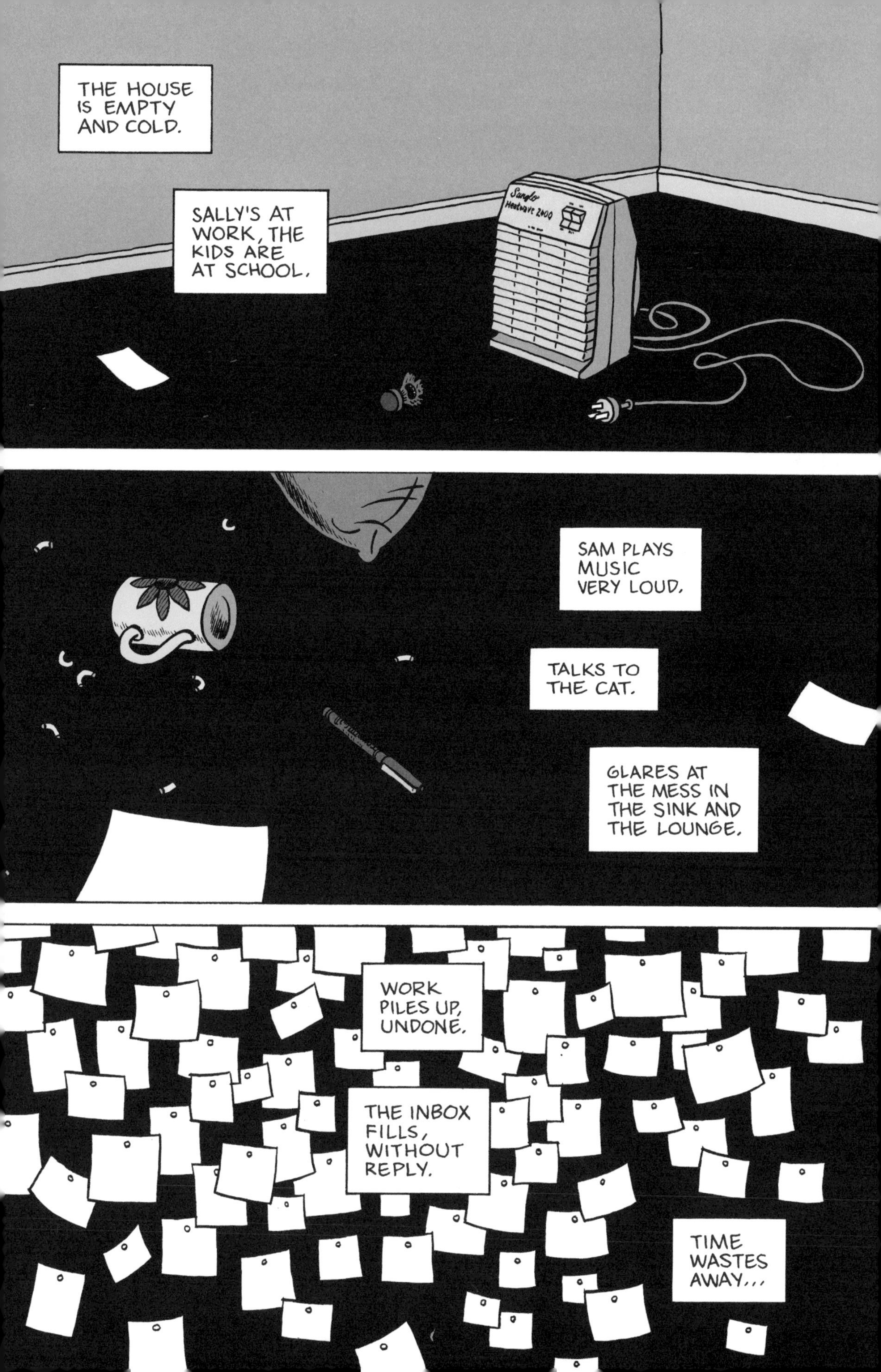
THE HOUSE IS EMPTY AND COLD.
SALLY'S AT WORK, THE KIDS ARE AT SCHOOL.
Sunglo Heatwave 2400
SAM PLAYS MUSIC VERY LOUD.
TALKS TO THE CAT.
GLARES AT THE MESS IN THE SINK AND THE LOUNGE.
WORK PILES UP, UNDONE.
THE INBOX FILLS, WITHOUT REPLY.
TIME WASTES AWAY...

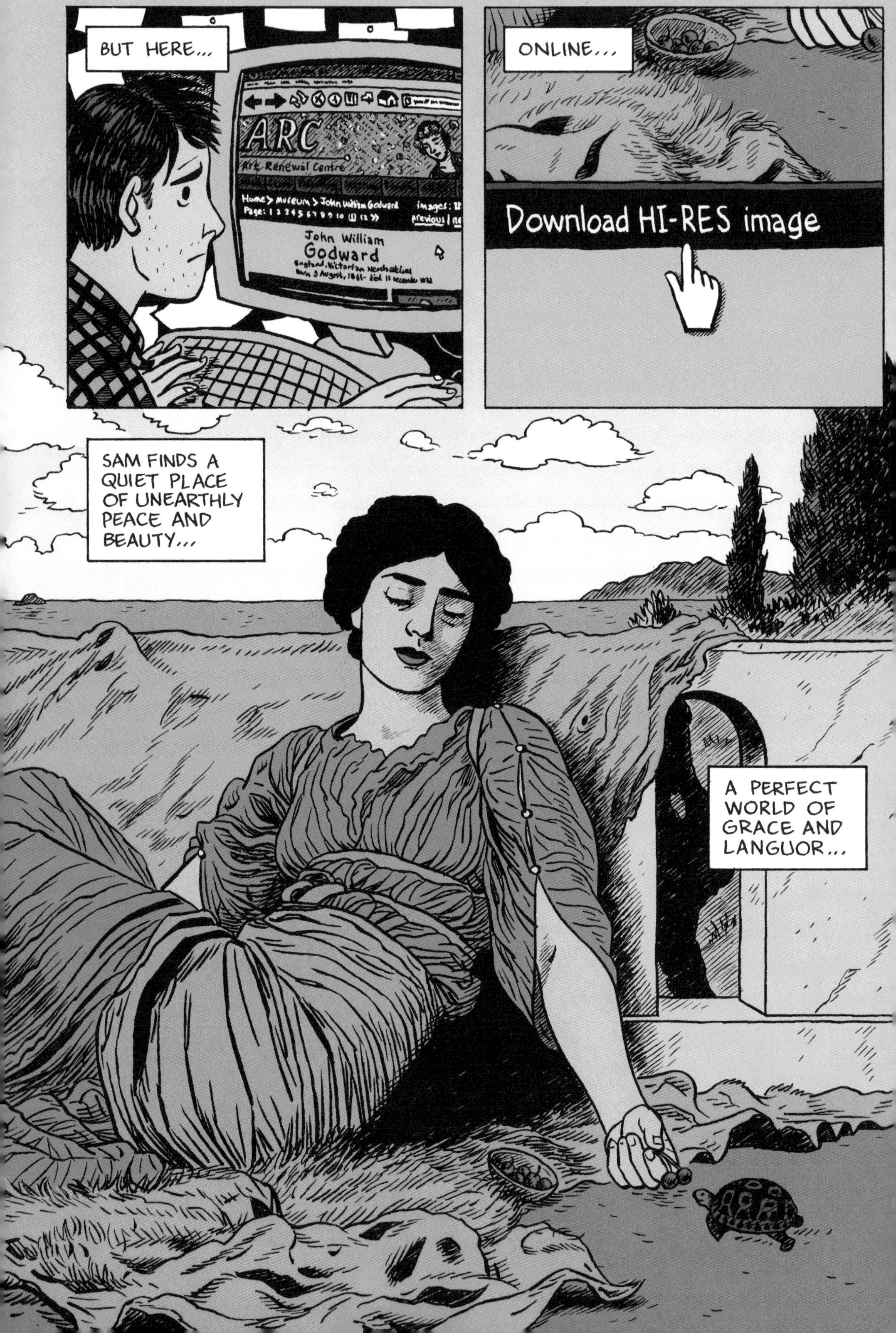
BUT HERE...
ARC
Art Renewal Centre
John William Godward
ONLINE...
Download HI-RES image
SAM FINDS A QUIET PLACE OF UNEARTHLY PEACE AND BEAUTY...
A PERFECT WORLD OF GRACE AND LANGUOR...

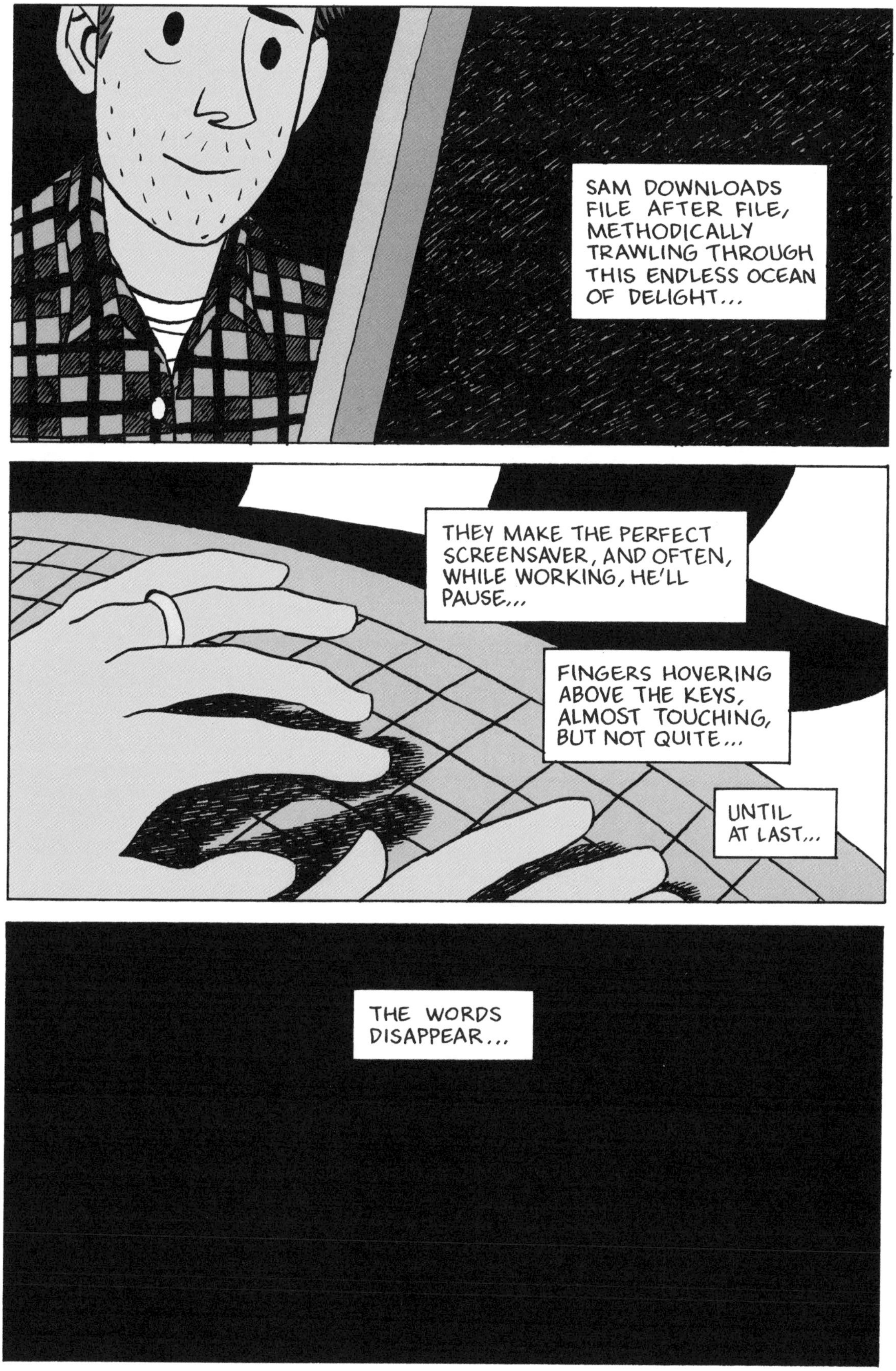
SAM DOWNLOADS FILE AFTER FILE, METHODICALLY TRAWLING THROUGH THIS ENDLESS OCEAN OF DELIGHT...
THEY MAKE THE PERFECT SCREENSAVER, AND OFTEN, WHILE WORKING, HE'LL PAUSE...
FINGERS HOVERING ABOVE THE KEYS, ALMOST TOUCHING, BUT NOT QUITE...
UNTIL AT LAST...
THE WORDS DISAPPEAR...

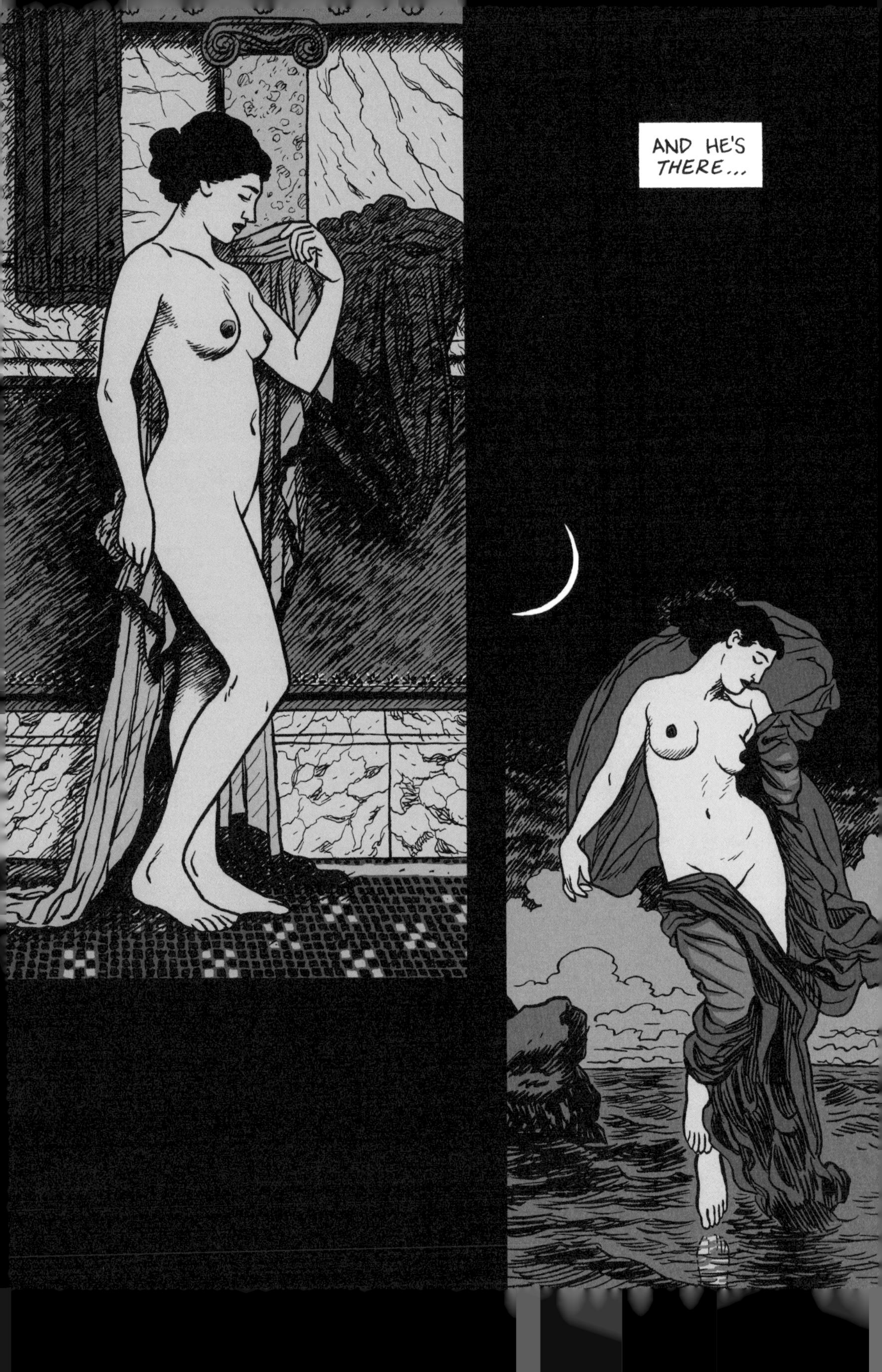
AND HE'S THERE...

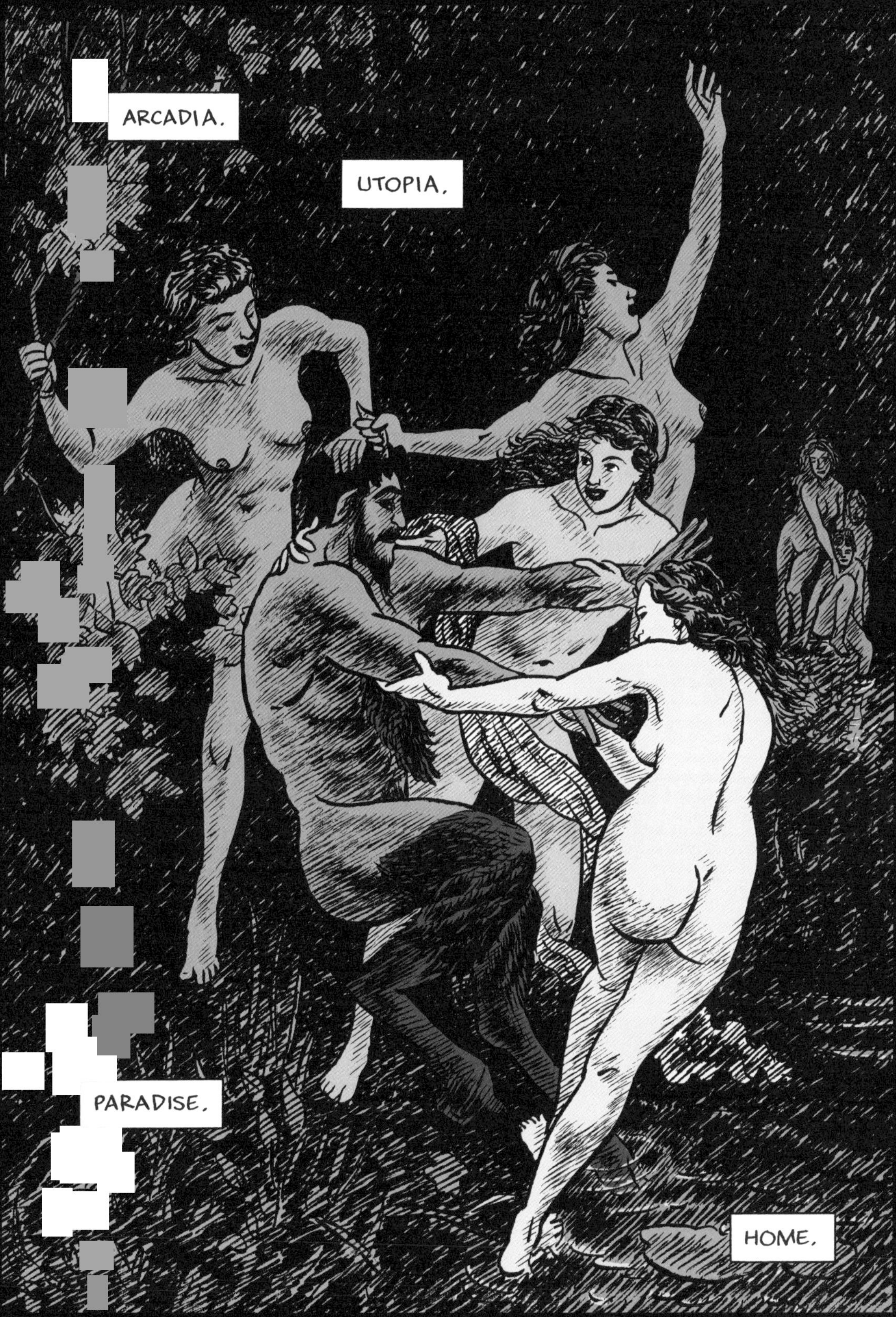
ARCADIA.
UTOPIA.
PARADISE.
HOME.

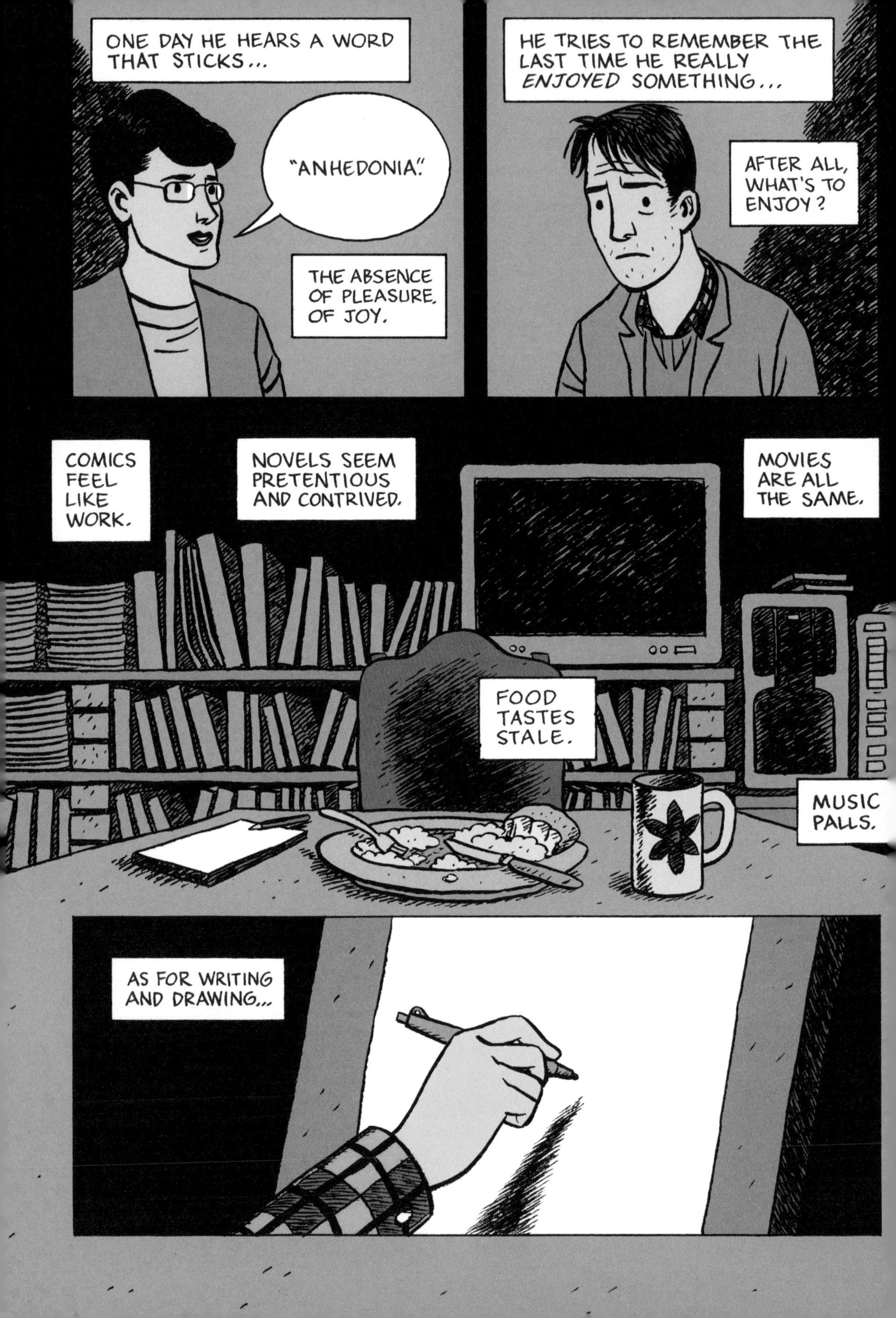
ONE DAY HE HEARS A WORD THAT STICKS...
"ANHEDONIA."
THE ABSENCE OF PLEASURE, OF JOY.
HE TRIES TO REMEMBER THE LAST TIME HE REALLY *ENJOYED* SOMETHING...
AFTER ALL, WHAT'S TO ENJOY?
COMICS FEEL LIKE WORK.
NOVELS SEEM PRETENTIOUS AND CONTRIVED.
MOVIES ARE ALL THE SAME.
FOOD TASTES STALE.
MUSIC PALLS.
AS FOR WRITING AND DRAWING...

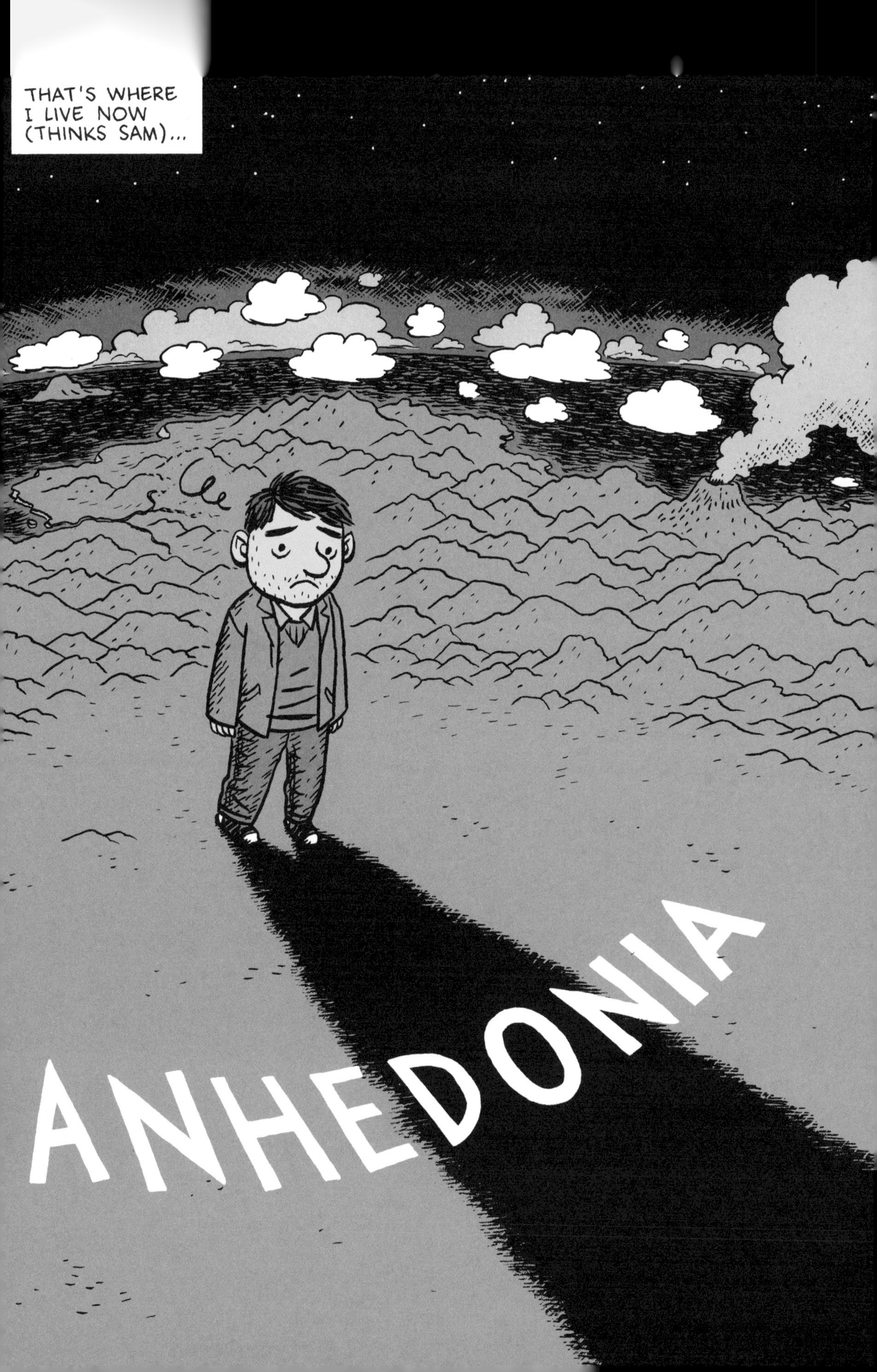
THAT'S WHERE I LIVE NOW (THINKS SAM)...
ANHEDONIA

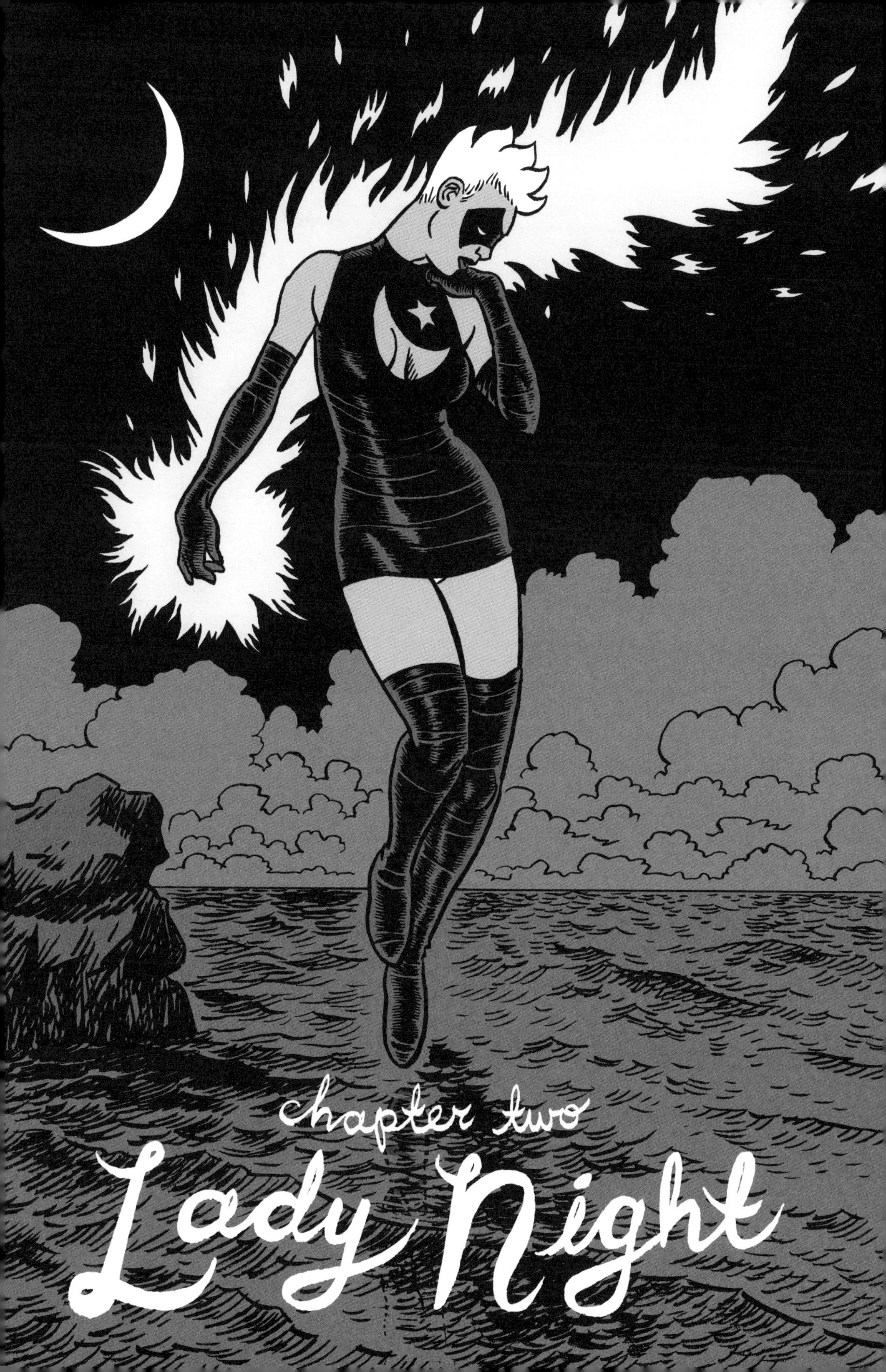
chapter two
Lady Night

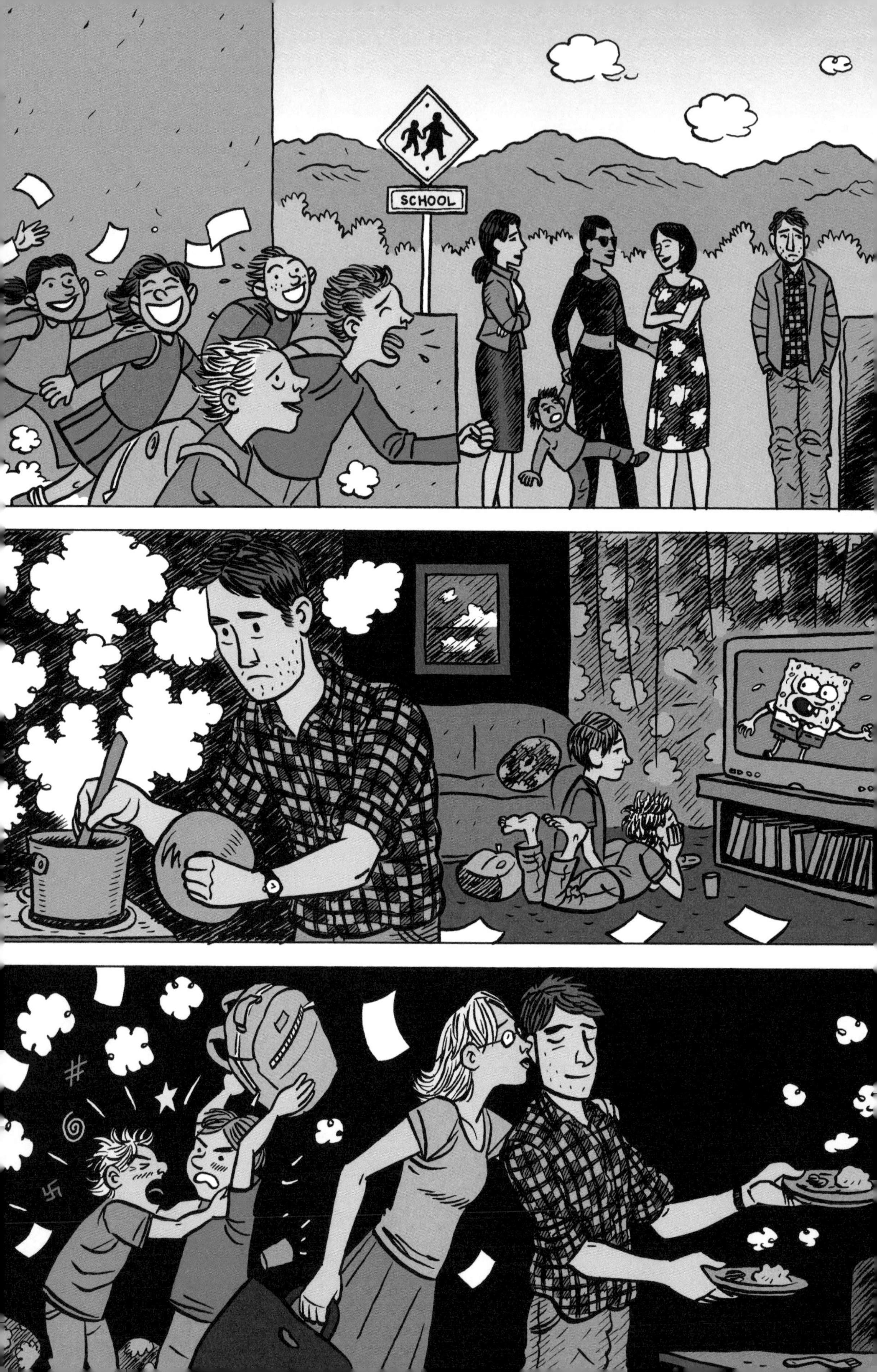
SCHOOL

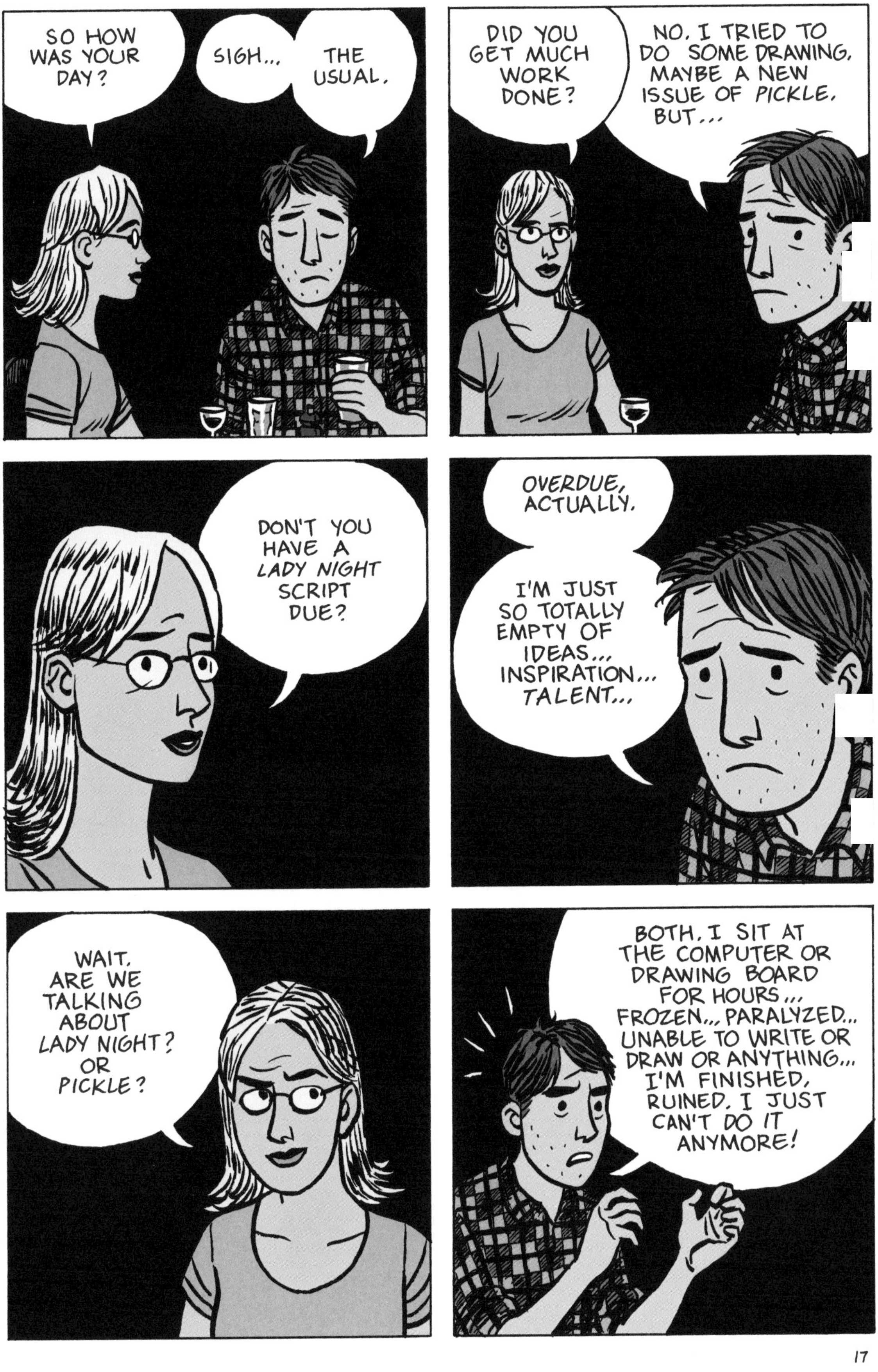
SO HOW WAS YOUR DAY?
SIGH...
THE USUAL.
DID YOU GET MUCH WORK DONE?
NO. I TRIED TO DO SOME DRAWING. MAYBE A NEW ISSUE OF *PICKLE*. BUT...
DON'T YOU HAVE A *LADY NIGHT* SCRIPT DUE?
OVERDUE, ACTUALLY.
I'M JUST SO TOTALLY EMPTY OF IDEAS... INSPIRATION... *TALENT*...
WAIT. ARE WE TALKING ABOUT *LADY NIGHT*? OR *PICKLE*?
BOTH. I SIT AT THE COMPUTER OR DRAWING BOARD FOR HOURS... FROZEN... PARALYZED... UNABLE TO WRITE OR DRAW OR ANYTHING... I'M FINISHED. RUINED. I JUST CAN'T *DO* IT ANYMORE!

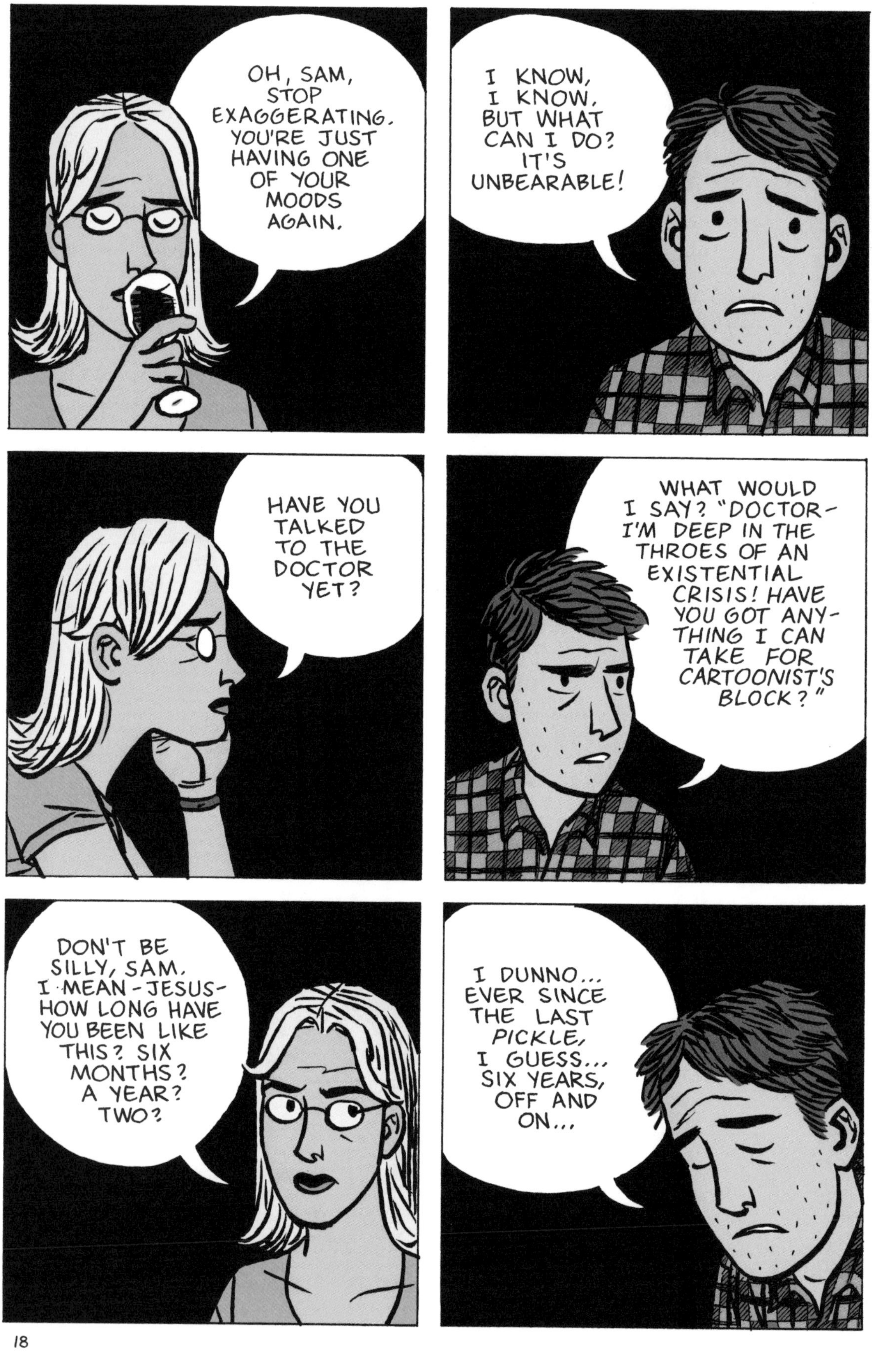
OH, SAM, STOP EXAGGERATING. YOU'RE JUST HAVING ONE OF YOUR MOODS AGAIN.
I KNOW, I KNOW, BUT WHAT CAN I DO? IT'S UNBEARABLE!
HAVE YOU TALKED TO THE DOCTOR YET?
WHAT WOULD I SAY? "DOCTOR- I'M DEEP IN THE THROES OF AN EXISTENTIAL CRISIS! HAVE YOU GOT ANY-THING I CAN TAKE FOR CARTOONIST'S BLOCK?"
DON'T BE SILLY, SAM. I MEAN - JESUS- HOW LONG HAVE YOU BEEN LIKE THIS? SIX MONTHS? A YEAR? TWO?
I DUNNO... EVER SINCE THE LAST *PICKLE*, I GUESS... SIX YEARS, OFF AND ON...

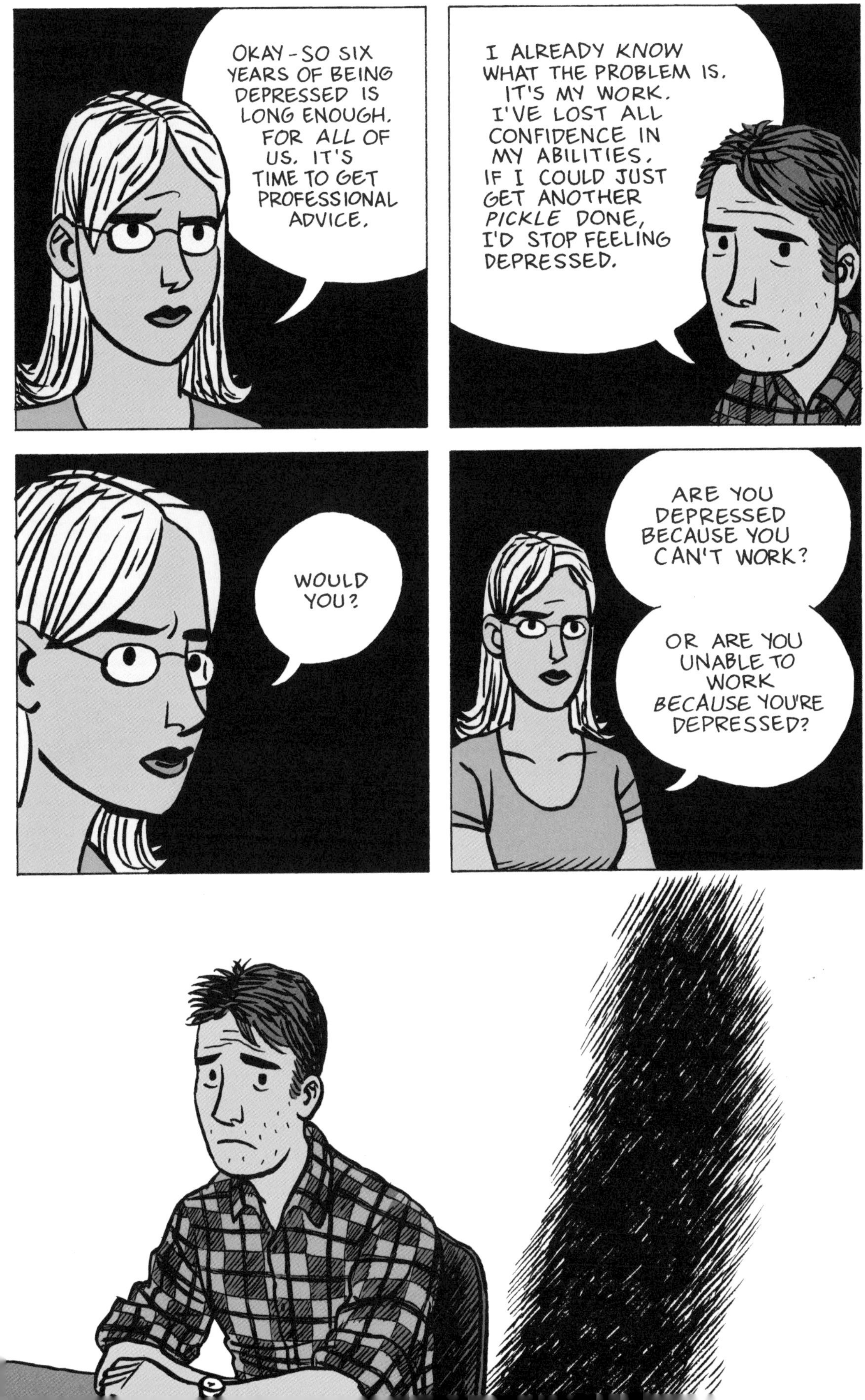
OKAY - SO SIX YEARS OF BEING DEPRESSED IS LONG ENOUGH. FOR ALL OF US. IT'S TIME TO GET PROFESSIONAL ADVICE.
I ALREADY KNOW WHAT THE PROBLEM IS. IT'S MY WORK. I'VE LOST ALL CONFIDENCE IN MY ABILITIES. IF I COULD JUST GET ANOTHER *PICKLE* DONE, I'D STOP FEELING DEPRESSED.
WOULD YOU?
ARE YOU DEPRESSED BECAUSE YOU CAN'T WORK?
OR ARE YOU UNABLE TO WORK *BECAUSE* YOU'RE DEPRESSED?

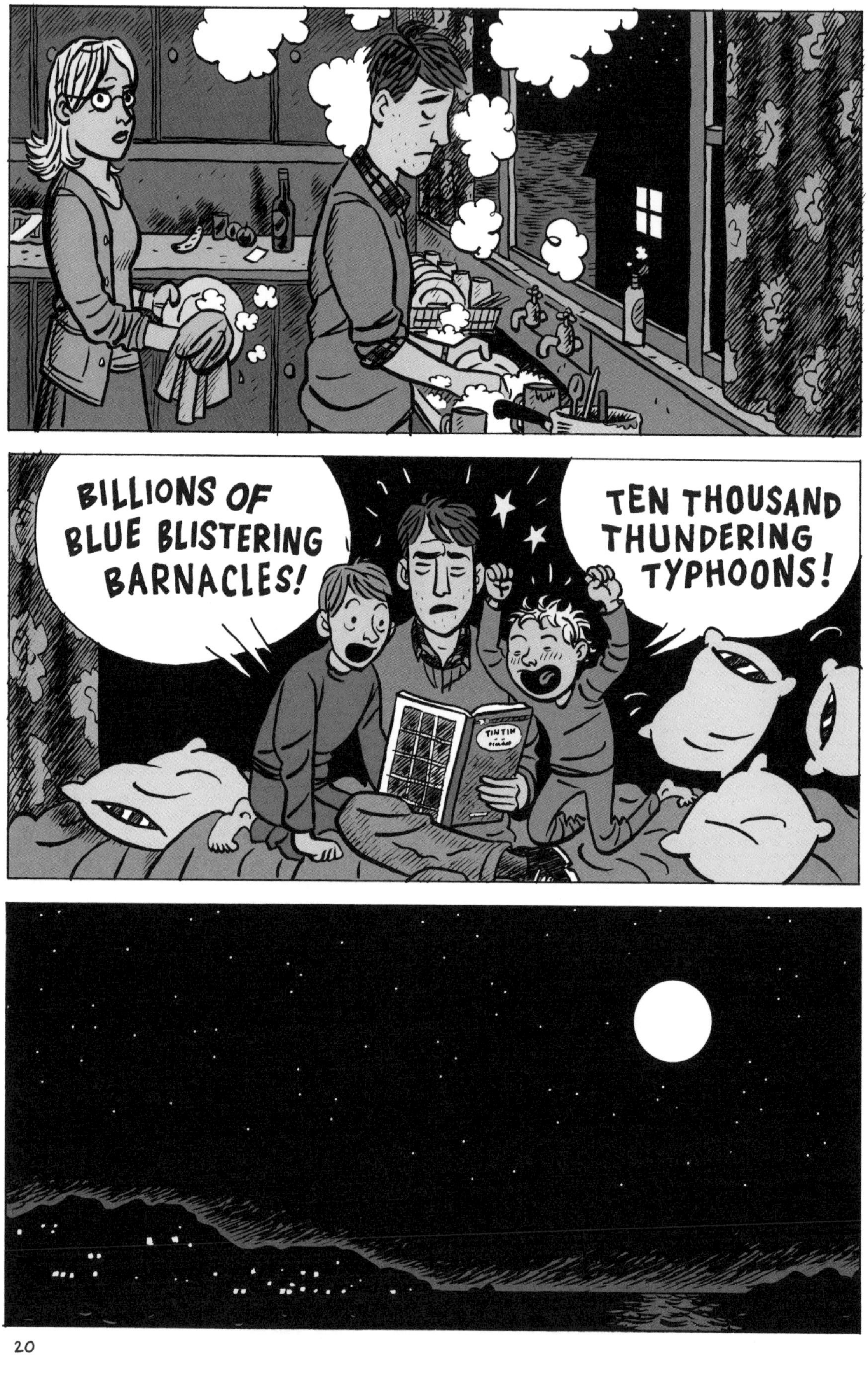
BILLIONS OF BLUE BLISTERING BARNACLES!
TEN THOUSAND THUNDERING TYPHOONS!

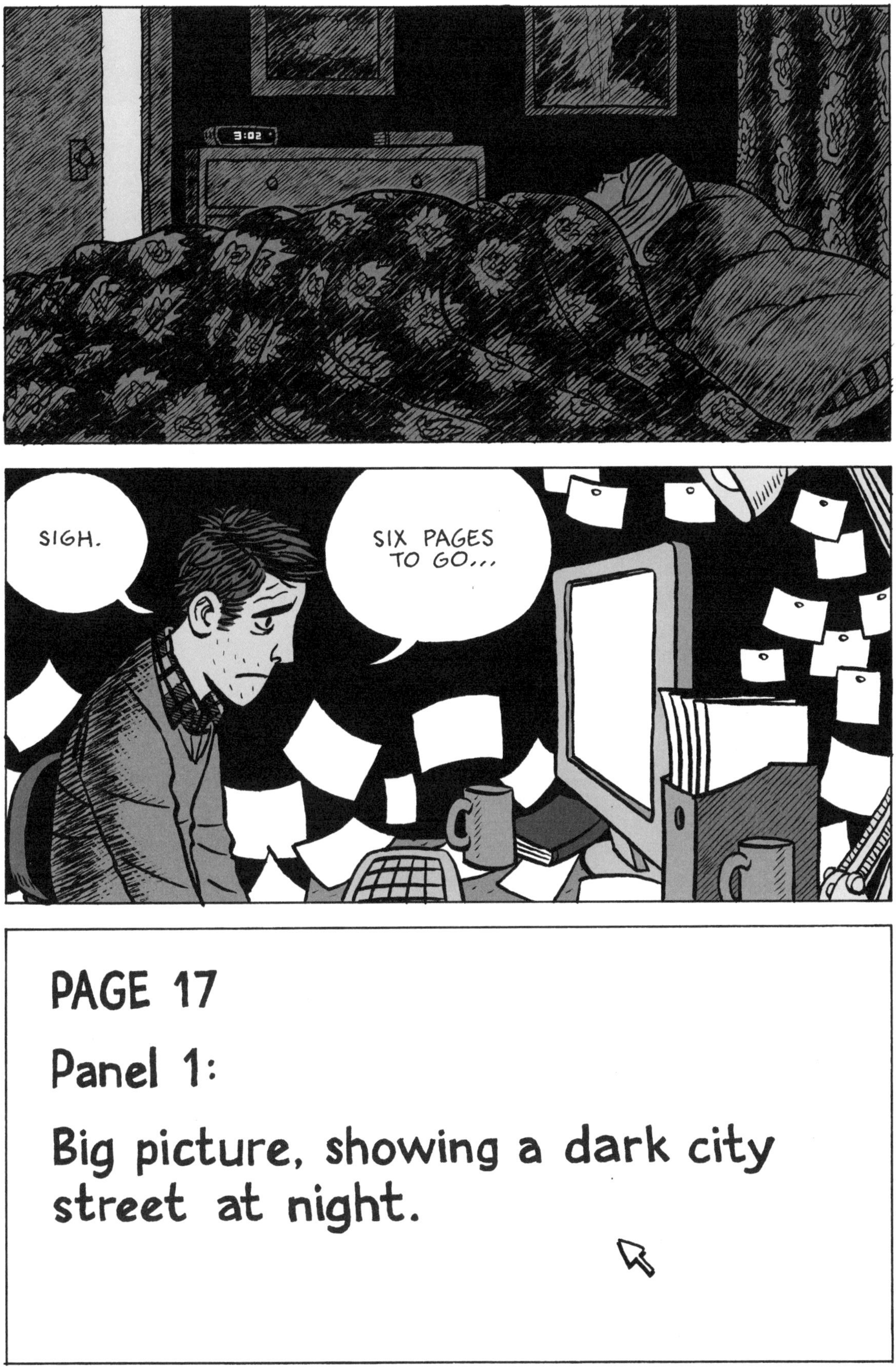
3:02
SIGH.
SIX PAGES TO GO...
PAGE 17
Panel 1:
Big picture, showing a dark city street at night.

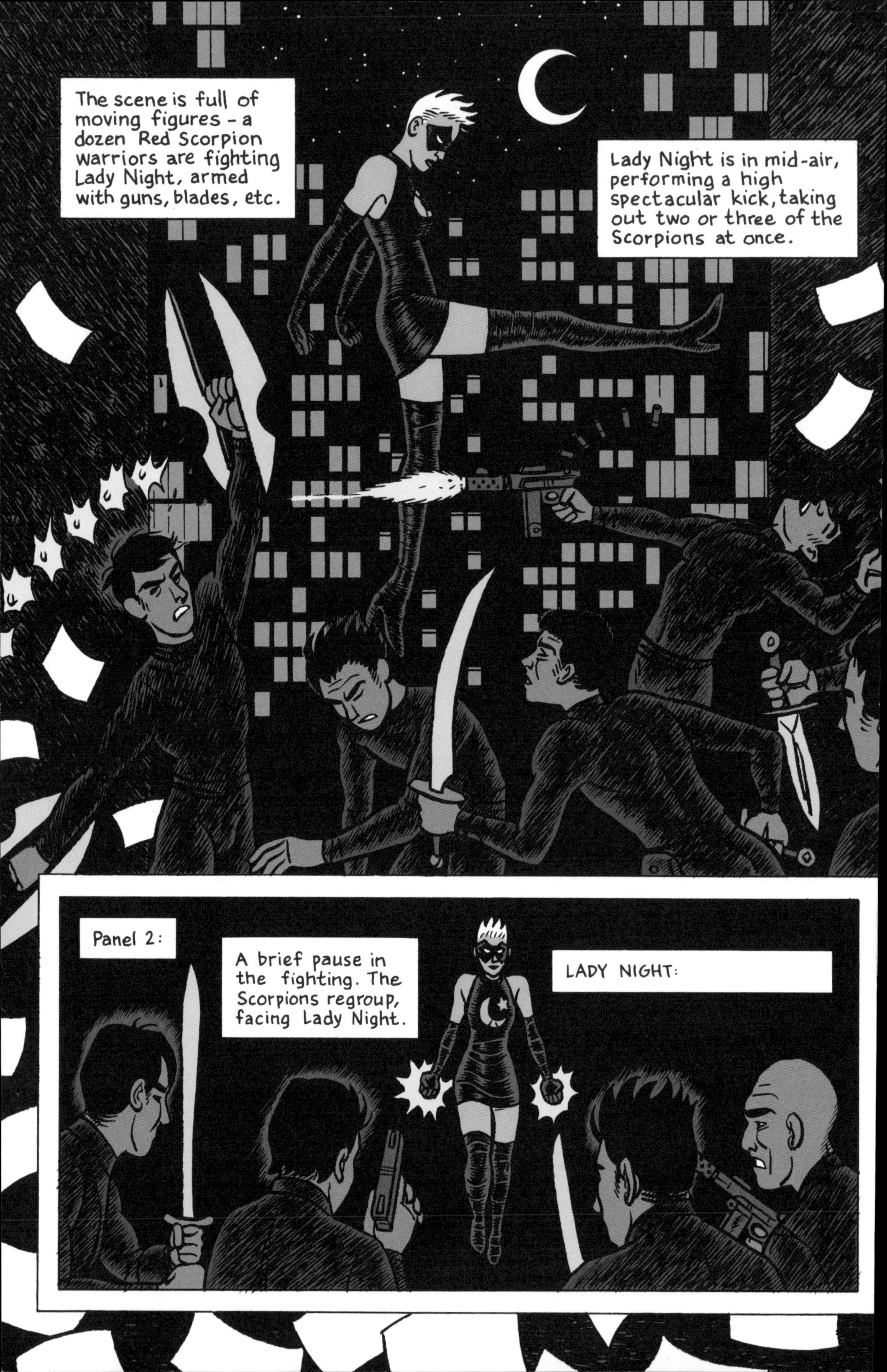
The scene is full of moving figures - a dozen Red Scorpion warriors are fighting Lady Night, armed with guns, blades, etc.
Lady Night is in mid-air, performing a high spectacular kick, taking out two or three of the Scorpions at once.
Panel 2:
A brief pause in the fighting. The Scorpions regroup, facing Lady Night.
LADY NIGHT:

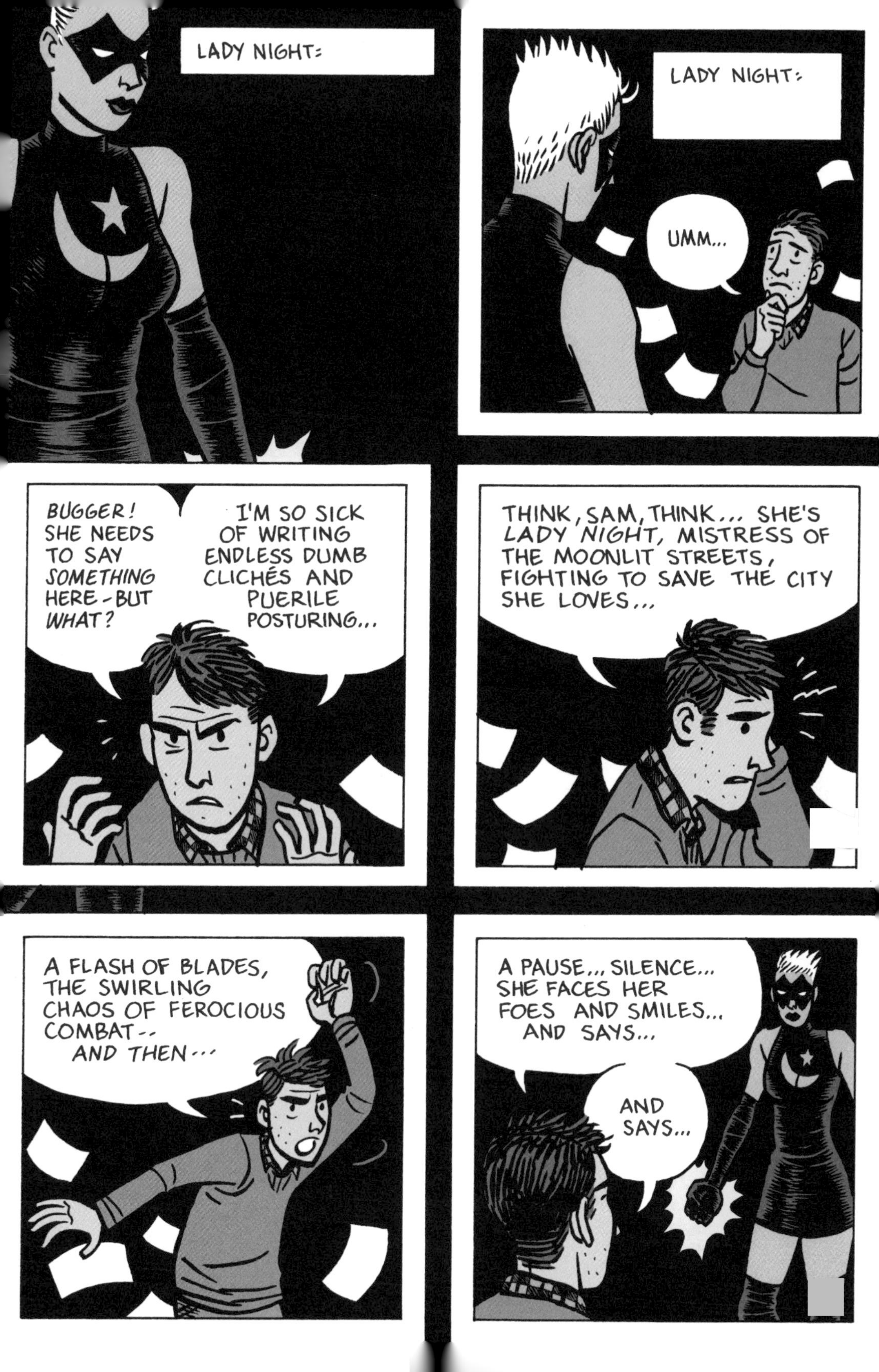
LADY NIGHT:
LADY NIGHT:
UMM...
BUGGER! SHE NEEDS TO SAY SOMETHING HERE - BUT WHAT?
I'M SO SICK OF WRITING ENDLESS DUMB CLICHÉS AND PUERILE POSTURING...
THINK, SAM, THINK... SHE'S LADY NIGHT, MISTRESS OF THE MOONLIT STREETS, FIGHTING TO SAVE THE CITY SHE LOVES...
A FLASH OF BLADES, THE SWIRLING CHAOS OF FEROCIOUS COMBAT -- AND THEN...
A PAUSE... SILENCE... SHE FACES HER FOES AND SMILES... AND SAYS...
AND SAYS...

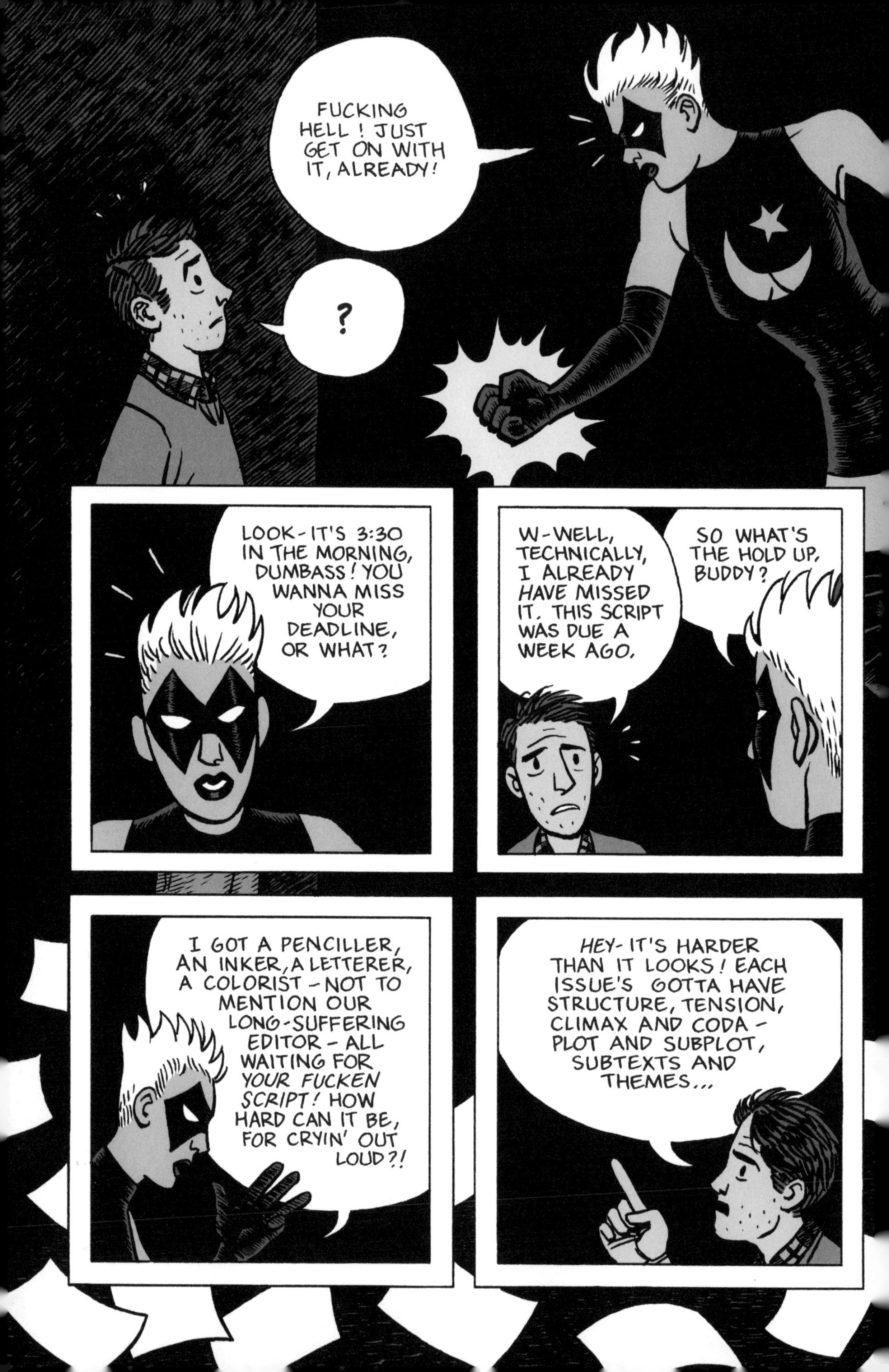
FUCKING HELL! JUST GET ON WITH IT, ALREADY!
?
LOOK- IT'S 3:30 IN THE MORNING, DUMBASS! YOU WANNA MISS YOUR DEADLINE, OR WHAT?
SO WHAT'S THE HOLD UP, BUDDY?
W-WELL, TECHNICALLY, I ALREADY *HAVE* MISSED IT. THIS SCRIPT WAS DUE A WEEK AGO.
I GOT A PENCILLER, AN INKER, A LETTERER, A COLORIST - NOT TO MENTION OUR LONG-SUFFERING EDITOR - ALL WAITING FOR *YOUR FUCKEN SCRIPT!* HOW HARD CAN IT BE, FOR CRYIN' OUT LOUD?!
HEY- IT'S HARDER THAN IT LOOKS! EACH ISSUE'S GOTTA HAVE STRUCTURE, TENSION, CLIMAX AND CODA - PLOT AND SUBPLOT, SUBTEXTS AND THEMES...

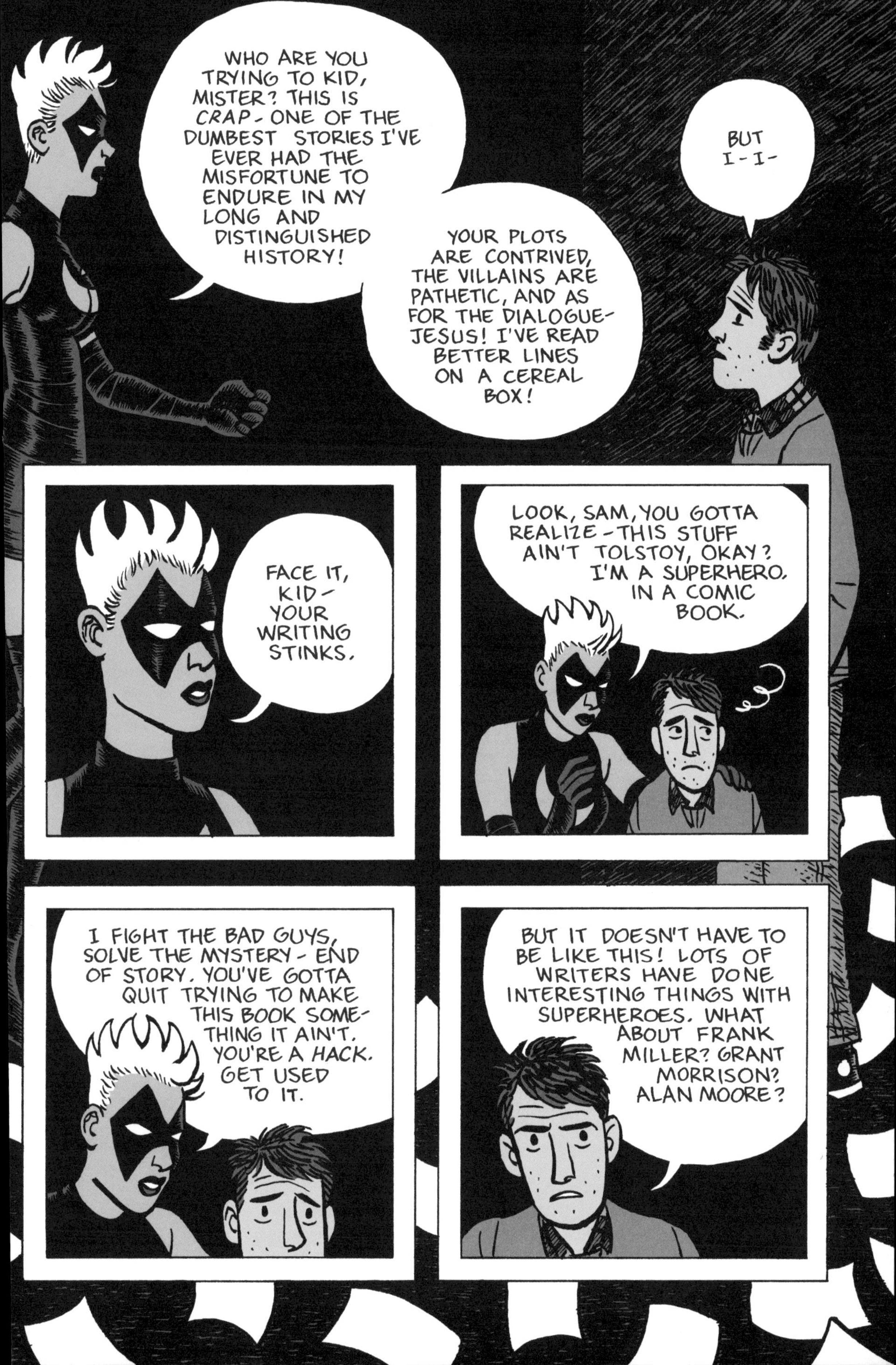
WHO ARE YOU TRYING TO KID, MISTER? THIS IS CRAP- ONE OF THE DUMBEST STORIES I'VE EVER HAD THE MISFORTUNE TO ENDURE IN MY LONG AND DISTINGUISHED HISTORY!
YOUR PLOTS ARE CONTRIVED, THE VILLAINS ARE PATHETIC, AND AS FOR THE DIALOGUE- JESUS! I'VE READ BETTER LINES ON A CEREAL BOX!
BUT I-I-
FACE IT, KID- YOUR WRITING STINKS.
LOOK, SAM, YOU GOTTA REALIZE - THIS STUFF AIN'T TOLSTOY, OKAY? I'M A SUPERHERO. IN A COMIC BOOK.
I FIGHT THE BAD GUYS, SOLVE THE MYSTERY - END OF STORY. YOU'VE GOTTA QUIT TRYING TO MAKE THIS BOOK SOMETHING IT AIN'T. YOU'RE A HACK. GET USED TO IT.
BUT IT DOESN'T HAVE TO BE LIKE THIS! LOTS OF WRITERS HAVE DONE INTERESTING THINGS WITH SUPERHEROES. WHAT ABOUT FRANK MILLER? GRANT MORRISON? ALAN MOORE?

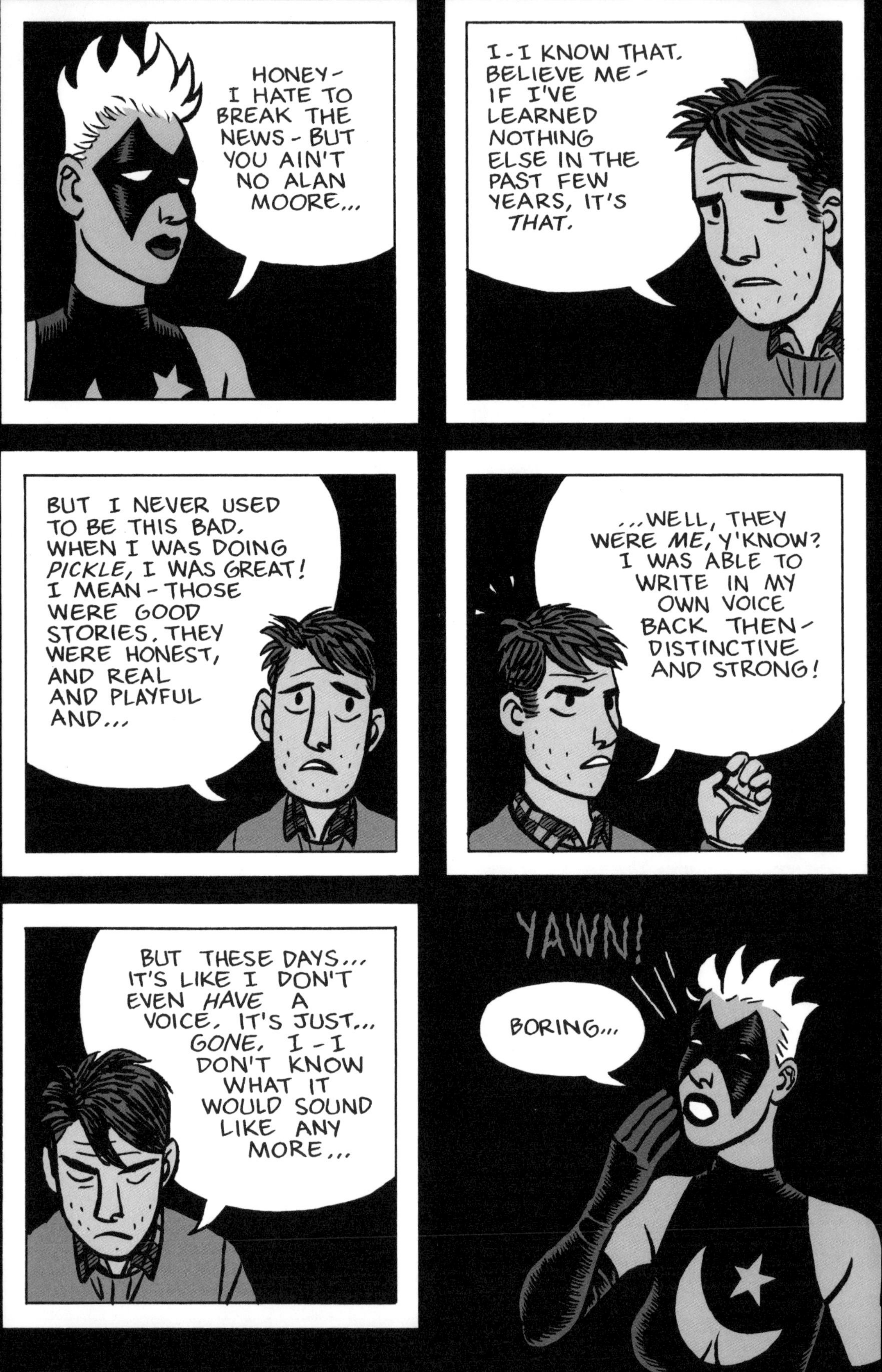
HONEY- I HATE TO BREAK THE NEWS - BUT YOU AIN'T NO ALAN MOORE...
I-I KNOW THAT. BELIEVE ME- IF I'VE LEARNED NOTHING ELSE IN THE PAST FEW YEARS, IT'S THAT.
BUT I NEVER USED TO BE THIS BAD. WHEN I WAS DOING PICKLE, I WAS GREAT! I MEAN - THOSE WERE GOOD STORIES. THEY WERE HONEST, AND REAL AND PLAYFUL AND...
...WELL, THEY WERE ME, Y'KNOW? I WAS ABLE TO WRITE IN MY OWN VOICE BACK THEN- DISTINCTIVE AND STRONG!
BUT THESE DAYS... IT'S LIKE I DON'T EVEN HAVE A VOICE. IT'S JUST... GONE. I-I DON'T KNOW WHAT IT WOULD SOUND LIKE ANY MORE...
YAWN!
BORING...

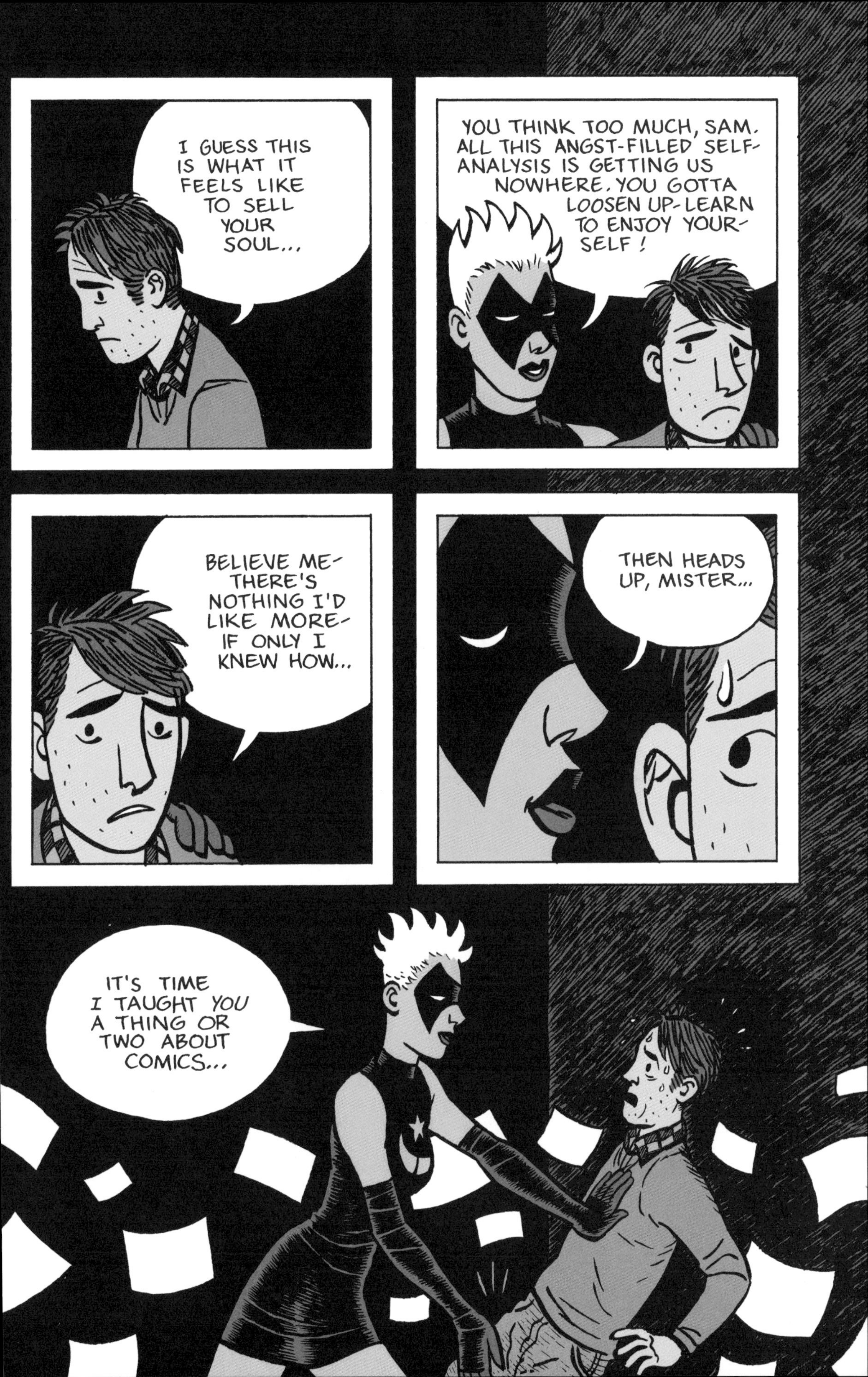
I GUESS THIS IS WHAT IT FEELS LIKE TO SELL YOUR SOUL...
YOU THINK TOO MUCH, SAM. ALL THIS ANGST-FILLED SELF-ANALYSIS IS GETTING US NOWHERE. YOU GOTTA LOOSEN UP- LEARN TO ENJOY YOURSELF!
BELIEVE ME- THERE'S NOTHING I'D LIKE MORE- IF ONLY I KNEW HOW...
THEN HEADS UP, MISTER...
IT'S TIME I TAUGHT *YOU* A THING OR TWO ABOUT COMICS...

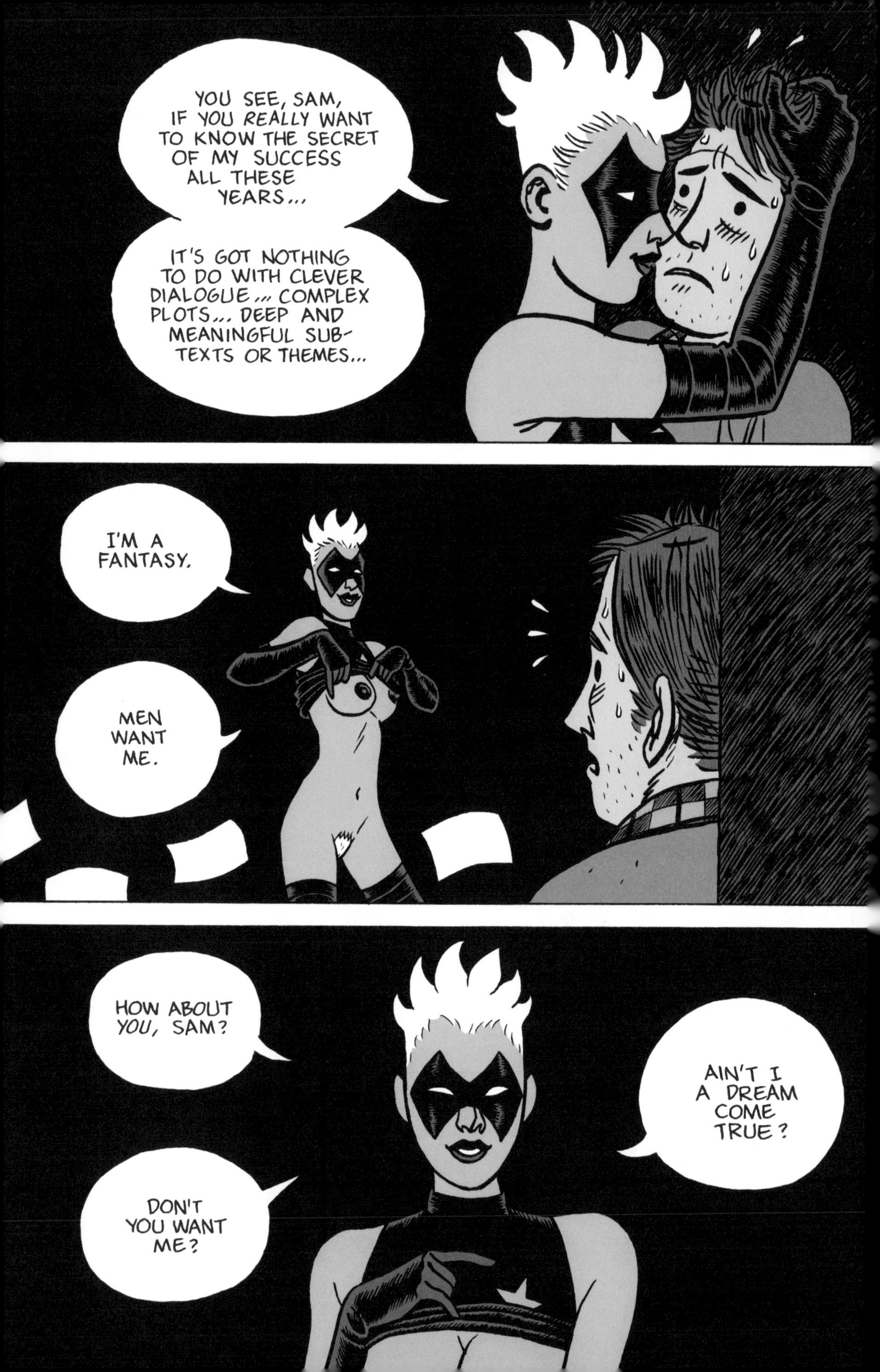
YOU SEE, SAM, IF YOU REALLY WANT TO KNOW THE SECRET OF MY SUCCESS ALL THESE YEARS...
IT'S GOT NOTHING TO DO WITH CLEVER DIALOGUE... COMPLEX PLOTS... DEEP AND MEANINGFUL SUB-TEXTS OR THEMES...
I'M A FANTASY.
MEN WANT ME.
HOW ABOUT YOU, SAM?
DON'T YOU WANT ME?
AIN'T I A DREAM COME TRUE?

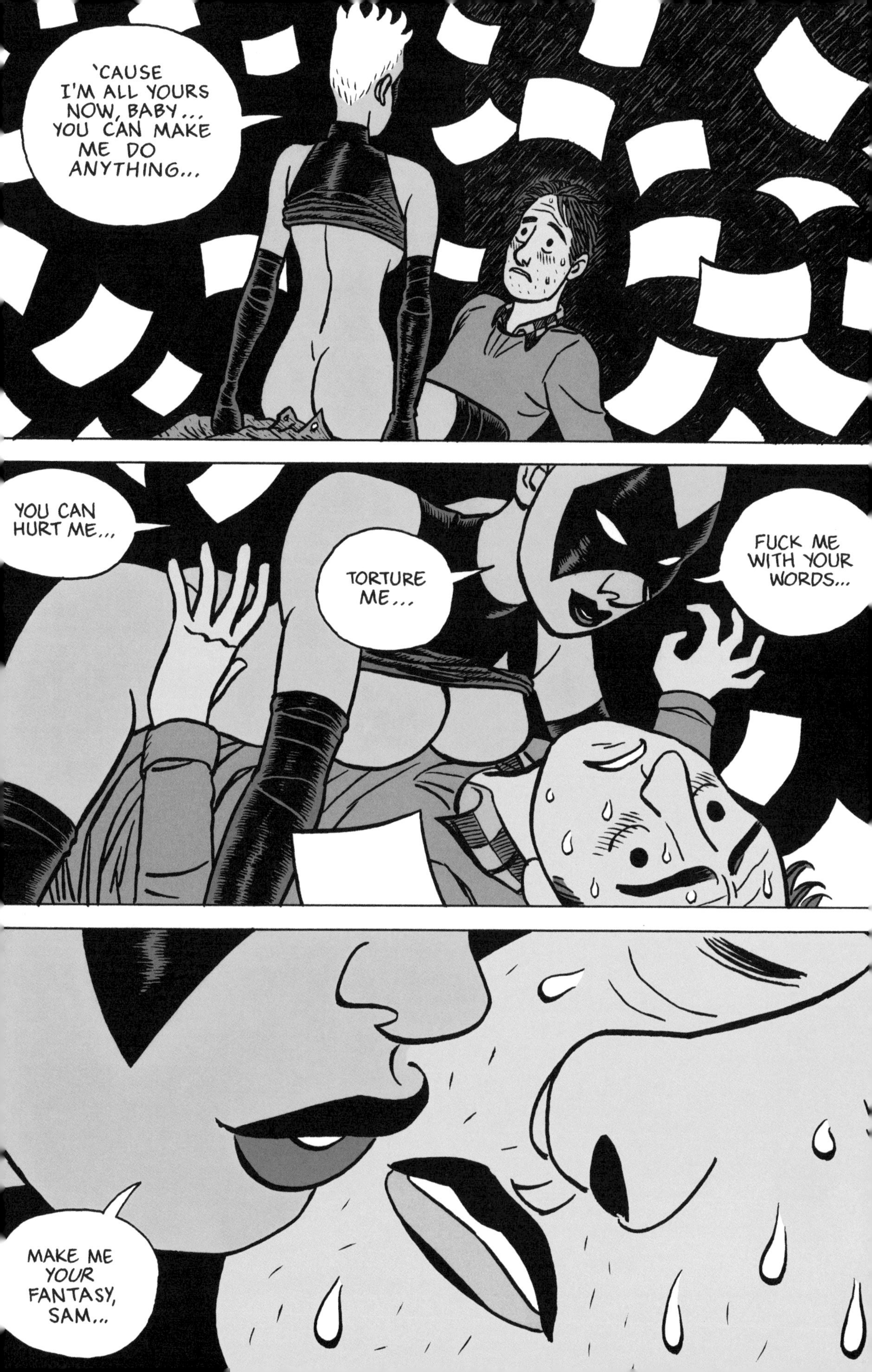
`CAUSE I'M ALL YOURS NOW, BABY... YOU CAN MAKE ME DO ANYTHING...
YOU CAN HURT ME...
TORTURE ME...
FUCK ME WITH YOUR WORDS...
MAKE ME *YOUR* FANTASY, SAM...

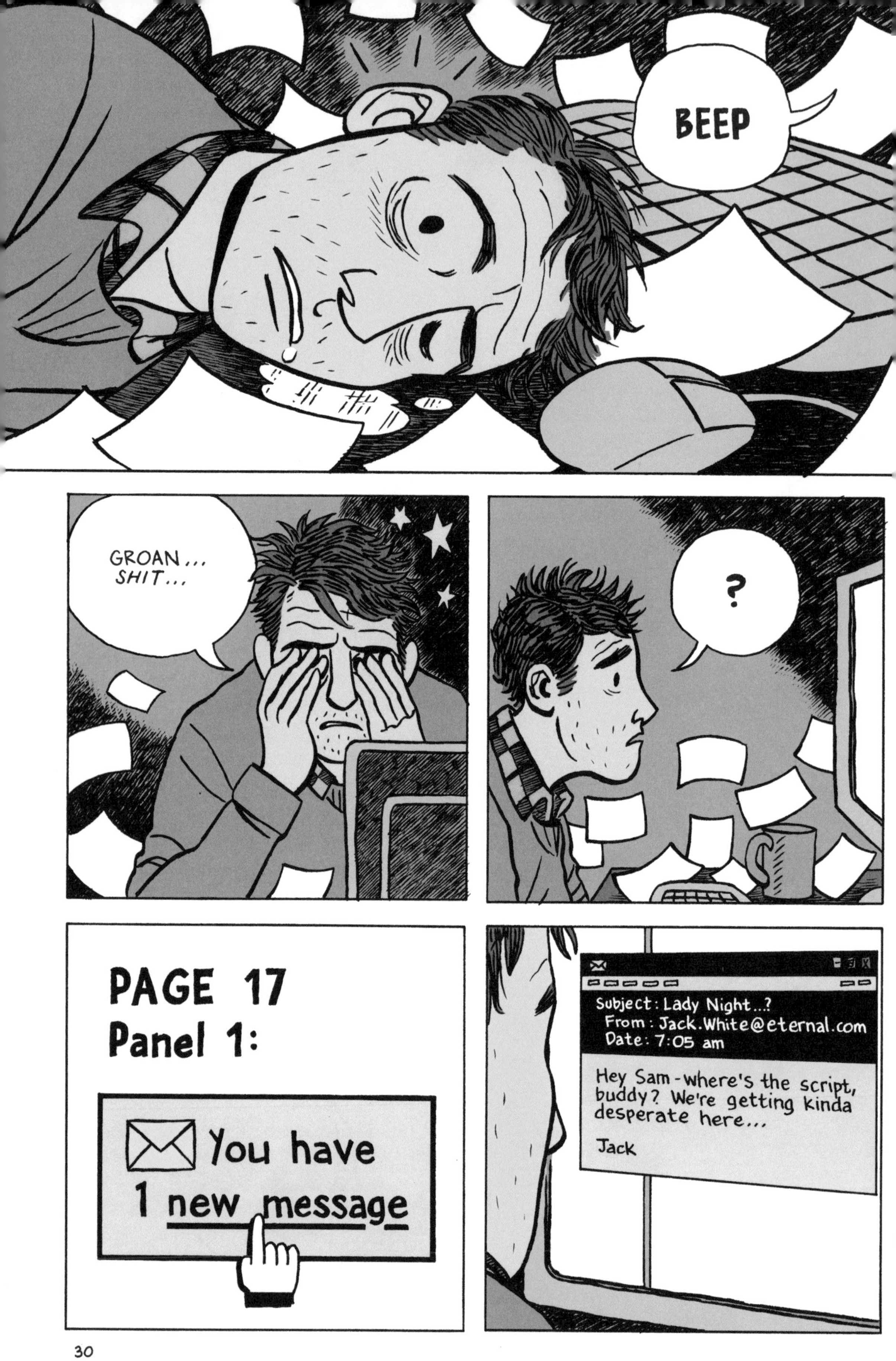
BEEP
GROAN... SHIT...
?
PAGE 17
Panel 1:
You have 1 new message
Subject: Lady Night...?
From: Jack.White@eternal.com
Date: 7:05 am
Hey Sam - where's the script, buddy? We're getting kinda desperate here...
Jack

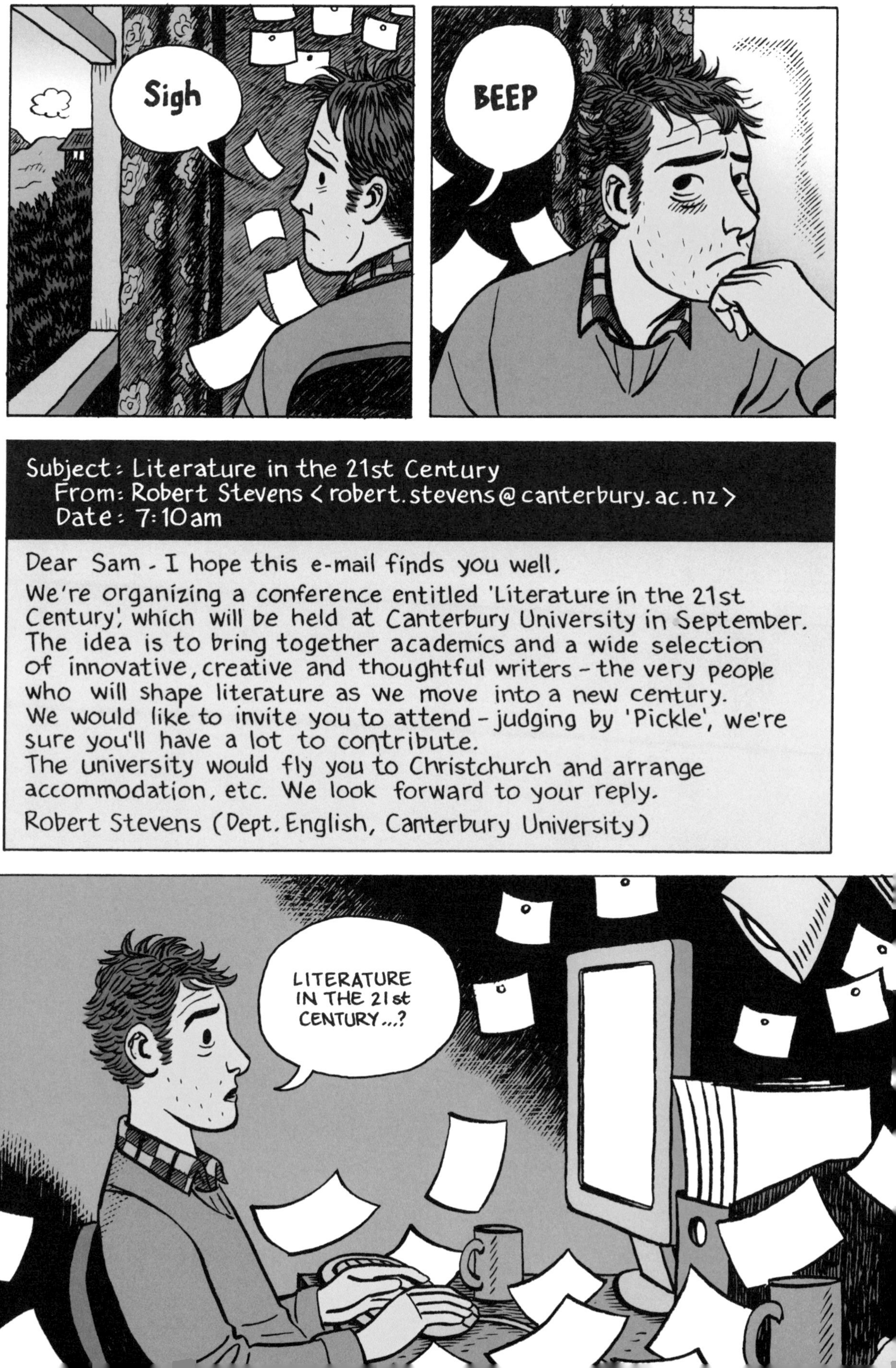
Sigh
BEEP
Subject: Literature in the 21st Century
From: Robert Stevens <robert.stevens@canterbury.ac.nz>
Date: 7:10am
Dear Sam - I hope this e-mail finds you well.
We're organizing a conference entitled 'Literature in the 21st Century', which will be held at Canterbury University in September. The idea is to bring together academics and a wide selection of innovative, creative and thoughtful writers - the very people who will shape literature as we move into a new century.
We would like to invite you to attend - judging by 'Pickle', we're sure you'll have a lot to contribute.
The university would fly you to Christchurch and arrange accommodation, etc. We look forward to your reply.
Robert Stevens (Dept. English, Canterbury University)
LITERATURE IN THE 21st CENTURY...?

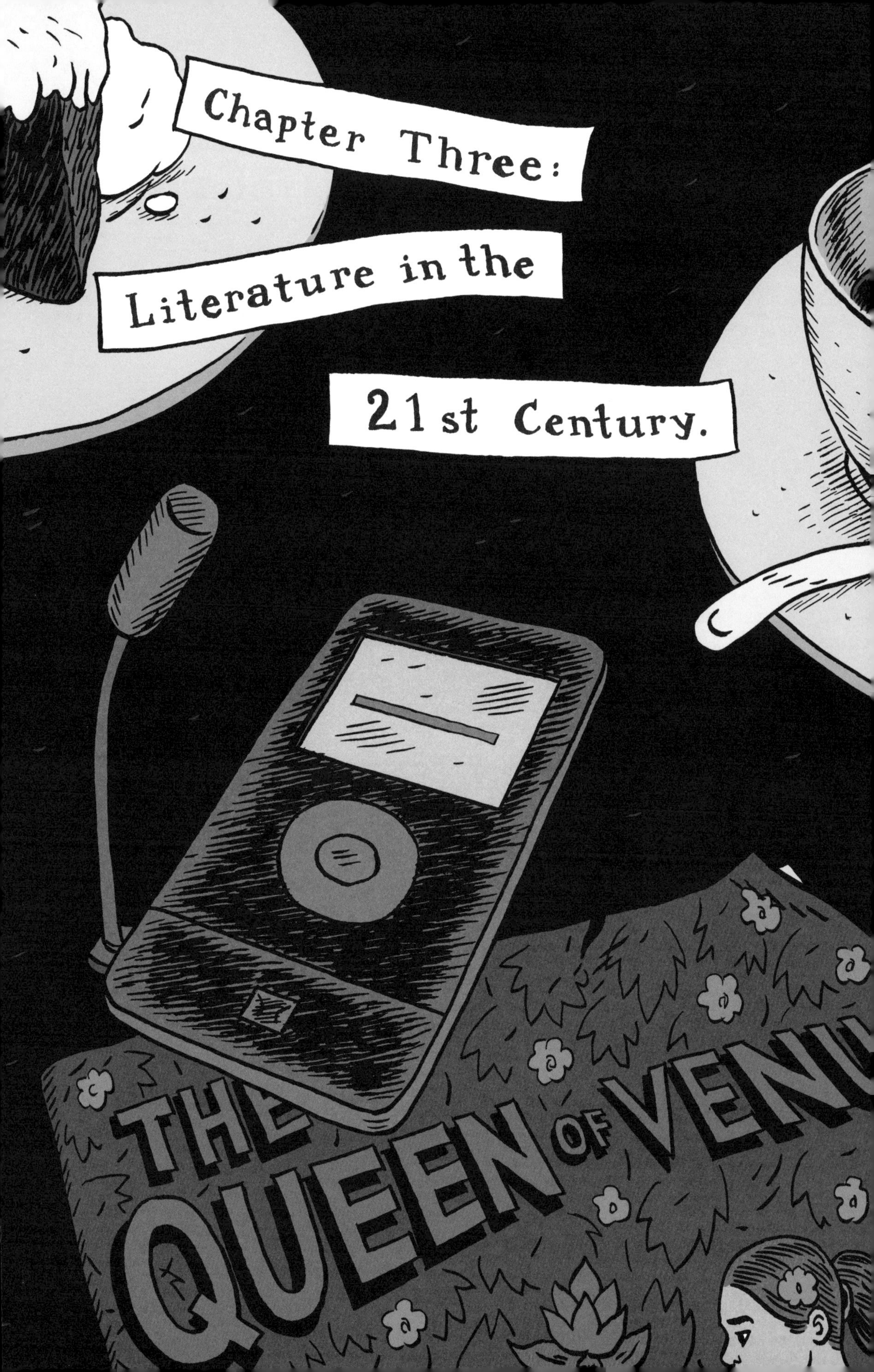

Chapter Three:
Literature in the
21st Century.
THE QUEEN OF VENU

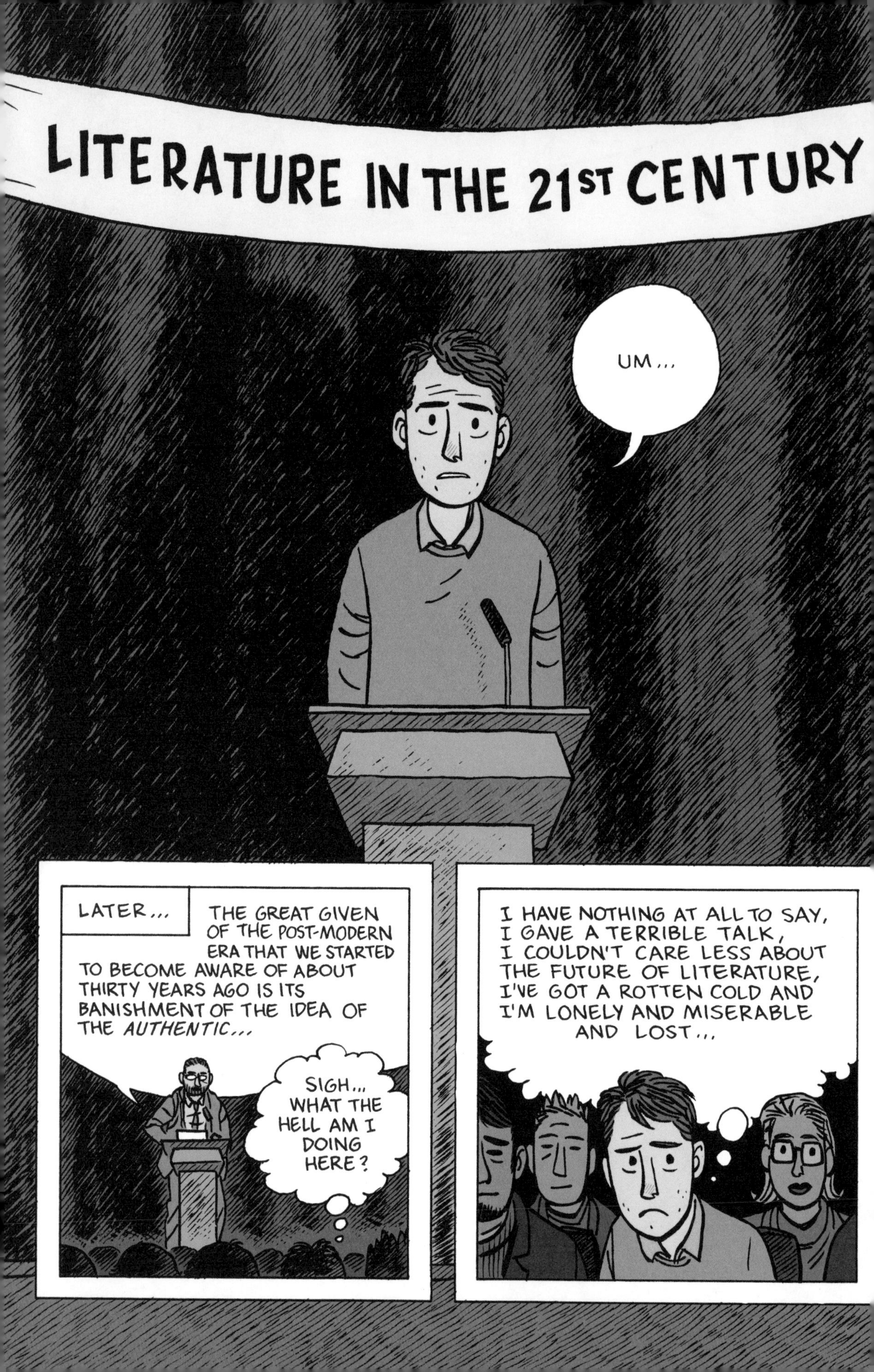
LITERATURE IN THE 21ST CENTURY
UM...
LATER...
THE GREAT GIVEN OF THE POST-MODERN ERA THAT WE STARTED TO BECOME AWARE OF ABOUT THIRTY YEARS AGO IS ITS BANISHMENT OF THE IDEA OF THE *AUTHENTIC*...
SIGH... WHAT THE HELL AM I DOING HERE?
I HAVE NOTHING AT ALL TO SAY, I GAVE A TERRIBLE TALK, I COULDN'T CARE LESS ABOUT THE FUTURE OF LITERATURE, I'VE GOT A ROTTEN COLD AND I'M LONELY AND MISERABLE AND LOST...

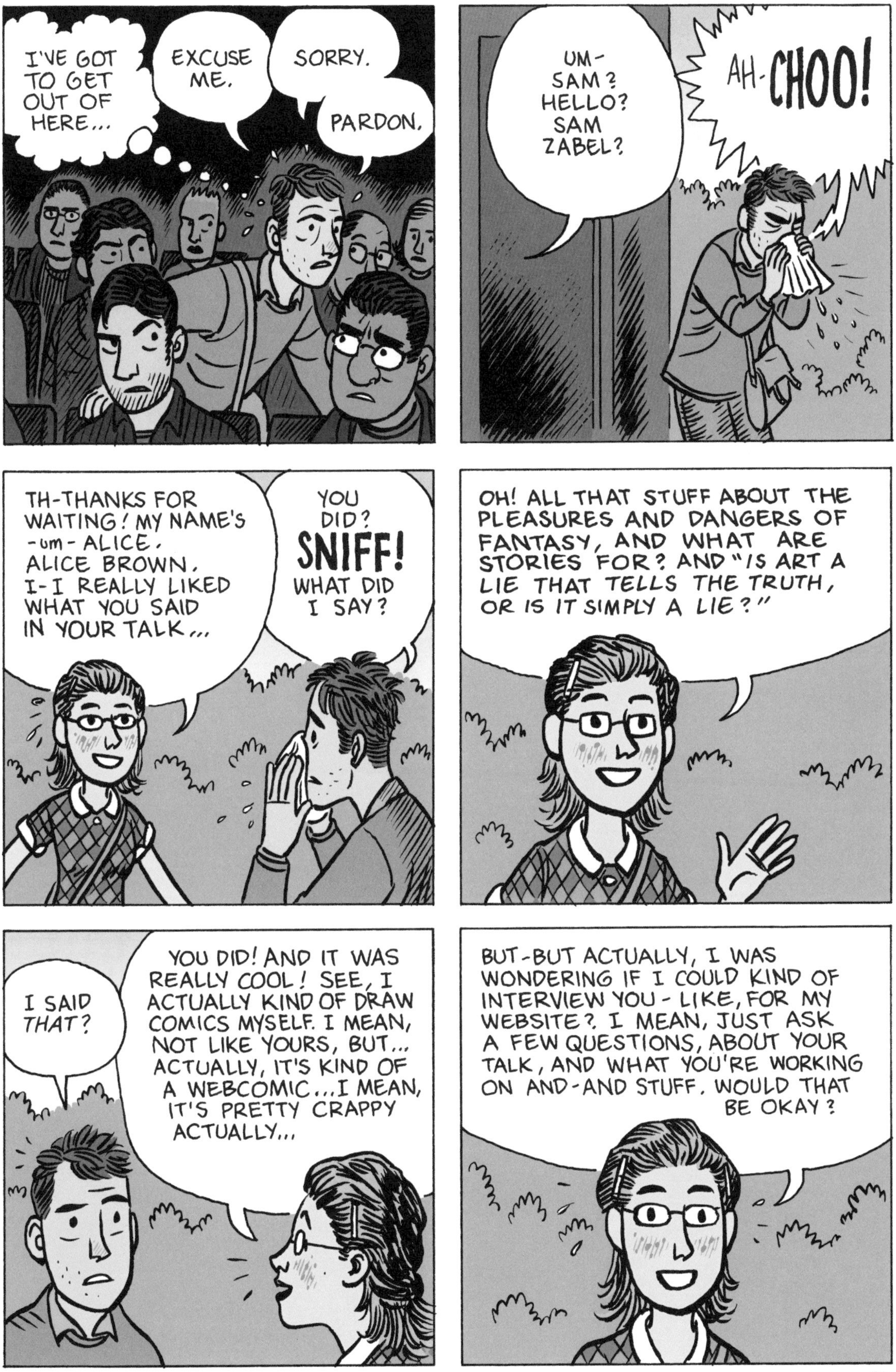
I'VE GOT TO GET OUT OF HERE...
EXCUSE ME.
SORRY.
PARDON.
UM- SAM? HELLO? SAM ZABEL?
AH-CHOO!
TH-THANKS FOR WAITING! MY NAME'S -um- ALICE. ALICE BROWN. I-I REALLY LIKED WHAT YOU SAID IN YOUR TALK...
YOU DID? SNIFF! WHAT DID I SAY?
OH! ALL THAT STUFF ABOUT THE PLEASURES AND DANGERS OF FANTASY, AND WHAT ARE STORIES FOR? AND "IS ART A LIE THAT TELLS THE TRUTH, OR IS IT SIMPLY A LIE?"
I SAID THAT?
YOU DID! AND IT WAS REALLY COOL! SEE, I ACTUALLY KIND OF DRAW COMICS MYSELF. I MEAN, NOT LIKE YOURS, BUT... ACTUALLY, IT'S KIND OF A WEBCOMIC...I MEAN, IT'S PRETTY CRAPPY ACTUALLY...
BUT-BUT ACTUALLY, I WAS WONDERING IF I COULD KIND OF INTERVIEW YOU- LIKE, FOR MY WEBSITE? I MEAN, JUST ASK A FEW QUESTIONS, ABOUT YOUR TALK, AND WHAT YOU'RE WORKING ON AND-AND STUFF. WOULD THAT BE OKAY?

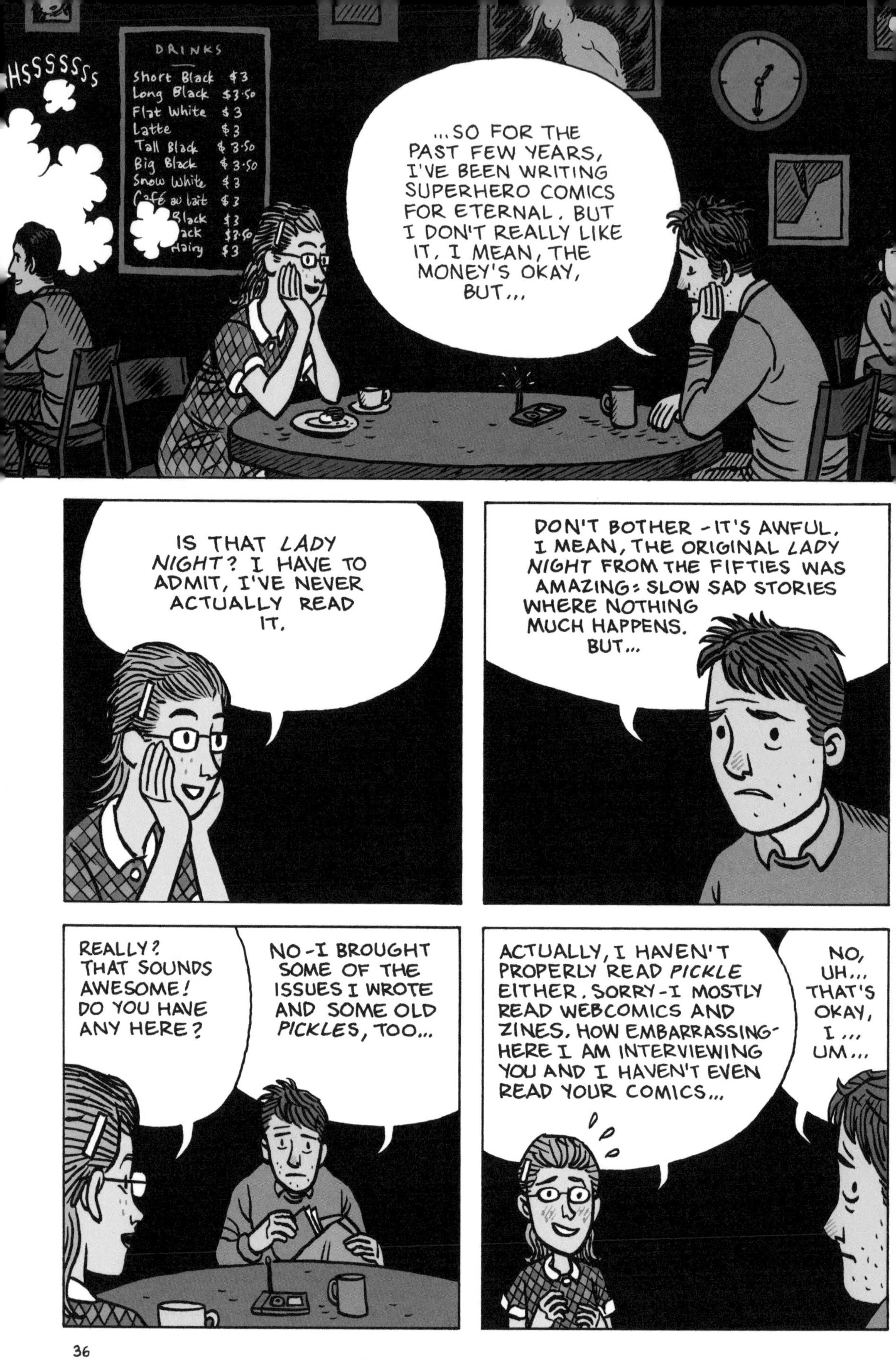
HSSSSSSs
DRINKS
Short Black $3
Long Black $3·50
Flat White $3
Latte $3
Tall Black $3·50
Big Black $3·50
Snow White $3
...SO FOR THE PAST FEW YEARS, I'VE BEEN WRITING SUPERHERO COMICS FOR ETERNAL. BUT I DON'T REALLY LIKE IT. I MEAN, THE MONEY'S OKAY, BUT...
IS THAT *LADY NIGHT*? I HAVE TO ADMIT, I'VE NEVER ACTUALLY READ IT.
DON'T BOTHER - IT'S AWFUL. I MEAN, THE ORIGINAL *LADY NIGHT* FROM THE FIFTIES WAS AMAZING: SLOW SAD STORIES WHERE NOTHING MUCH HAPPENS. BUT...
REALLY? THAT SOUNDS AWESOME! DO YOU HAVE ANY HERE?
NO - I BROUGHT SOME OF THE ISSUES I WROTE AND SOME OLD *PICKLES*, TOO...
ACTUALLY, I HAVEN'T PROPERLY READ *PICKLE* EITHER. SORRY - I MOSTLY READ WEBCOMICS AND ZINES. HOW EMBARRASSING - HERE I AM INTERVIEWING YOU AND I HAVEN'T EVEN READ YOUR COMICS...
NO, UH... THAT'S OKAY, I... UM...

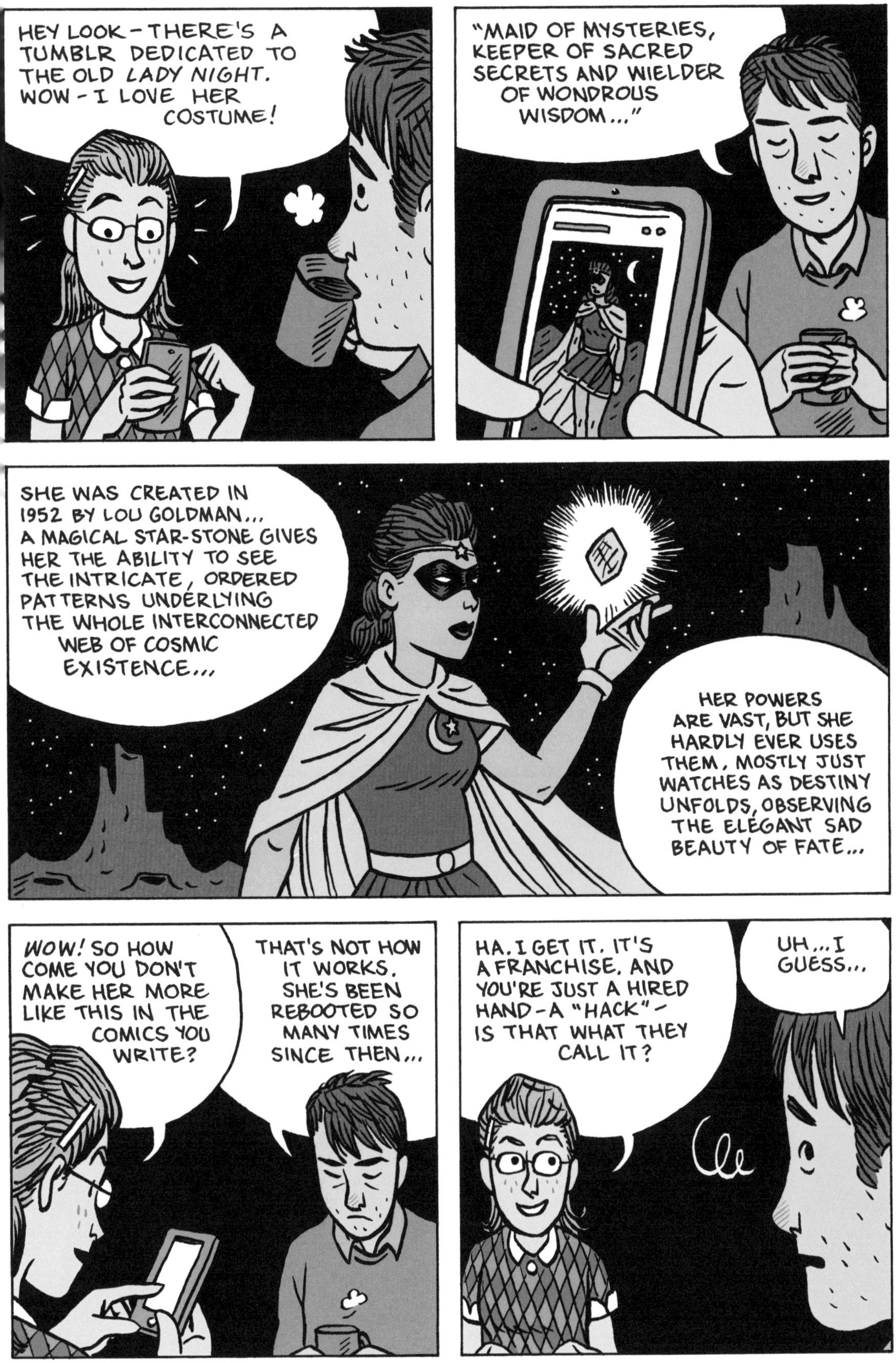
HEY LOOK - THERE'S A TUMBLR DEDICATED TO THE OLD *LADY NIGHT*. WOW - I LOVE HER COSTUME!
"MAID OF MYSTERIES, KEEPER OF SACRED SECRETS AND WIELDER OF WONDROUS WISDOM..."
SHE WAS CREATED IN 1952 BY LOU GOLDMAN... A MAGICAL STAR-STONE GIVES HER THE ABILITY TO SEE THE INTRICATE, ORDERED PATTERNS UNDERLYING THE WHOLE INTERCONNECTED WEB OF COSMIC EXISTENCE...
HER POWERS ARE VAST, BUT SHE HARDLY EVER USES THEM, MOSTLY JUST WATCHES AS DESTINY UNFOLDS, OBSERVING THE ELEGANT SAD BEAUTY OF FATE...
WOW! SO HOW COME YOU DON'T MAKE HER MORE LIKE THIS IN THE COMICS YOU WRITE?
THAT'S NOT HOW IT WORKS. SHE'S BEEN REBOOTED SO MANY TIMES SINCE THEN...
HA. I GET IT. IT'S A FRANCHISE. AND YOU'RE JUST A HIRED HAND - A "HACK" - IS THAT WHAT THEY CALL IT?
UH... I GUESS...

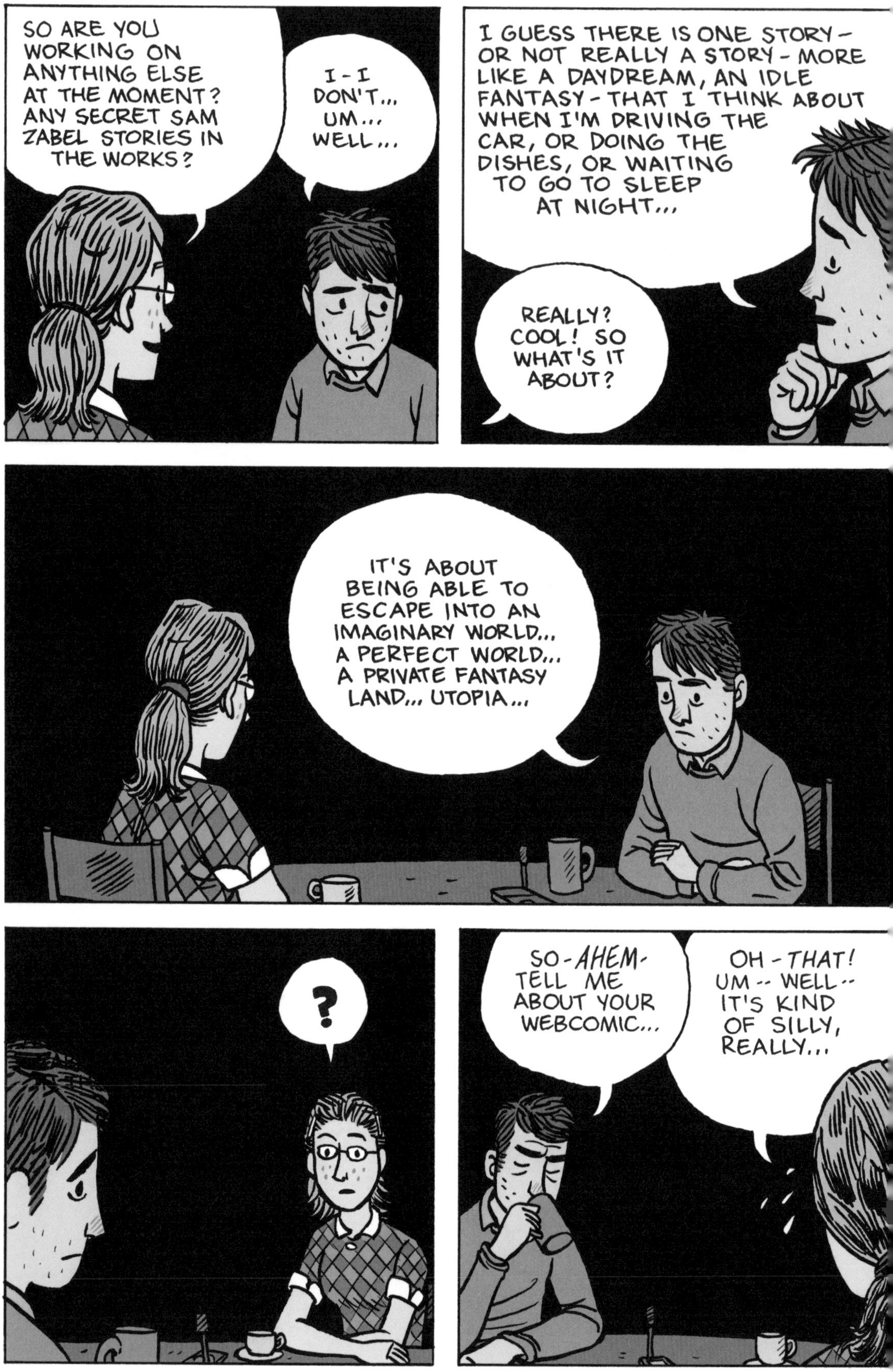
SO ARE YOU WORKING ON ANYTHING ELSE AT THE MOMENT? ANY SECRET SAM ZABEL STORIES IN THE WORKS?
I-I DON'T... UM... WELL...
I GUESS THERE IS ONE STORY— OR NOT REALLY A STORY—MORE LIKE A DAYDREAM, AN IDLE FANTASY—THAT I THINK ABOUT WHEN I'M DRIVING THE CAR, OR DOING THE DISHES, OR WAITING TO GO TO SLEEP AT NIGHT...
REALLY? COOL! SO WHAT'S IT ABOUT?
IT'S ABOUT BEING ABLE TO ESCAPE INTO AN IMAGINARY WORLD... A PERFECT WORLD... A PRIVATE FANTASY LAND... UTOPIA...
?
SO-*AHEM*-TELL ME ABOUT YOUR WEBCOMIC...
OH-*THAT*! UM-- WELL-- IT'S KIND OF SILLY, REALLY...

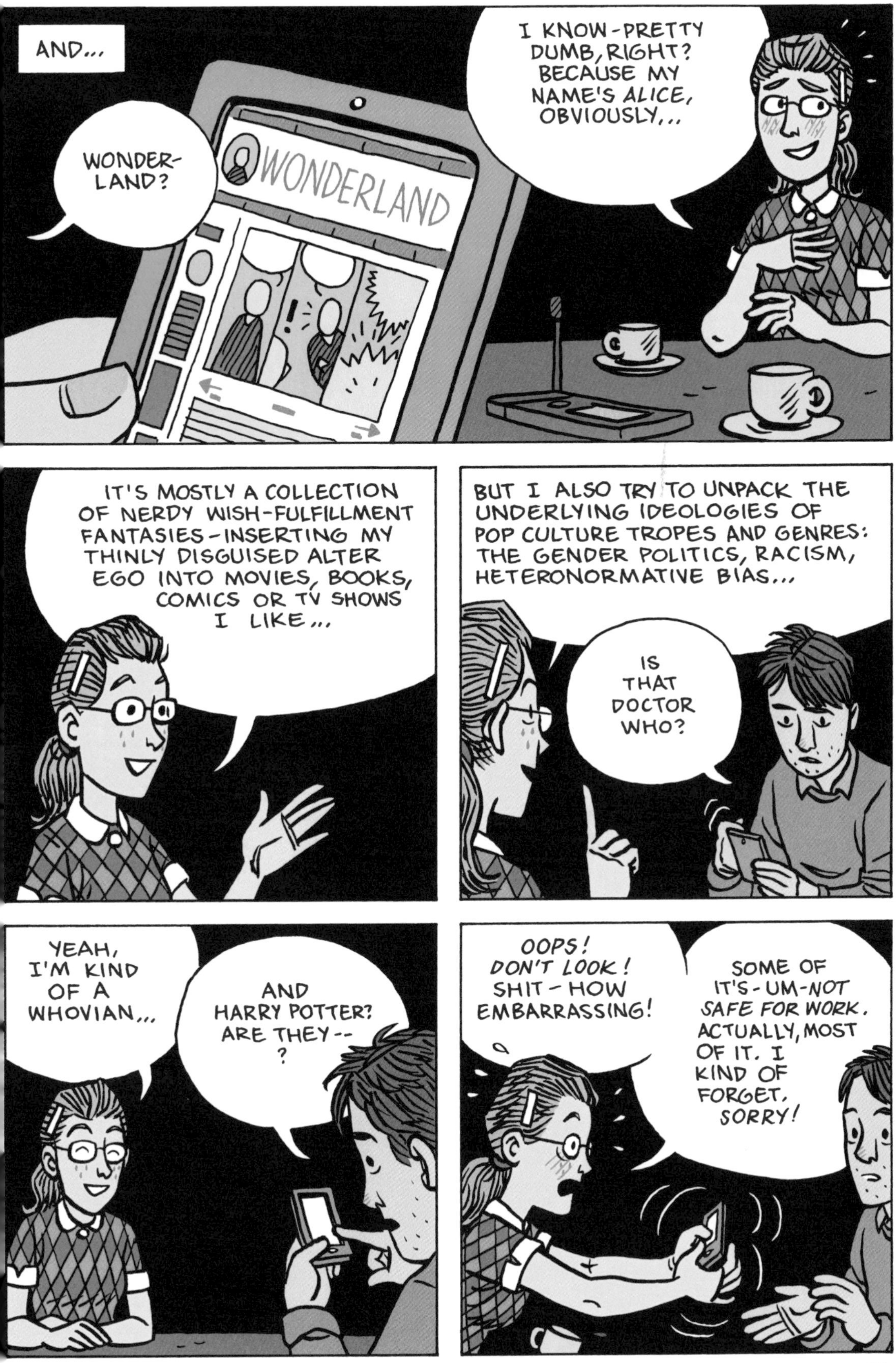
AND...
WONDER-LAND?
WONDERLAND
I KNOW-PRETTY DUMB, RIGHT? BECAUSE MY NAME'S ALICE, OBVIOUSLY...
IT'S MOSTLY A COLLECTION OF NERDY WISH-FULFILLMENT FANTASIES-INSERTING MY THINLY DISGUISED ALTER EGO INTO MOVIES, BOOKS, COMICS OR TV SHOWS I LIKE...
BUT I ALSO TRY TO UNPACK THE UNDERLYING IDEOLOGIES OF POP CULTURE TROPES AND GENRES: THE GENDER POLITICS, RACISM, HETERONORMATIVE BIAS...
IS THAT DOCTOR WHO?
YEAH, I'M KIND OF A WHOVIAN...
AND HARRY POTTER? ARE THEY-- ?
OOPS! DON'T LOOK! SHIT-HOW EMBARRASSING!
SOME OF IT'S-UM-NOT SAFE FOR WORK. ACTUALLY, MOST OF IT. I KIND OF FORGET. SORRY!

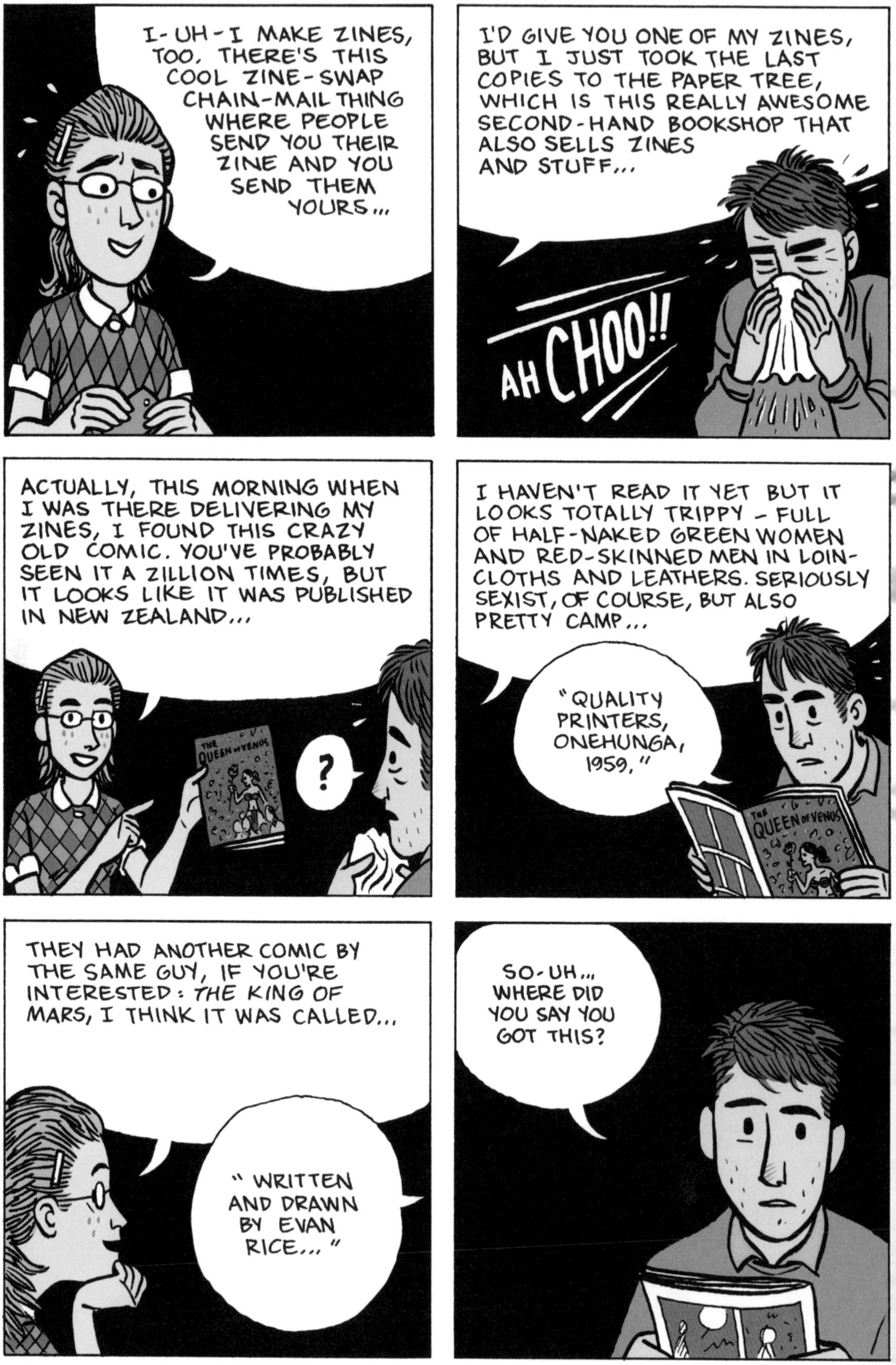
I- UH - I MAKE ZINES, TOO. THERE'S THIS COOL ZINE-SWAP CHAIN-MAIL THING WHERE PEOPLE SEND YOU THEIR ZINE AND YOU SEND THEM YOURS...
I'D GIVE YOU ONE OF MY ZINES, BUT I JUST TOOK THE LAST COPIES TO THE PAPER TREE, WHICH IS THIS REALLY AWESOME SECOND-HAND BOOKSHOP THAT ALSO SELLS ZINES AND STUFF...
AH CHOO!!
ACTUALLY, THIS MORNING WHEN I WAS THERE DELIVERING MY ZINES, I FOUND THIS CRAZY OLD COMIC. YOU'VE PROBABLY SEEN IT A ZILLION TIMES, BUT IT LOOKS LIKE IT WAS PUBLISHED IN NEW ZEALAND...
THE QUEEN OF VENUS
?
I HAVEN'T READ IT YET BUT IT LOOKS TOTALLY TRIPPY - FULL OF HALF-NAKED GREEN WOMEN AND RED-SKINNED MEN IN LOIN-CLOTHS AND LEATHERS. SERIOUSLY SEXIST, OF COURSE, BUT ALSO PRETTY CAMP...
"QUALITY PRINTERS, ONEHUNGA, 1959."
THE QUEEN OF VENUS
THEY HAD ANOTHER COMIC BY THE SAME GUY, IF YOU'RE INTERESTED: THE KING OF MARS, I THINK IT WAS CALLED...
" WRITTEN AND DRAWN BY EVAN RICE..."
SO-UH... WHERE DID YOU SAY YOU GOT THIS?

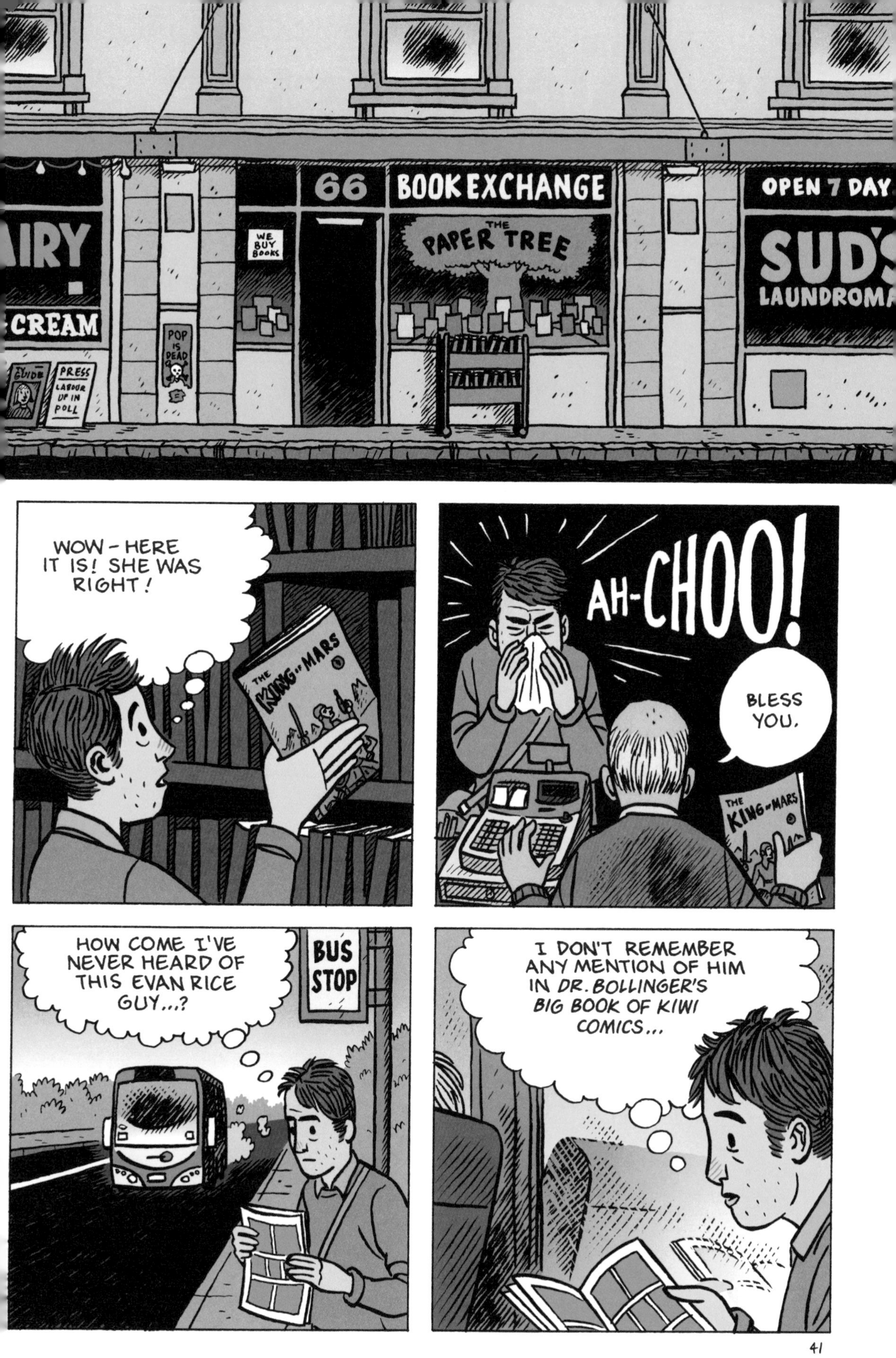
66
BOOK EXCHANGE
THE PAPER TREE
WE BUY BOOKS
OPEN 7 DAY
SUD'S LAUNDROMA
AIRY
CREAM
POP IS DEAD
PRESS LABOUR UP IN POLL
WOW - HERE IT IS! SHE WAS RIGHT!
THE KING OF MARS
AH-CHOO!
BLESS YOU.
THE KING OF MARS
HOW COME I'VE NEVER HEARD OF THIS EVAN RICE GUY...?
BUS STOP
I DON'T REMEMBER ANY MENTION OF HIM IN *DR. BOLLINGER'S BIG BOOK OF KIWI COMICS*...

THE KING OF MARS

by Evan Rice

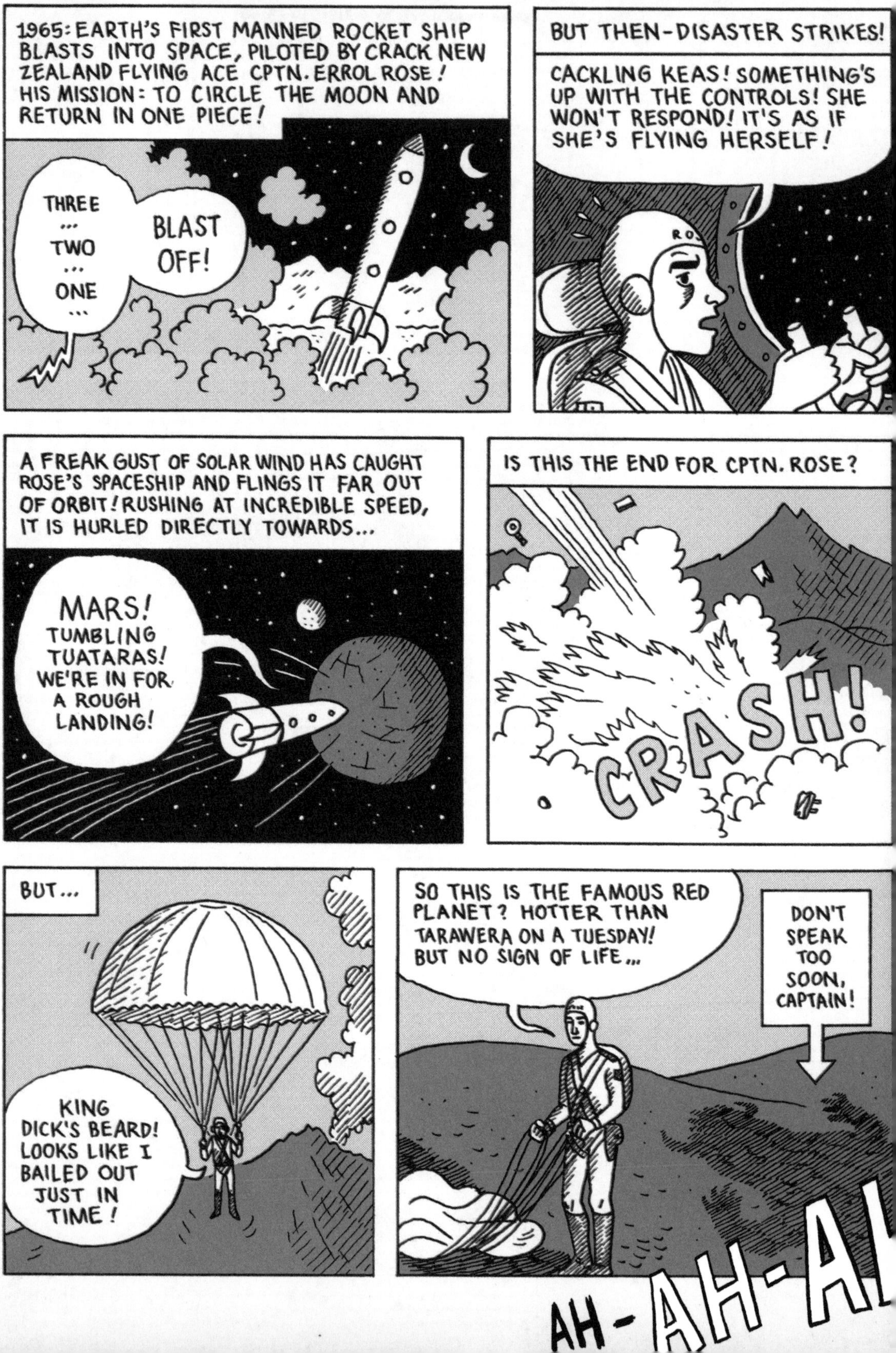
1965: EARTH'S FIRST MANNED ROCKET SHIP BLASTS INTO SPACE, PILOTED BY CRACK NEW ZEALAND FLYING ACE CPTN. ERROL ROSE! HIS MISSION: TO CIRCLE THE MOON AND RETURN IN ONE PIECE!
THREE ... TWO ... ONE ...
BLAST OFF!
BUT THEN-DISASTER STRIKES!
CACKLING KEAS! SOMETHING'S UP WITH THE CONTROLS! SHE WON'T RESPOND! IT'S AS IF SHE'S FLYING HERSELF!
A FREAK GUST OF SOLAR WIND HAS CAUGHT ROSE'S SPACESHIP AND FLINGS IT FAR OUT OF ORBIT! RUSHING AT INCREDIBLE SPEED, IT IS HURLED DIRECTLY TOWARDS...
MARS! TUMBLING TUATARAS! WE'RE IN FOR A ROUGH LANDING!
IS THIS THE END FOR CPTN. ROSE?
CRASH!
BUT...
KING DICK'S BEARD! LOOKS LIKE I BAILED OUT JUST IN TIME!
SO THIS IS THE FAMOUS RED PLANET? HOTTER THAN TARAWERA ON A TUESDAY! BUT NO SIGN OF LIFE...
DON'T SPEAK TOO SOON, CAPTAIN!
AH-AH-A

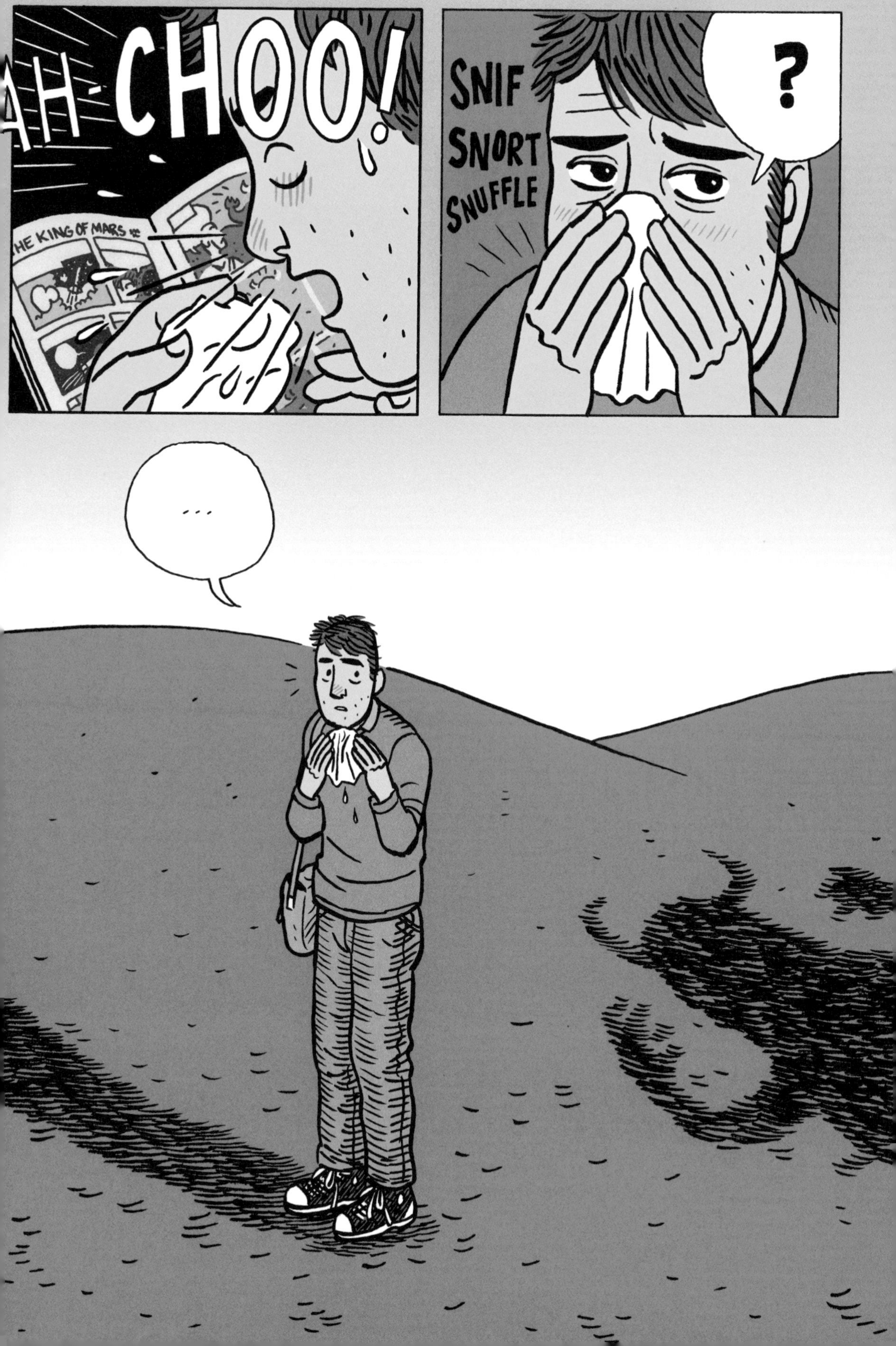
AH-CHOO!
HE KING OF MARS
SNIF
SNORT
SNUFFLE
?
...

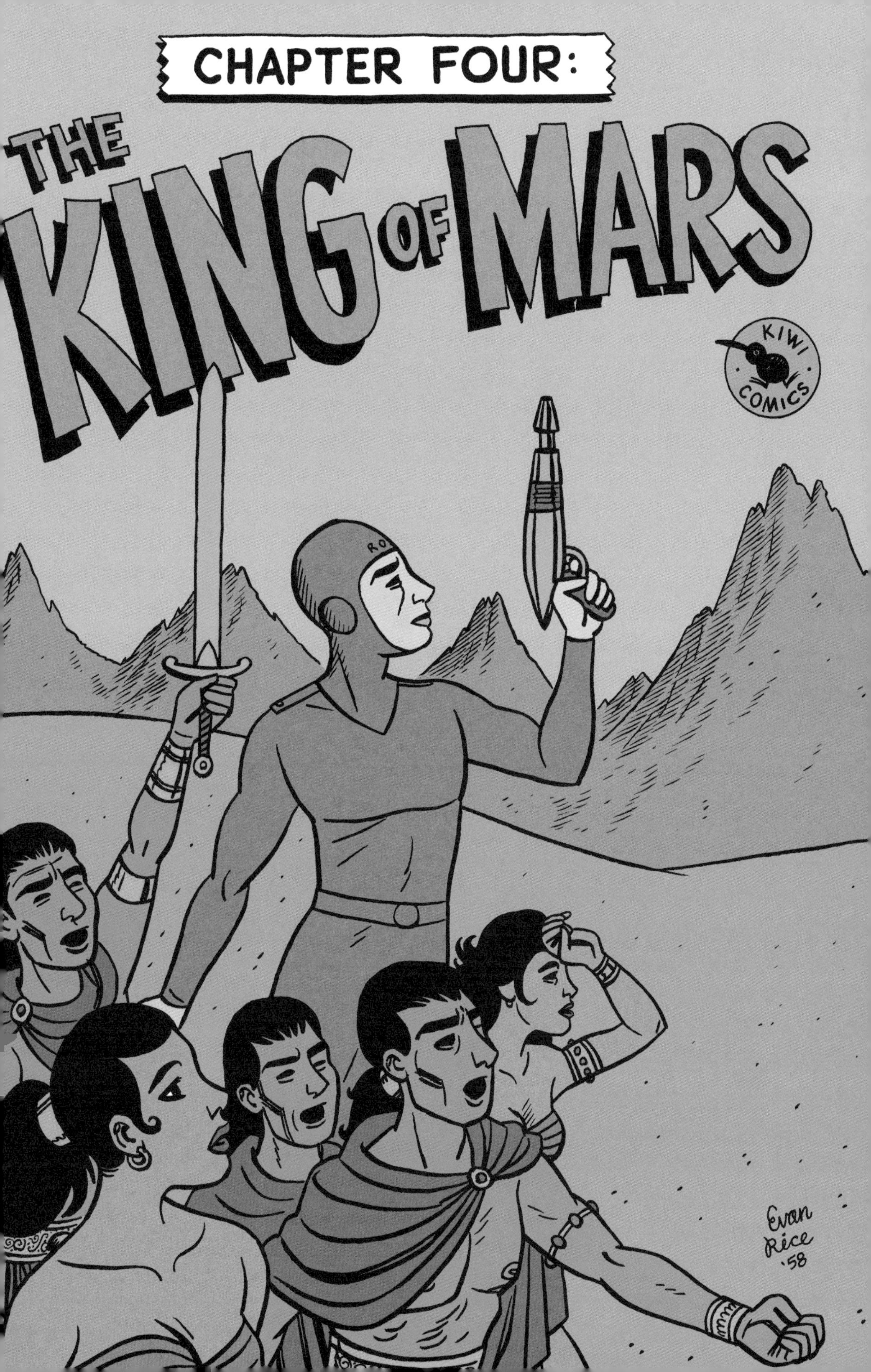
CHAPTER FOUR:
THE KING OF MARS
KIWI COMICS
RO
Evan Rice '58

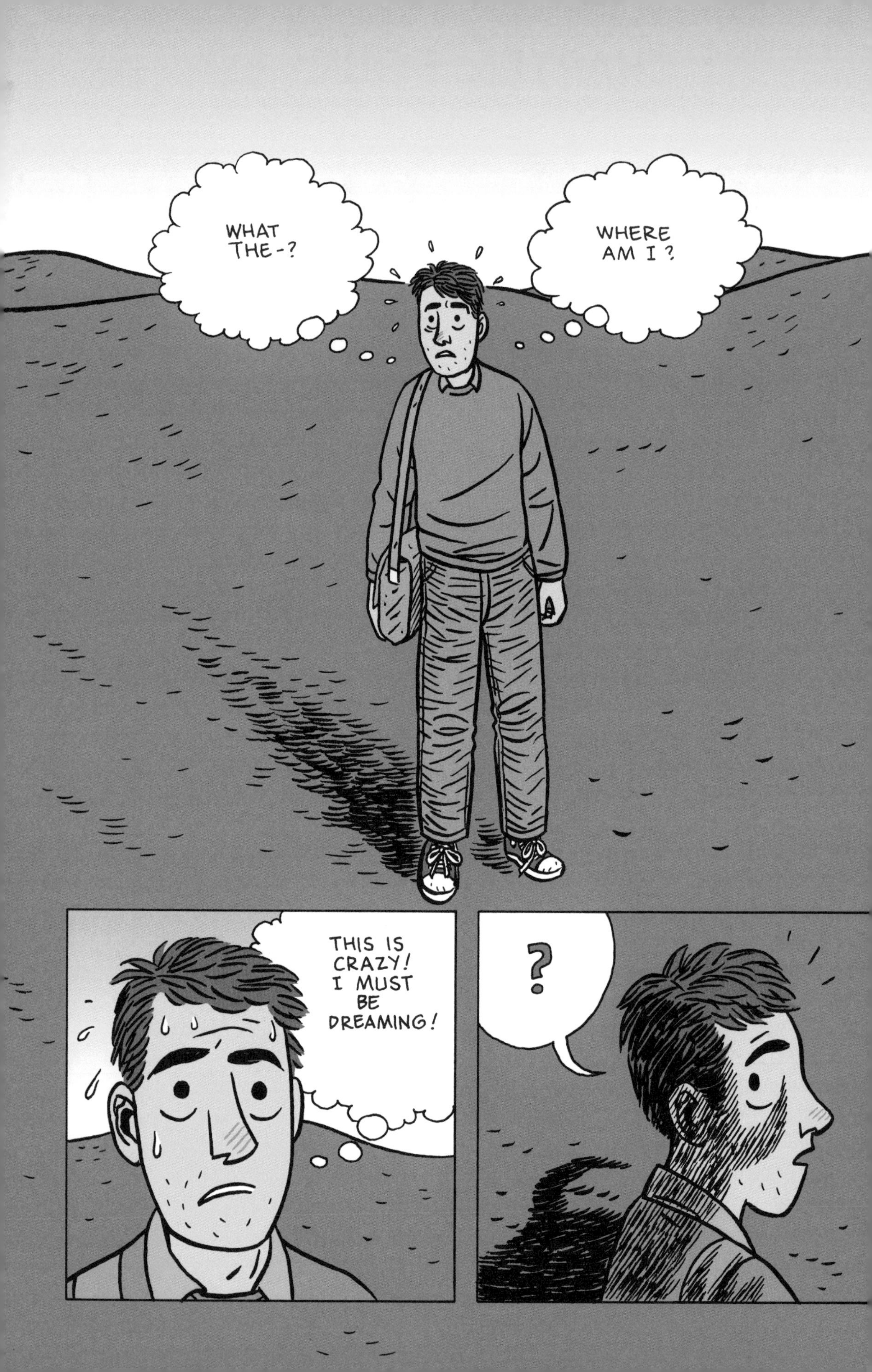
WHAT THE-?
WHERE AM I?
THIS IS CRAZY! I MUST BE DREAMING!
?

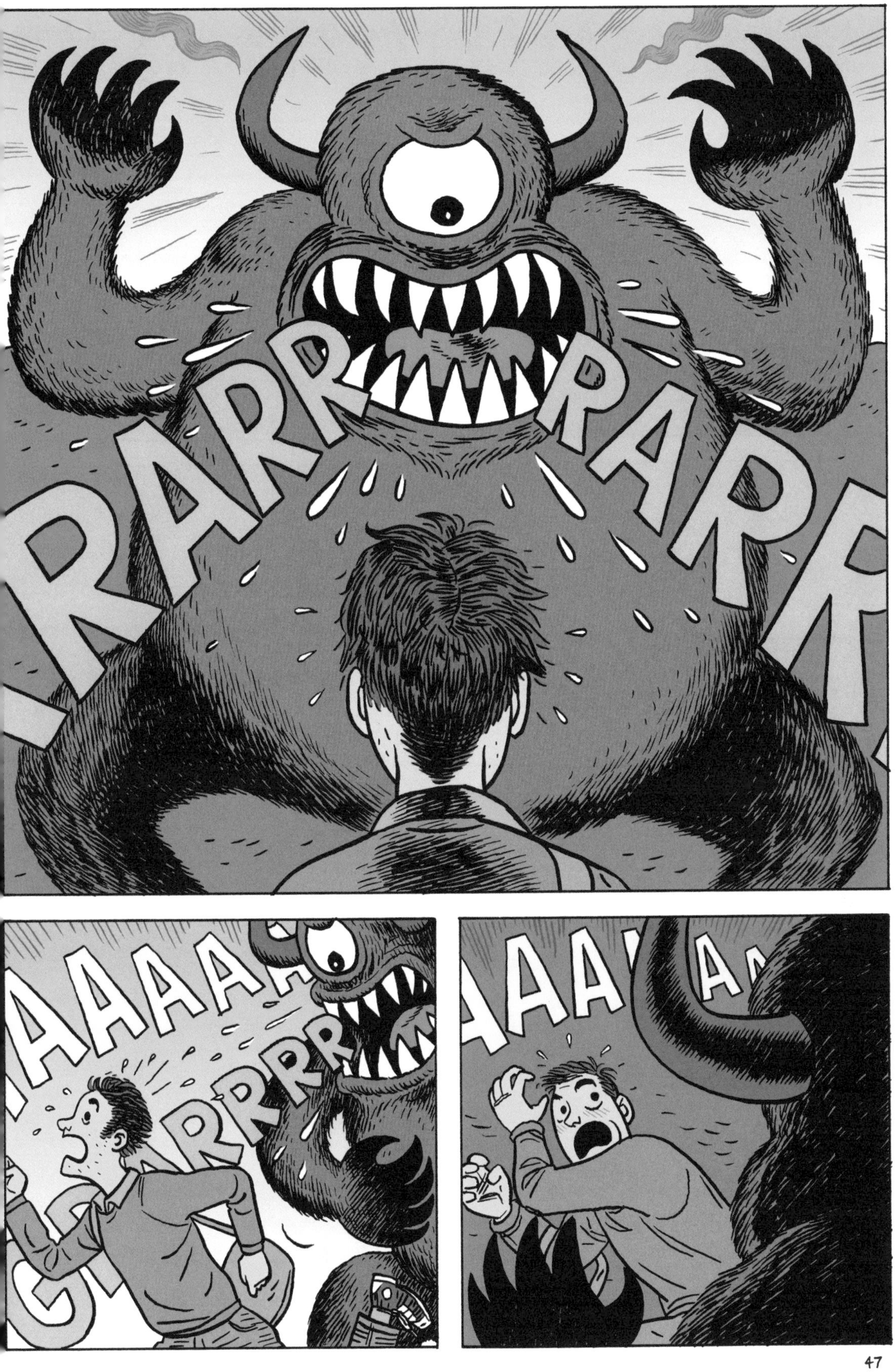
RARR
RARR
AAAA
GRRRR
AAA

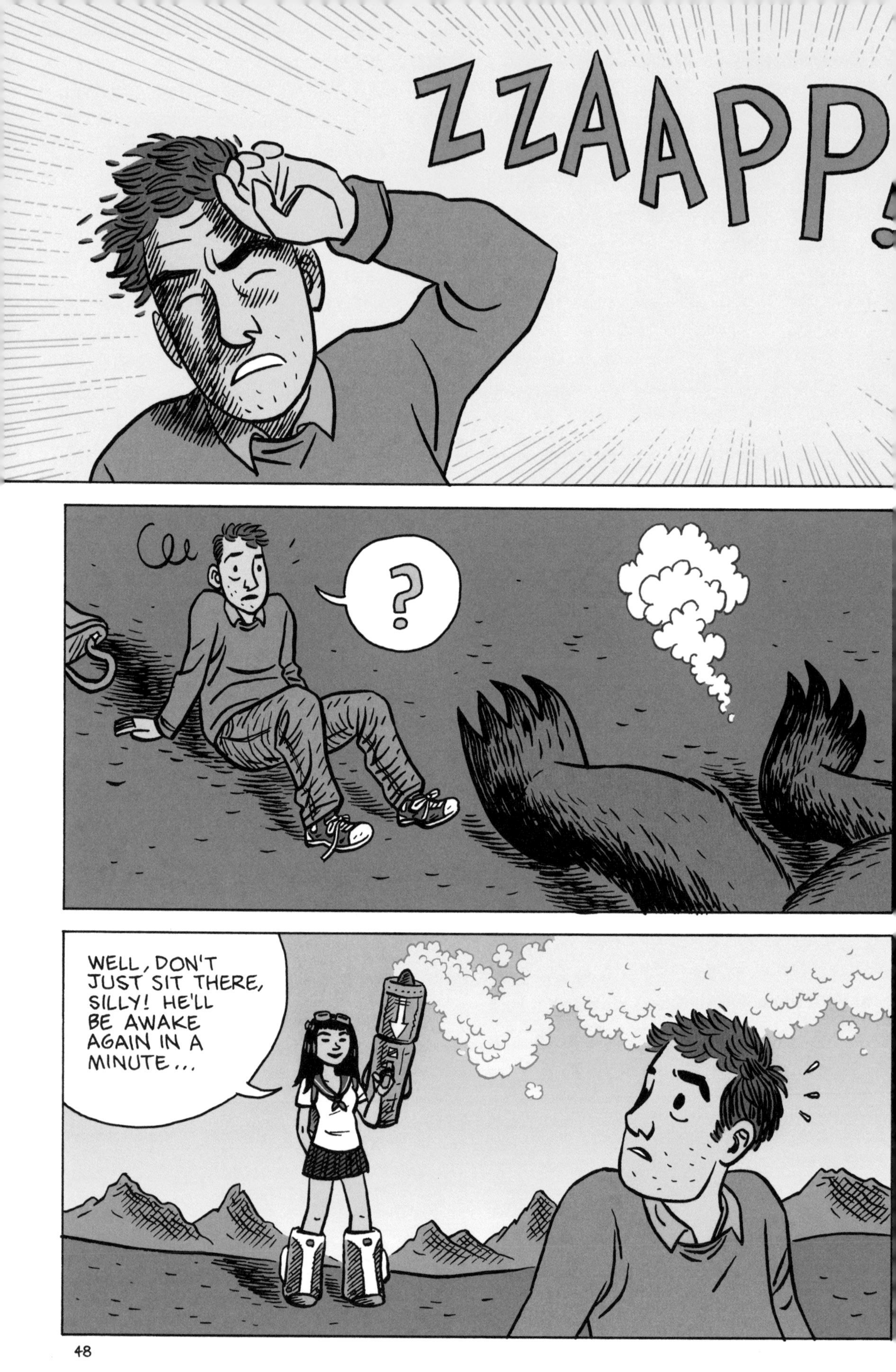
ZZAAPP!
?
WELL, DON'T JUST SIT THERE, SILLY! HE'LL BE AWAKE AGAIN IN A MINUTE...

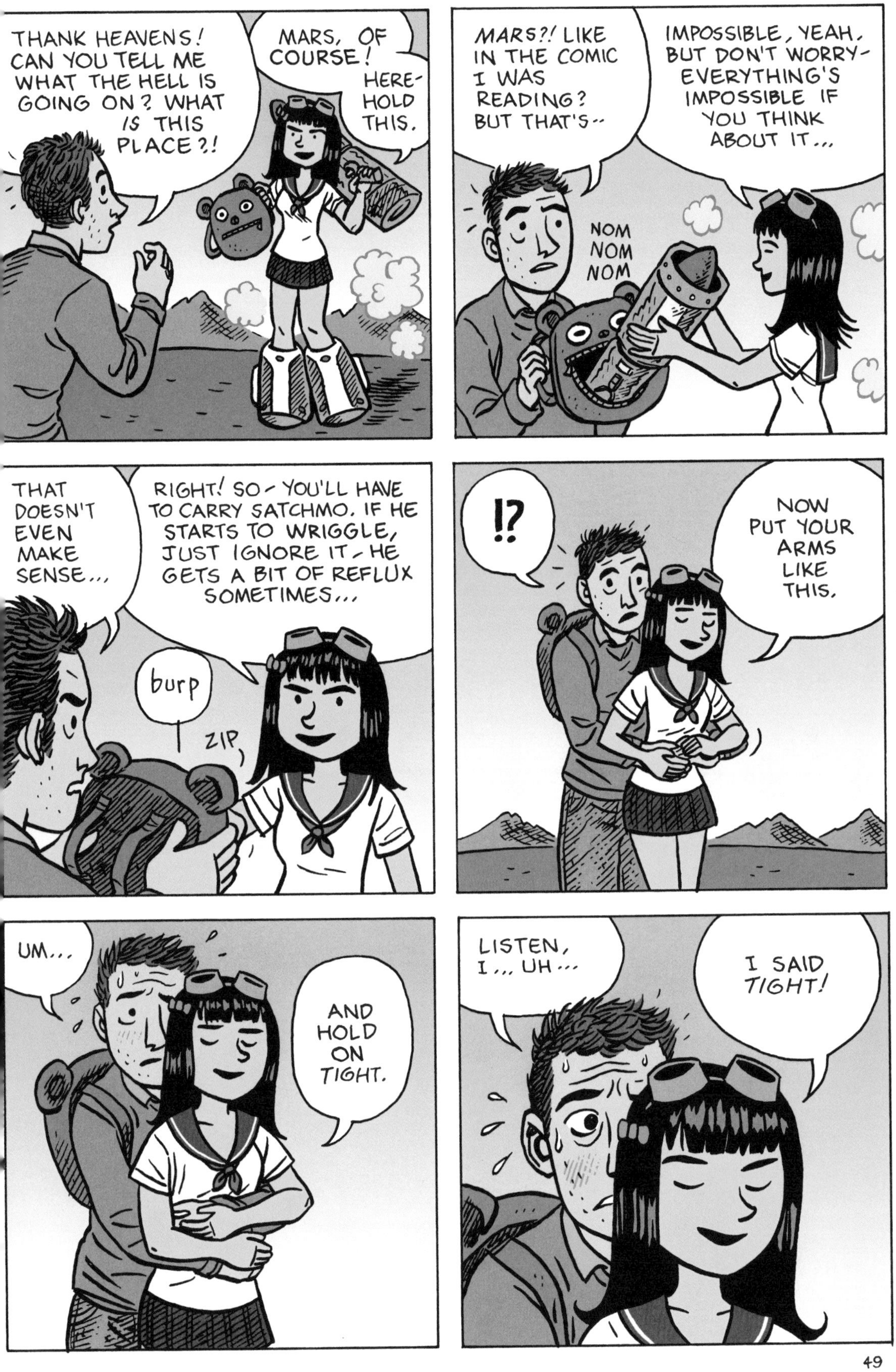
THANK HEAVENS! CAN YOU TELL ME WHAT THE HELL IS GOING ON? WHAT *IS* THIS PLACE?!
MARS, OF COURSE!
HERE- HOLD THIS.
MARS?! LIKE IN THE COMIC I WAS READING? BUT THAT'S--
IMPOSSIBLE, YEAH, BUT DON'T WORRY- EVERYTHING'S IMPOSSIBLE IF YOU THINK ABOUT IT...
NOM NOM NOM
THAT DOESN'T EVEN MAKE SENSE...
RIGHT! SO- YOU'LL HAVE TO CARRY SATCHMO. IF HE STARTS TO WRIGGLE, JUST IGNORE IT- HE GETS A BIT OF REFLUX SOMETIMES...
burp
ZIP
!?
NOW PUT YOUR ARMS LIKE THIS.
UM...
AND HOLD ON *TIGHT*.
LISTEN, I... UH...
I SAID *TIGHT!*

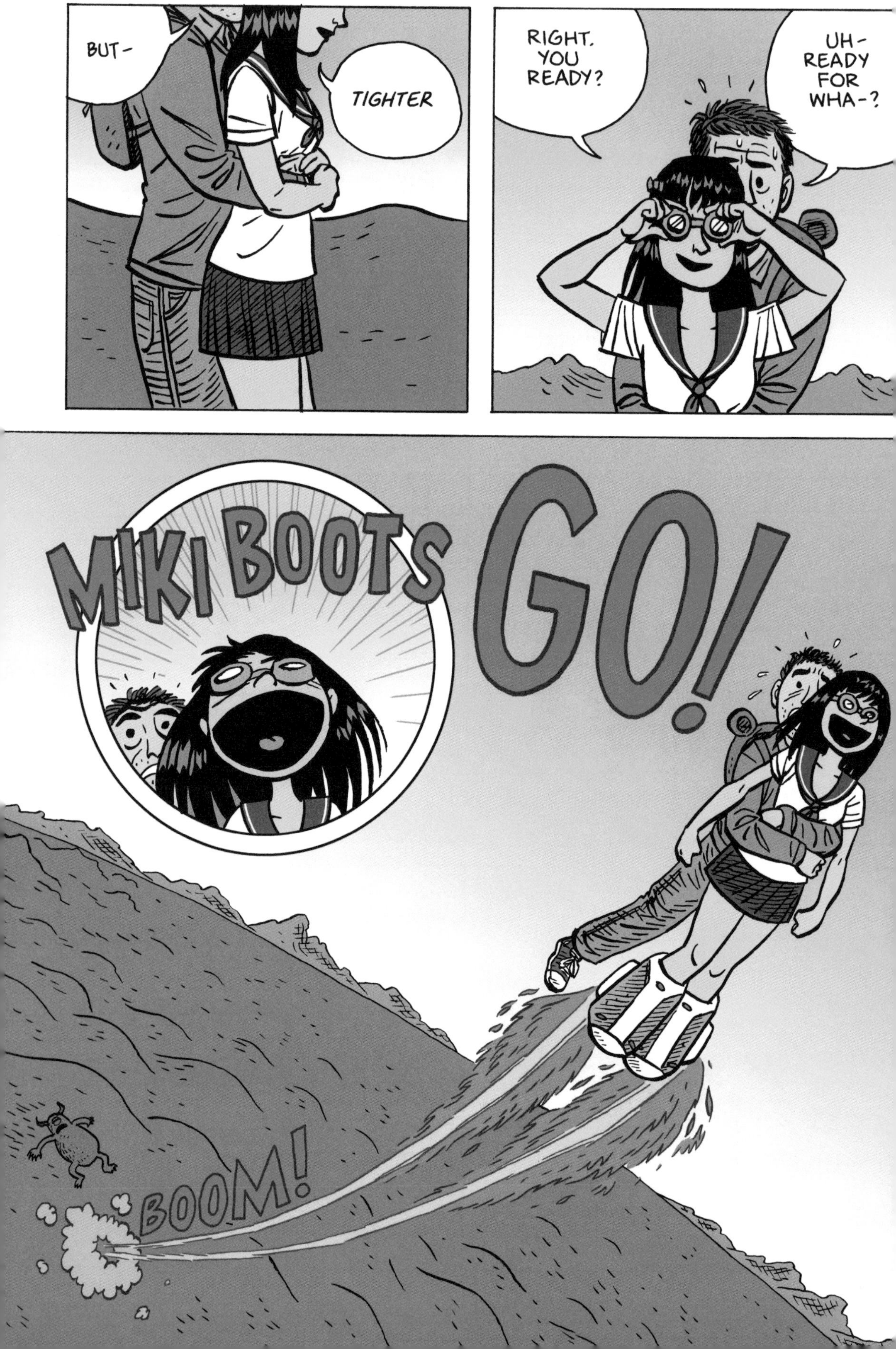
BUT-
TIGHTER
RIGHT. YOU READY?
UH-READY FOR WHA-?
MIKI BOOTS GO!
BOOM!

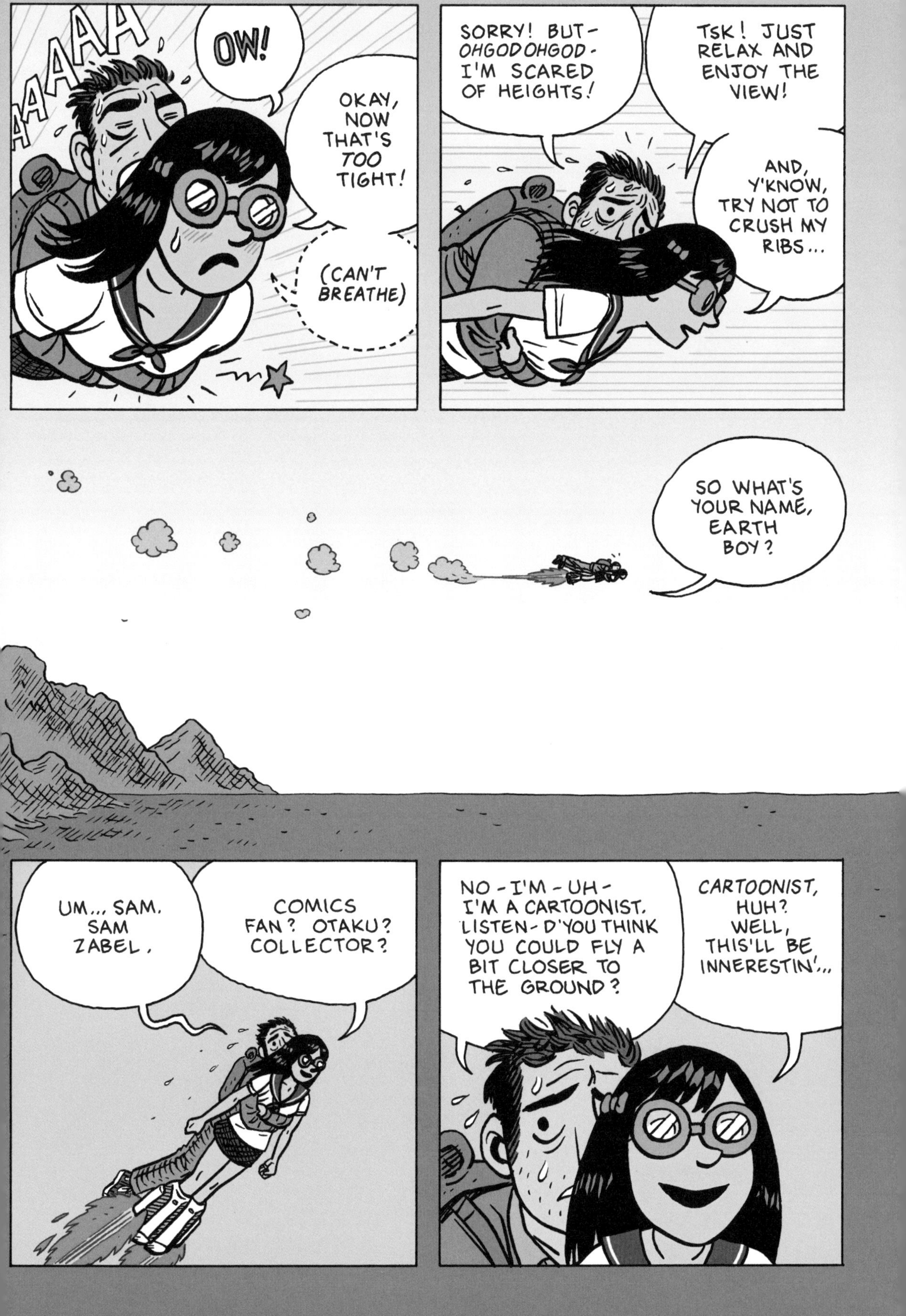
AAAAAA
OW!
OKAY, NOW THAT'S *TOO* TIGHT!
(CAN'T BREATHE)
SORRY! BUT- OHGODOHGOD- I'M SCARED OF HEIGHTS!
TSK! JUST RELAX AND ENJOY THE VIEW!
AND, Y'KNOW, TRY NOT TO CRUSH MY RIBS...
SO WHAT'S YOUR NAME, EARTH BOY?
UM... SAM. SAM ZABEL.
COMICS FAN? OTAKU? COLLECTOR?
NO - I'M - UH - I'M A CARTOONIST. LISTEN- D'YOU THINK YOU COULD FLY A BIT CLOSER TO THE GROUND?
CARTOONIST, HUH? WELL, THIS'LL BE INNERESTIN'...

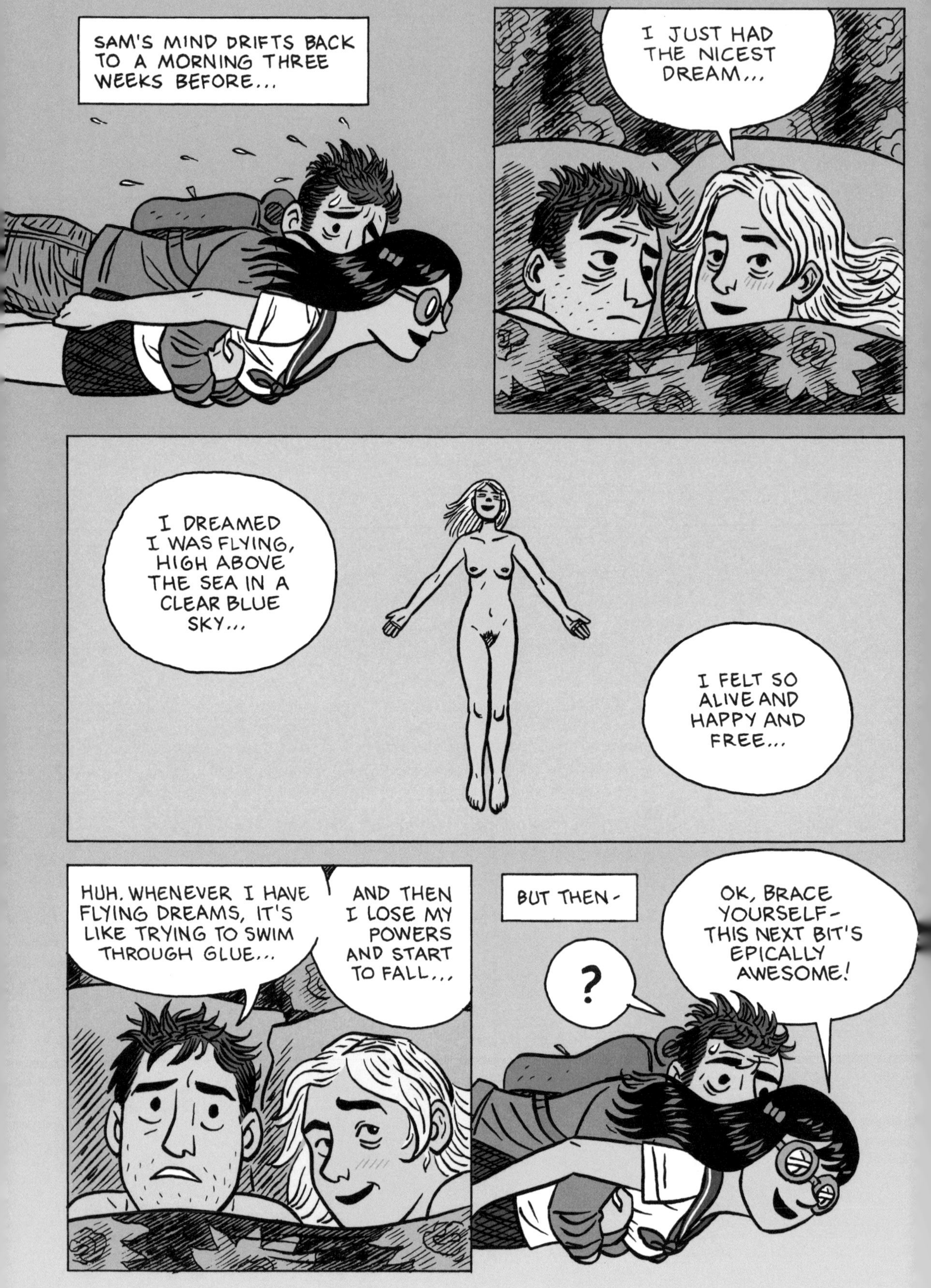
SAM'S MIND DRIFTS BACK TO A MORNING THREE WEEKS BEFORE...
I JUST HAD THE NICEST DREAM...
I DREAMED I WAS FLYING, HIGH ABOVE THE SEA IN A CLEAR BLUE SKY...
I FELT SO ALIVE AND HAPPY AND FREE...
HUH. WHENEVER I HAVE FLYING DREAMS, IT'S LIKE TRYING TO SWIM THROUGH GLUE...
AND THEN I LOSE MY POWERS AND START TO FALL...
BUT THEN-
?
OK, BRACE YOURSELF- THIS NEXT BIT'S EPICALLY AWESOME!

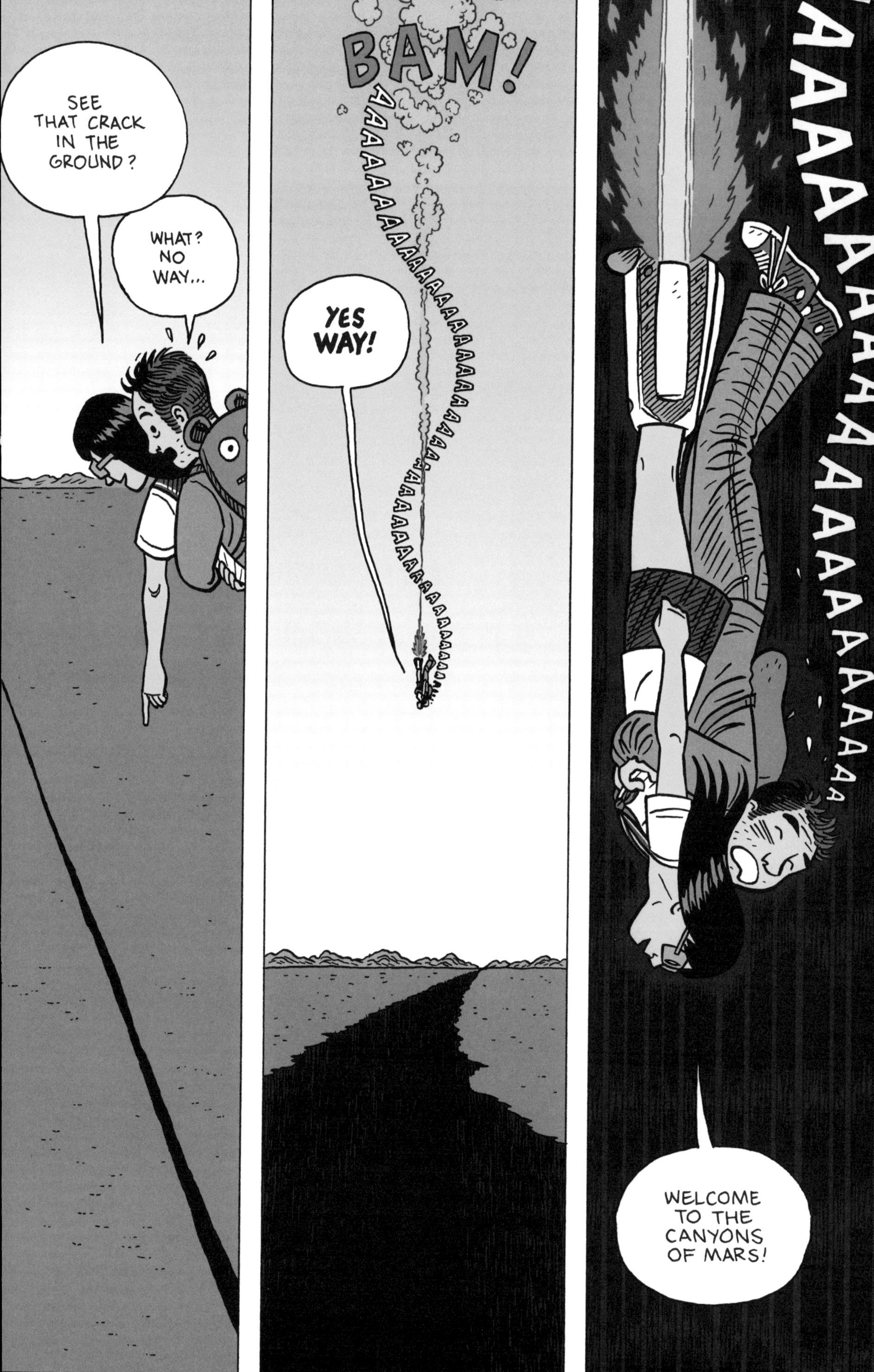
SEE THAT CRACK IN THE GROUND?
WHAT? NO WAY...
BAM!
AAAAAAAAAAAAAAAAAAAAAAAAAAAAAAAA
YES WAY!
AAAAAAAAAAAAAAAAAAAA
WELCOME TO THE CANYONS OF MARS!

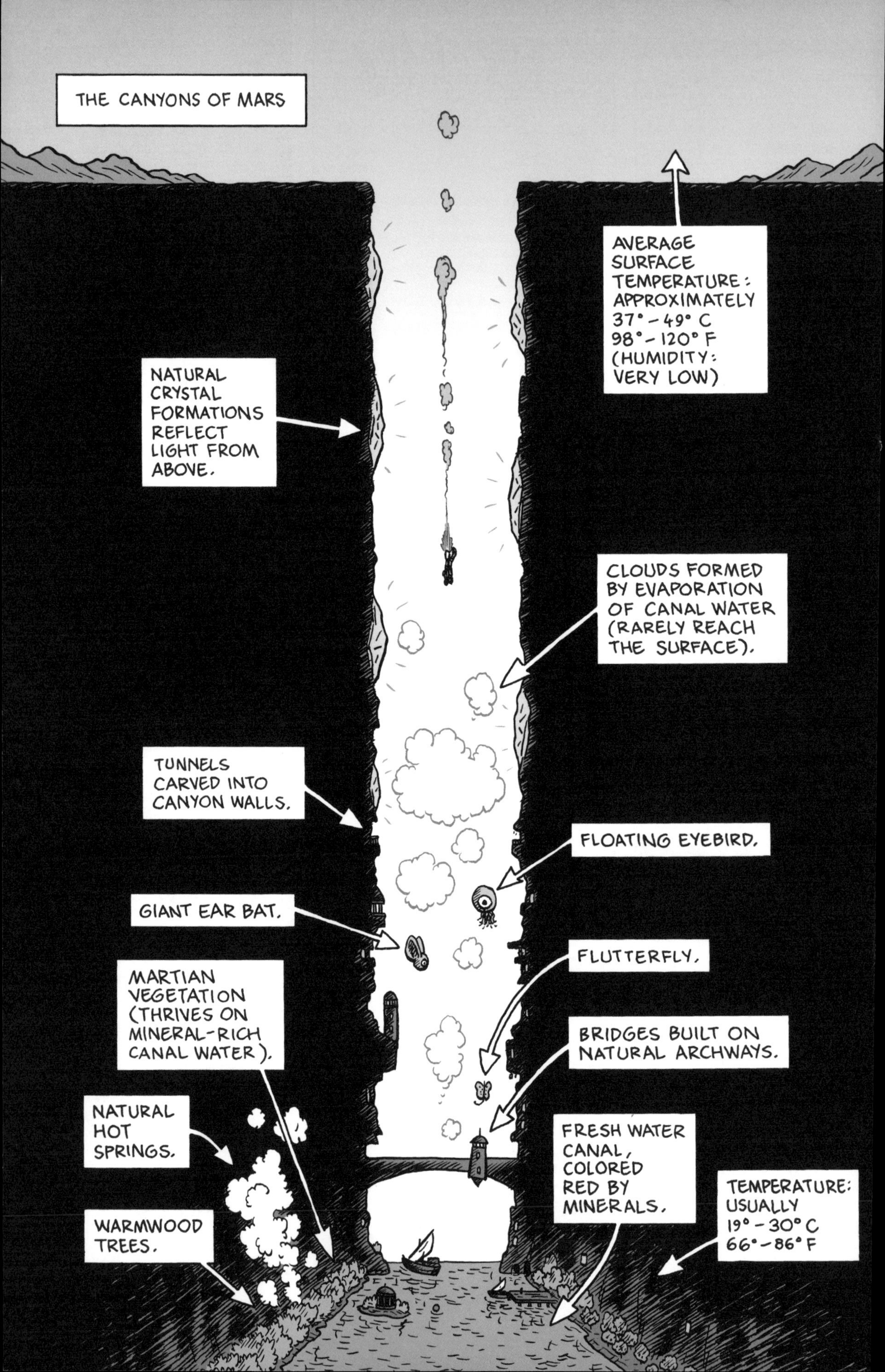
THE CANYONS OF MARS
AVERAGE SURFACE TEMPERATURE: APPROXIMATELY 37° – 49° C 98° – 120° F (HUMIDITY: VERY LOW)
NATURAL CRYSTAL FORMATIONS REFLECT LIGHT FROM ABOVE.
CLOUDS FORMED BY EVAPORATION OF CANAL WATER (RARELY REACH THE SURFACE).
TUNNELS CARVED INTO CANYON WALLS.
FLOATING EYEBIRD.
GIANT EAR BAT.
FLUTTERFLY.
MARTIAN VEGETATION (THRIVES ON MINERAL-RICH CANAL WATER).
BRIDGES BUILT ON NATURAL ARCHWAYS.
NATURAL HOT SPRINGS.
FRESH WATER CANAL, COLORED RED BY MINERALS.
TEMPERATURE: USUALLY 19° – 30° C 66° – 86° F
WARMWOOD TREES.

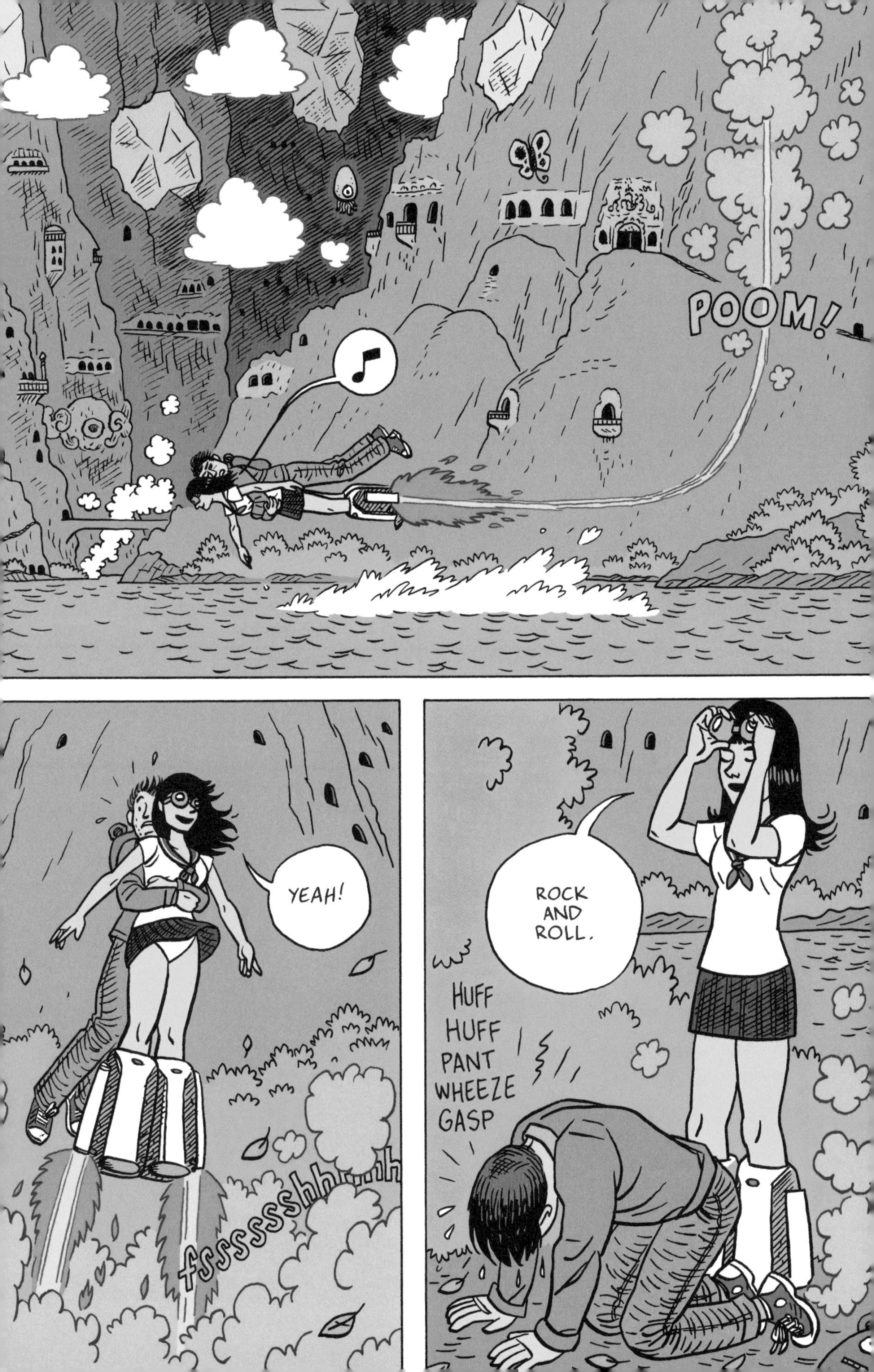
POOM!
YEAH!
fsssssshhh...h
ROCK AND ROLL.
HUFF
HUFF
PANT
WHEEZE
GASP

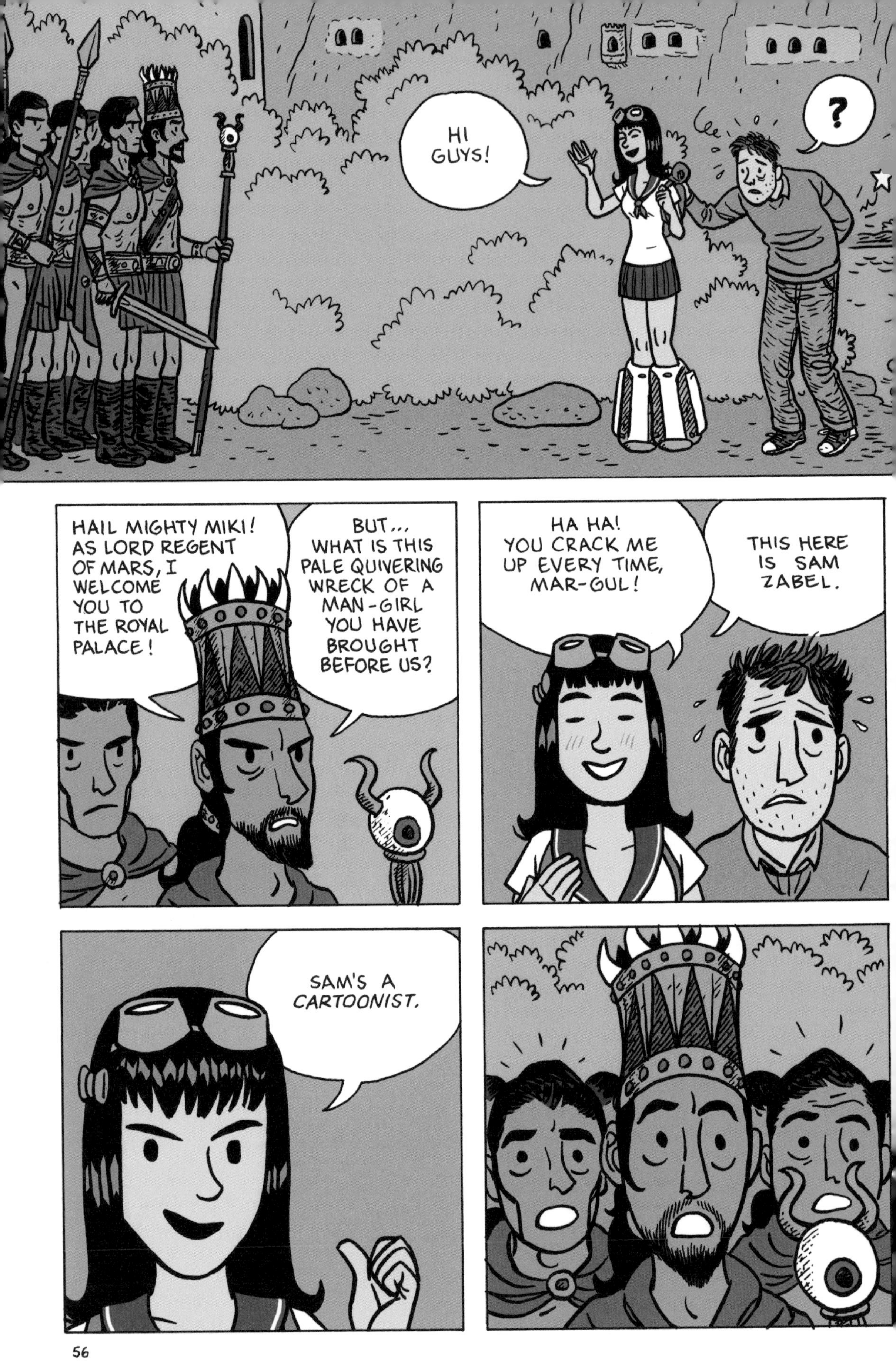
HI GUYS!
?
HAIL MIGHTY MIKI! AS LORD REGENT OF MARS, I WELCOME YOU TO THE ROYAL PALACE!
BUT... WHAT IS THIS PALE QUIVERING WRECK OF A MAN-GIRL YOU HAVE BROUGHT BEFORE US?
HA HA! YOU CRACK ME UP EVERY TIME, MAR-GUL!
THIS HERE IS SAM ZABEL.
SAM'S A *CARTOONIST.*

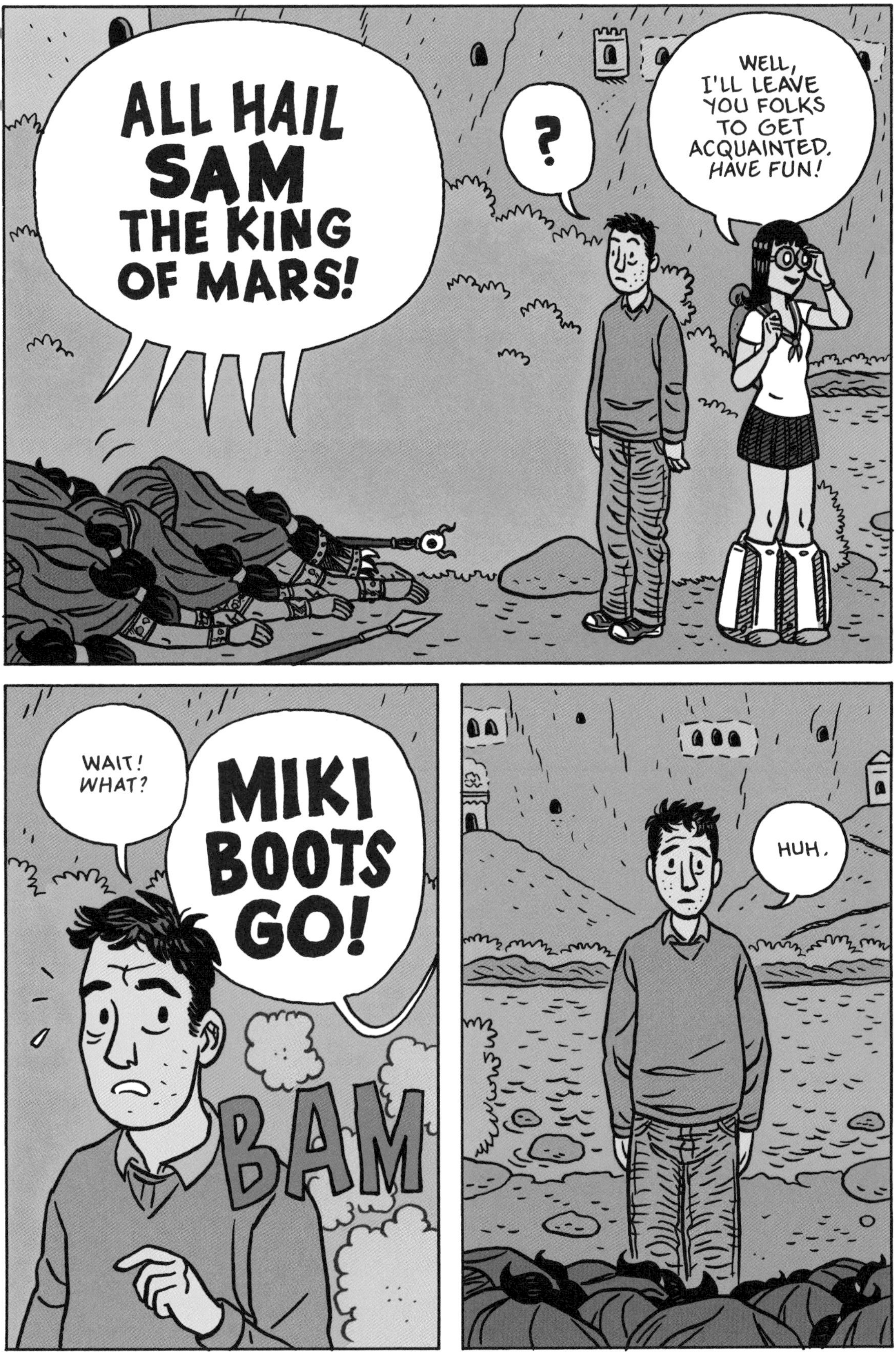
ALL HAIL SAM THE KING OF MARS!
?
WELL, I'LL LEAVE YOU FOLKS TO GET ACQUAINTED. HAVE FUN!
WAIT! WHAT?
MIKI BOOTS GO!
BAM
HUH.

Chapter Five

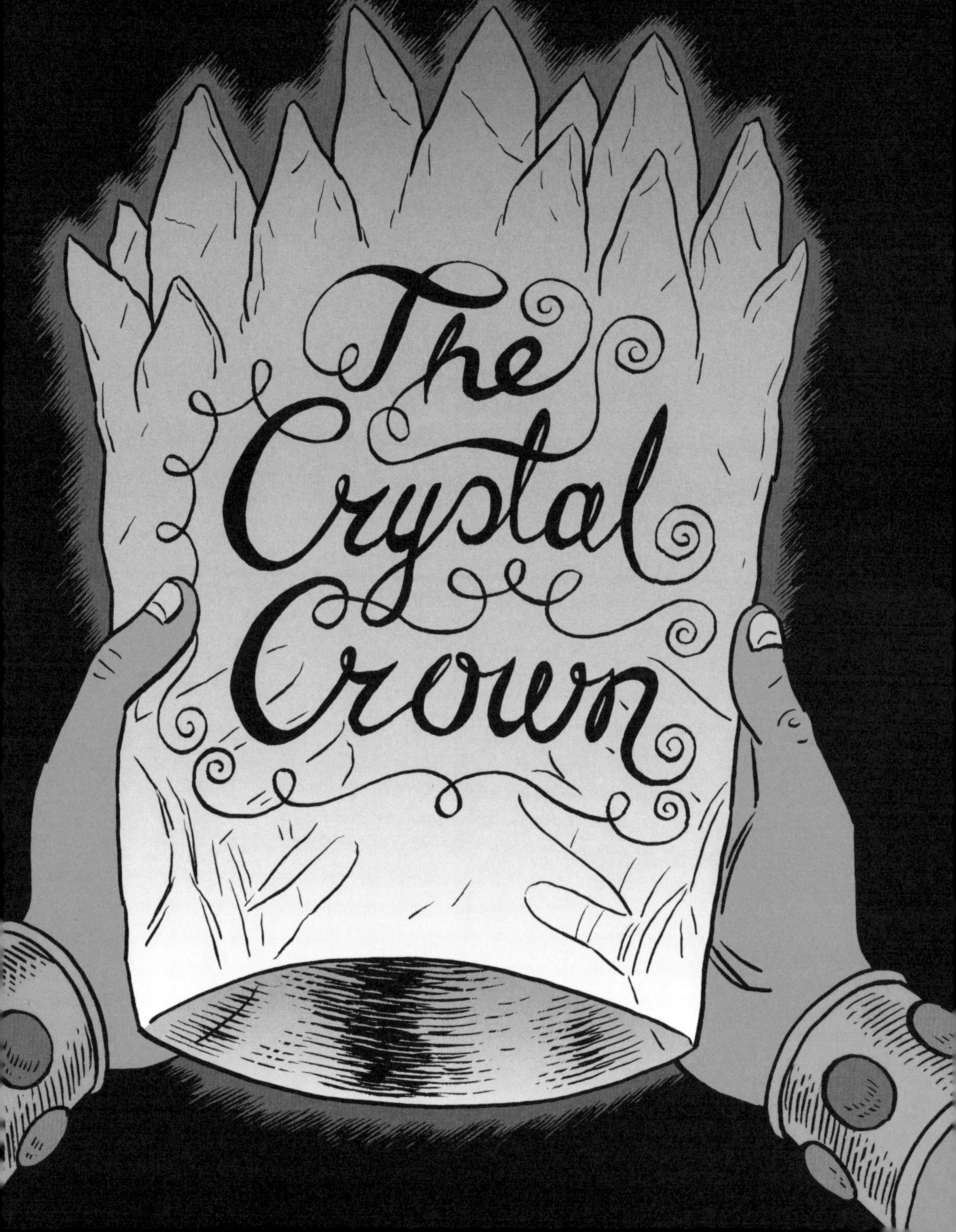
The Crystal Crown

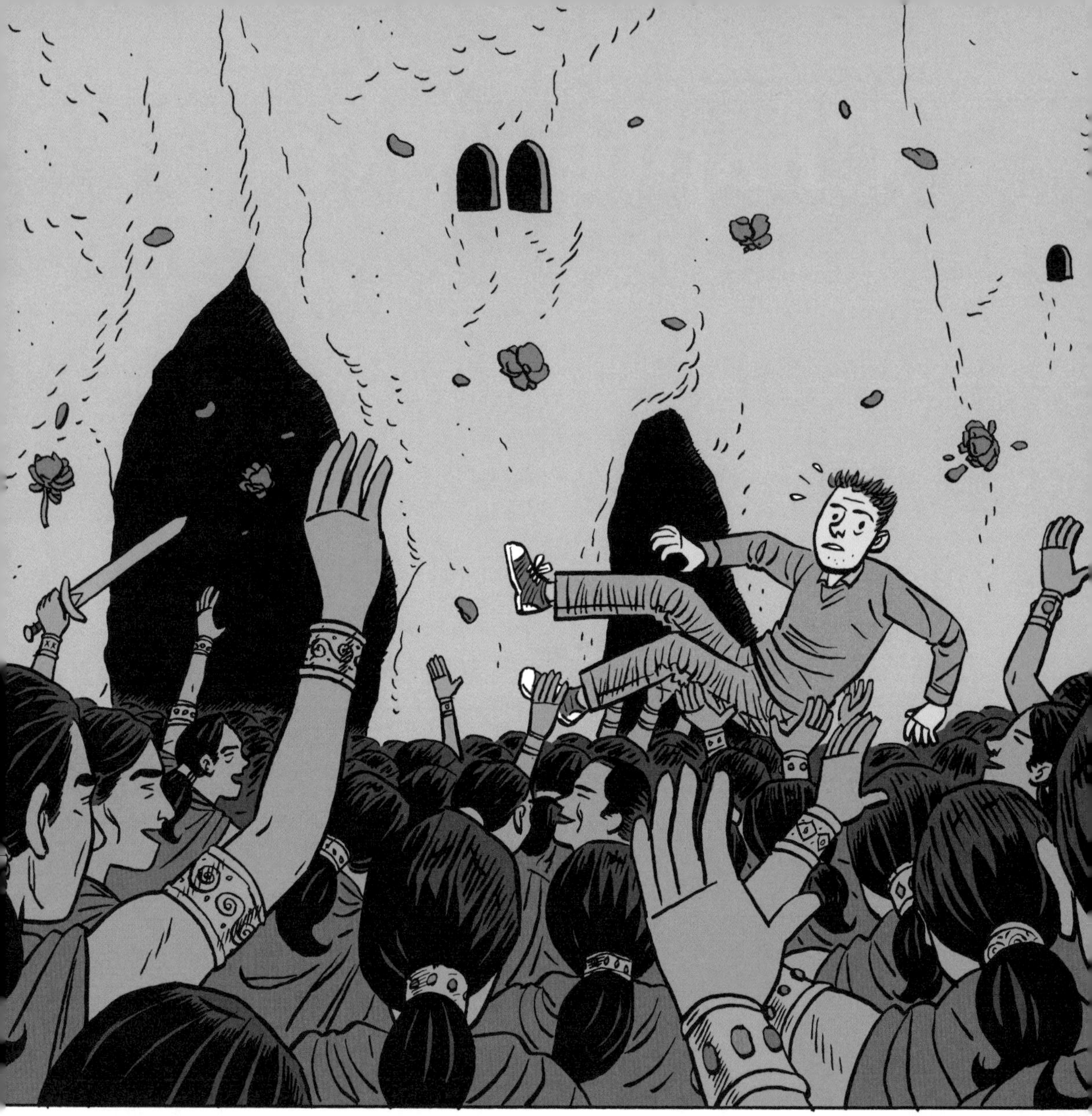

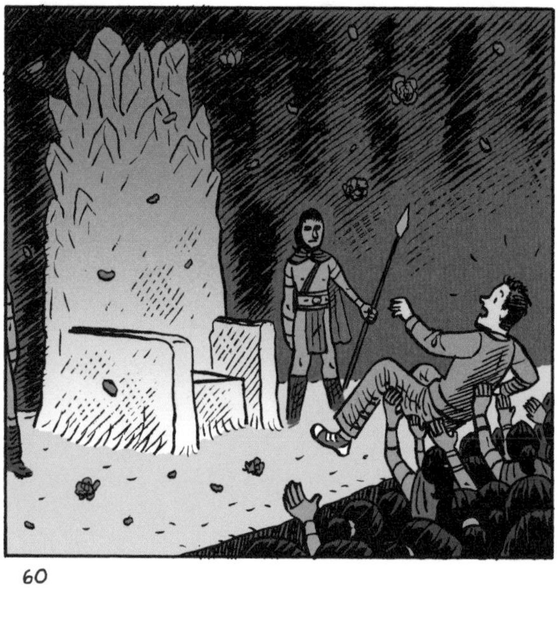

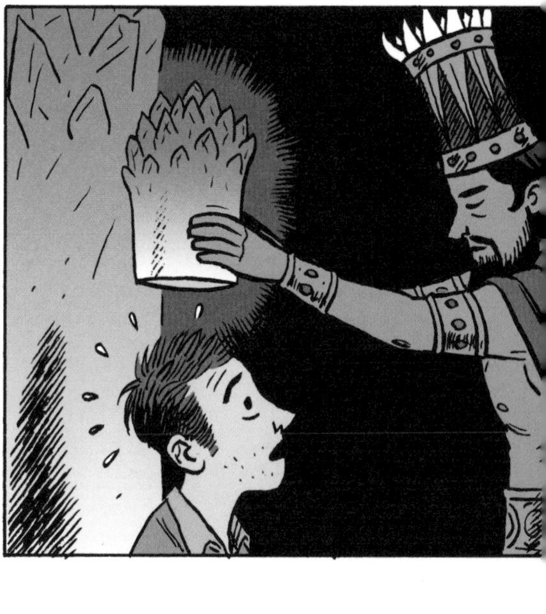

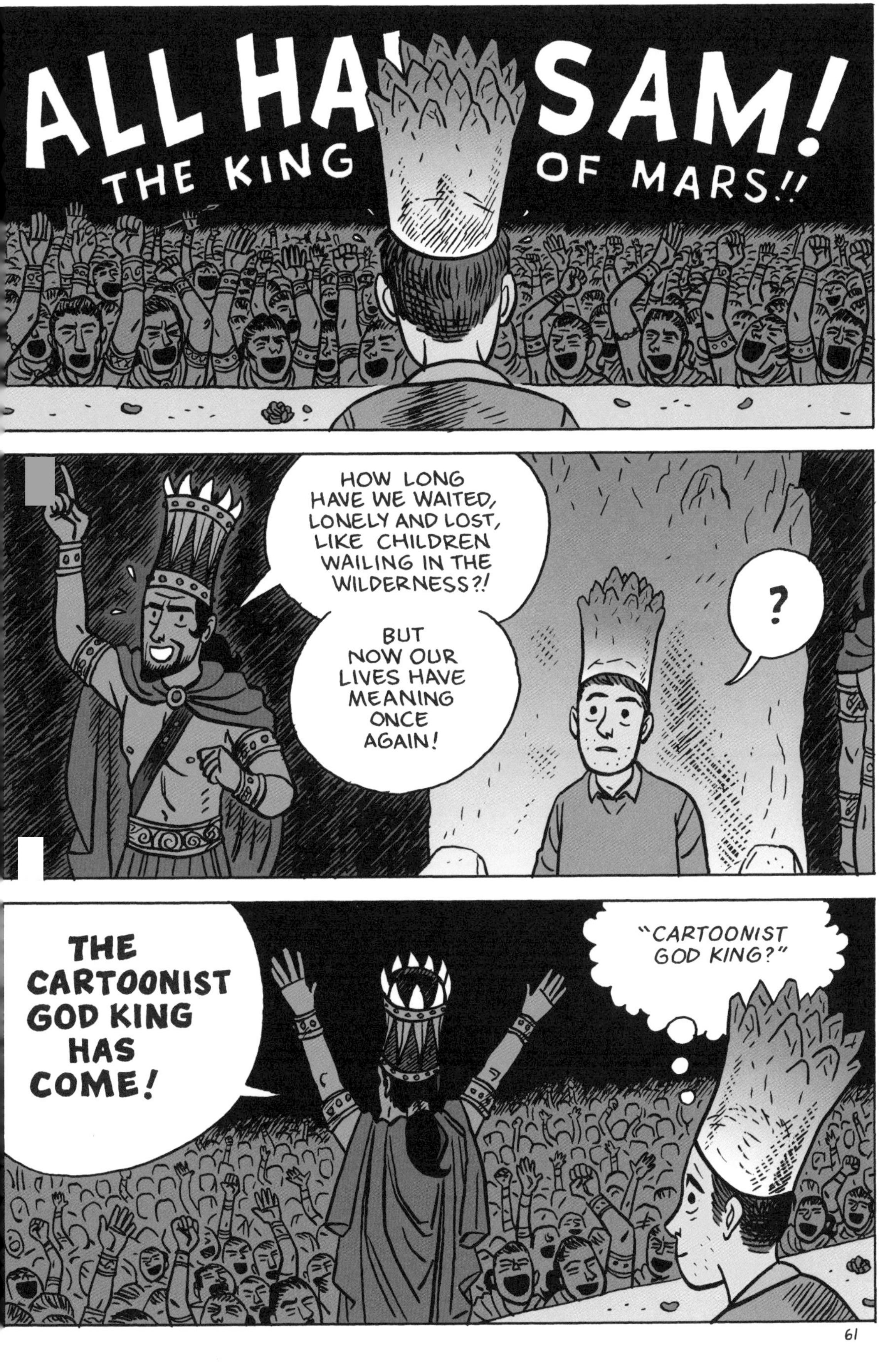
ALL HA SAM!
THE KING OF MARS!!
HOW LONG HAVE WE WAITED, LONELY AND LOST, LIKE CHILDREN WAILING IN THE WILDERNESS?!
BUT NOW OUR LIVES HAVE MEANING ONCE AGAIN!
?
THE CARTOONIST GOD KING HAS COME!
"CARTOONIST GOD KING?"

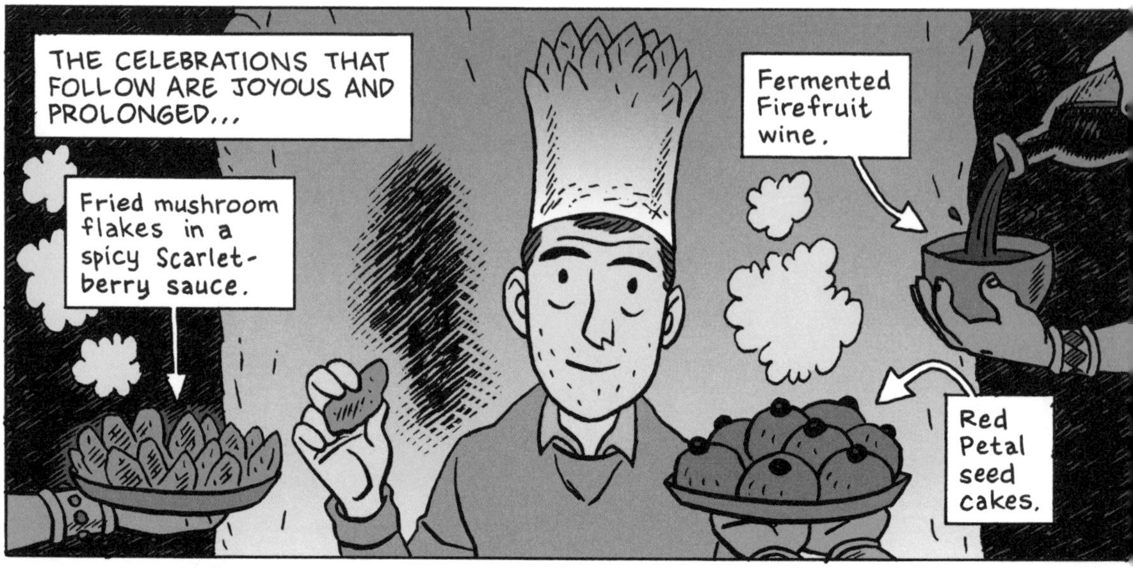
THE CELEBRATIONS THAT FOLLOW ARE JOYOUS AND PROLONGED...
Fried mushroom flakes in a spicy Scarlet-berry sauce.
Fermented Firefruit wine.
Red Petal seed cakes.

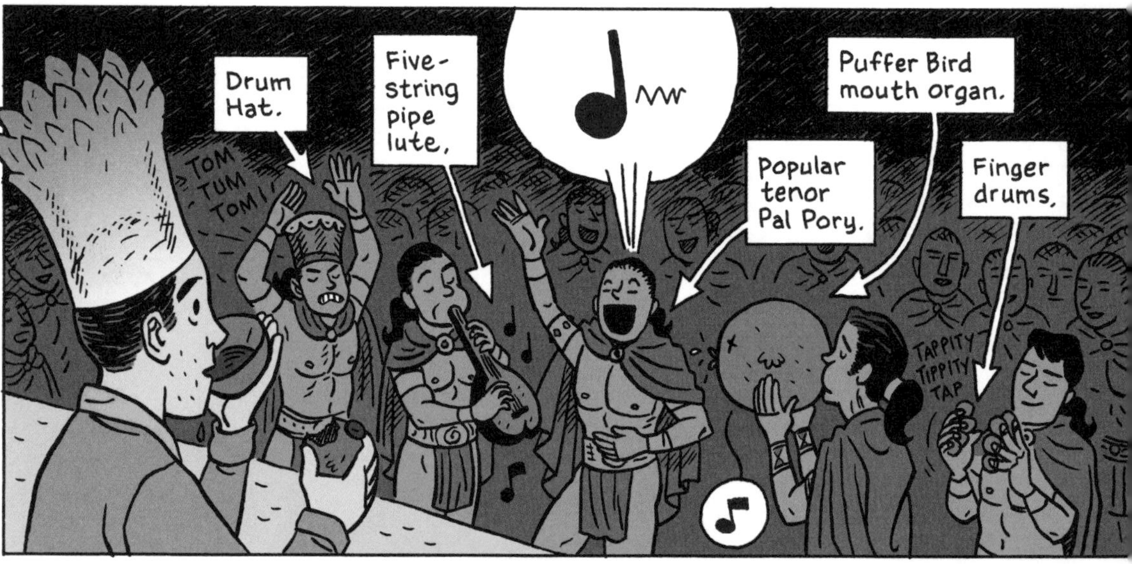
Drum Hat.
TOM TUM TOM!
Five-string pipe lute.
Popular tenor Pal Pory.
Puffer Bird mouth organ.
Finger drums.
TAPPITY TIPPITY TAP

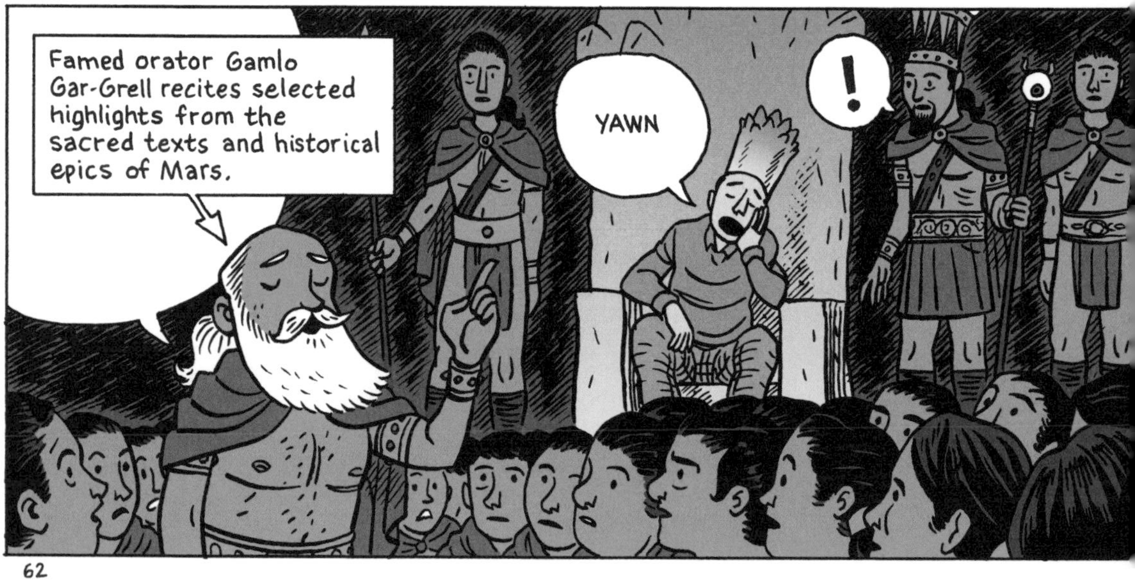
Famed orator Gamlo Gar-Grell recites selected highlights from the sacred texts and historical epics of Mars.
YAWN
!

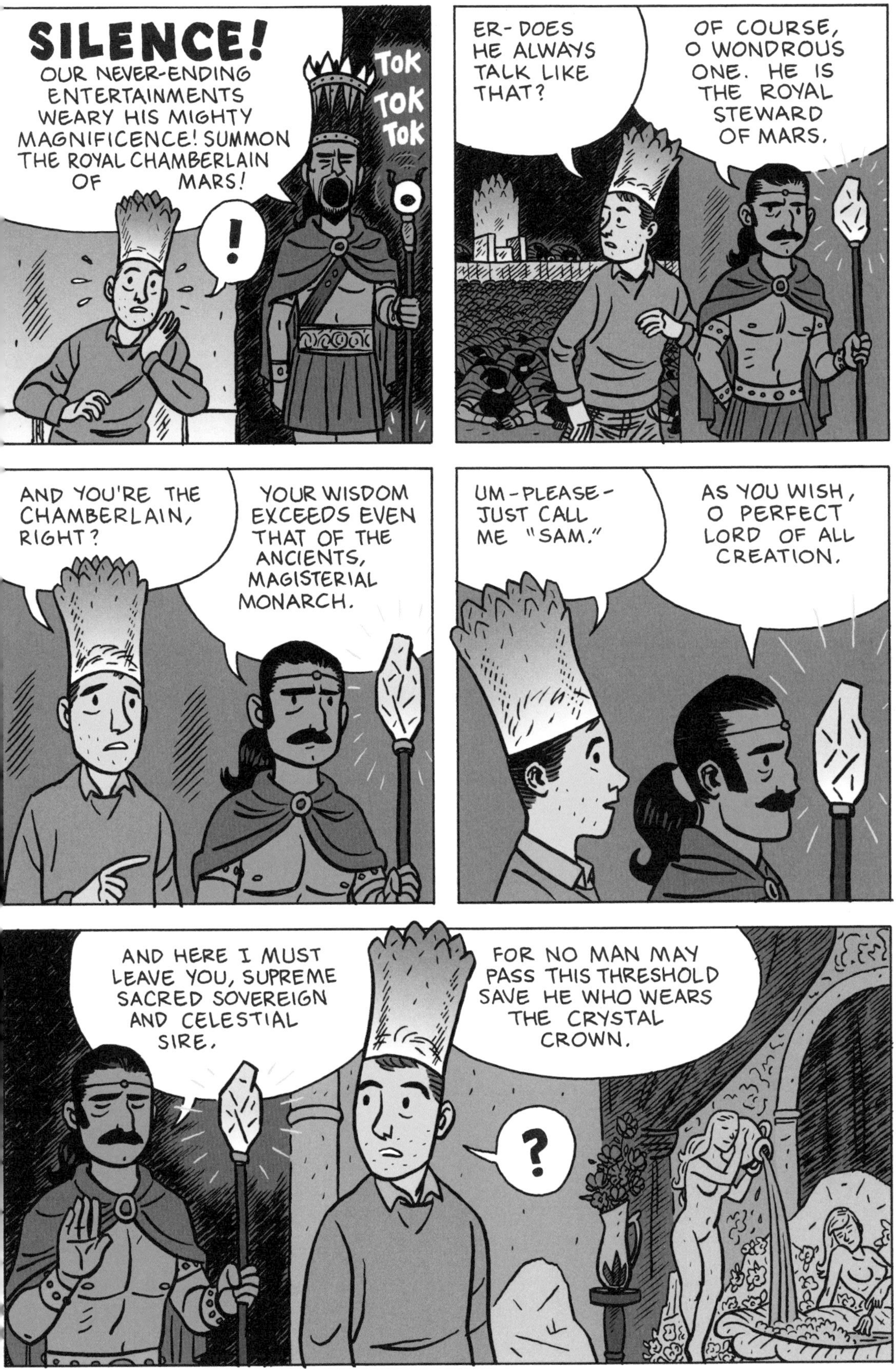
SILENCE! OUR NEVER-ENDING ENTERTAINMENTS WEARY HIS MIGHTY MAGNIFICENCE! SUMMON THE ROYAL CHAMBERLAIN OF MARS!
!
TOK TOK TOK
ER- DOES HE ALWAYS TALK LIKE THAT?
OF COURSE, O WONDROUS ONE. HE IS THE ROYAL STEWARD OF MARS.
AND YOU'RE THE CHAMBERLAIN, RIGHT?
YOUR WISDOM EXCEEDS EVEN THAT OF THE ANCIENTS, MAGISTERIAL MONARCH.
UM - PLEASE - JUST CALL ME "SAM."
AS YOU WISH, O PERFECT LORD OF ALL CREATION.
AND HERE I MUST LEAVE YOU, SUPREME SACRED SOVEREIGN AND CELESTIAL SIRE.
FOR NO MAN MAY PASS THIS THRESHOLD SAVE HE WHO WEARS THE CRYSTAL CROWN.
?

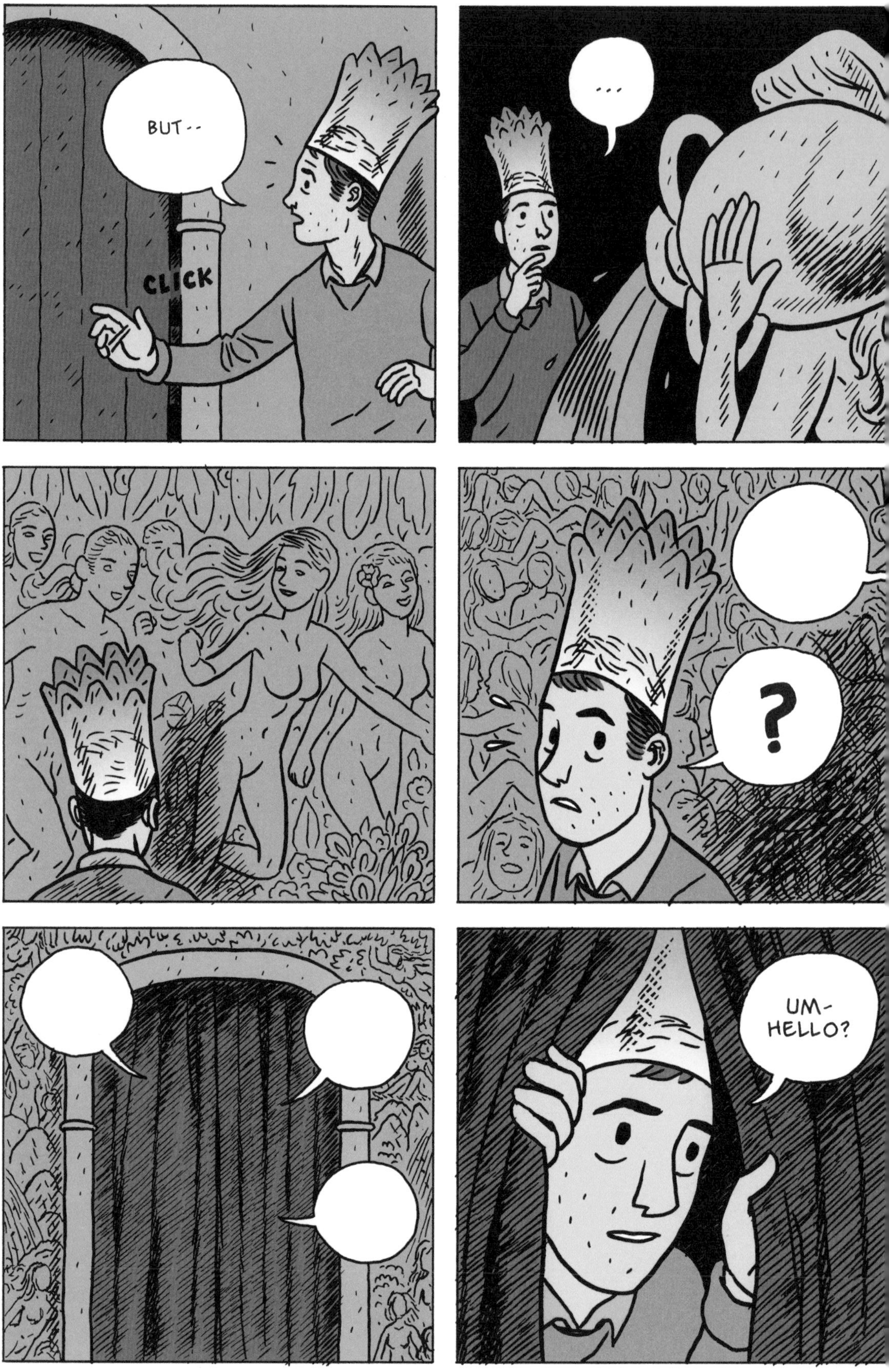
BUT--
CLICK
...
?
UM-
HELLO?

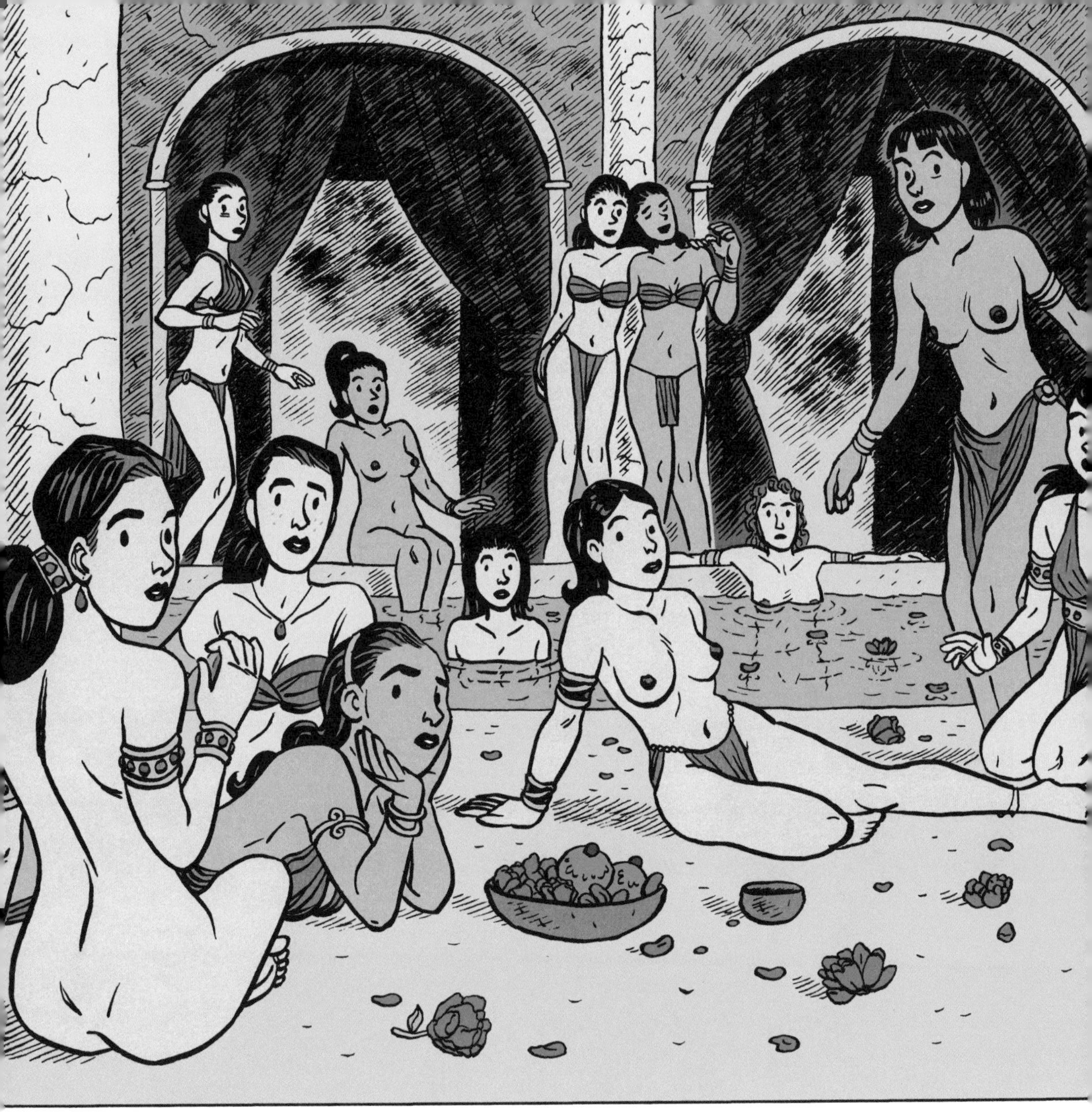

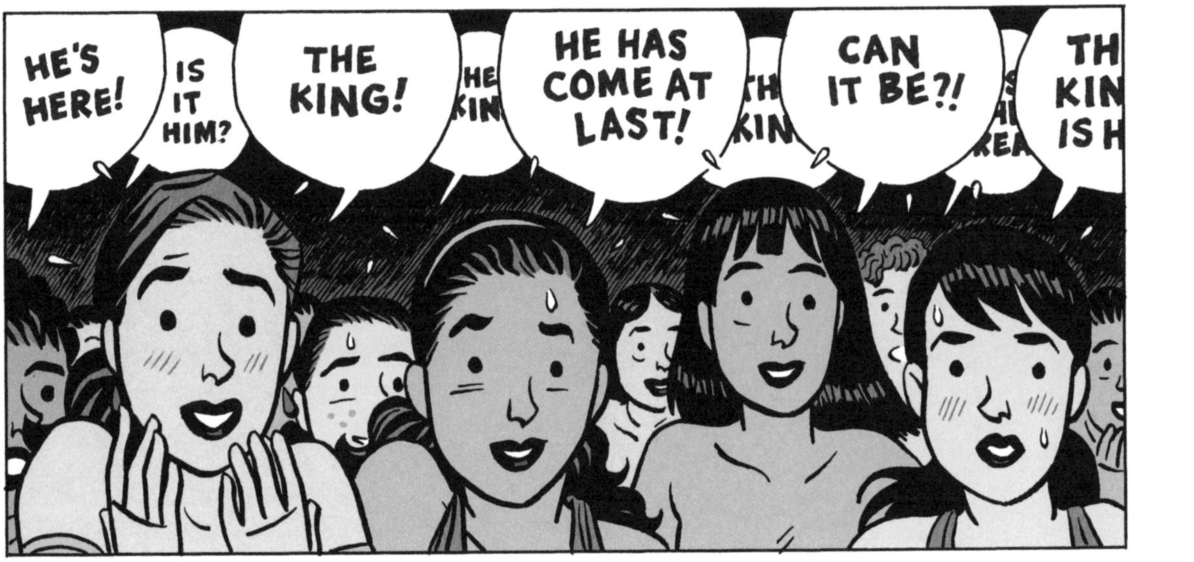
HE'S HERE!
IS IT HIM?
THE KING!
HE HAS COME AT LAST!
CAN IT BE?!

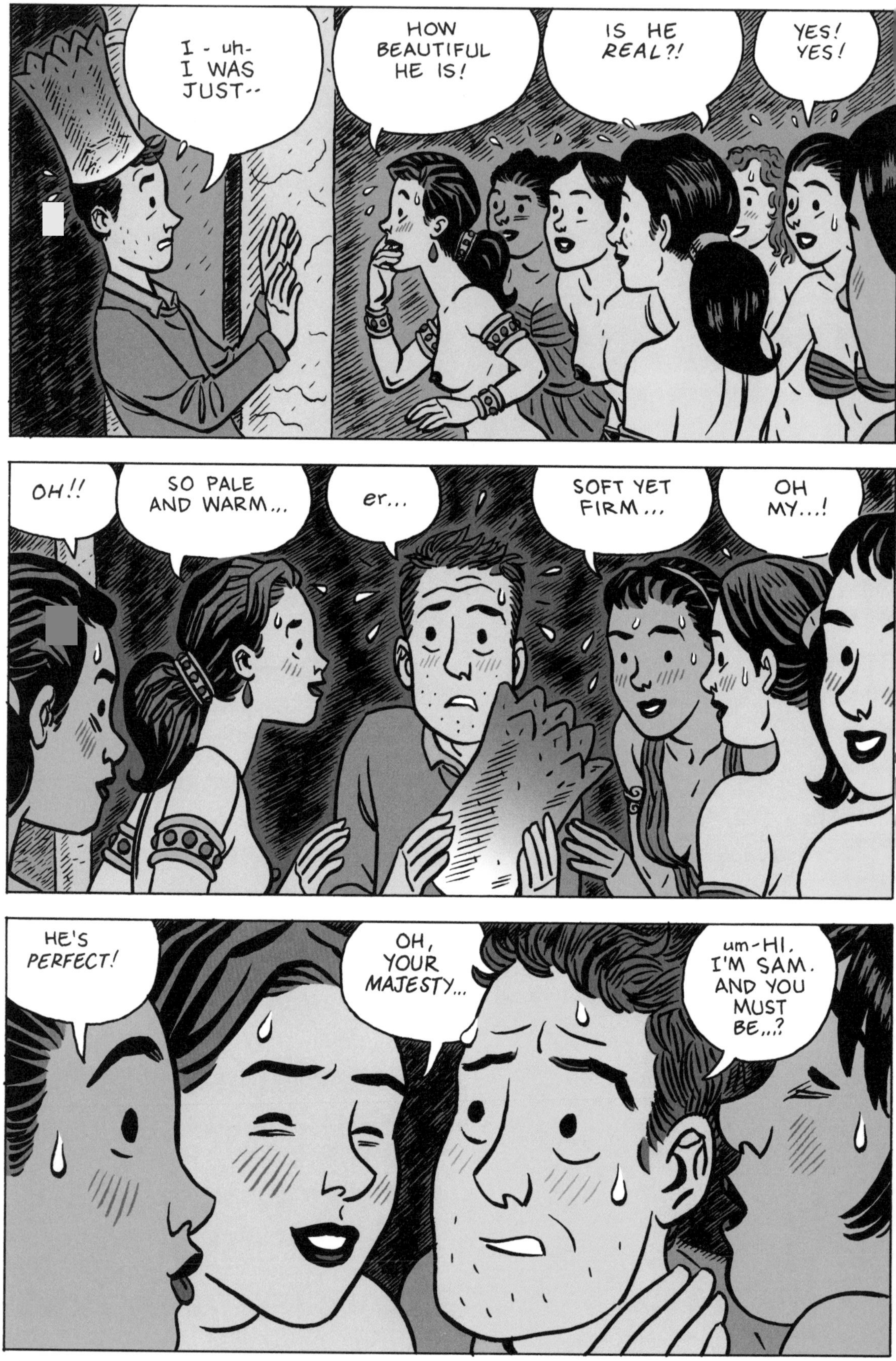
I - uh-
I WAS
JUST--
HOW
BEAUTIFUL
HE IS!
IS HE
REAL?!
YES!
YES!
OH!!
SO PALE
AND WARM...
er...
SOFT YET
FIRM...
OH
MY...!
HE'S
PERFECT!
OH,
YOUR
MAJESTY...
um-HI.
I'M SAM.
AND YOU
MUST
BE...?

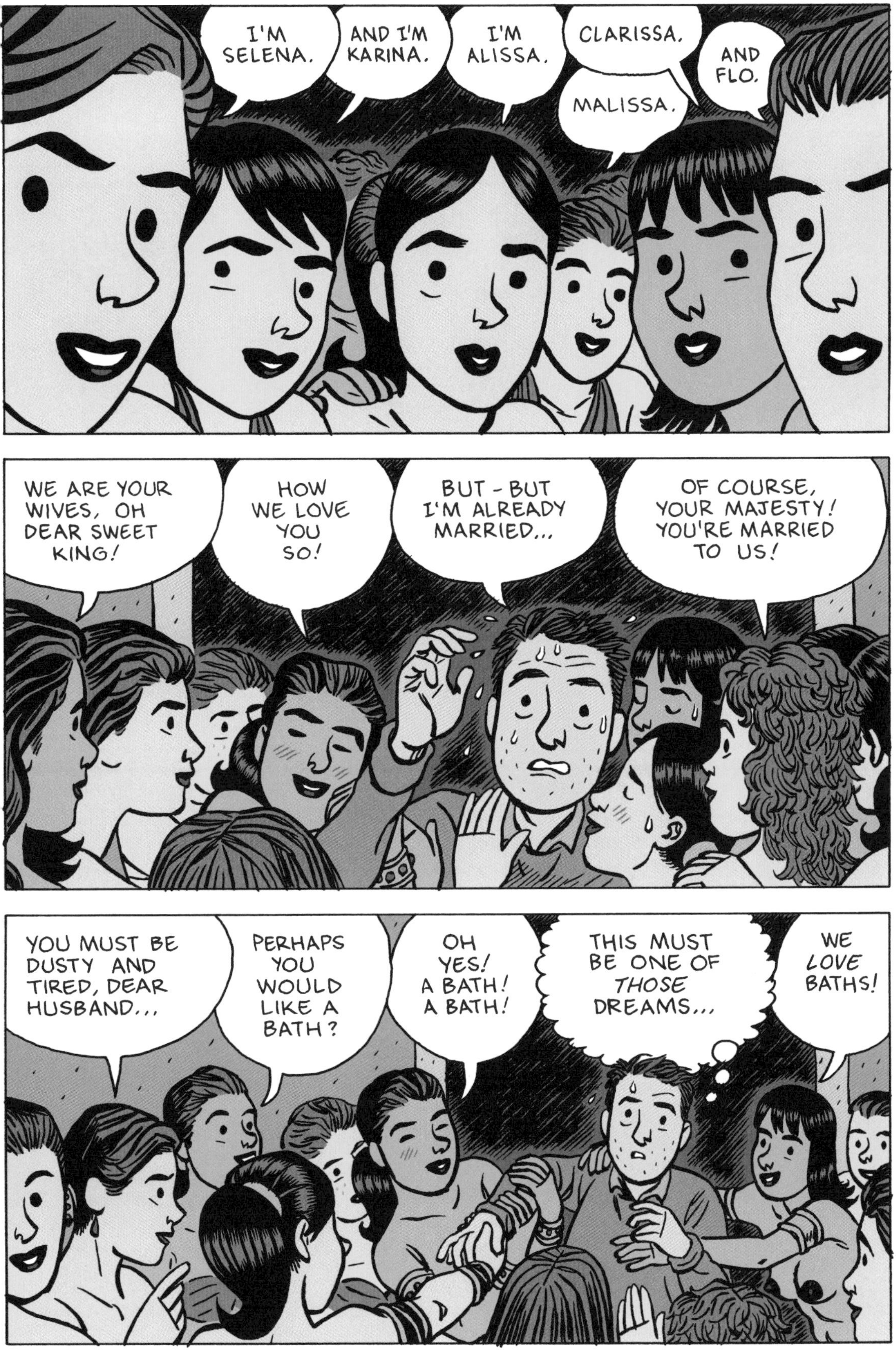
I'M SELENA.
AND I'M KARINA.
I'M ALISSA.
CLARISSA.
MALISSA.
AND FLO.
WE ARE YOUR WIVES, OH DEAR SWEET KING!
HOW WE LOVE YOU SO!
BUT - BUT I'M ALREADY MARRIED...
OF COURSE, YOUR MAJESTY! YOU'RE MARRIED TO US!
YOU MUST BE DUSTY AND TIRED, DEAR HUSBAND...
PERHAPS YOU WOULD LIKE A BATH?
OH YES! A BATH! A BATH!
THIS MUST BE ONE OF *THOSE* DREAMS...
WE *LOVE* BATHS!

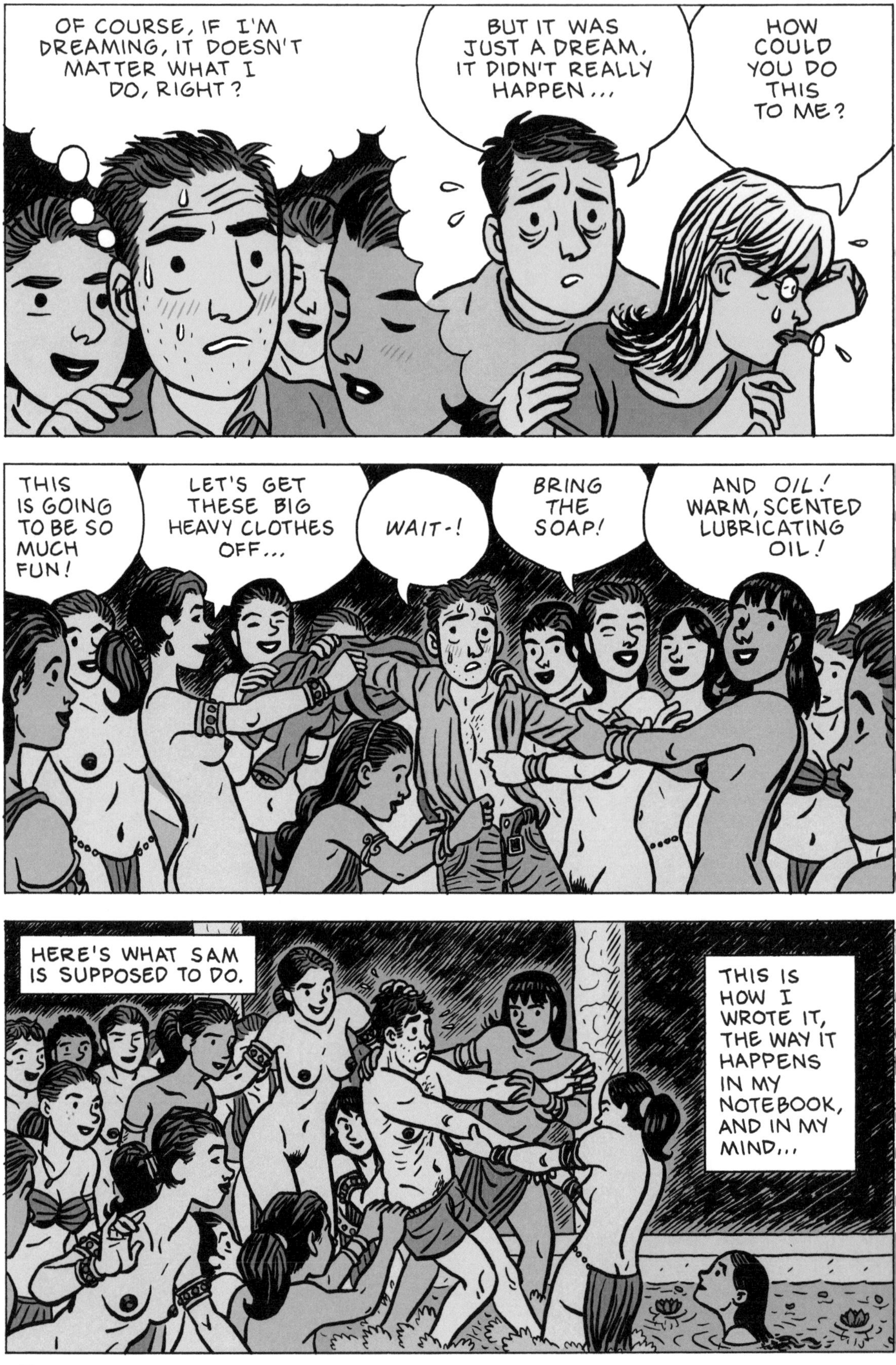
OF COURSE, IF I'M DREAMING, IT DOESN'T MATTER WHAT I DO, RIGHT?
BUT IT WAS JUST A DREAM. IT DIDN'T REALLY HAPPEN...
HOW COULD YOU DO THIS TO ME?
THIS IS GOING TO BE SO MUCH FUN!
LET'S GET THESE BIG HEAVY CLOTHES OFF...
WAIT-!
BRING THE SOAP!
AND OIL! WARM, SCENTED LUBRICATING OIL!
HERE'S WHAT SAM IS SUPPOSED TO DO.
THIS IS HOW I WROTE IT, THE WAY IT HAPPENS IN MY NOTEBOOK, AND IN MY MIND...

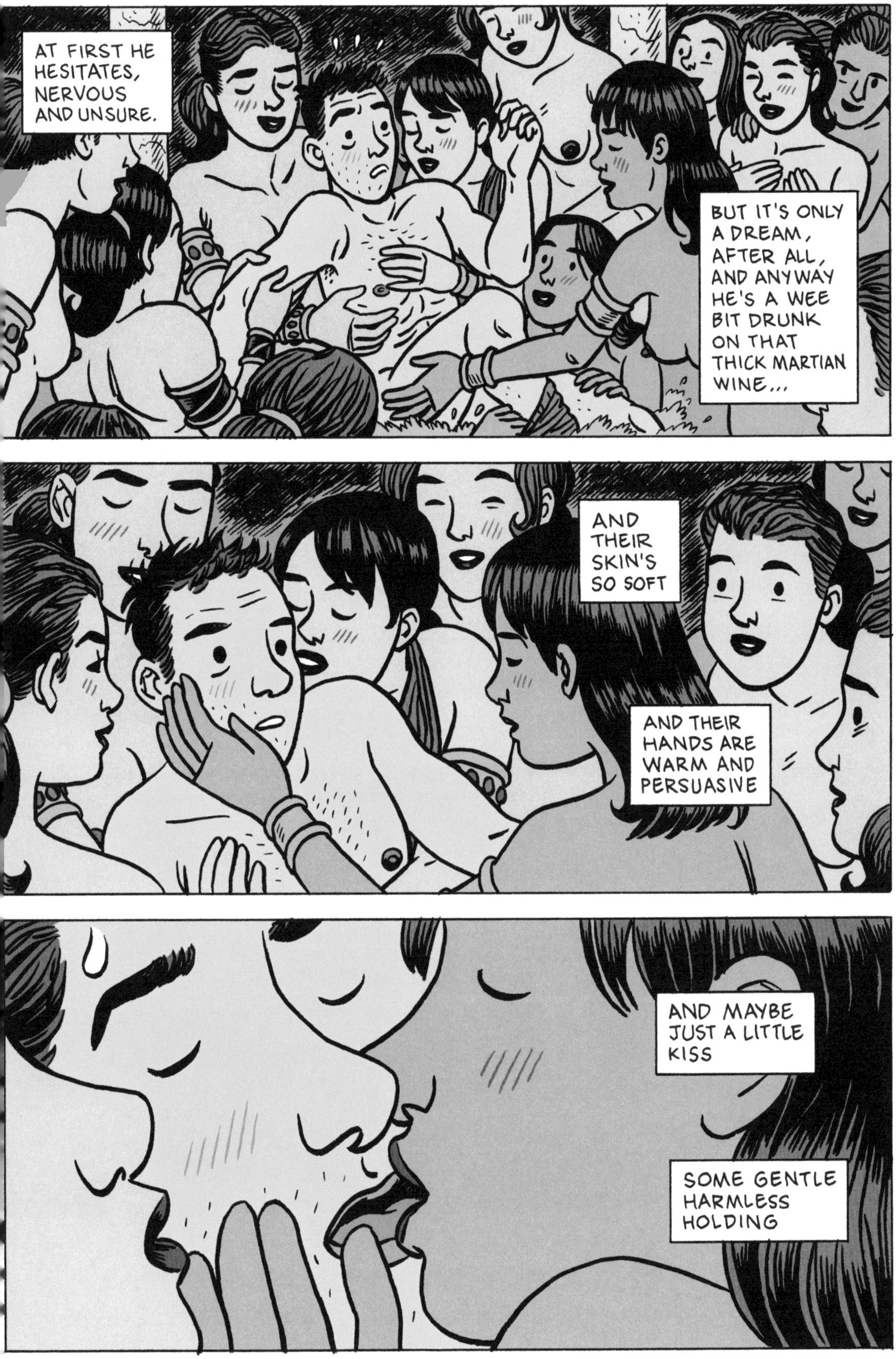
AT FIRST HE HESITATES, NERVOUS AND UNSURE.
BUT IT'S ONLY A DREAM, AFTER ALL, AND ANYWAY HE'S A WEE BIT DRUNK ON THAT THICK MARTIAN WINE...
AND THEIR SKIN'S SO SOFT
AND THEIR HANDS ARE WARM AND PERSUASIVE
AND MAYBE JUST A LITTLE KISS
SOME GENTLE HARMLESS HOLDING

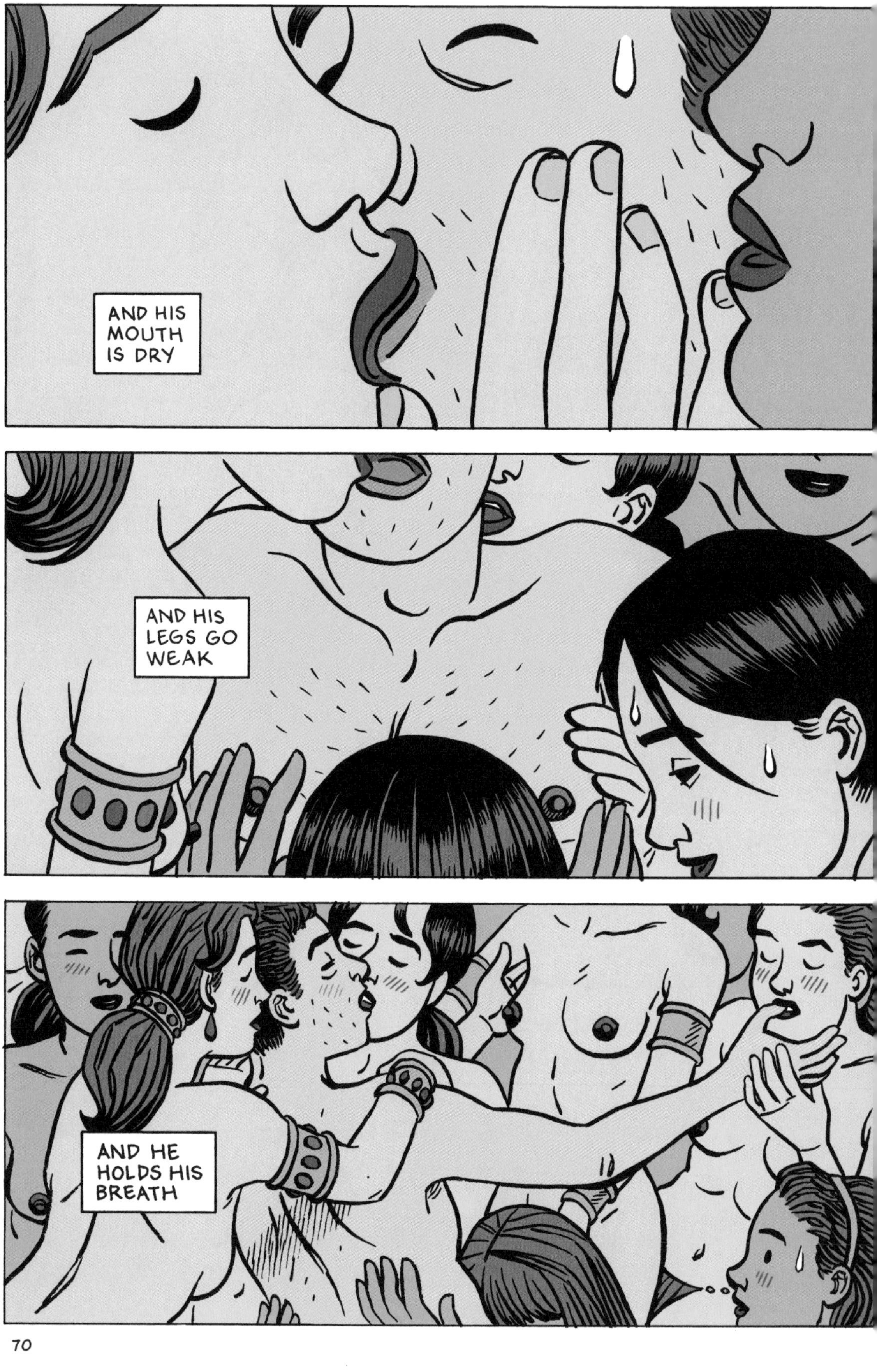
AND HIS MOUTH IS DRY
AND HIS LEGS GO WEAK
AND HE HOLDS HIS BREATH

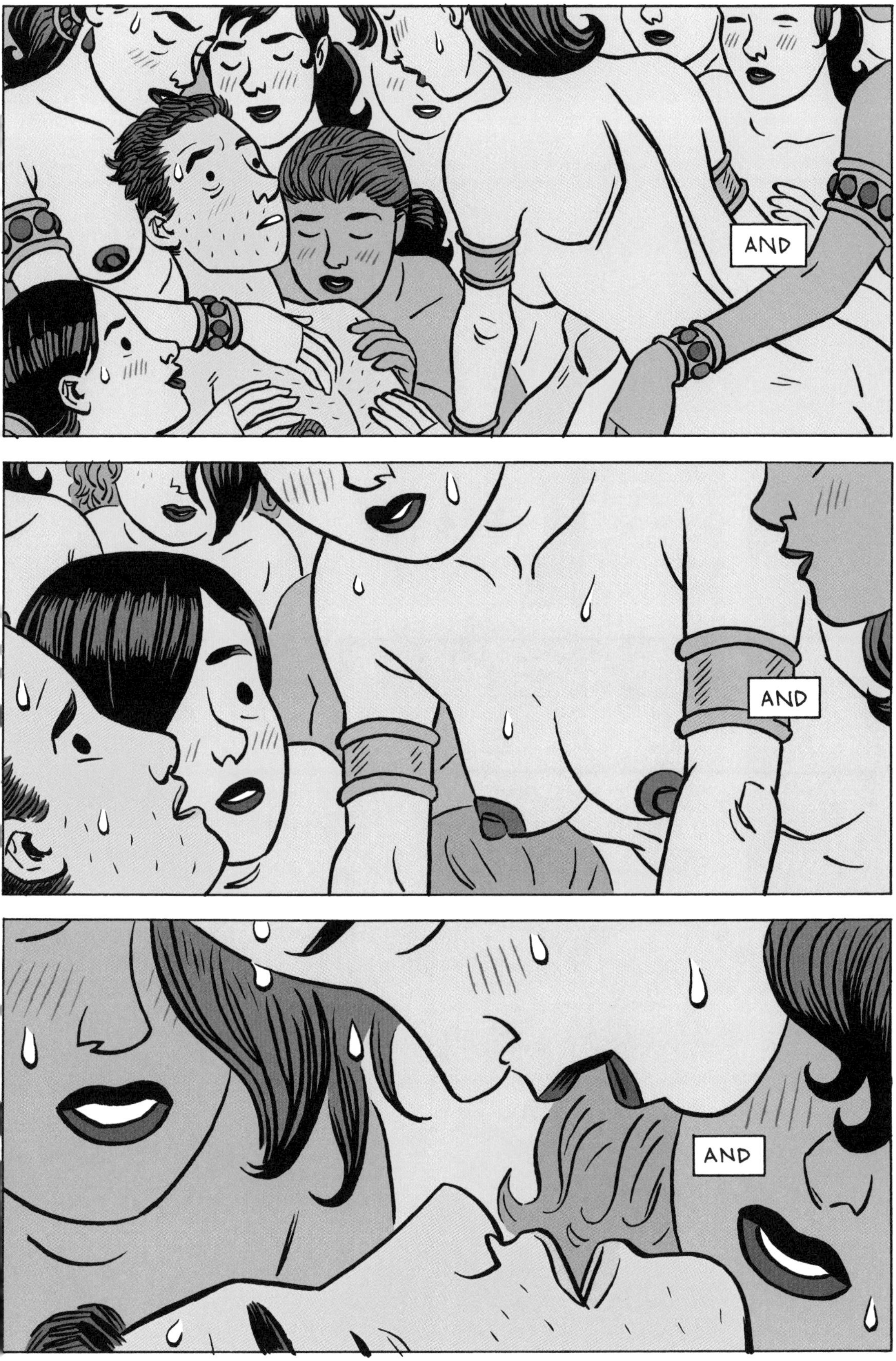
AND
AND
AND

THAT'S HOW IT'S *MEANT* TO GO.

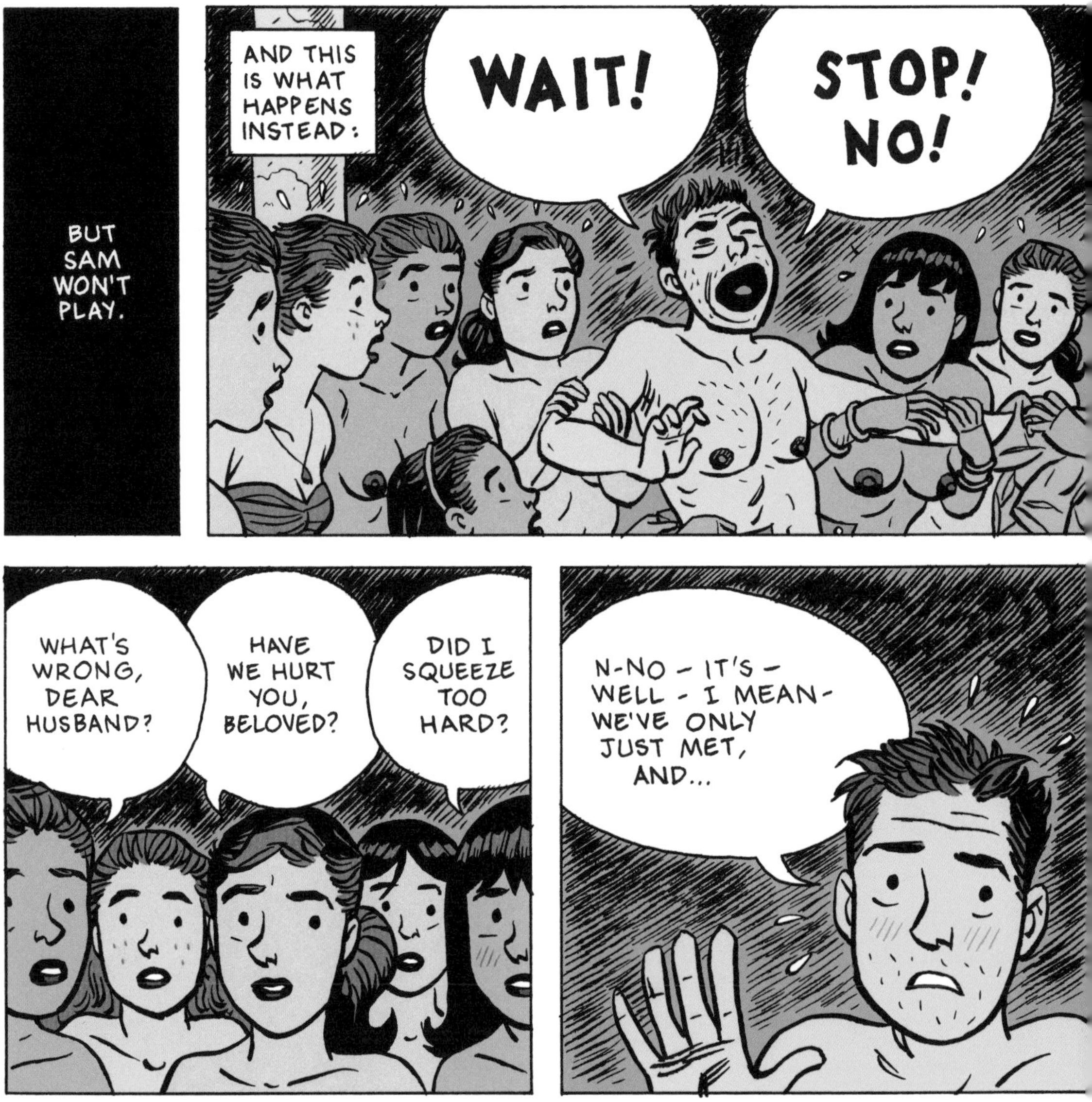
BUT SAM WON'T PLAY.
AND THIS IS WHAT HAPPENS INSTEAD:
WAIT!
STOP! NO!
WHAT'S WRONG, DEAR HUSBAND?
HAVE WE HURT YOU, BELOVED?
DID I SQUEEZE TOO HARD?
N-NO – IT'S – WELL – I MEAN – WE'VE ONLY JUST MET, AND...

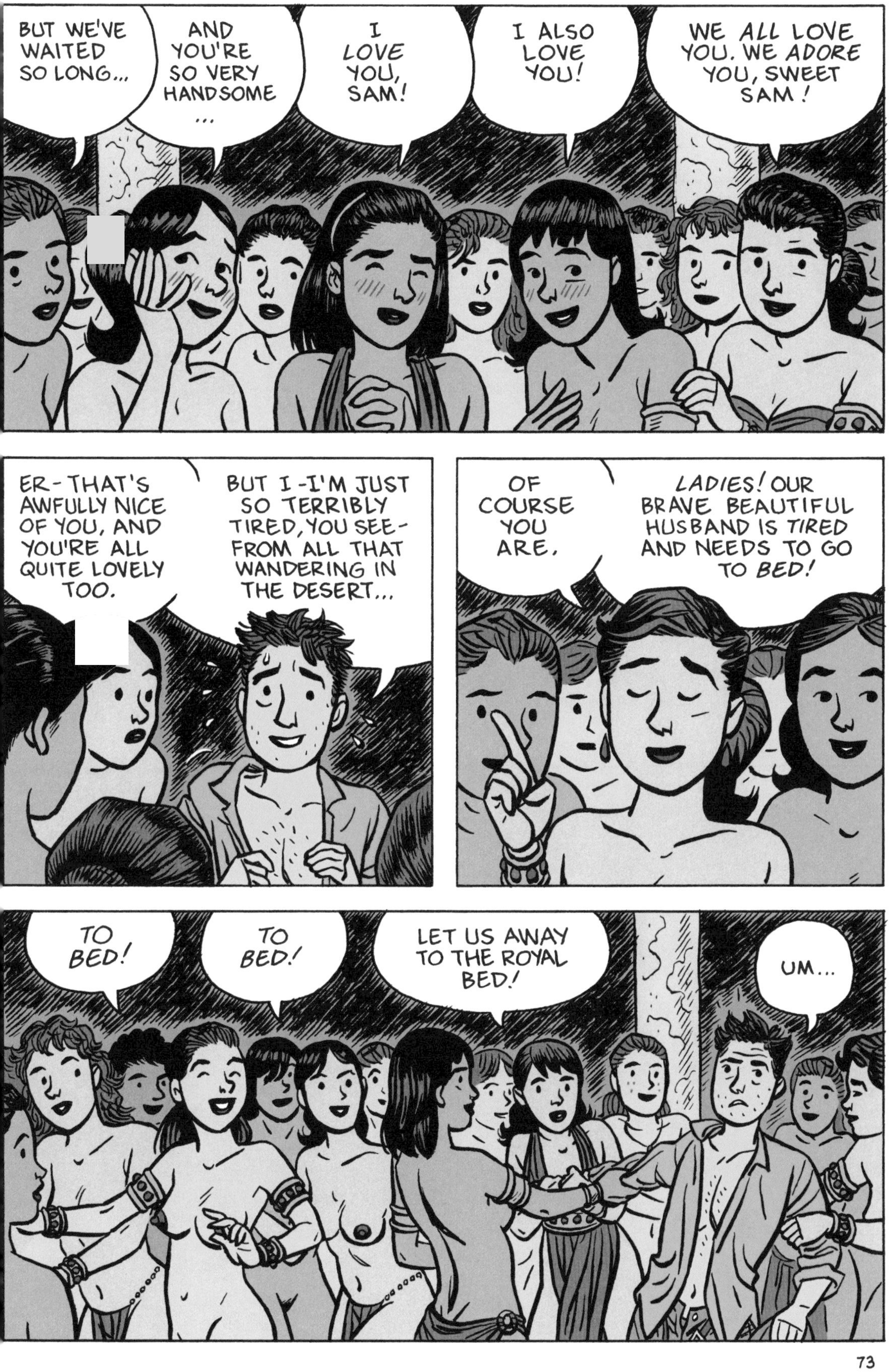
BUT WE'VE WAITED SO LONG...
AND YOU'RE SO VERY HANDSOME ...
I LOVE YOU, SAM!
I ALSO LOVE YOU!
WE ALL LOVE YOU. WE ADORE YOU, SWEET SAM!
ER-THAT'S AWFULLY NICE OF YOU, AND YOU'RE ALL QUITE LOVELY TOO.
BUT I-I'M JUST SO TERRIBLY TIRED, YOU SEE- FROM ALL THAT WANDERING IN THE DESERT...
OF COURSE YOU ARE.
LADIES! OUR BRAVE BEAUTIFUL HUSBAND IS TIRED AND NEEDS TO GO TO BED!
TO BED!
TO BED!
LET US AWAY TO THE ROYAL BED!
UM...

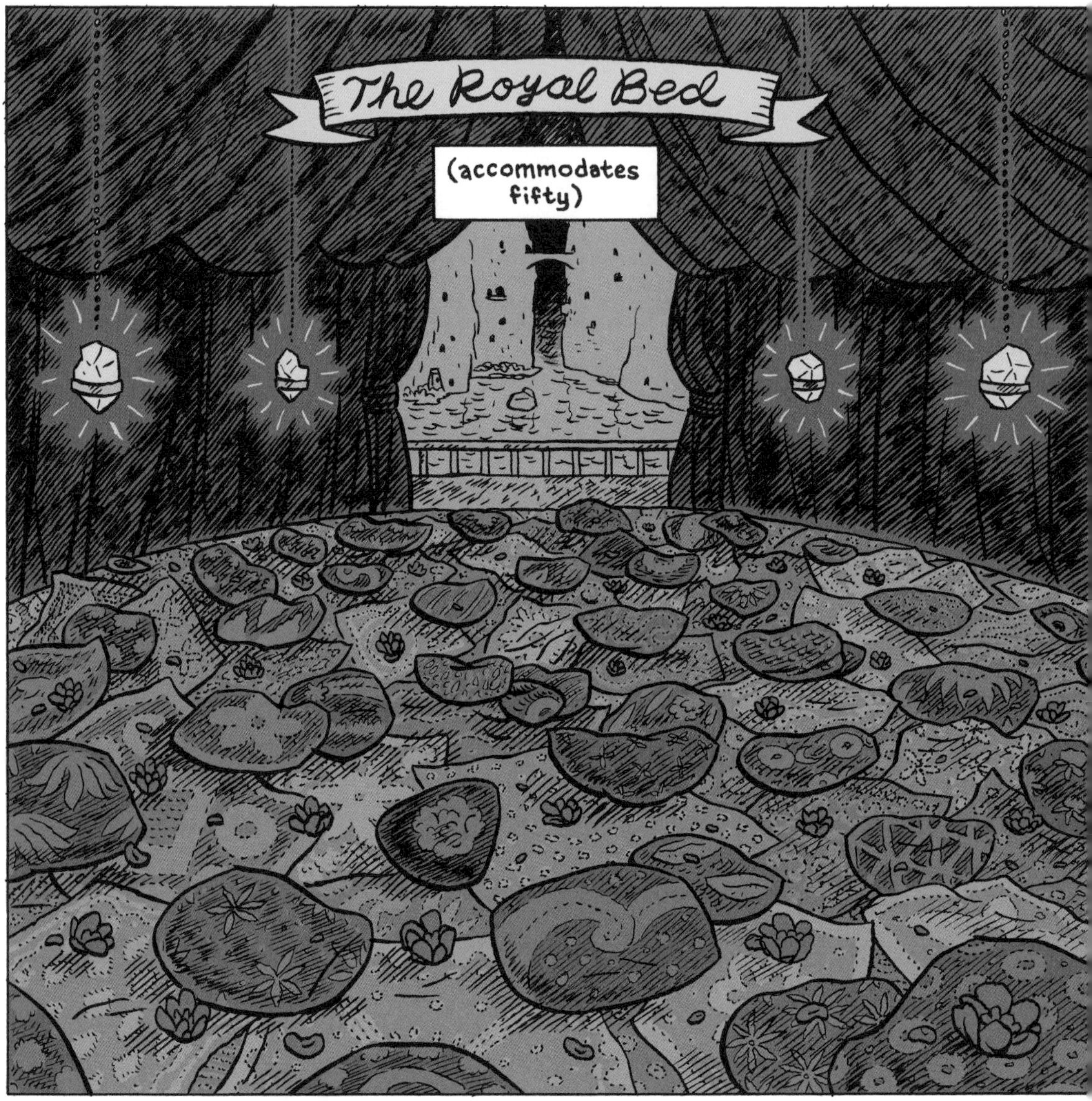
The Royal Bed
(accommodates fifty)

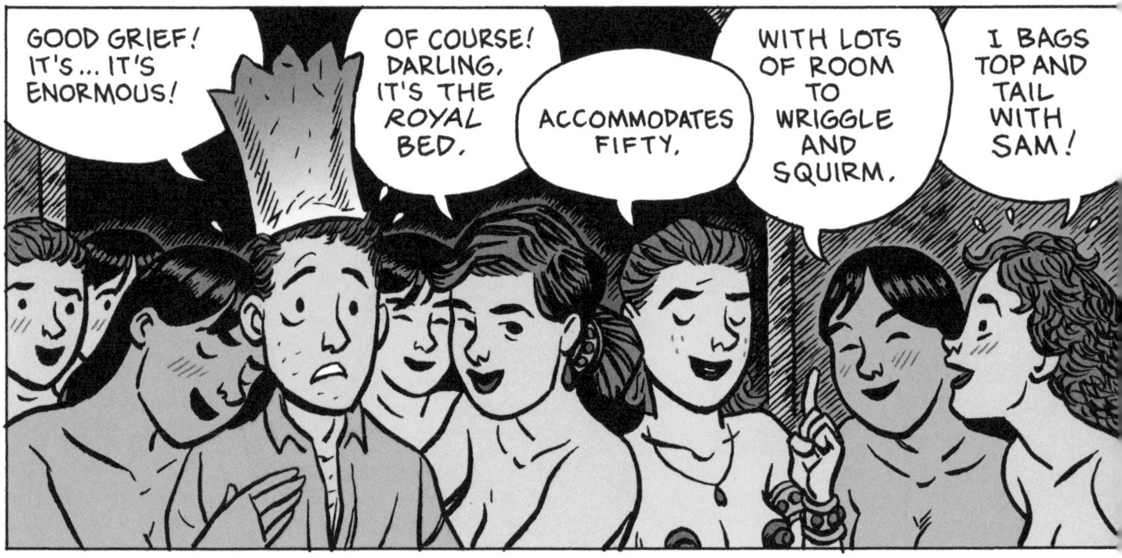
GOOD GRIEF! IT'S... IT'S ENORMOUS!
OF COURSE! DARLING, IT'S THE ROYAL BED.
ACCOMMODATES FIFTY.
WITH LOTS OF ROOM TO WRIGGLE AND SQUIRM.
I BAGS TOP AND TAIL WITH SAM!

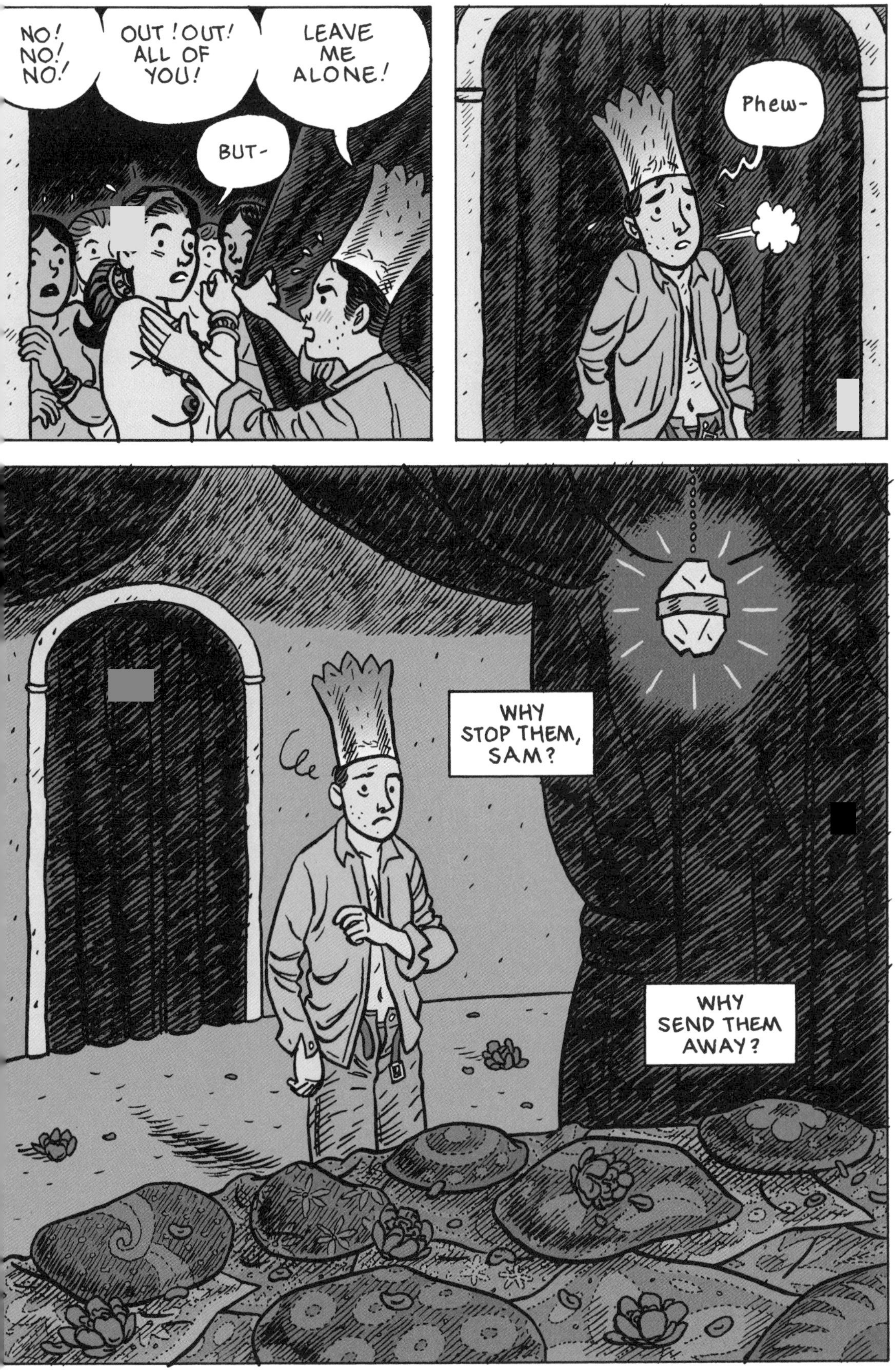
NO! NO! NO!
OUT! OUT! ALL OF YOU!
LEAVE ME ALONE!
BUT-
Phew-
WHY STOP THEM, SAM?
WHY SEND THEM AWAY?

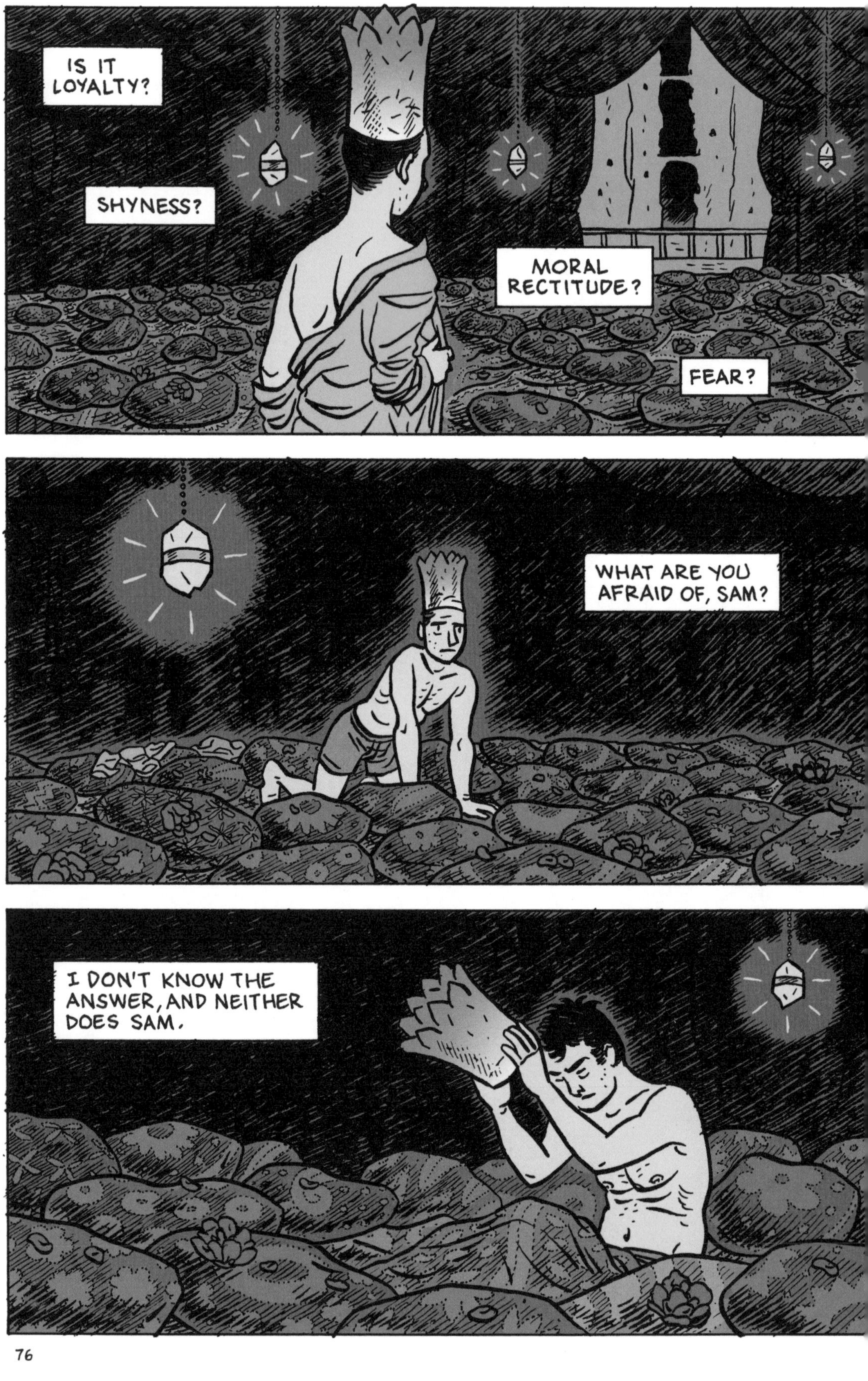
IS IT LOYALTY?
SHYNESS?
MORAL RECTITUDE?
FEAR?
WHAT ARE YOU AFRAID OF, SAM?
I DON'T KNOW THE ANSWER, AND NEITHER DOES SAM.

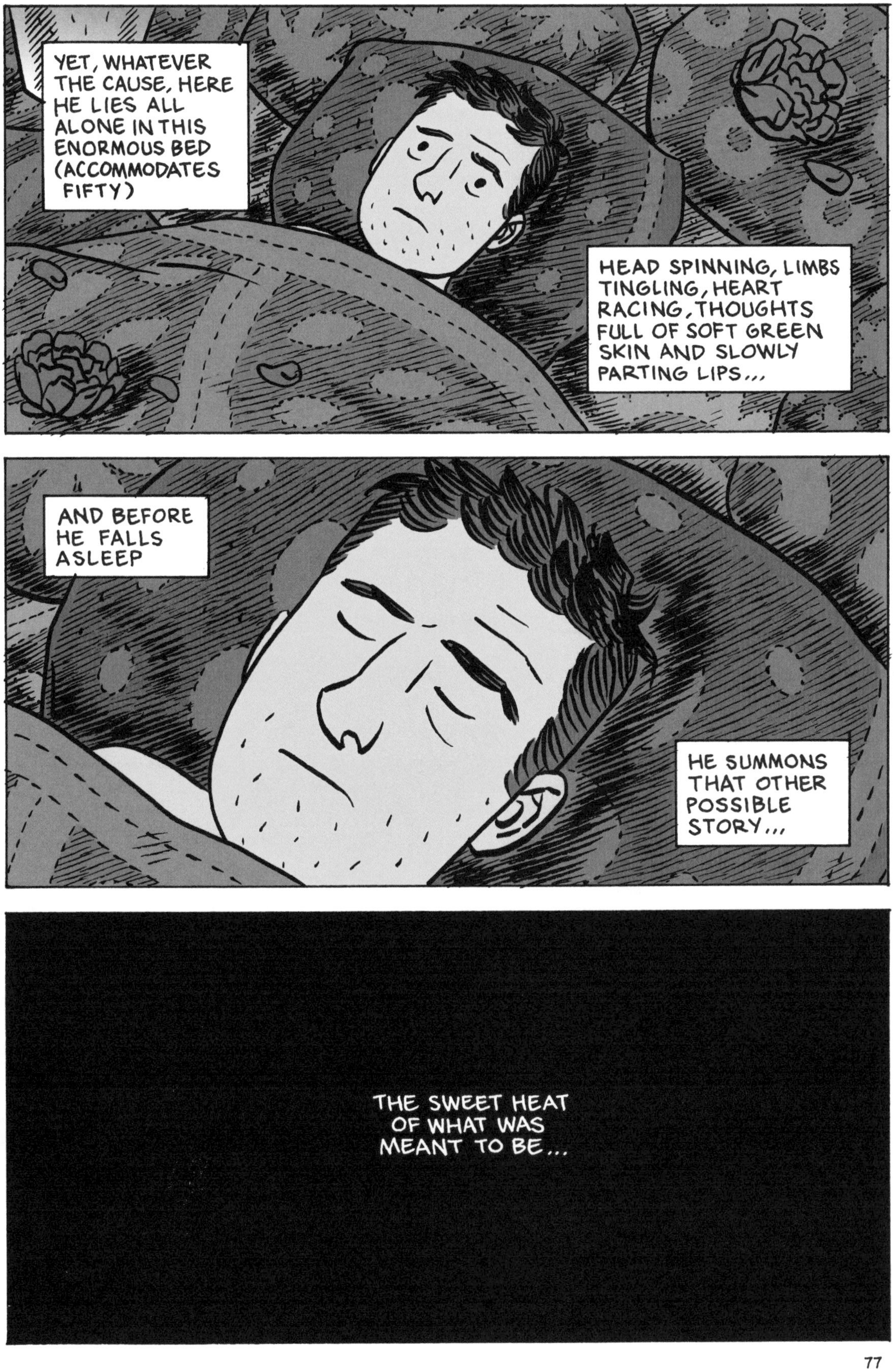
YET, WHATEVER THE CAUSE, HERE HE LIES ALL ALONE IN THIS ENORMOUS BED (ACCOMMODATES FIFTY)
HEAD SPINNING, LIMBS TINGLING, HEART RACING, THOUGHTS FULL OF SOFT GREEN SKIN AND SLOWLY PARTING LIPS...
AND BEFORE HE FALLS ASLEEP
HE SUMMONS THAT OTHER POSSIBLE STORY...
THE SWEET HEAT OF WHAT WAS MEANT TO BE...

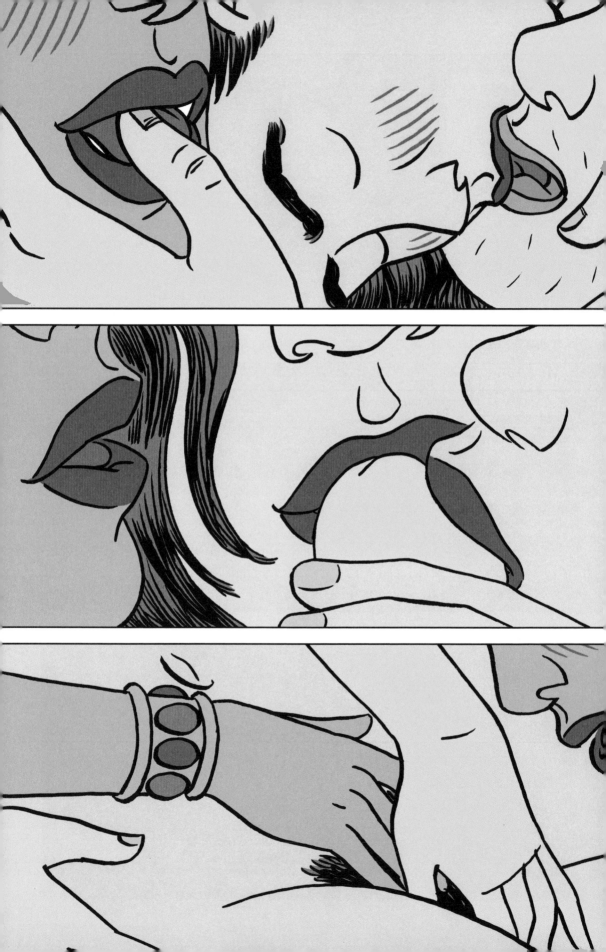

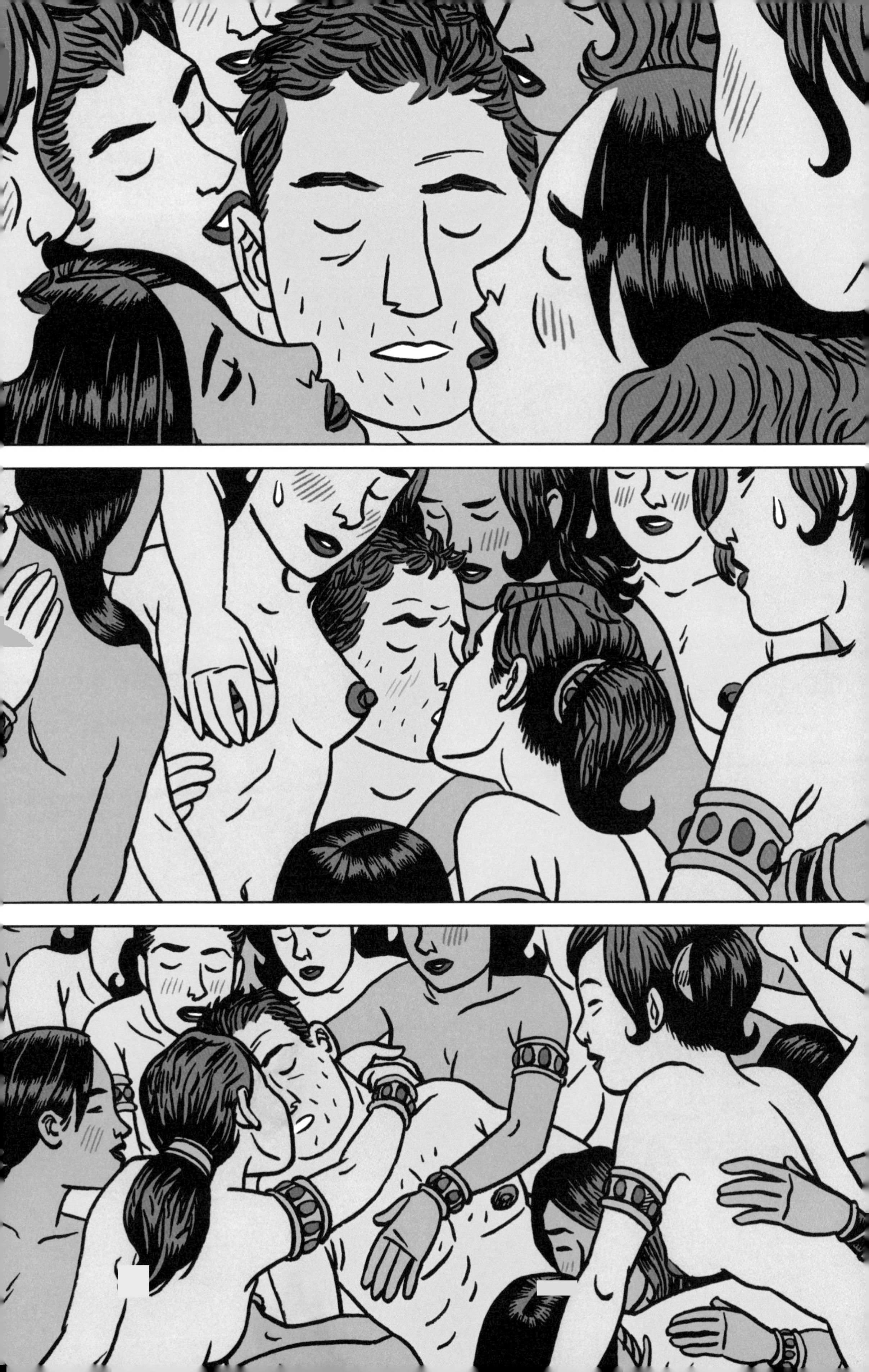

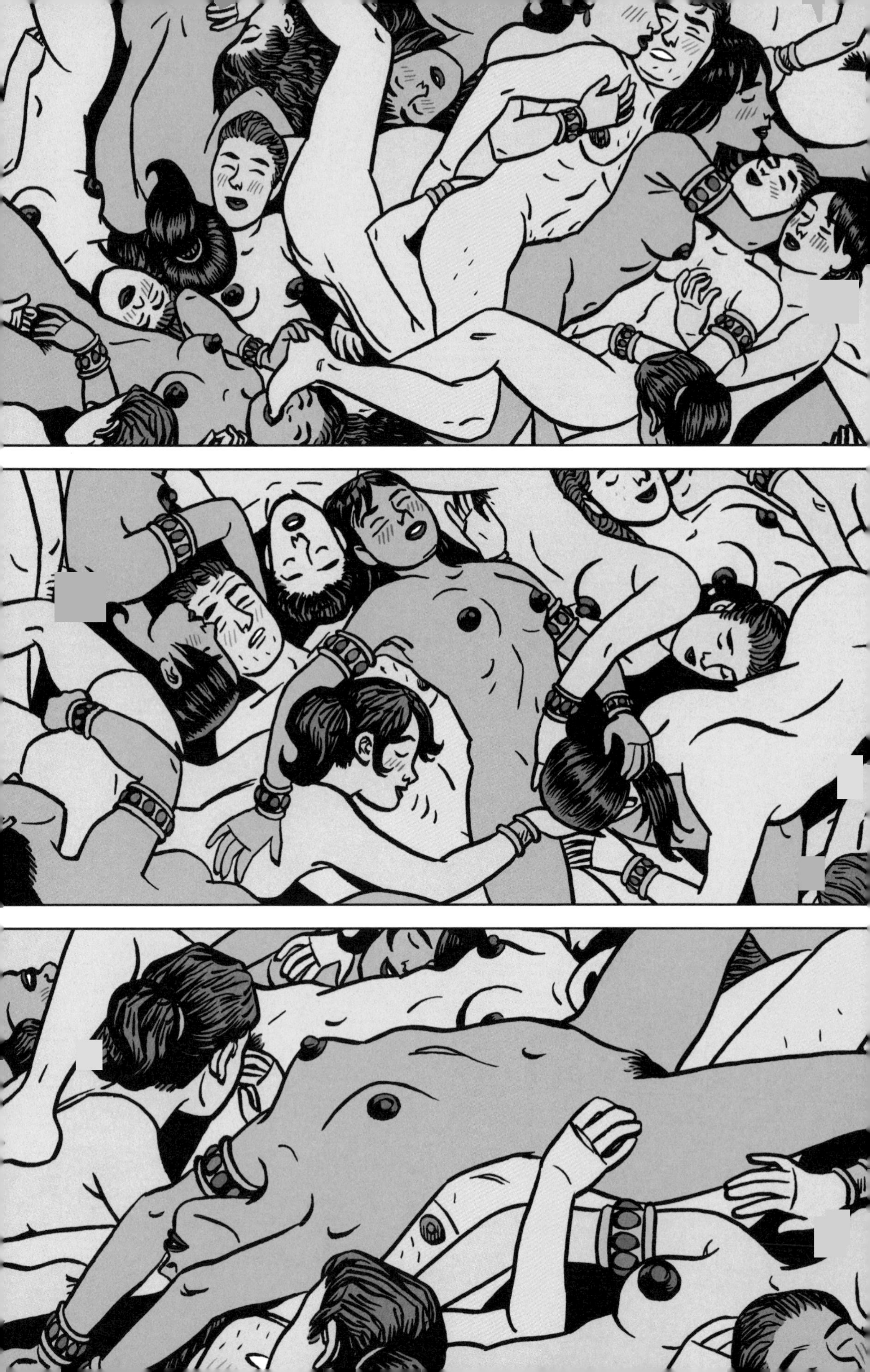

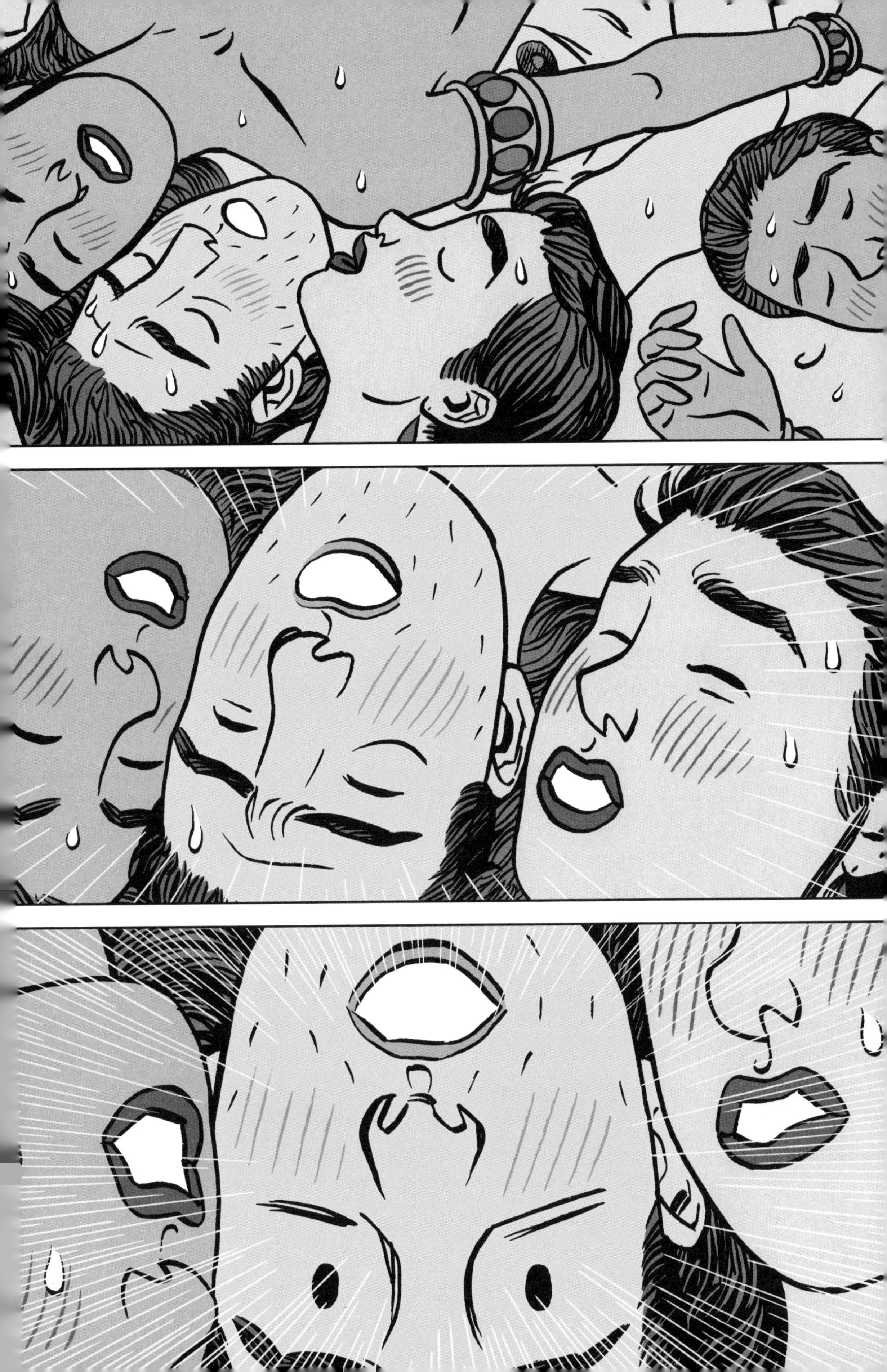

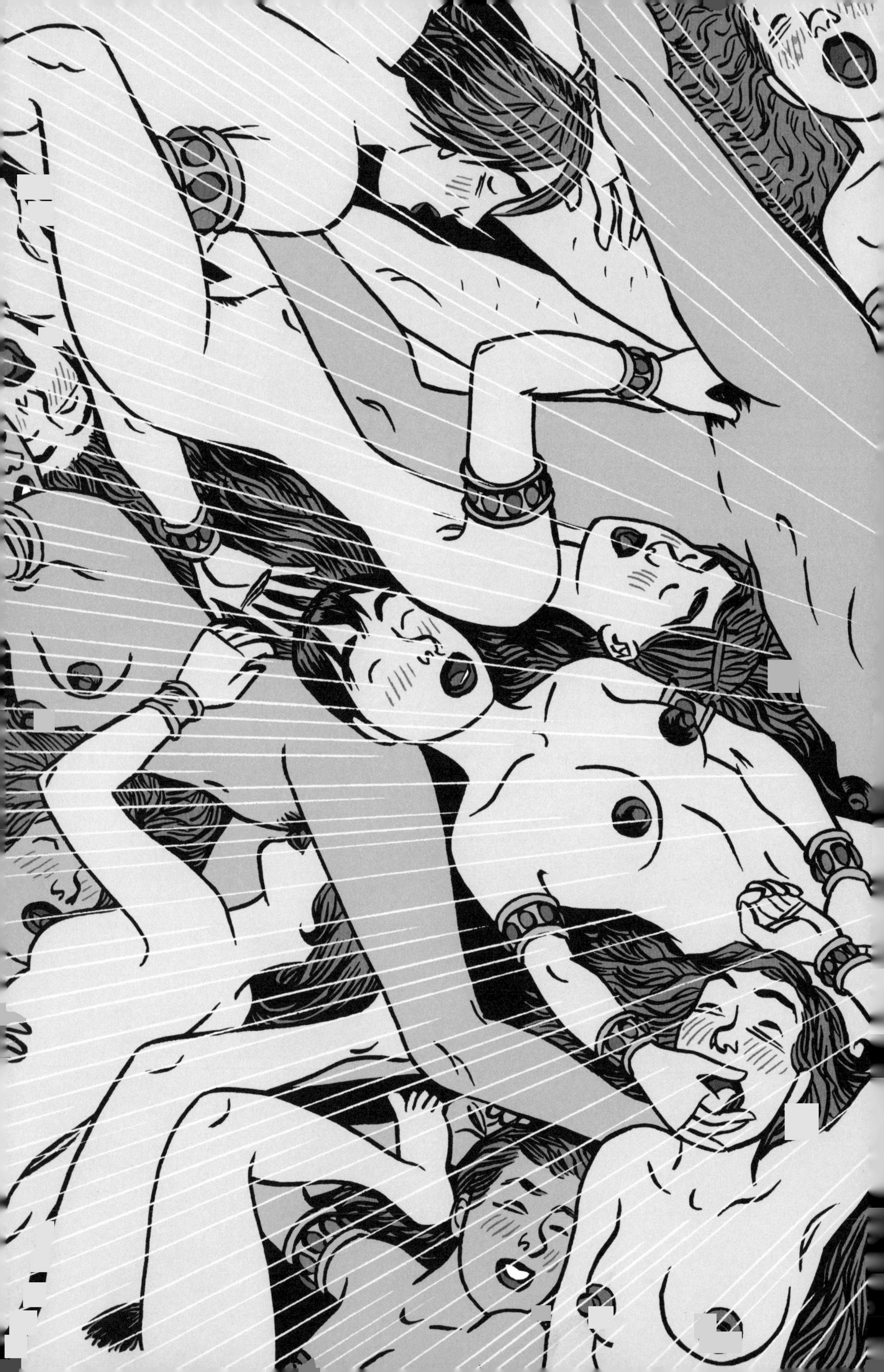

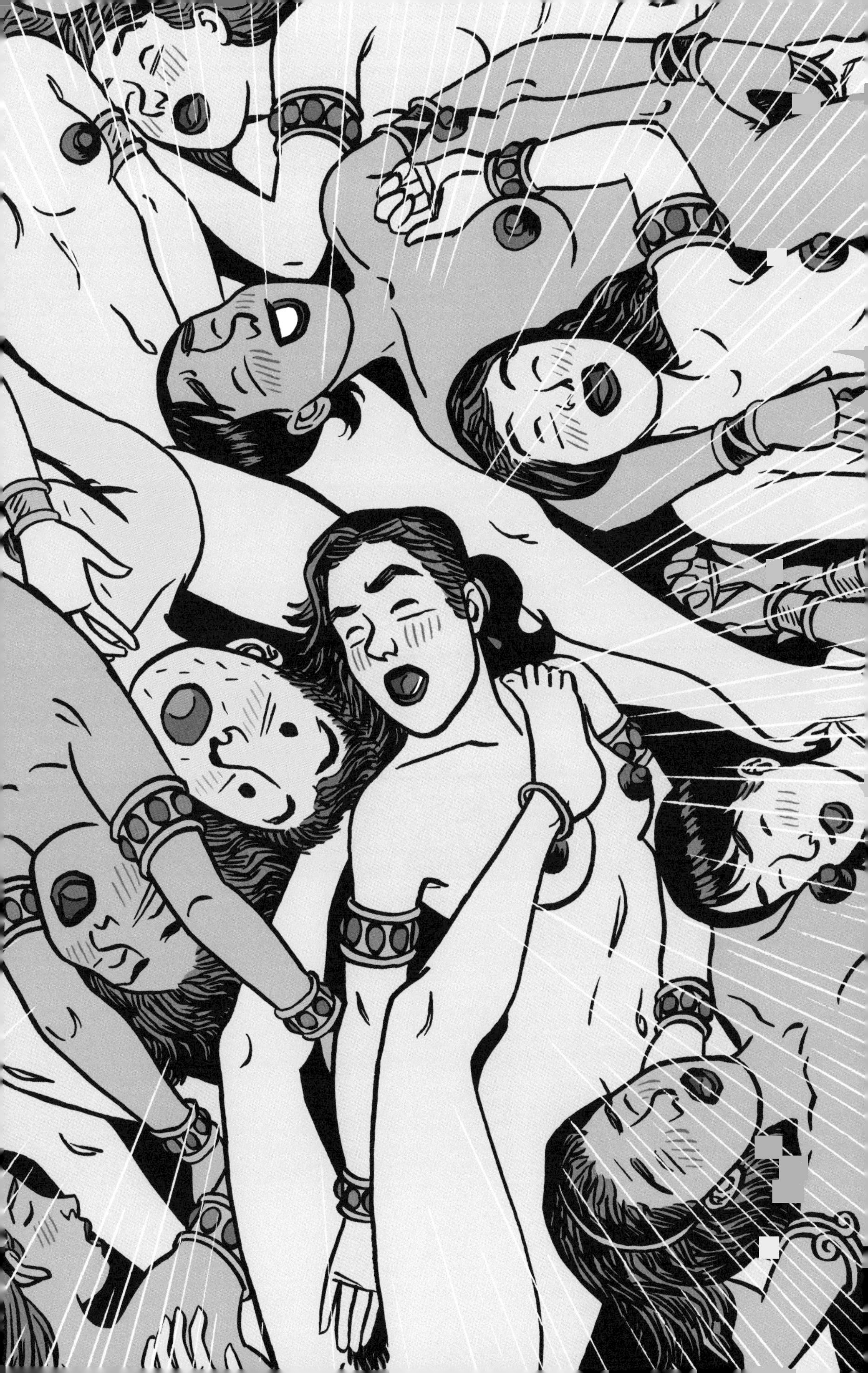

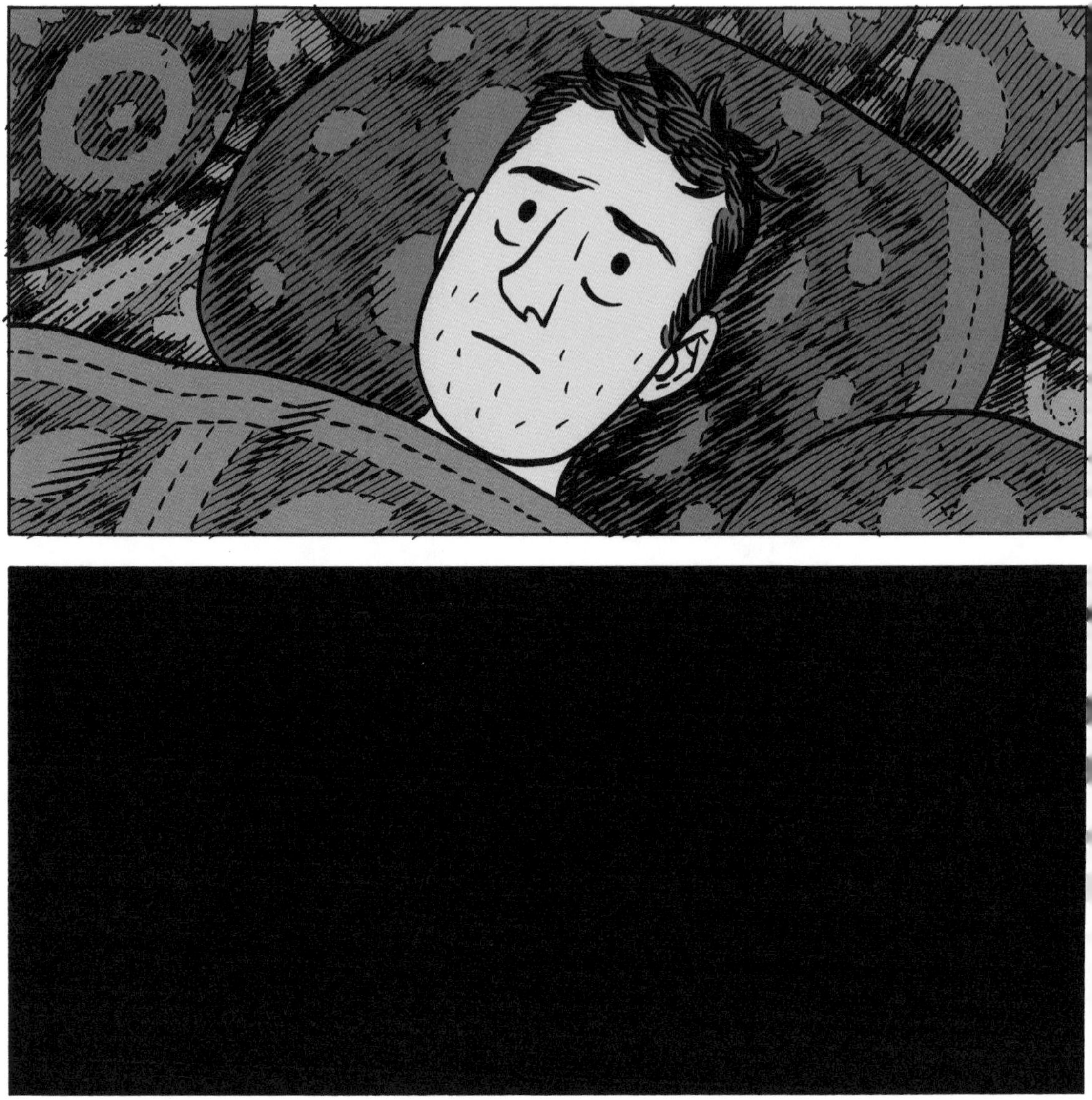

chapter six
The Sacred Comic

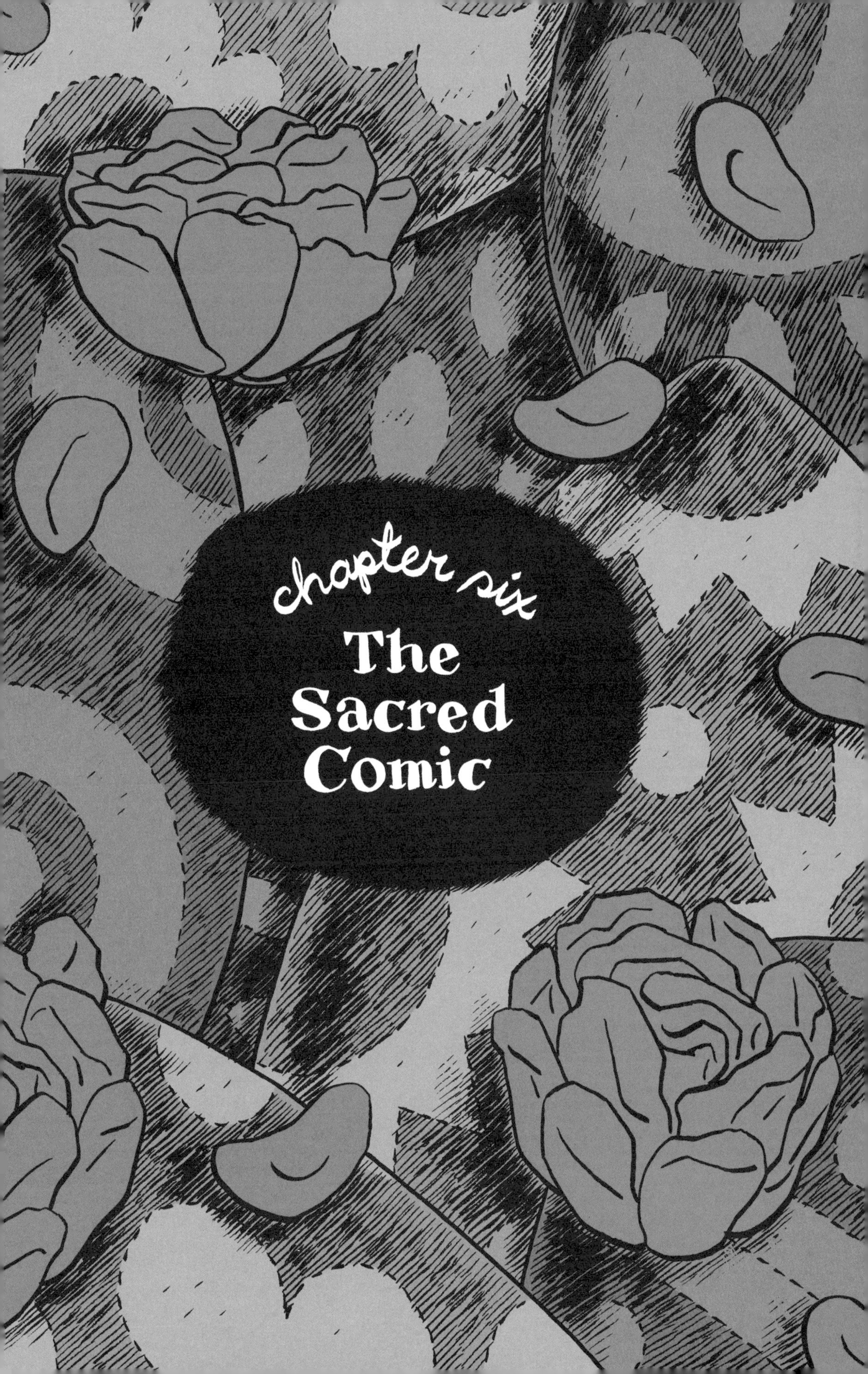

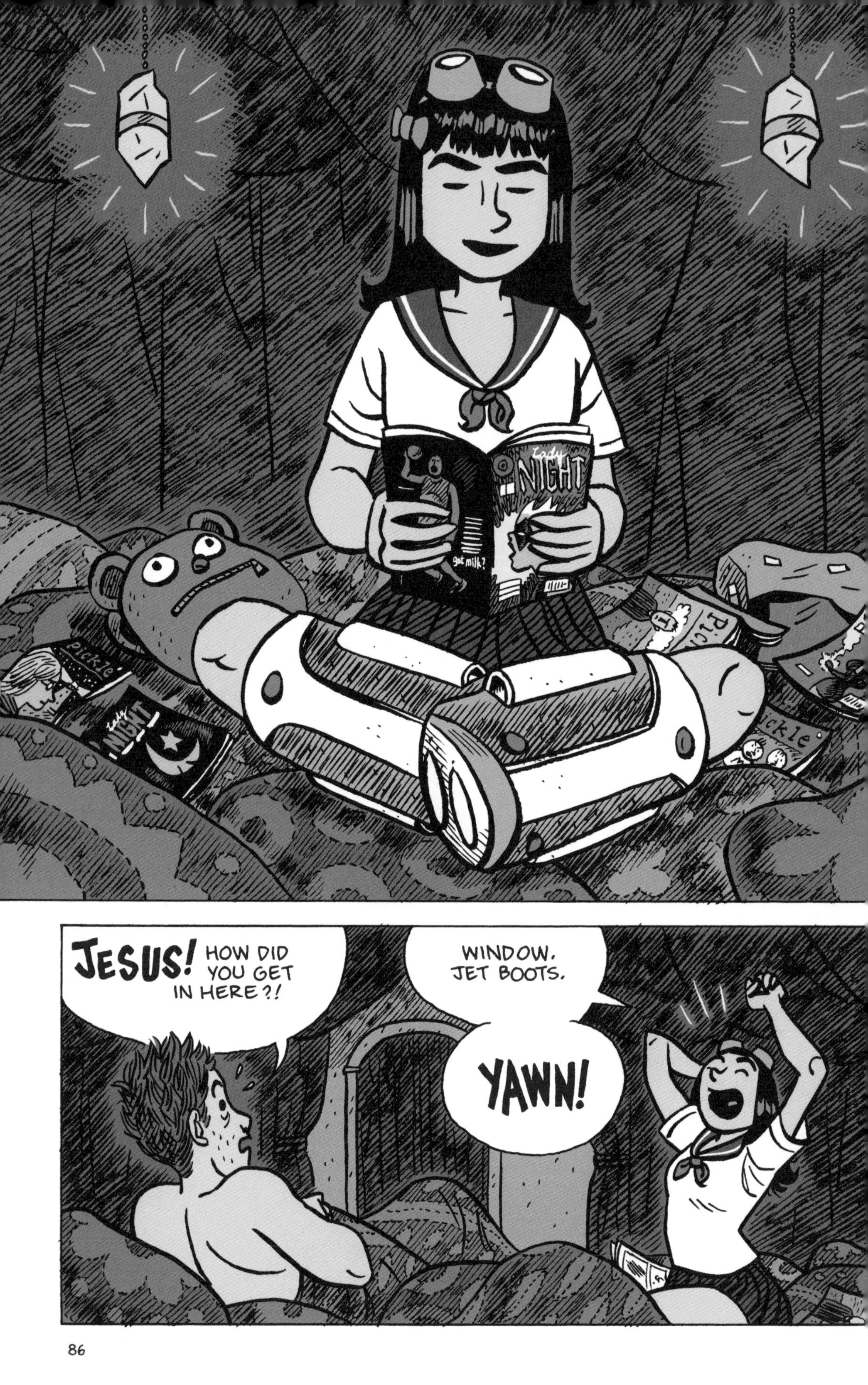
JESUS! HOW DID YOU GET IN HERE?!
WINDOW. JET BOOTS.
YAWN!

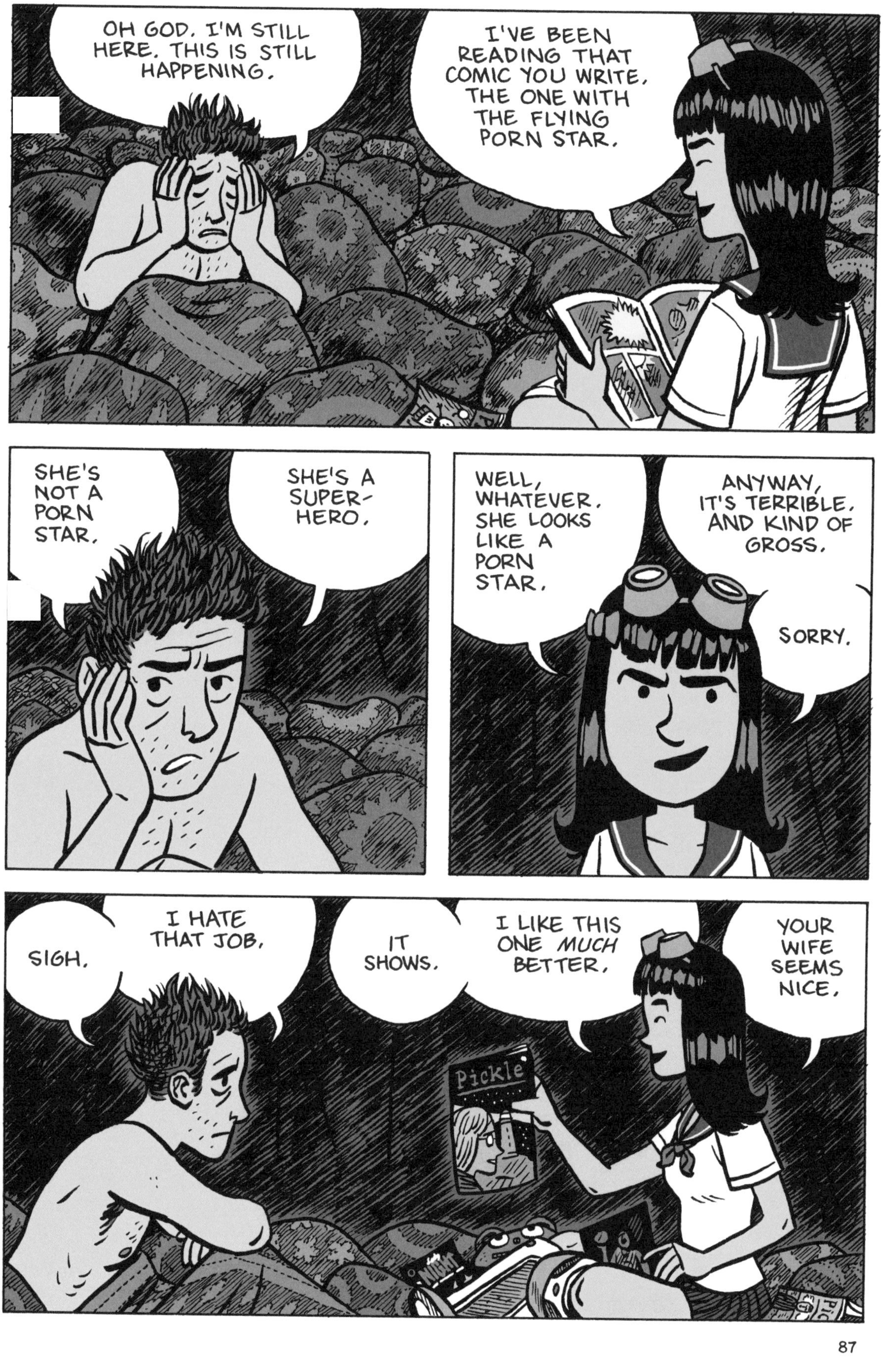
OH GOD. I'M STILL HERE. THIS IS STILL HAPPENING.
I'VE BEEN READING THAT COMIC YOU WRITE. THE ONE WITH THE FLYING PORN STAR.
SHE'S NOT A PORN STAR.
SHE'S A SUPER-HERO.
WELL, WHATEVER. SHE LOOKS LIKE A PORN STAR.
ANYWAY, IT'S TERRIBLE. AND KIND OF GROSS.
SORRY.
SIGH.
I HATE THAT JOB.
IT SHOWS.
I LIKE THIS ONE *MUCH* BETTER.
YOUR WIFE SEEMS NICE.
Pickle

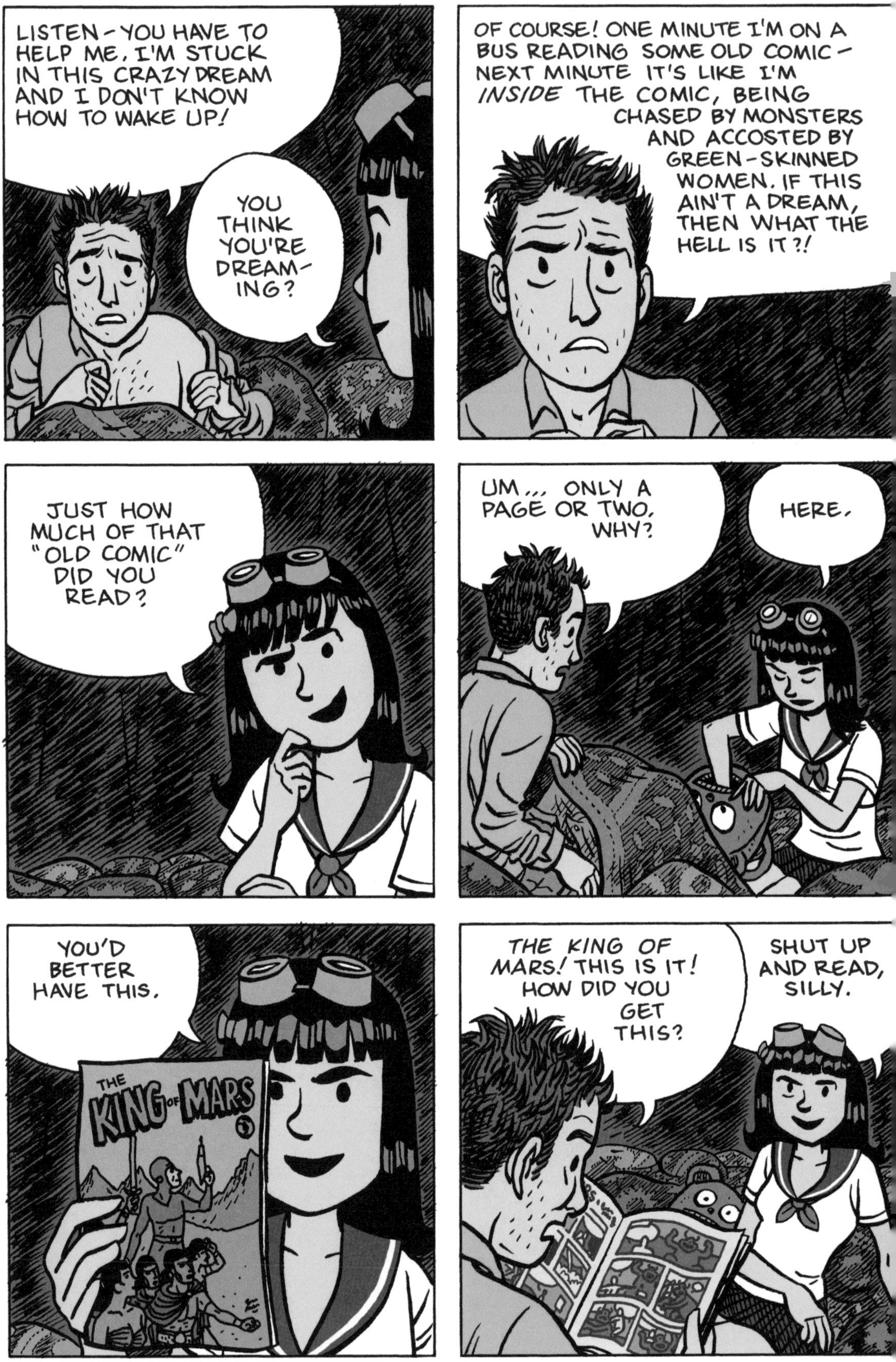
LISTEN - YOU HAVE TO HELP ME. I'M STUCK IN THIS CRAZY DREAM AND I DON'T KNOW HOW TO WAKE UP!
YOU THINK YOU'RE DREAMING?
OF COURSE! ONE MINUTE I'M ON A BUS READING SOME OLD COMIC - NEXT MINUTE IT'S LIKE I'M *INSIDE* THE COMIC, BEING CHASED BY MONSTERS AND ACCOSTED BY GREEN-SKINNED WOMEN. IF THIS AIN'T A DREAM, THEN WHAT THE HELL IS IT?!
JUST HOW MUCH OF THAT "OLD COMIC" DID YOU READ?
UM... ONLY A PAGE OR TWO. WHY?
HERE.
YOU'D BETTER HAVE THIS.
THE KING OF MARS
THE KING OF MARS! THIS IS IT! HOW DID YOU GET THIS?
SHUT UP AND READ, SILLY.

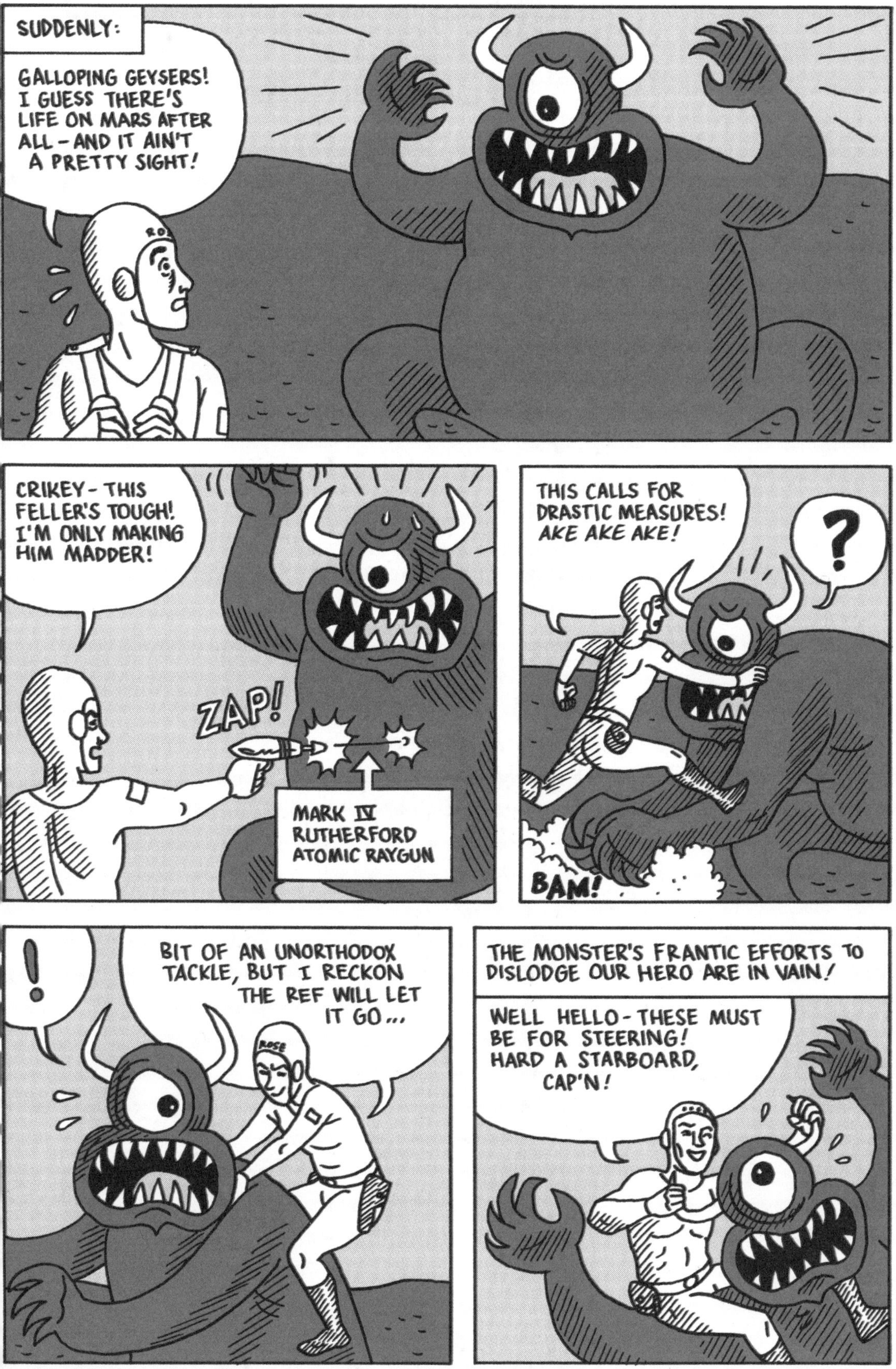
SUDDENLY:
GALLOPING GEYSERS! I GUESS THERE'S LIFE ON MARS AFTER ALL – AND IT AIN'T A PRETTY SIGHT!
CRIKEY – THIS FELLER'S TOUGH! I'M ONLY MAKING HIM MADDER!
ZAP!
MARK IV RUTHERFORD ATOMIC RAYGUN
THIS CALLS FOR DRASTIC MEASURES! AKE AKE AKE!
?
BAM!
!
BIT OF AN UNORTHODOX TACKLE, BUT I RECKON THE REF WILL LET IT GO...
ROSE
THE MONSTER'S FRANTIC EFFORTS TO DISLODGE OUR HERO ARE IN VAIN!
WELL HELLO – THESE MUST BE FOR STEERING! HARD A STARBOARD, CAP'N!

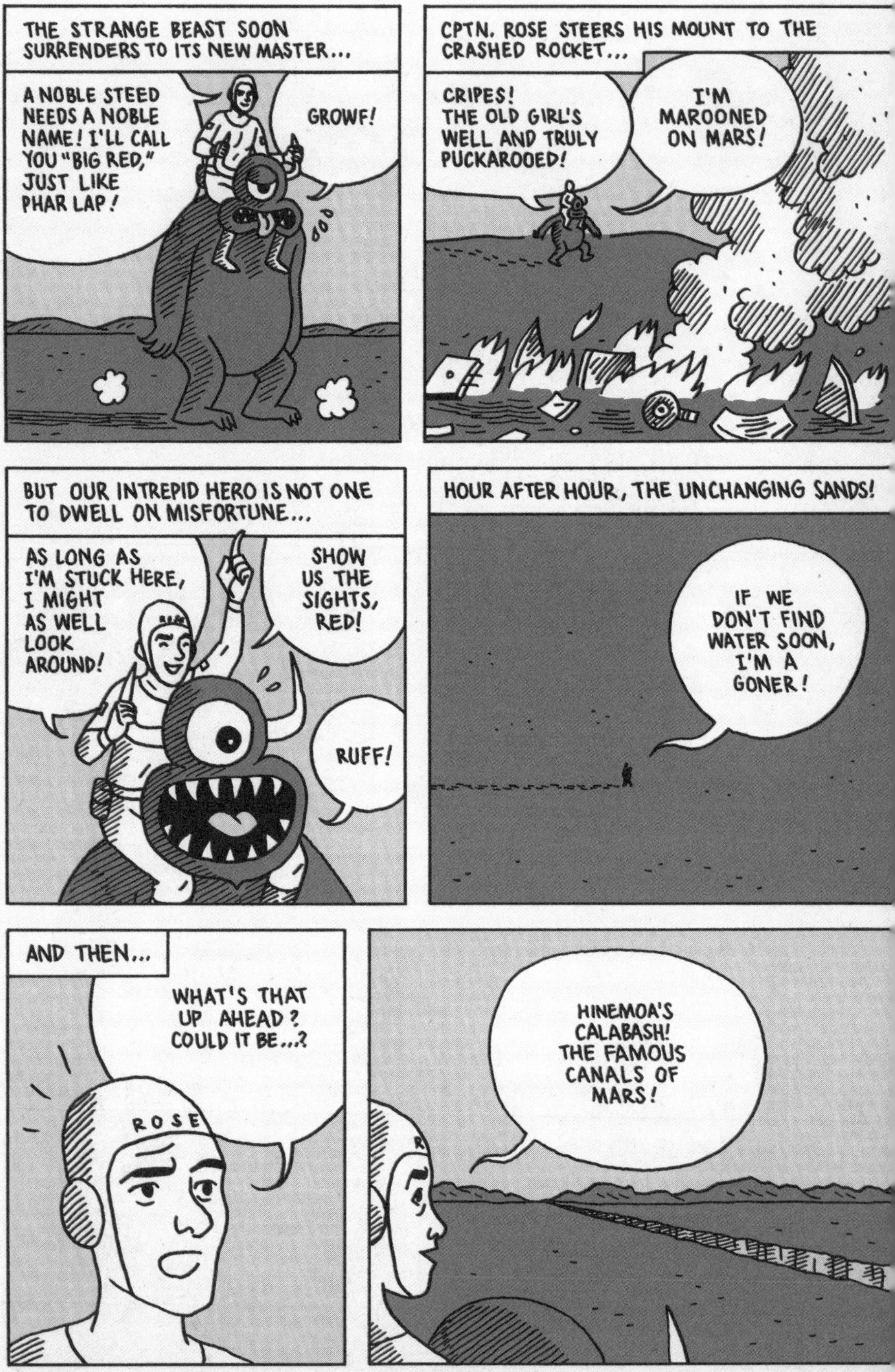
THE STRANGE BEAST SOON SURRENDERS TO ITS NEW MASTER...
A NOBLE STEED NEEDS A NOBLE NAME! I'LL CALL YOU "BIG RED," JUST LIKE PHAR LAP!
GROWF!
CPTN. ROSE STEERS HIS MOUNT TO THE CRASHED ROCKET...
CRIPES! THE OLD GIRL'S WELL AND TRULY PUCKAROOED!
I'M MAROONED ON MARS!
BUT OUR INTREPID HERO IS NOT ONE TO DWELL ON MISFORTUNE...
AS LONG AS I'M STUCK HERE, I MIGHT AS WELL LOOK AROUND!
SHOW US THE SIGHTS, RED!
RUFF!
HOUR AFTER HOUR, THE UNCHANGING SANDS!
IF WE DON'T FIND WATER SOON, I'M A GONER!
AND THEN...
WHAT'S THAT UP AHEAD? COULD IT BE...?
ROSE
HINEMOA'S CALABASH! THE FAMOUS CANALS OF MARS!

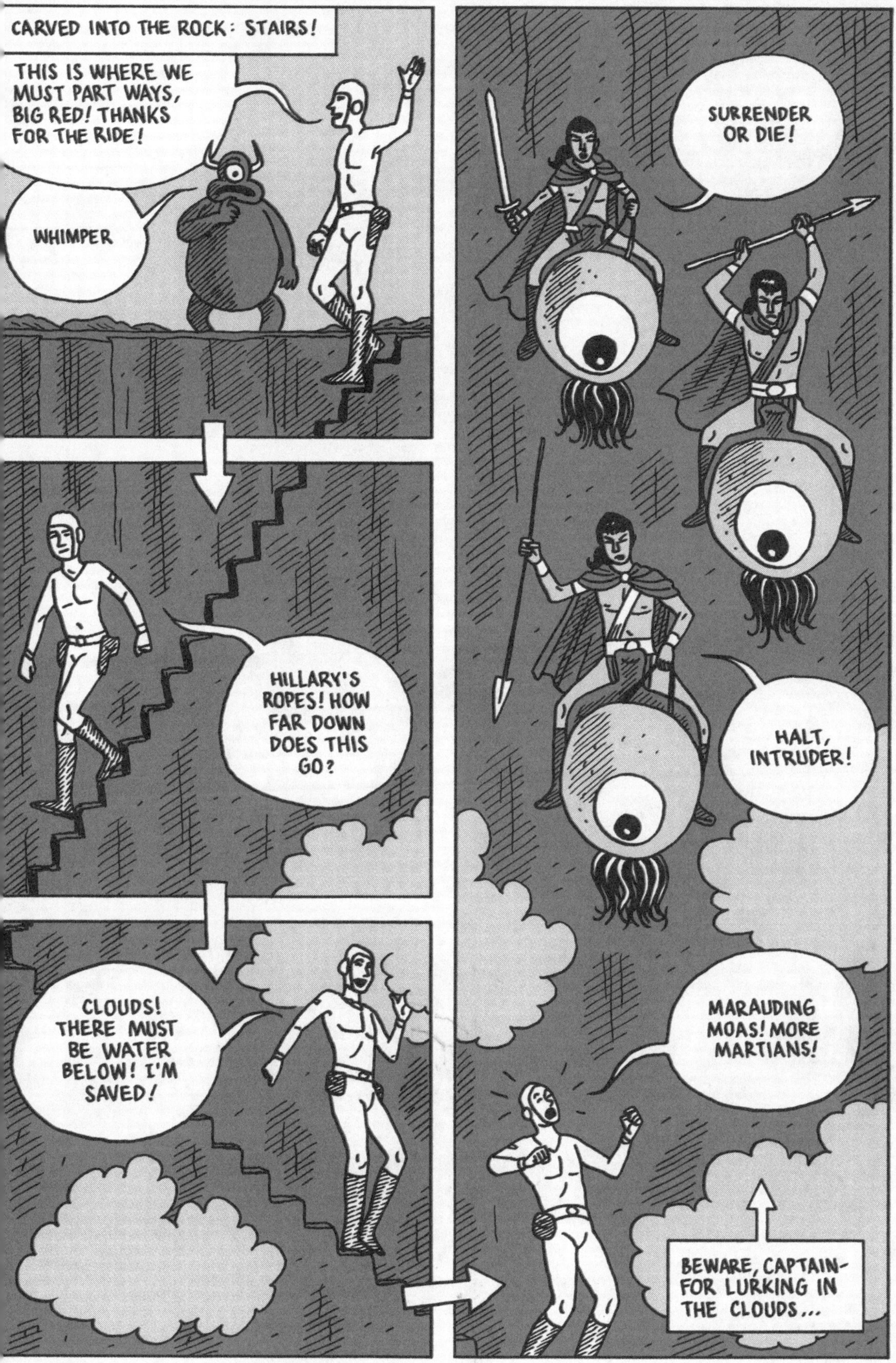
CARVED INTO THE ROCK: STAIRS!
THIS IS WHERE WE MUST PART WAYS, BIG RED! THANKS FOR THE RIDE!
WHIMPER
HILLARY'S ROPES! HOW FAR DOWN DOES THIS GO?
CLOUDS! THERE MUST BE WATER BELOW! I'M SAVED!
SURRENDER OR DIE!
HALT, INTRUDER!
MARAUDING MOAS! MORE MARTIANS!
BEWARE, CAPTAIN- FOR LURKING IN THE CLOUDS...

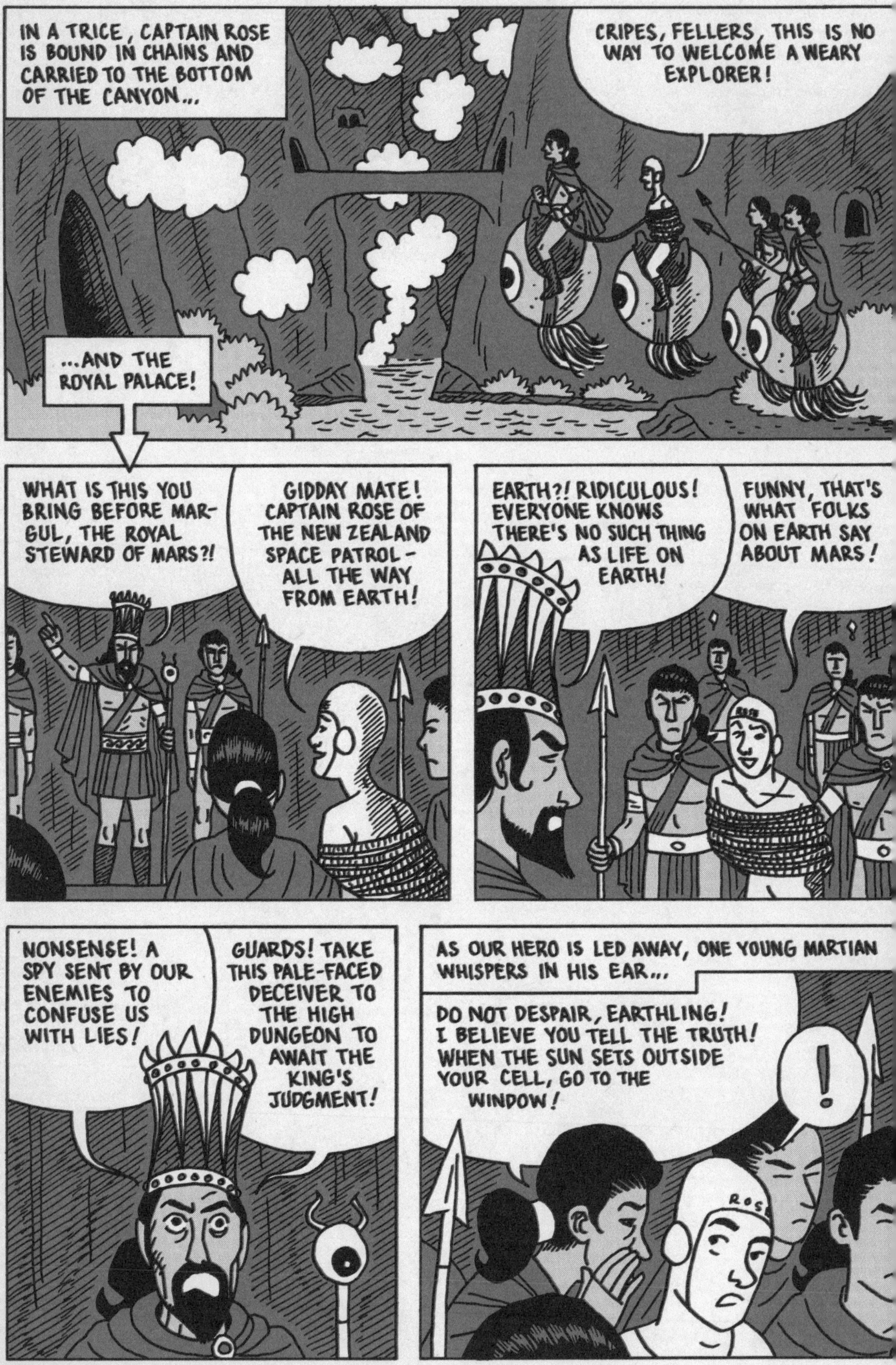
IN A TRICE, CAPTAIN ROSE IS BOUND IN CHAINS AND CARRIED TO THE BOTTOM OF THE CANYON...
CRIPES, FELLERS, THIS IS NO WAY TO WELCOME A WEARY EXPLORER!
...AND THE ROYAL PALACE!
WHAT IS THIS YOU BRING BEFORE MAR-GUL, THE ROYAL STEWARD OF MARS?!
GIDDAY MATE! CAPTAIN ROSE OF THE NEW ZEALAND SPACE PATROL - ALL THE WAY FROM EARTH!
EARTH?! RIDICULOUS! EVERYONE KNOWS THERE'S NO SUCH THING AS LIFE ON EARTH!
FUNNY, THAT'S WHAT FOLKS ON EARTH SAY ABOUT MARS!
NONSENSE! A SPY SENT BY OUR ENEMIES TO CONFUSE US WITH LIES!
GUARDS! TAKE THIS PALE-FACED DECEIVER TO THE HIGH DUNGEON TO AWAIT THE KING'S JUDGMENT!
AS OUR HERO IS LED AWAY, ONE YOUNG MARTIAN WHISPERS IN HIS EAR...
DO NOT DESPAIR, EARTHLING! I BELIEVE YOU TELL THE TRUTH! WHEN THE SUN SETS OUTSIDE YOUR CELL, GO TO THE WINDOW!
!
ROSE

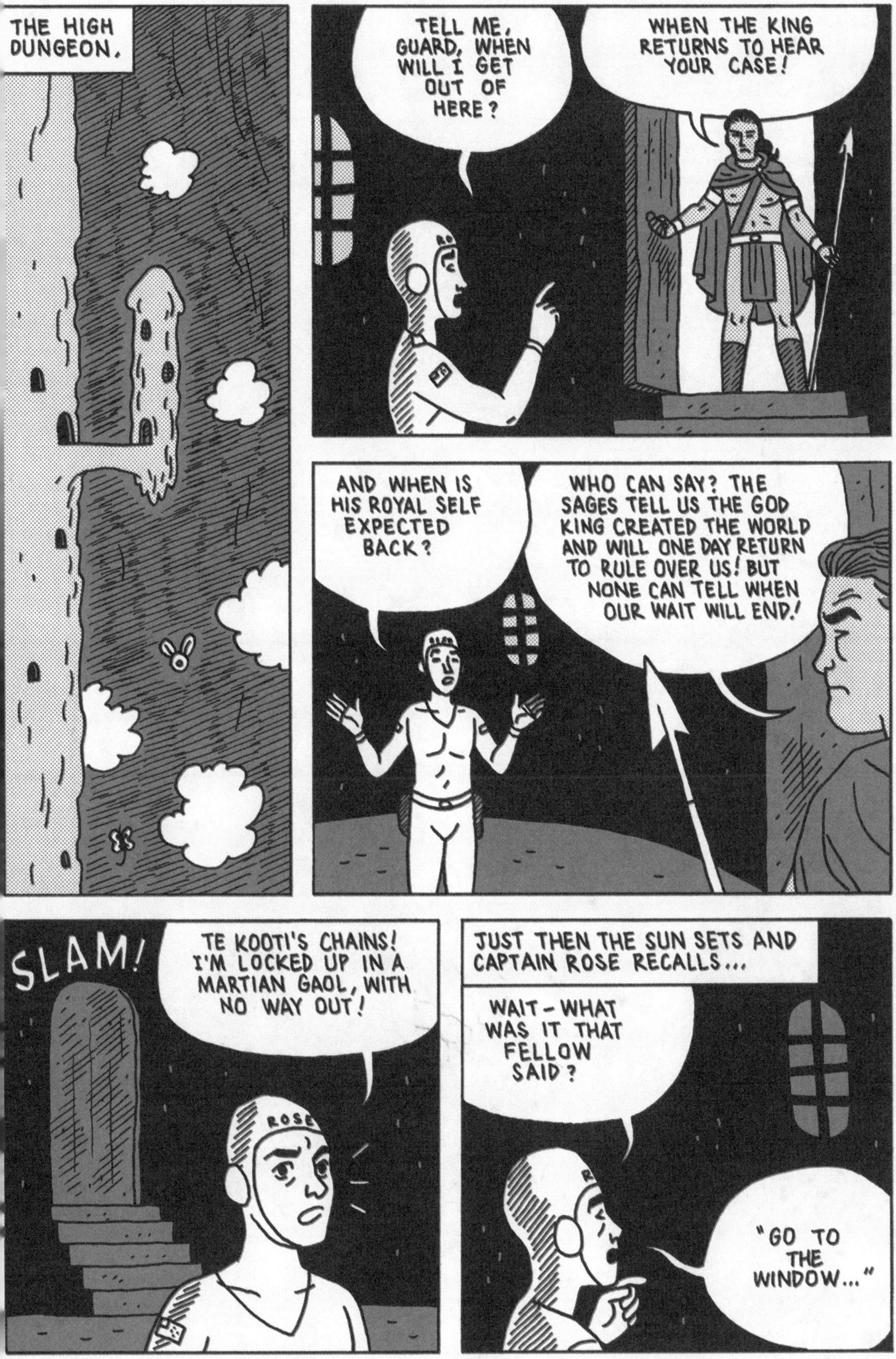

THE HIGH DUNGEON.
TELL ME, GUARD, WHEN WILL I GET OUT OF HERE?
WHEN THE KING RETURNS TO HEAR YOUR CASE!
AND WHEN IS HIS ROYAL SELF EXPECTED BACK?
WHO CAN SAY? THE SAGES TELL US THE GOD KING CREATED THE WORLD AND WILL ONE DAY RETURN TO RULE OVER US! BUT NONE CAN TELL WHEN OUR WAIT WILL END!
SLAM!
TE KOOTI'S CHAINS! I'M LOCKED UP IN A MARTIAN GAOL, WITH NO WAY OUT!
ROSE
JUST THEN THE SUN SETS AND CAPTAIN ROSE RECALLS...
WAIT - WHAT WAS IT THAT FELLOW SAID?
"GO TO THE WINDOW..."

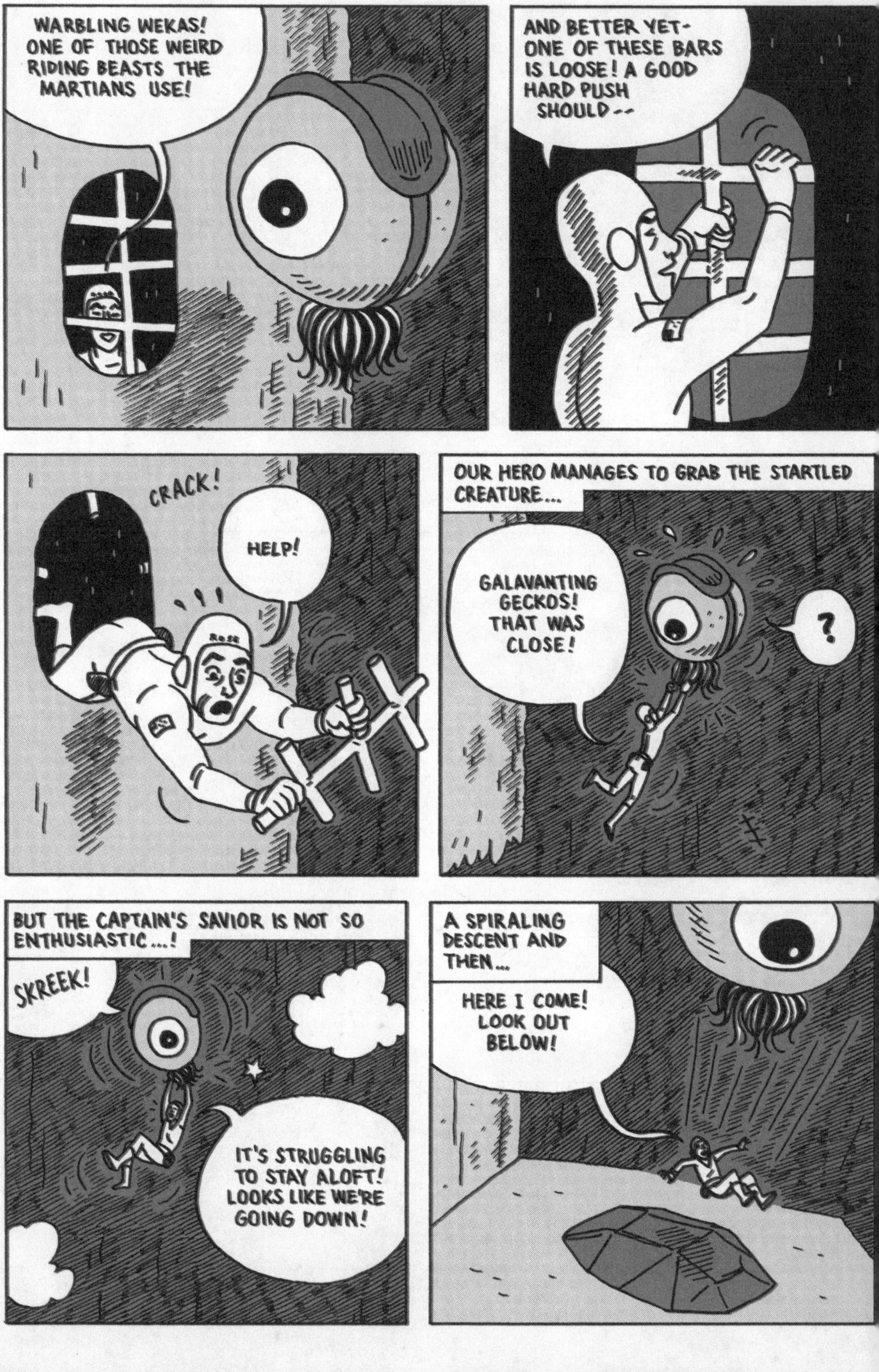
WARBLING WEKAS! ONE OF THOSE WEIRD RIDING BEASTS THE MARTIANS USE!
AND BETTER YET- ONE OF THESE BARS IS LOOSE! A GOOD HARD PUSH SHOULD--
CRACK!
HELP!
OUR HERO MANAGES TO GRAB THE STARTLED CREATURE....
GALAVANTING GECKOS! THAT WAS CLOSE!
?
BUT THE CAPTAIN'S SAVIOR IS NOT SO ENTHUSIASTIC....!
SKREEK!
IT'S STRUGGLING TO STAY ALOFT! LOOKS LIKE WE'RE GOING DOWN!
A SPIRALING DESCENT AND THEN...
HERE I COME! LOOK OUT BELOW!

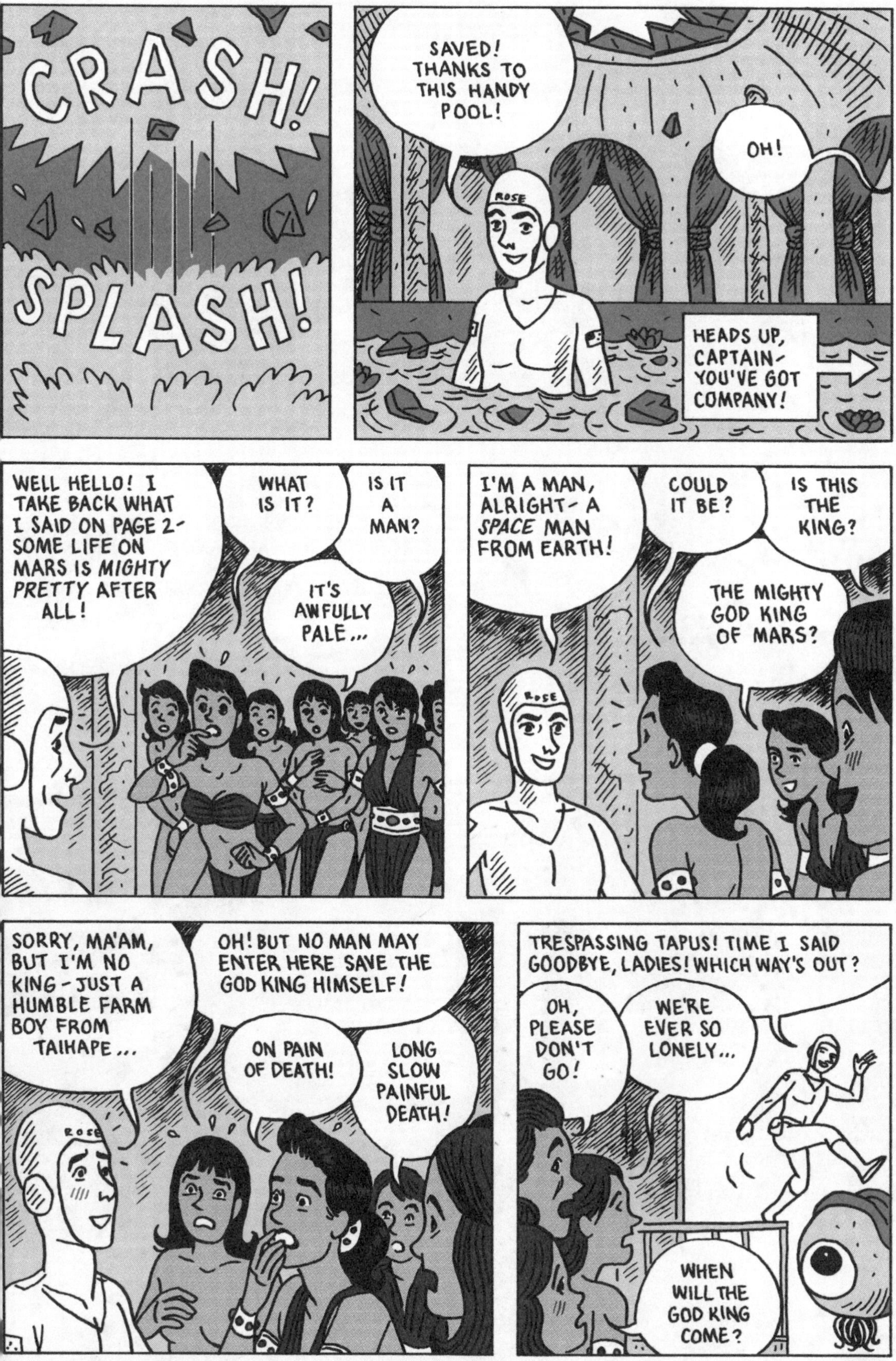
CRASH!
SPLASH!
SAVED! THANKS TO THIS HANDY POOL!
OH!
HEADS UP, CAPTAIN- YOU'VE GOT COMPANY!
WELL HELLO! I TAKE BACK WHAT I SAID ON PAGE 2- SOME LIFE ON MARS IS *MIGHTY PRETTY* AFTER ALL!
WHAT IS IT?
IS IT A MAN?
IT'S AWFULLY PALE...
I'M A MAN, ALRIGHT- A *SPACE* MAN FROM EARTH!
COULD IT BE?
IS THIS THE KING?
THE MIGHTY GOD KING OF MARS?
SORRY, MA'AM, BUT I'M NO KING - JUST A HUMBLE FARM BOY FROM TAIHAPE...
OH! BUT NO MAN MAY ENTER HERE SAVE THE GOD KING HIMSELF!
ON PAIN OF DEATH!
LONG SLOW PAINFUL DEATH!
TRESPASSING TAPUS! TIME I SAID GOODBYE, LADIES! WHICH WAY'S OUT?
OH, PLEASE DON'T GO!
WE'RE EVER SO LONELY...
WHEN WILL THE GOD KING COME?

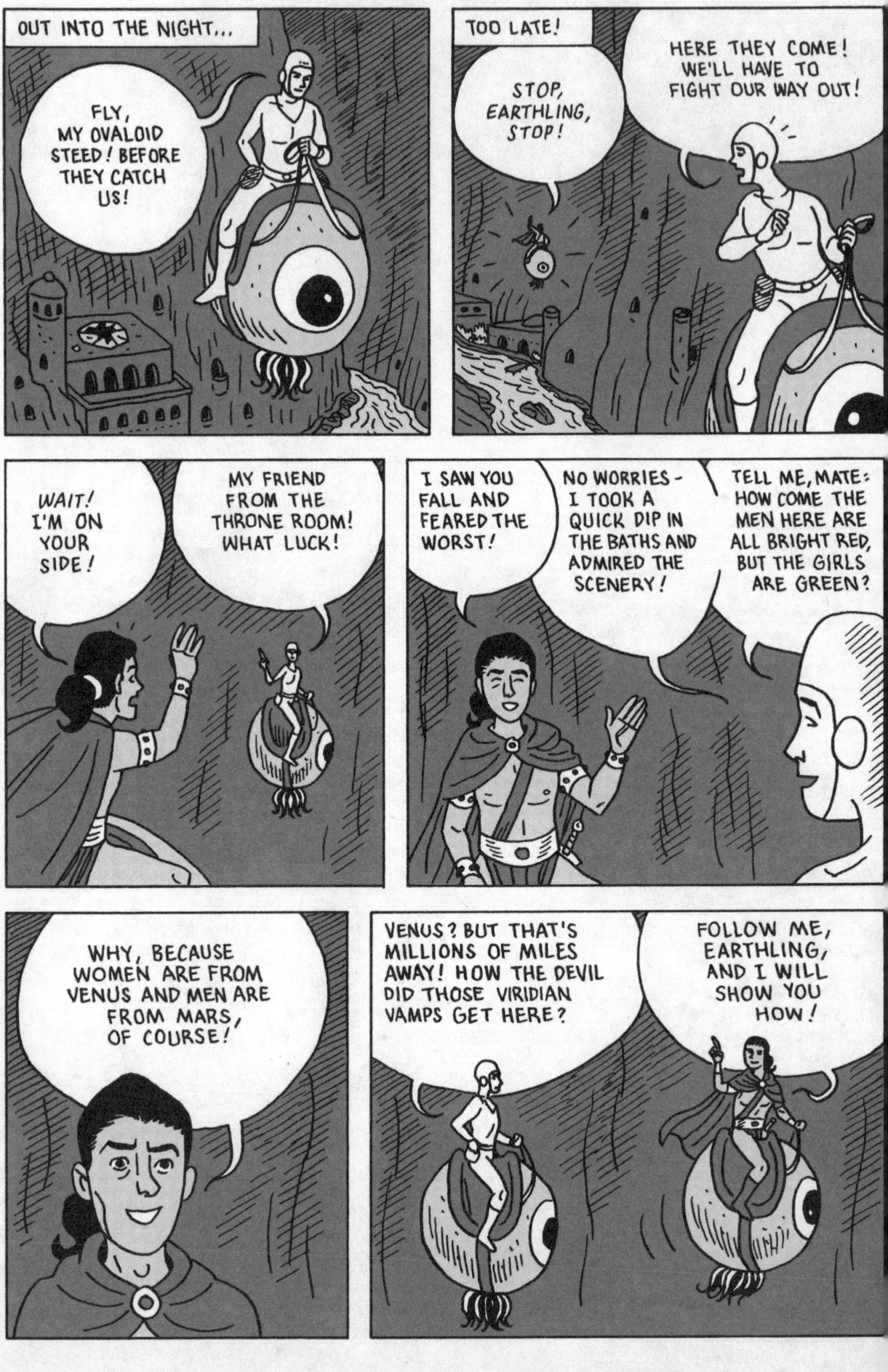
OUT INTO THE NIGHT...
FLY, MY OVALOID STEED! BEFORE THEY CATCH US!
TOO LATE!
STOP, EARTHLING, STOP!
HERE THEY COME! WE'LL HAVE TO FIGHT OUR WAY OUT!
WAIT! I'M ON YOUR SIDE!
MY FRIEND FROM THE THRONE ROOM! WHAT LUCK!
I SAW YOU FALL AND FEARED THE WORST!
NO WORRIES - I TOOK A QUICK DIP IN THE BATHS AND ADMIRED THE SCENERY!
TELL ME, MATE: HOW COME THE MEN HERE ARE ALL BRIGHT RED, BUT THE GIRLS ARE GREEN?
WHY, BECAUSE WOMEN ARE FROM VENUS AND MEN ARE FROM MARS, OF COURSE!
VENUS? BUT THAT'S MILLIONS OF MILES AWAY! HOW THE DEVIL DID THOSE VIRIDIAN VAMPS GET HERE?
FOLLOW ME, EARTHLING, AND I WILL SHOW YOU HOW!

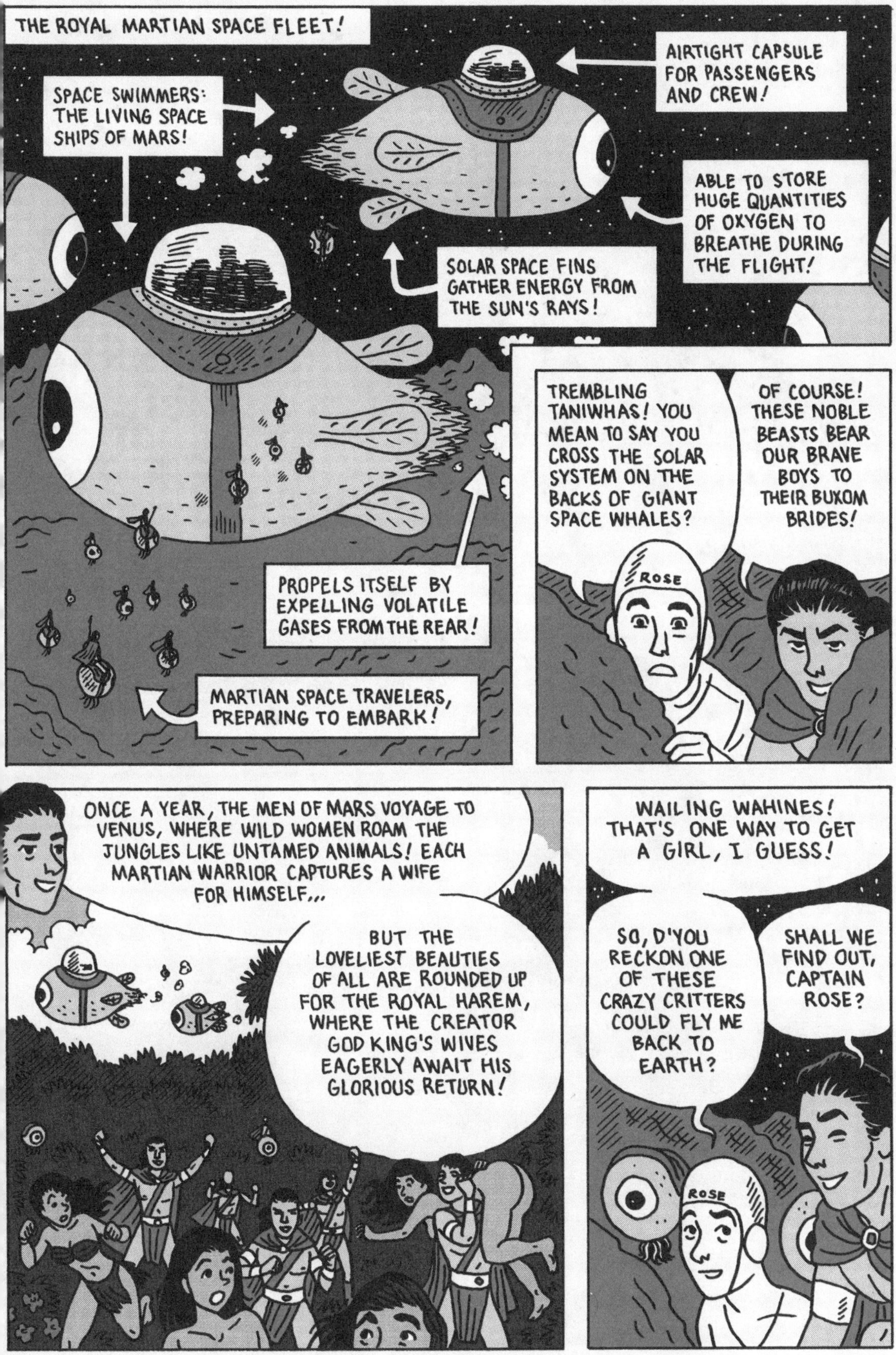
THE ROYAL MARTIAN SPACE FLEET!
SPACE SWIMMERS: THE LIVING SPACE SHIPS OF MARS!
AIRTIGHT CAPSULE FOR PASSENGERS AND CREW!
ABLE TO STORE HUGE QUANTITIES OF OXYGEN TO BREATHE DURING THE FLIGHT!
SOLAR SPACE FINS GATHER ENERGY FROM THE SUN'S RAYS!
PROPELS ITSELF BY EXPELLING VOLATILE GASES FROM THE REAR!
MARTIAN SPACE TRAVELERS, PREPARING TO EMBARK!
TREMBLING TANIWHAS! YOU MEAN TO SAY YOU CROSS THE SOLAR SYSTEM ON THE BACKS OF GIANT SPACE WHALES?
OF COURSE! THESE NOBLE BEASTS BEAR OUR BRAVE BOYS TO THEIR BUXOM BRIDES!
ROSE
ONCE A YEAR, THE MEN OF MARS VOYAGE TO VENUS, WHERE WILD WOMEN ROAM THE JUNGLES LIKE UNTAMED ANIMALS! EACH MARTIAN WARRIOR CAPTURES A WIFE FOR HIMSELF...
BUT THE LOVELIEST BEAUTIES OF ALL ARE ROUNDED UP FOR THE ROYAL HAREM, WHERE THE CREATOR GOD KING'S WIVES EAGERLY AWAIT HIS GLORIOUS RETURN!
WAILING WAHINES! THAT'S ONE WAY TO GET A GIRL, I GUESS!
SO, D'YOU RECKON ONE OF THESE CRAZY CRITTERS COULD FLY ME BACK TO EARTH?
SHALL WE FIND OUT, CAPTAIN ROSE?
ROSE

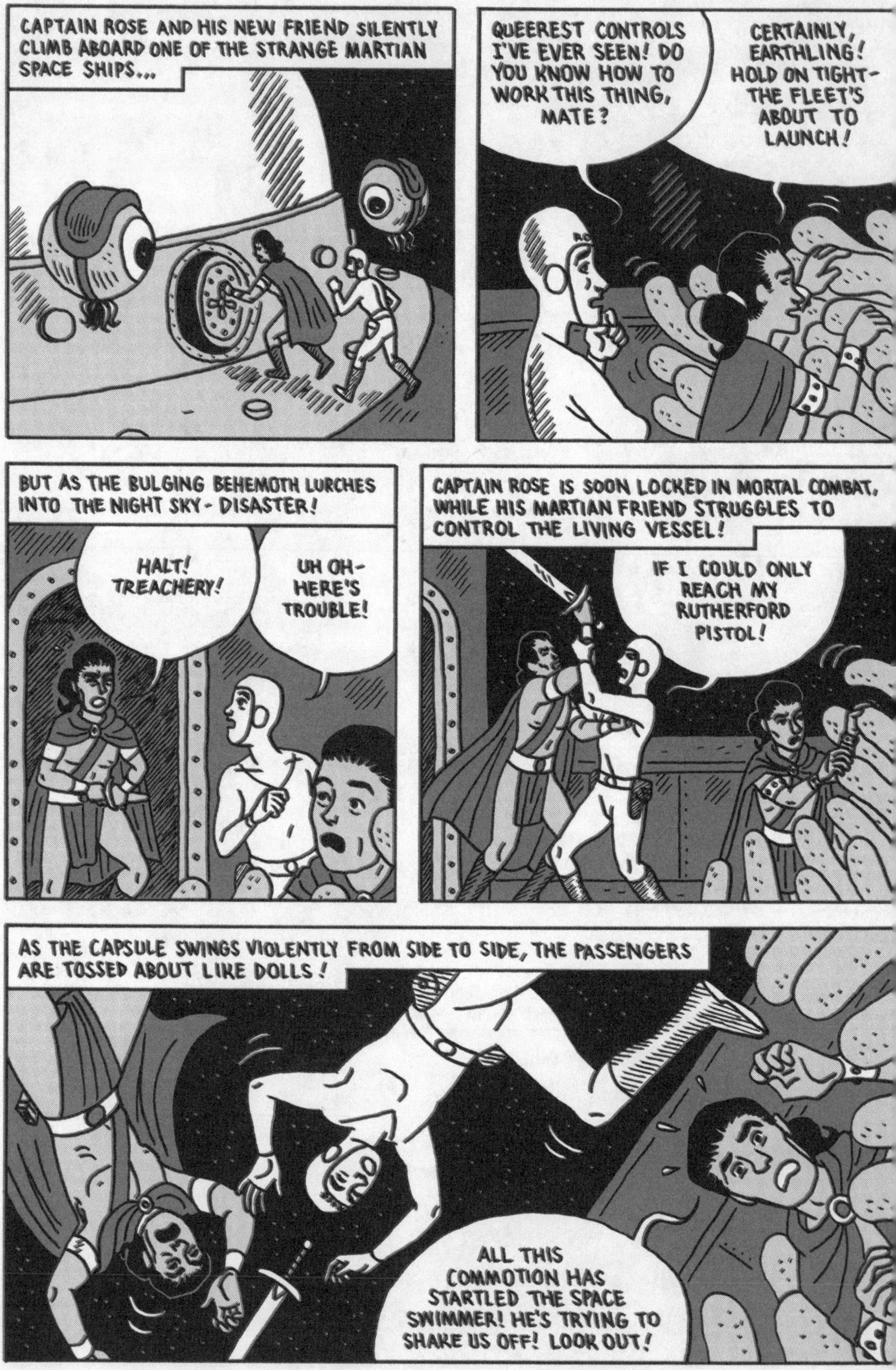
CAPTAIN ROSE AND HIS NEW FRIEND SILENTLY CLIMB ABOARD ONE OF THE STRANGE MARTIAN SPACE SHIPS...
QUEEREST CONTROLS I'VE EVER SEEN! DO YOU KNOW HOW TO WORK THIS THING, MATE?
CERTAINLY, EARTHLING! HOLD ON TIGHT- THE FLEET'S ABOUT TO LAUNCH!
BUT AS THE BULGING BEHEMOTH LURCHES INTO THE NIGHT SKY - DISASTER!
HALT! TREACHERY!
UH OH- HERE'S TROUBLE!
CAPTAIN ROSE IS SOON LOCKED IN MORTAL COMBAT, WHILE HIS MARTIAN FRIEND STRUGGLES TO CONTROL THE LIVING VESSEL!
IF I COULD ONLY REACH MY RUTHERFORD PISTOL!
AS THE CAPSULE SWINGS VIOLENTLY FROM SIDE TO SIDE, THE PASSENGERS ARE TOSSED ABOUT LIKE DOLLS!
ALL THIS COMMOTION HAS STARTLED THE SPACE SWIMMER! HE'S TRYING TO SHAKE US OFF! LOOK OUT!

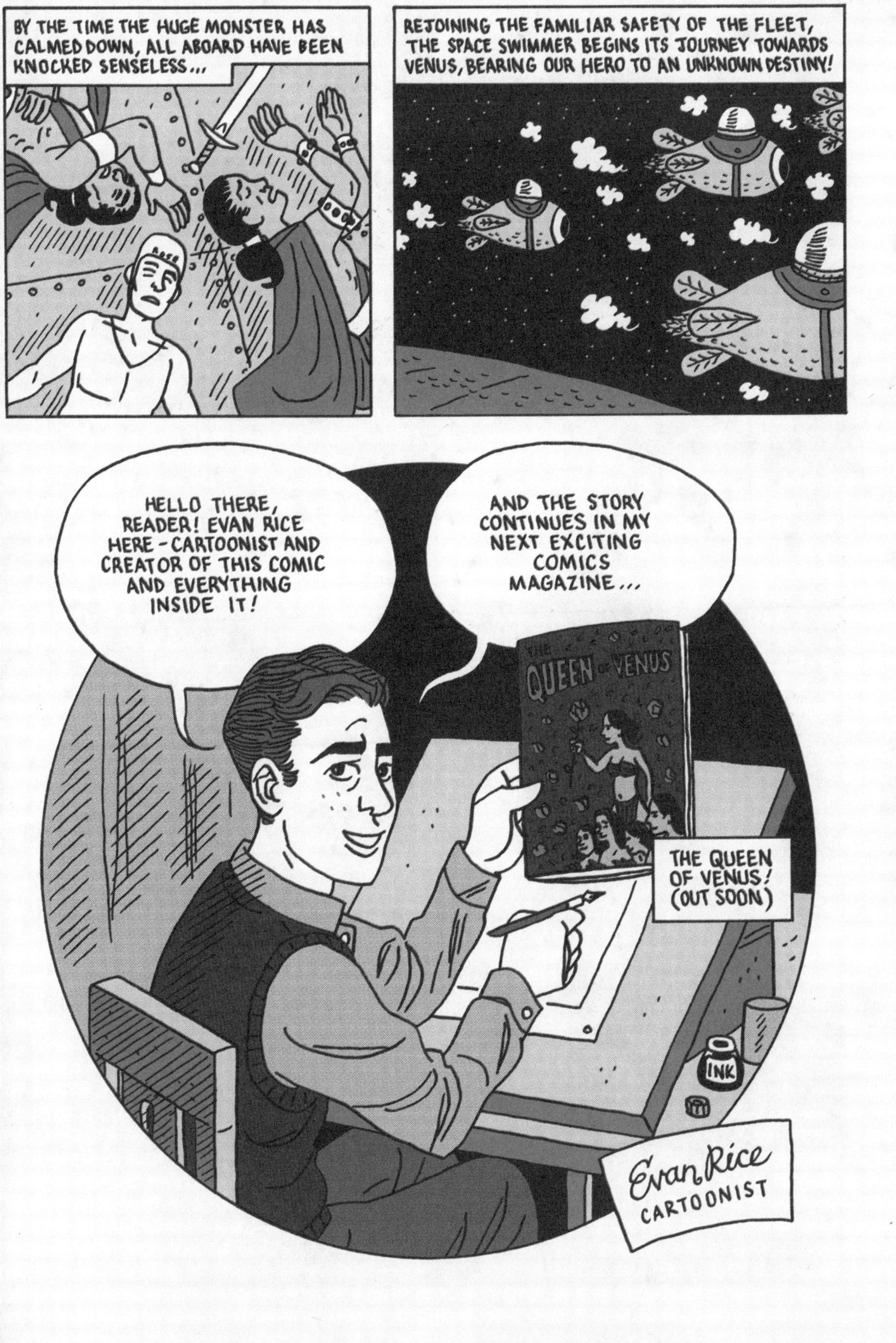
BY THE TIME THE HUGE MONSTER HAS CALMED DOWN, ALL ABOARD HAVE BEEN KNOCKED SENSELESS...
ROSE
REJOINING THE FAMILIAR SAFETY OF THE FLEET, THE SPACE SWIMMER BEGINS ITS JOURNEY TOWARDS VENUS, BEARING OUR HERO TO AN UNKNOWN DESTINY!
HELLO THERE, READER! EVAN RICE HERE - CARTOONIST AND CREATOR OF THIS COMIC AND EVERYTHING INSIDE IT!
AND THE STORY CONTINUES IN MY NEXT EXCITING COMICS MAGAZINE...
THE QUEEN OF VENUS
THE QUEEN OF VENUS! (OUT SOON)
INK
Evan Rice
CARTOONIST

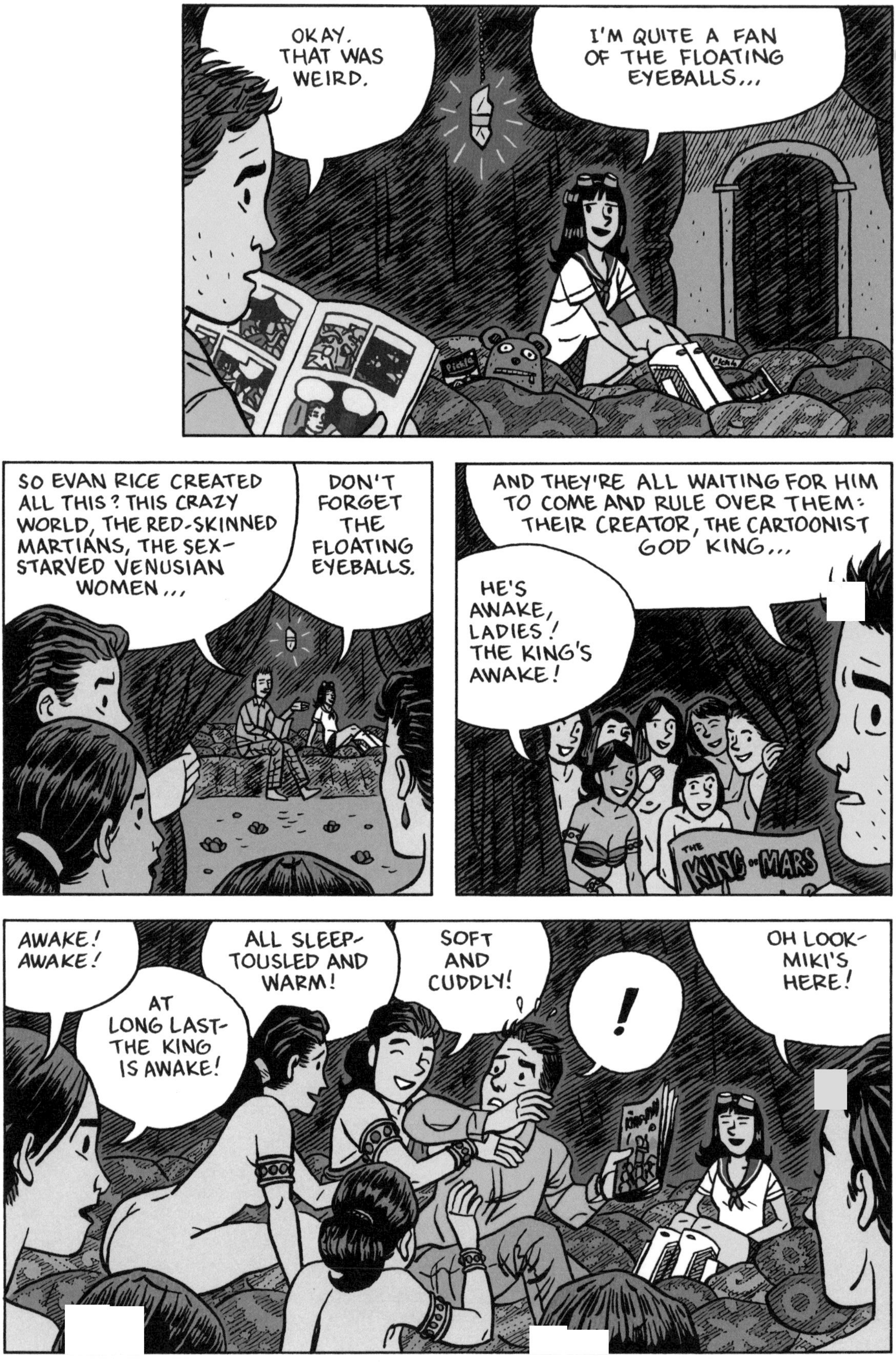
OKAY. THAT WAS WEIRD.
I'M QUITE A FAN OF THE FLOATING EYEBALLS...
SO EVAN RICE CREATED ALL THIS? THIS CRAZY WORLD, THE RED-SKINNED MARTIANS, THE SEX-STARVED VENUSIAN WOMEN...
DON'T FORGET THE FLOATING EYEBALLS.
AND THEY'RE ALL WAITING FOR HIM TO COME AND RULE OVER THEM: THEIR CREATOR, THE CARTOONIST GOD KING...
HE'S AWAKE, LADIES! THE KING'S AWAKE!
THE KING OF MARS
AWAKE! AWAKE!
AT LONG LAST-THE KING IS AWAKE!
ALL SLEEP-TOUSLED AND WARM!
SOFT AND CUDDLY!
!
OH LOOK-MIKI'S HERE!

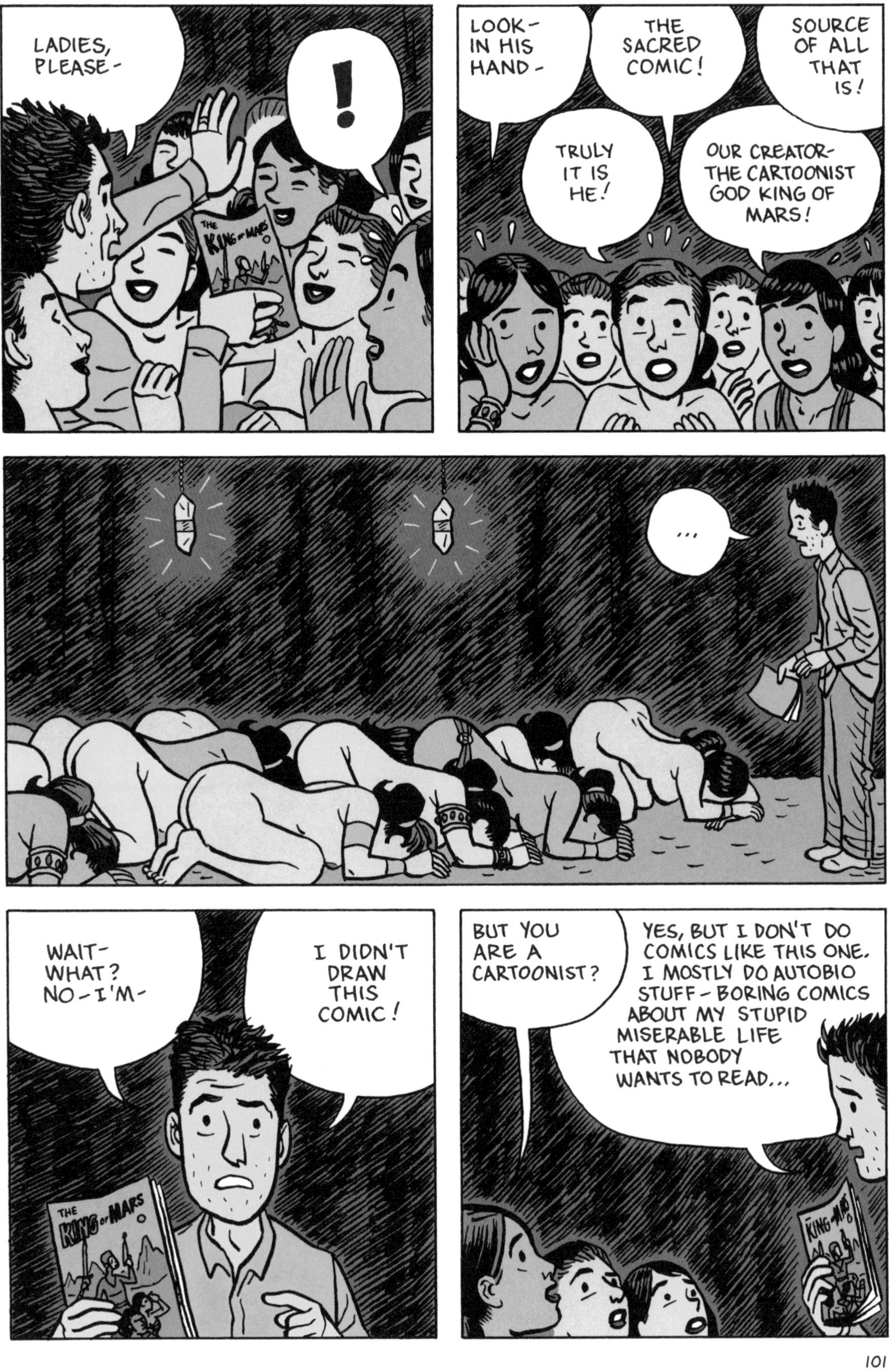
LADIES, PLEASE-
!
THE KING OF MARS
LOOK- IN HIS HAND-
THE SACRED COMIC!
SOURCE OF ALL THAT IS!
TRULY IT IS HE!
OUR CREATOR- THE CARTOONIST GOD KING OF MARS!
...
WAIT- WHAT? NO-I'M-
I DIDN'T DRAW THIS COMIC!
THE KING OF MARS
BUT YOU ARE A CARTOONIST?
YES, BUT I DON'T DO COMICS LIKE THIS ONE. I MOSTLY DO AUTOBIO STUFF- BORING COMICS ABOUT MY STUPID MISERABLE LIFE THAT NOBODY WANTS TO READ...

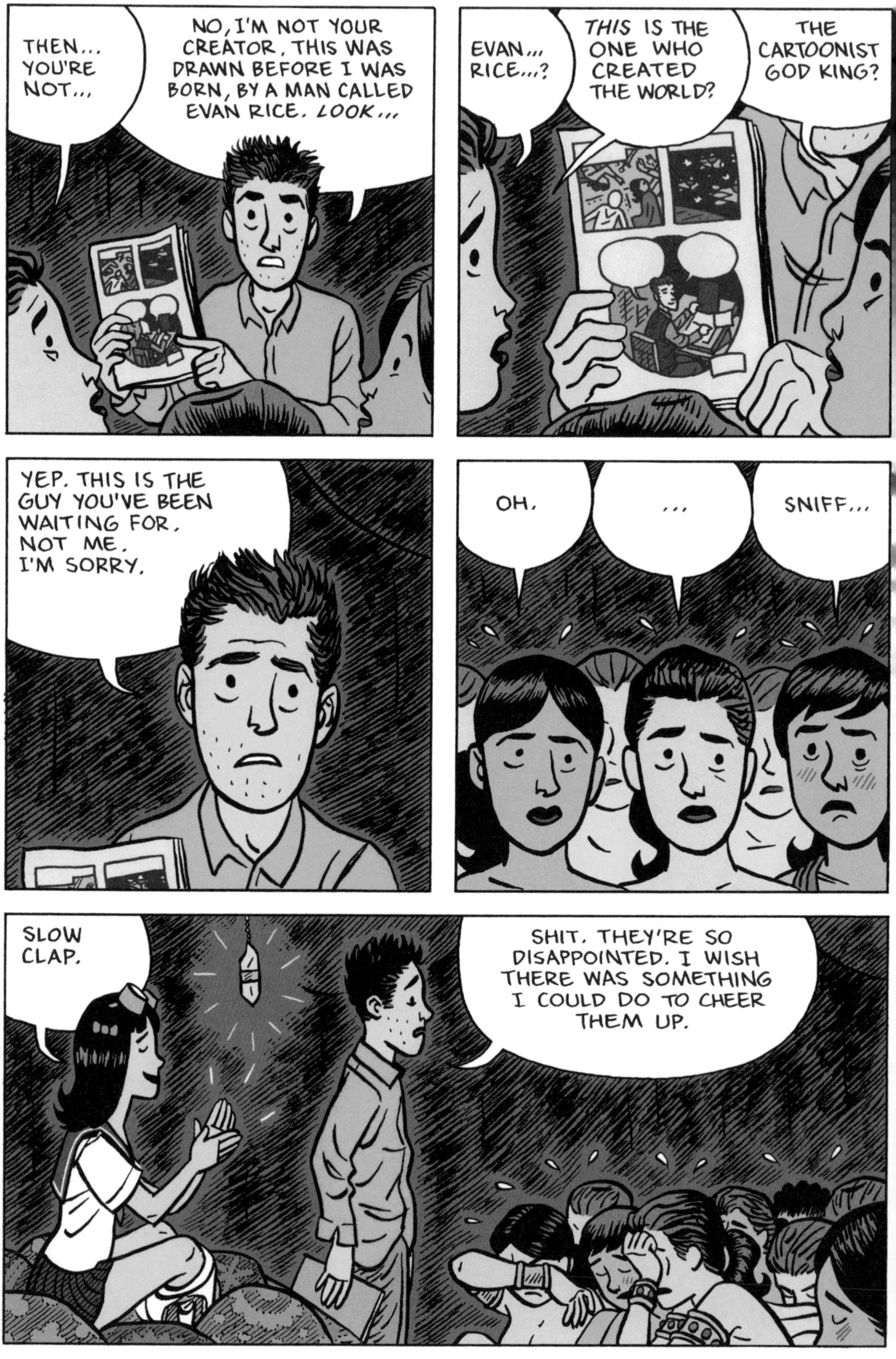
THEN... YOU'RE NOT...
NO, I'M NOT YOUR CREATOR. THIS WAS DRAWN BEFORE I WAS BORN, BY A MAN CALLED EVAN RICE. LOOK...
EVAN... RICE...?
THIS IS THE ONE WHO CREATED THE WORLD?
THE CARTOONIST GOD KING?
YEP. THIS IS THE GUY YOU'VE BEEN WAITING FOR. NOT ME. I'M SORRY.
OH.
...
SNIFF...
SLOW CLAP.
SHIT. THEY'RE SO DISAPPOINTED. I WISH THERE WAS SOMETHING I COULD DO TO CHEER THEM UP.

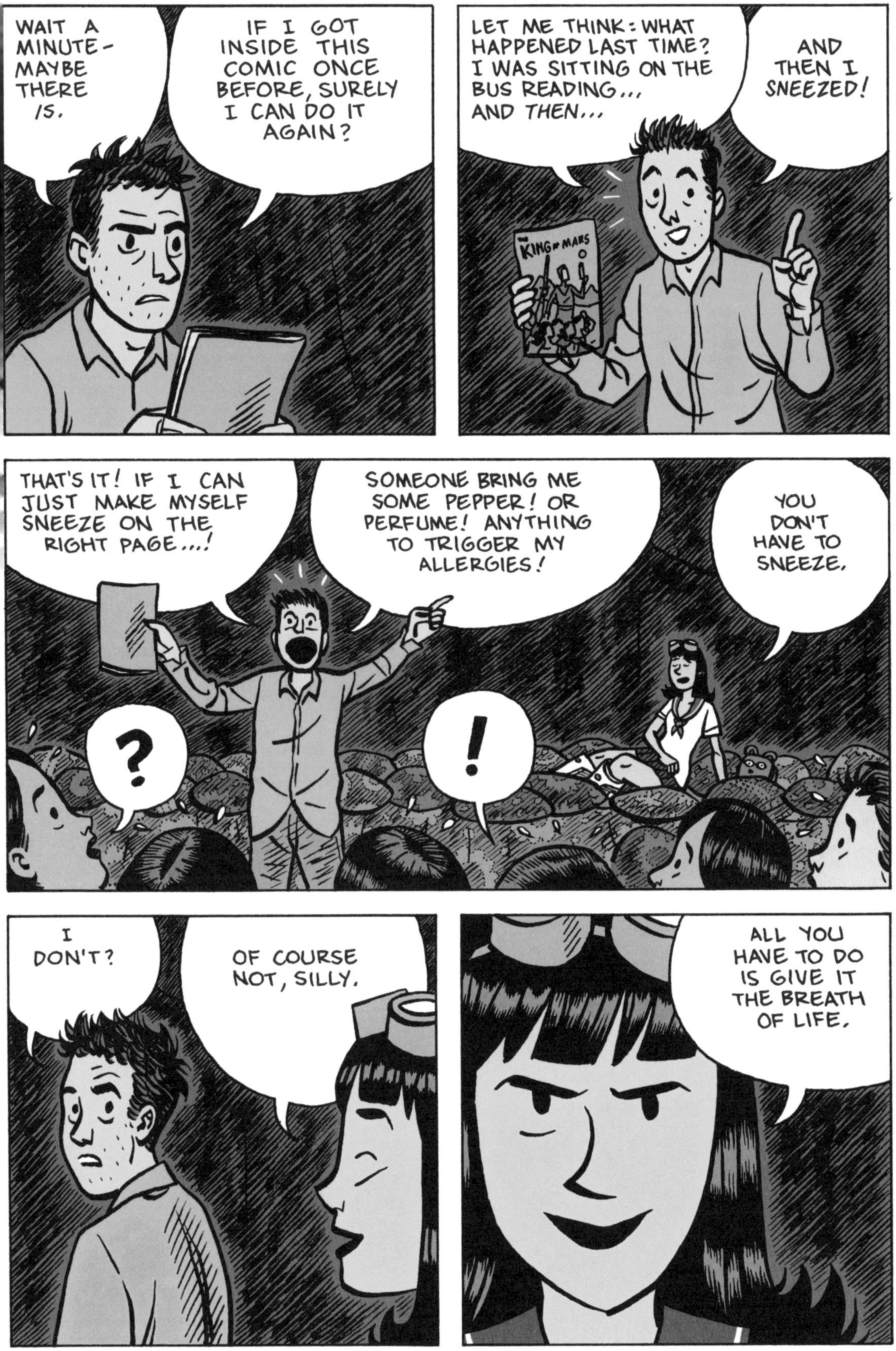
WAIT A MINUTE- MAYBE THERE IS.
IF I GOT INSIDE THIS COMIC ONCE BEFORE, SURELY I CAN DO IT AGAIN?
LET ME THINK: WHAT HAPPENED LAST TIME? I WAS SITTING ON THE BUS READING... AND THEN...
AND THEN I SNEEZED!
KING OF MARS
THAT'S IT! IF I CAN JUST MAKE MYSELF SNEEZE ON THE RIGHT PAGE...!
SOMEONE BRING ME SOME PEPPER! OR PERFUME! ANYTHING TO TRIGGER MY ALLERGIES!
YOU DON'T HAVE TO SNEEZE.
?
!
I DON'T?
OF COURSE NOT, SILLY.
ALL YOU HAVE TO DO IS GIVE IT THE BREATH OF LIFE.

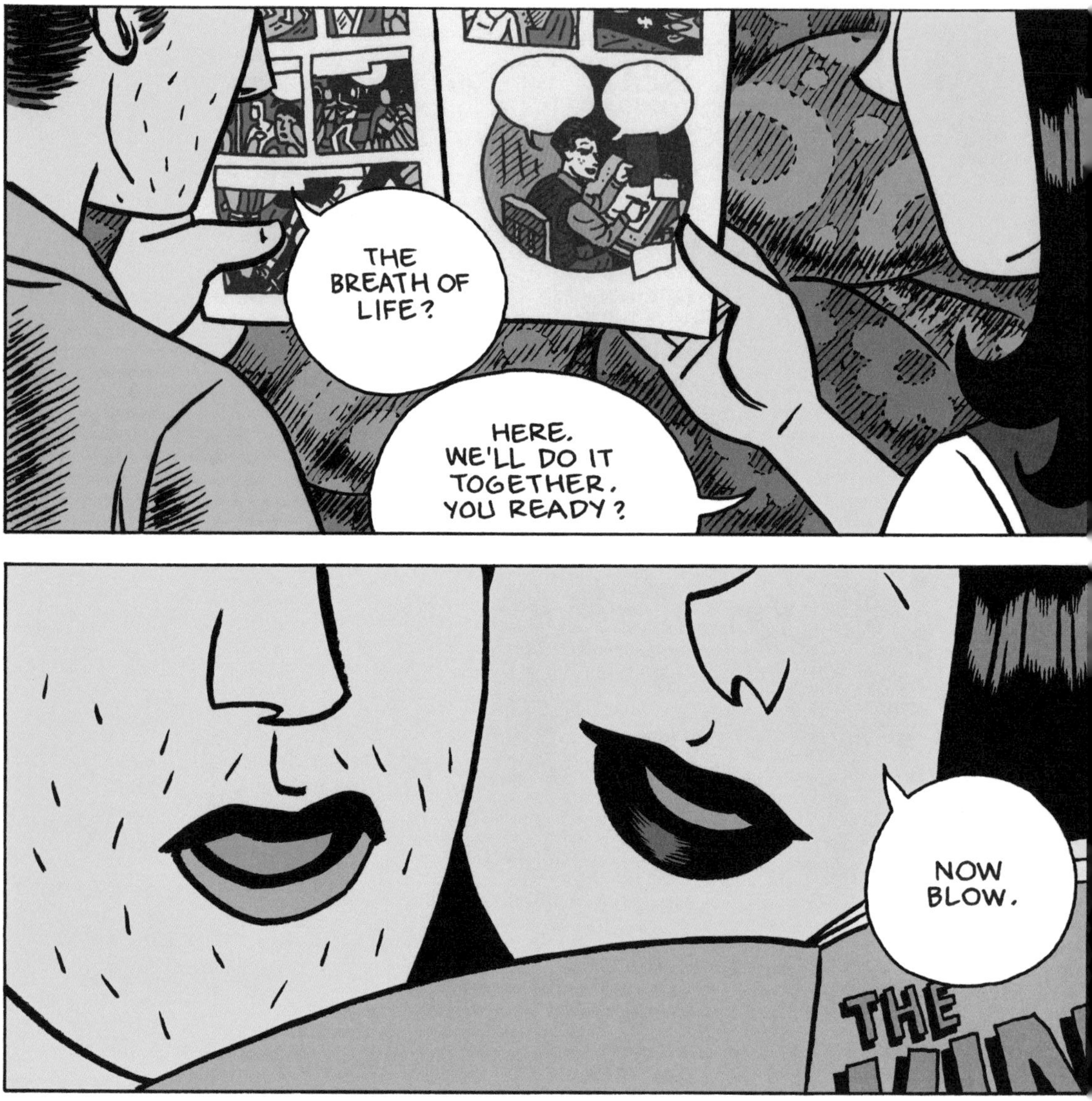
THE BREATH OF LIFE?
HERE. WE'LL DO IT TOGETHER. YOU READY?
NOW BLOW.
THE

CHAPTER SEVEN

THE CARTOONIST GOD KING!

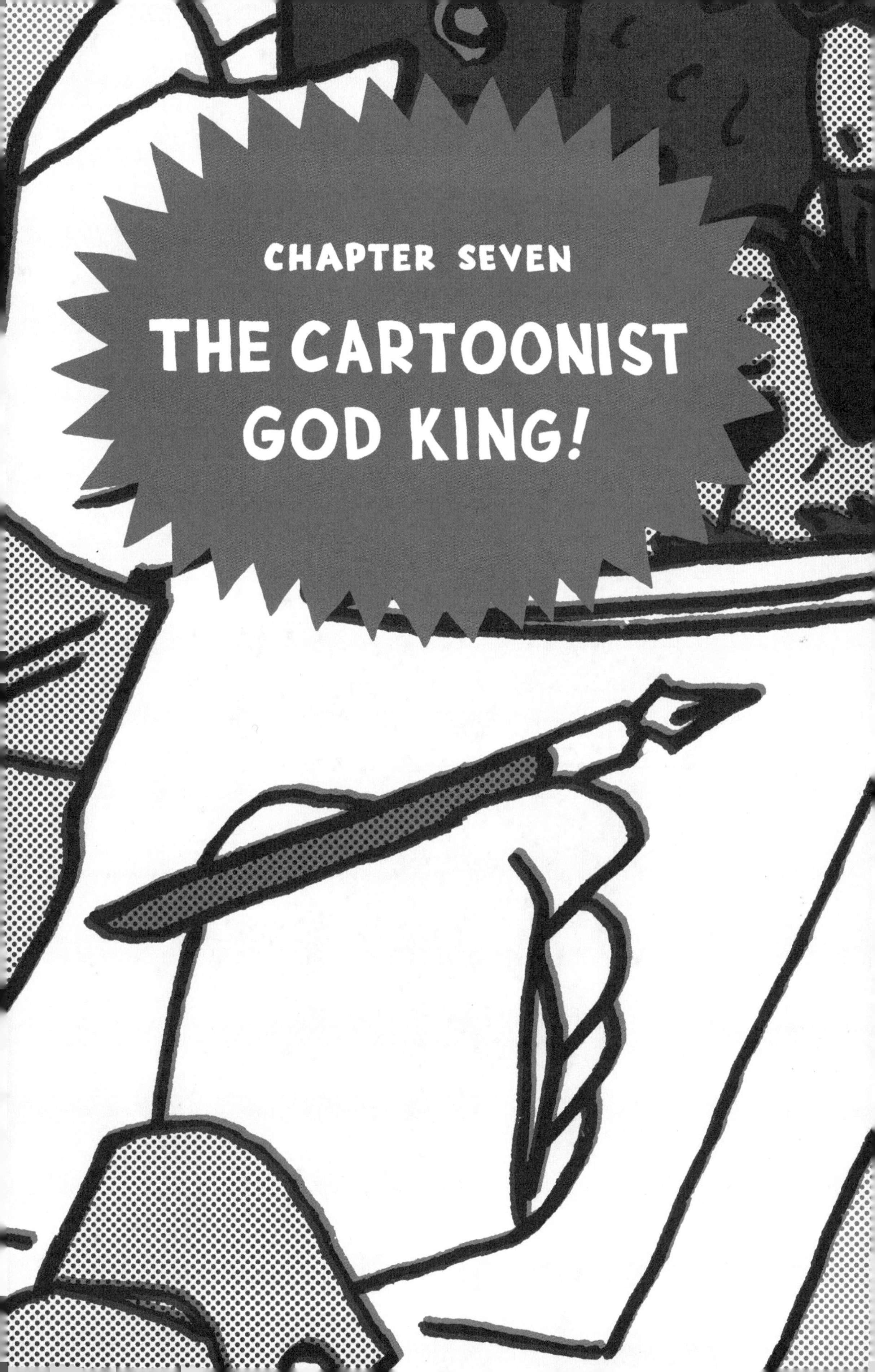

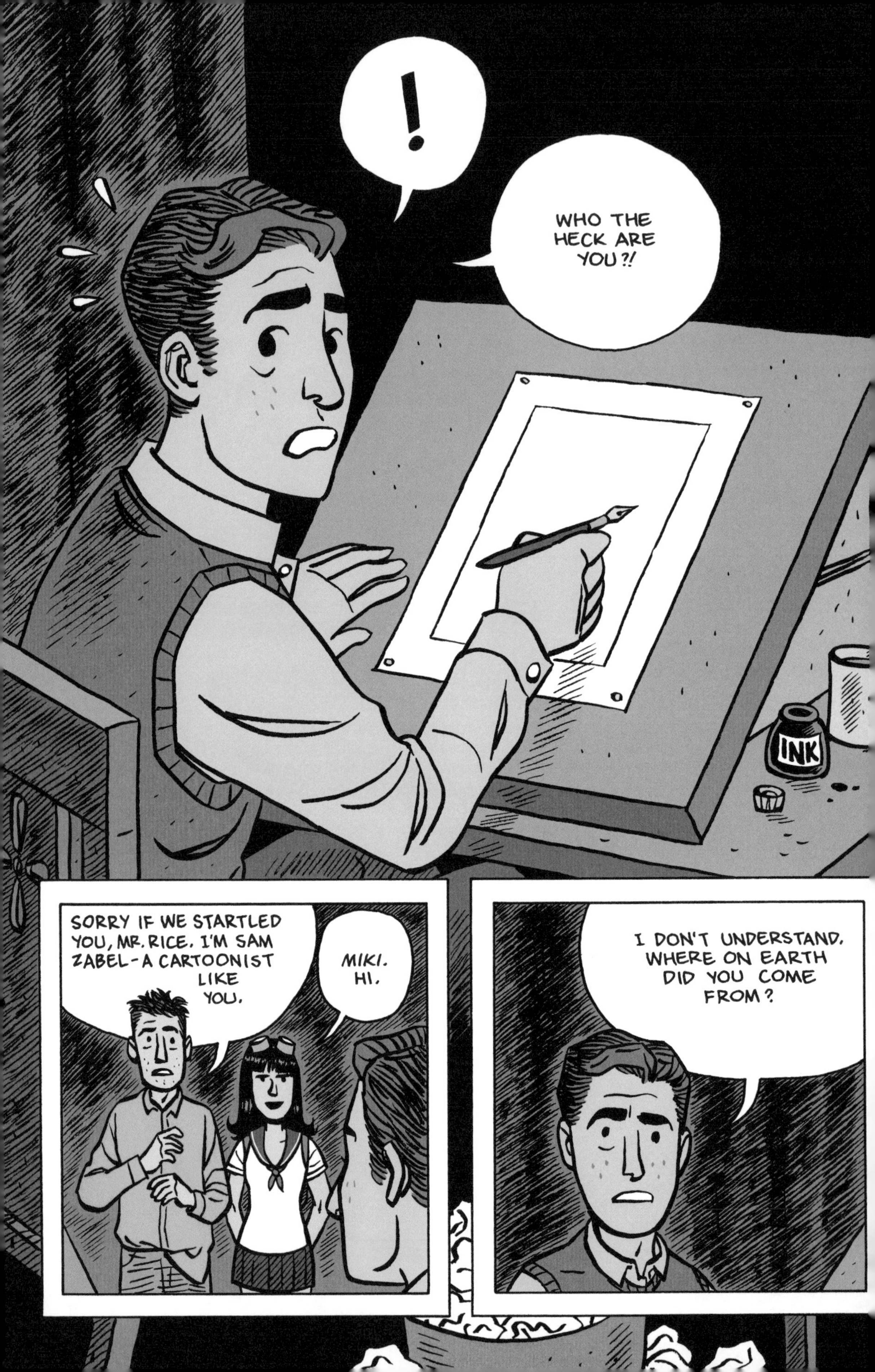
!
WHO THE HECK ARE YOU?!
INK
SORRY IF WE STARTLED YOU, MR. RICE. I'M SAM ZABEL - A CARTOONIST LIKE YOU.
MIKI. HI.
I DON'T UNDERSTAND. WHERE ON EARTH DID YOU COME FROM?

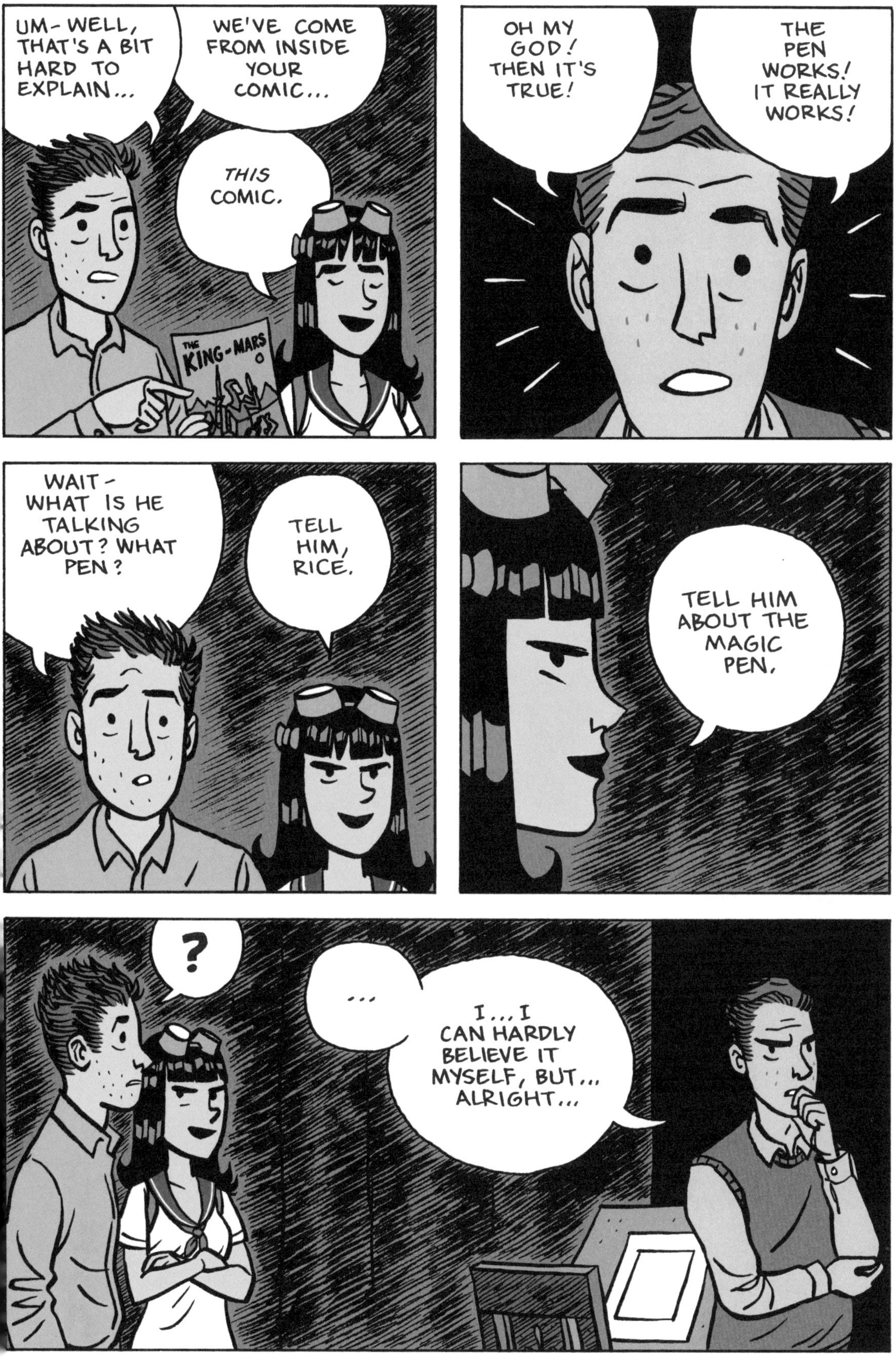
UM-WELL, THAT'S A BIT HARD TO EXPLAIN...
WE'VE COME FROM INSIDE YOUR COMIC...
THIS COMIC.
THE KING-MARS
OH MY GOD! THEN IT'S TRUE!
THE PEN WORKS! IT REALLY WORKS!
WAIT- WHAT IS HE TALKING ABOUT? WHAT PEN?
TELL HIM, RICE.
TELL HIM ABOUT THE MAGIC PEN.
?
...
I... I CAN HARDLY BELIEVE IT MYSELF, BUT... ALRIGHT...

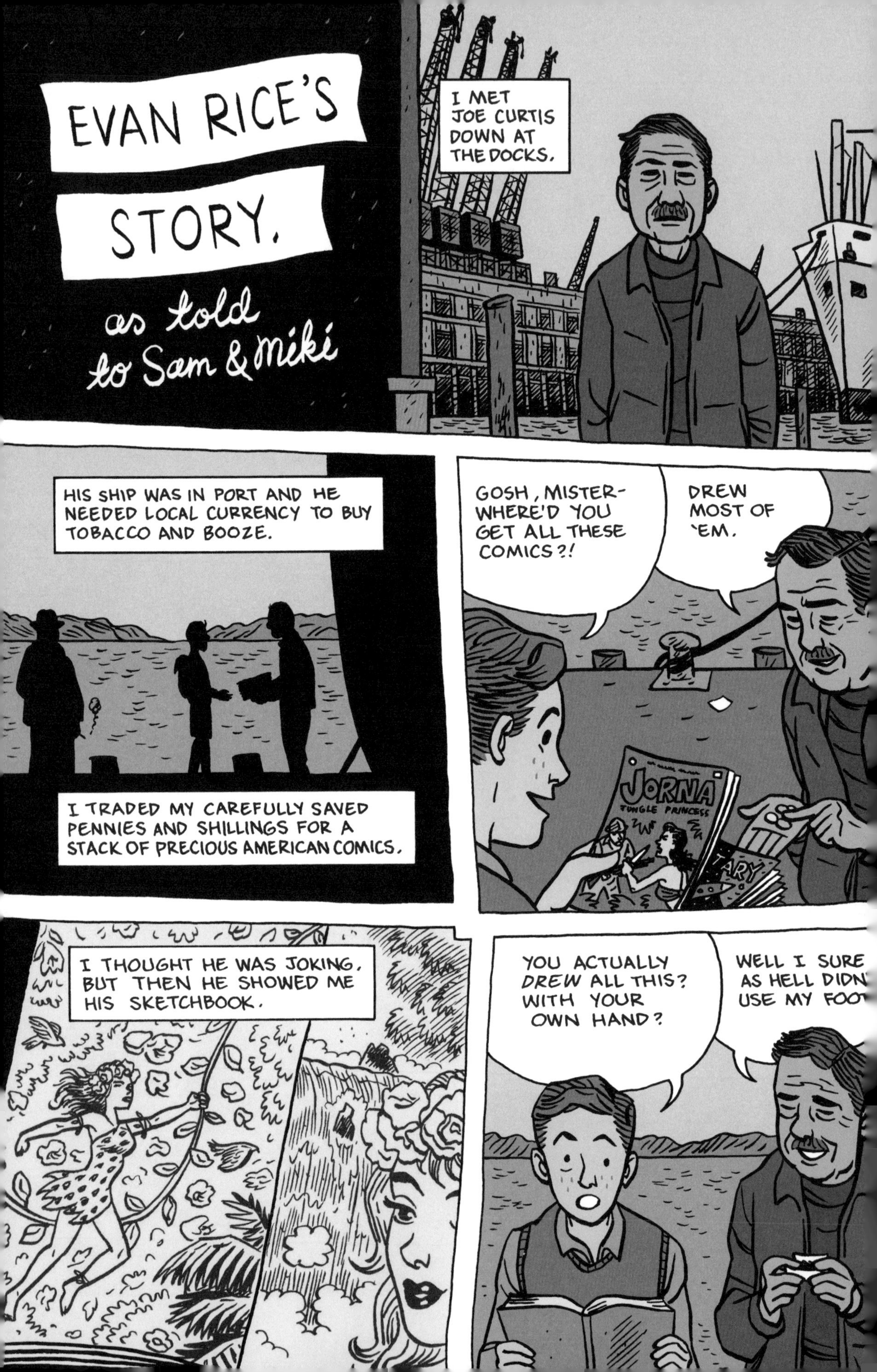
EVAN RICE'S
STORY.
as told to Sam & Miki
I MET JOE CURTIS DOWN AT THE DOCKS.
HIS SHIP WAS IN PORT AND HE NEEDED LOCAL CURRENCY TO BUY TOBACCO AND BOOZE.
I TRADED MY CAREFULLY SAVED PENNIES AND SHILLINGS FOR A STACK OF PRECIOUS AMERICAN COMICS.
GOSH, MISTER- WHERE'D YOU GET ALL THESE COMICS?!
DREW MOST OF 'EM.
JORNA
JUNGLE PRINCESS
I THOUGHT HE WAS JOKING, BUT THEN HE SHOWED ME HIS SKETCHBOOK.
YOU ACTUALLY DREW ALL THIS? WITH YOUR OWN HAND?
WELL I SURE AS HELL DIDN' USE MY FOO

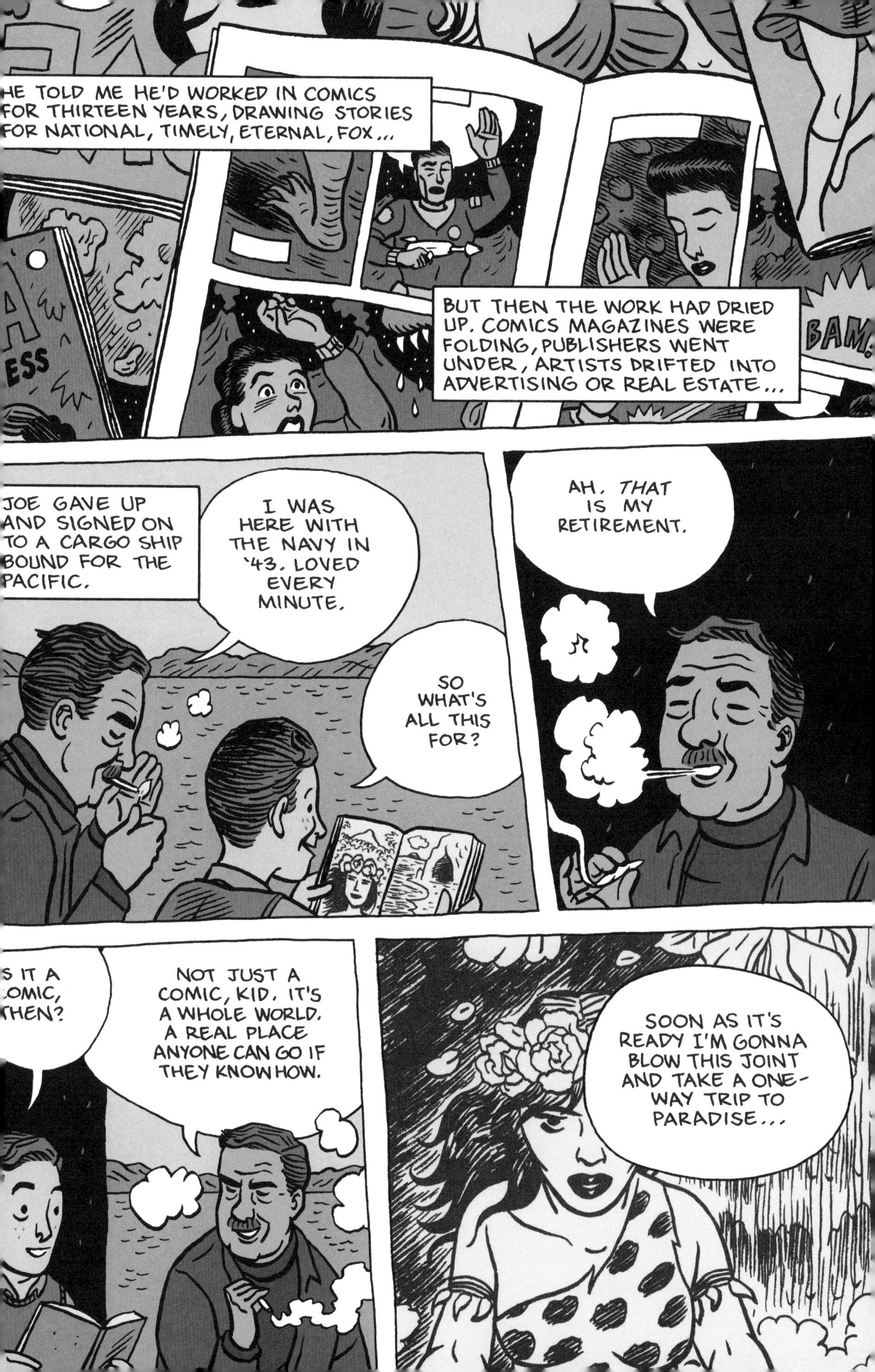

HE TOLD ME HE'D WORKED IN COMICS FOR THIRTEEN YEARS, DRAWING STORIES FOR NATIONAL, TIMELY, ETERNAL, FOX...
BUT THEN THE WORK HAD DRIED UP. COMICS MAGAZINES WERE FOLDING, PUBLISHERS WENT UNDER, ARTISTS DRIFTED INTO ADVERTISING OR REAL ESTATE...
BAM
JOE GAVE UP AND SIGNED ON TO A CARGO SHIP BOUND FOR THE PACIFIC.
I WAS HERE WITH THE NAVY IN '43. LOVED EVERY MINUTE.
SO WHAT'S ALL THIS FOR?
AH. *THAT* IS MY RETIREMENT.
S IT A OMIC, THEN?
NOT JUST A COMIC, KID. IT'S A WHOLE WORLD. A REAL PLACE ANYONE CAN GO IF THEY KNOW HOW.
SOON AS IT'S READY I'M GONNA BLOW THIS JOINT AND TAKE A ONE-WAY TRIP TO PARADISE...

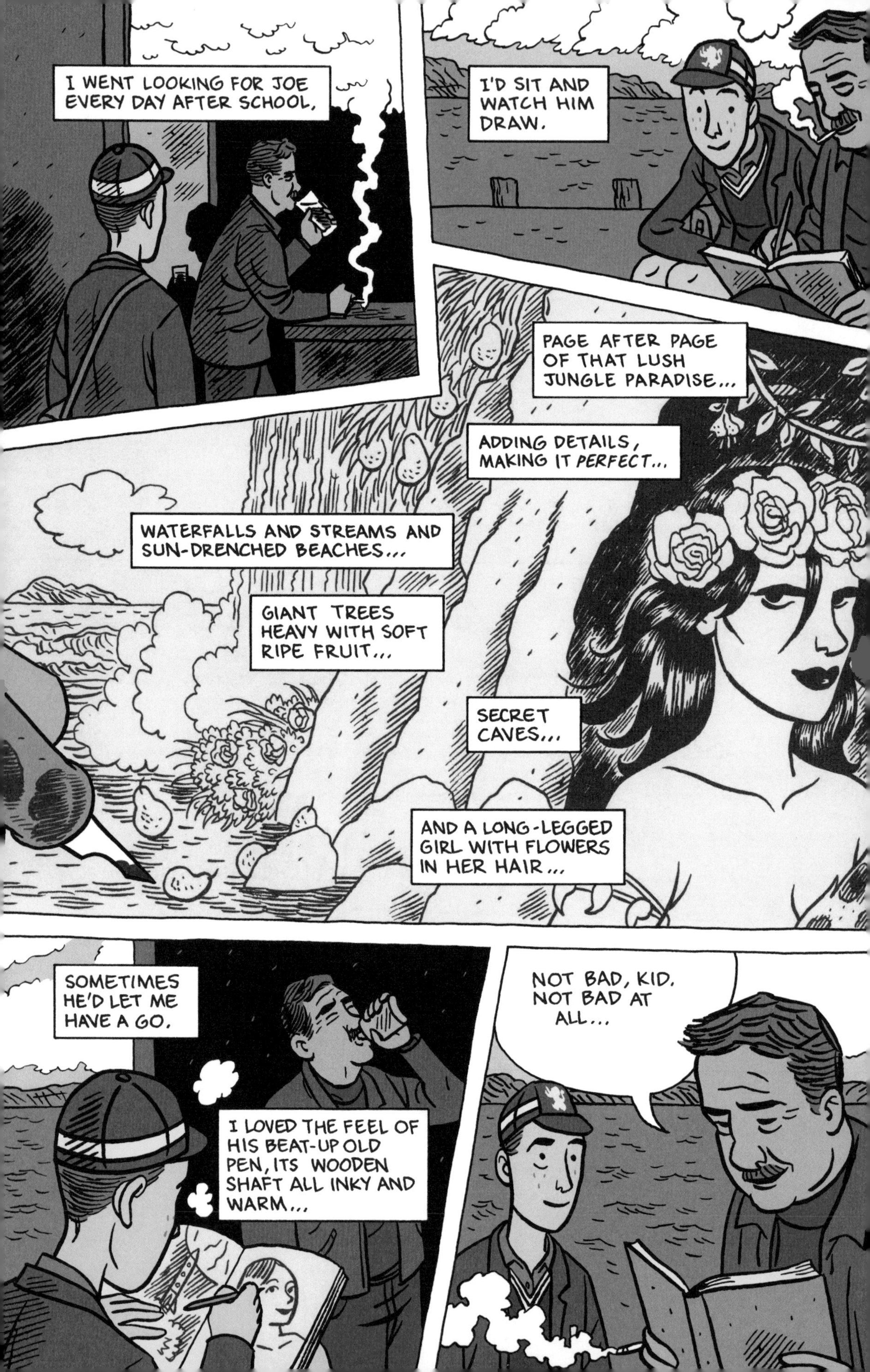
I WENT LOOKING FOR JOE EVERY DAY AFTER SCHOOL,
I'D SIT AND WATCH HIM DRAW.
PAGE AFTER PAGE OF THAT LUSH JUNGLE PARADISE...
ADDING DETAILS, MAKING IT *PERFECT*...
WATERFALLS AND STREAMS AND SUN-DRENCHED BEACHES...
GIANT TREES HEAVY WITH SOFT RIPE FRUIT...
SECRET CAVES...
AND A LONG-LEGGED GIRL WITH FLOWERS IN HER HAIR...
SOMETIMES HE'D LET ME HAVE A GO.
I LOVED THE FEEL OF HIS BEAT-UP OLD PEN, ITS WOODEN SHAFT ALL INKY AND WARM...
NOT BAD, KID. NOT BAD AT ALL...

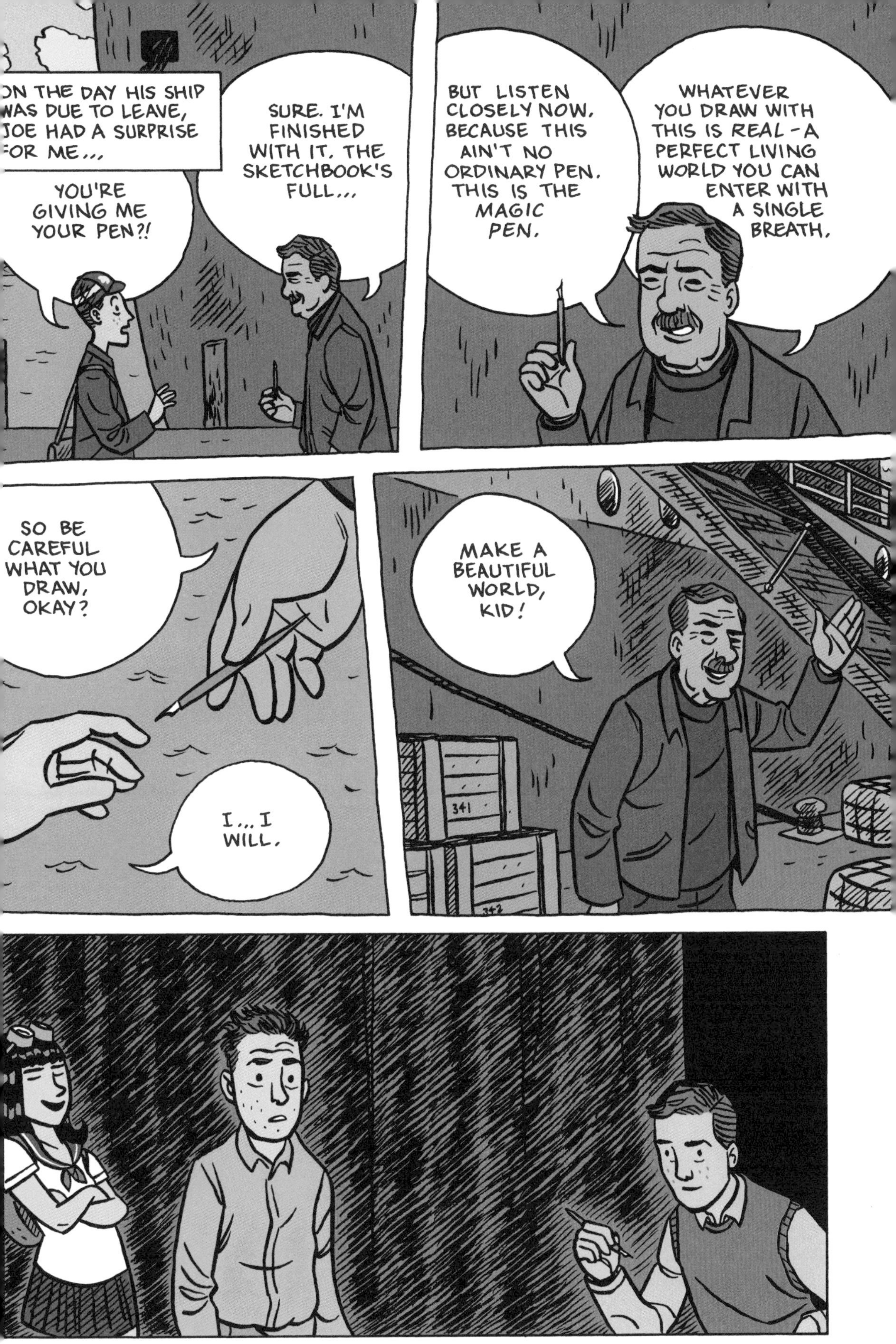
ON THE DAY HIS SHIP WAS DUE TO LEAVE, JOE HAD A SURPRISE FOR ME...
YOU'RE GIVING ME YOUR PEN?!
SURE. I'M FINISHED WITH IT. THE SKETCHBOOK'S FULL...
BUT LISTEN CLOSELY NOW, BECAUSE THIS AIN'T NO ORDINARY PEN. THIS IS THE MAGIC PEN.
WHATEVER YOU DRAW WITH THIS IS REAL - A PERFECT LIVING WORLD YOU CAN ENTER WITH A SINGLE BREATH.
SO BE CAREFUL WHAT YOU DRAW, OKAY?
I... I WILL.
MAKE A BEAUTIFUL WORLD, KID!
341
342

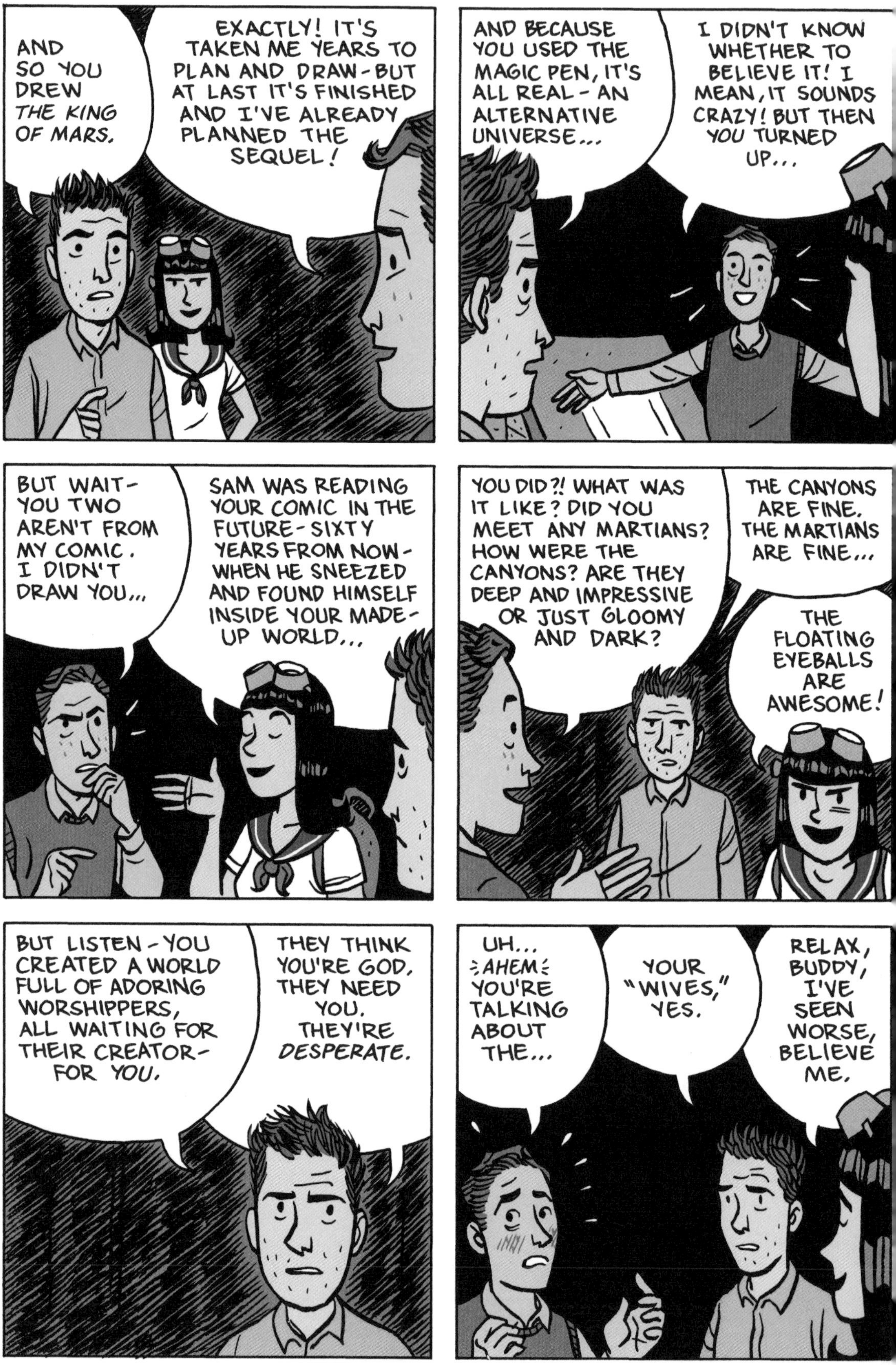
AND SO YOU DREW *THE KING OF MARS.*
EXACTLY! IT'S TAKEN ME YEARS TO PLAN AND DRAW - BUT AT LAST IT'S FINISHED AND I'VE ALREADY PLANNED THE SEQUEL!
AND BECAUSE YOU USED THE MAGIC PEN, IT'S ALL REAL - AN ALTERNATIVE UNIVERSE...
I DIDN'T KNOW WHETHER TO BELIEVE IT! I MEAN, IT SOUNDS CRAZY! BUT THEN *YOU* TURNED UP...
BUT WAIT - YOU TWO AREN'T FROM MY COMIC. I DIDN'T DRAW YOU...
SAM WAS READING YOUR COMIC IN THE FUTURE - SIXTY YEARS FROM NOW - WHEN HE SNEEZED AND FOUND HIMSELF INSIDE YOUR MADE-UP WORLD...
YOU DID?! WHAT WAS IT LIKE? DID YOU MEET ANY MARTIANS? HOW WERE THE CANYONS? ARE THEY DEEP AND IMPRESSIVE OR JUST GLOOMY AND DARK?
THE CANYONS ARE FINE. THE MARTIANS ARE FINE...
THE FLOATING EYEBALLS ARE AWESOME!
BUT LISTEN - YOU CREATED A WORLD FULL OF ADORING WORSHIPPERS, ALL WAITING FOR THEIR CREATOR - FOR *YOU.*
THEY THINK YOU'RE GOD, THEY NEED YOU. THEY'RE *DESPERATE.*
UH... AHEM YOU'RE TALKING ABOUT THE...
YOUR "WIVES," YES.
RELAX, BUDDY, I'VE SEEN WORSE, BELIEVE ME.

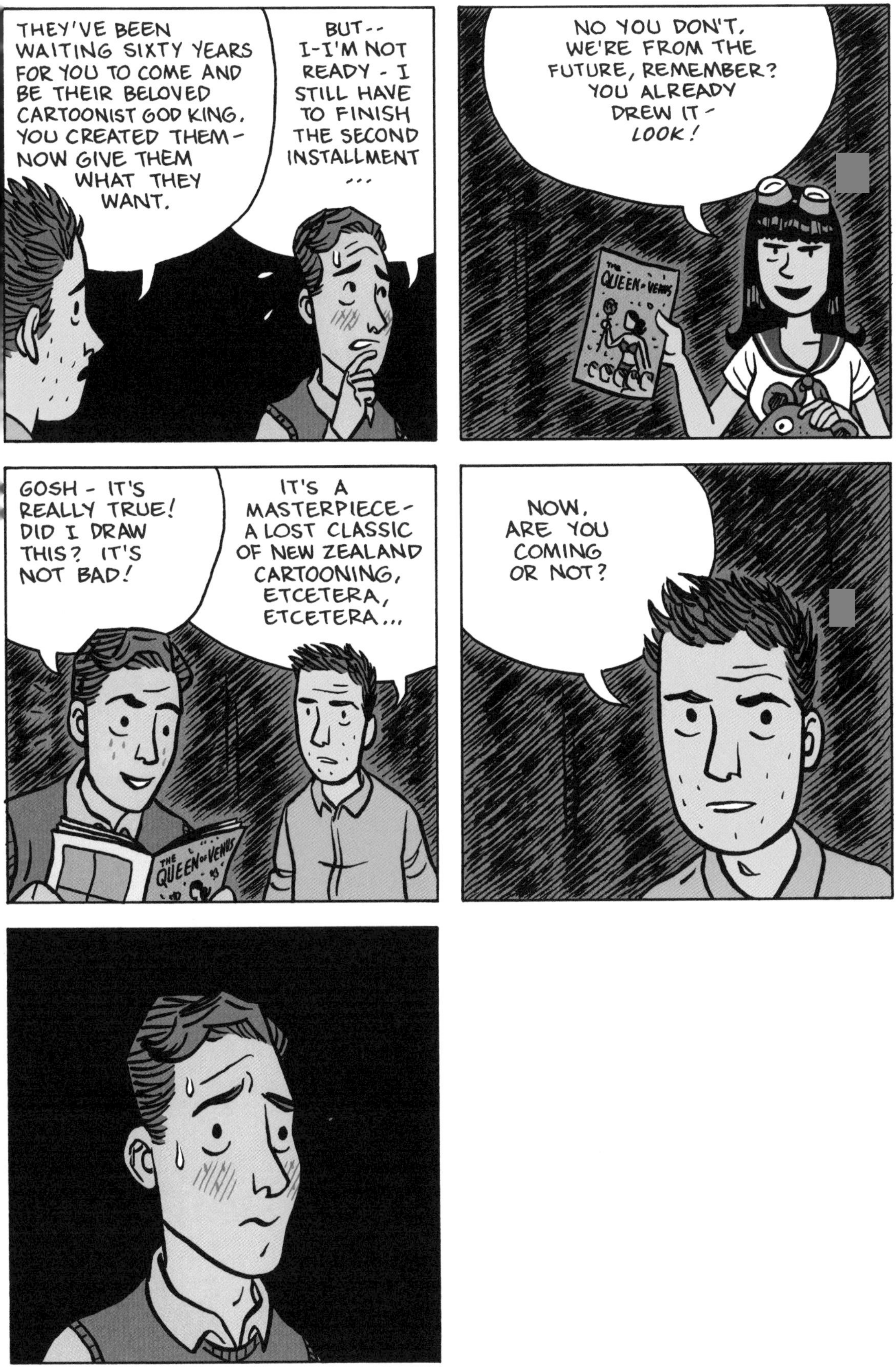
THEY'VE BEEN WAITING SIXTY YEARS FOR YOU TO COME AND BE THEIR BELOVED CARTOONIST GOD KING. YOU CREATED THEM - NOW GIVE THEM WHAT THEY WANT.
BUT-- I-I'M NOT READY - I STILL HAVE TO FINISH THE SECOND INSTALLMENT ...
NO YOU DON'T. WE'RE FROM THE FUTURE, REMEMBER? YOU ALREADY DREW IT - LOOK!
THE QUEEN OF VENUS
GOSH - IT'S REALLY TRUE! DID I DRAW THIS? IT'S NOT BAD!
IT'S A MASTERPIECE - A LOST CLASSIC OF NEW ZEALAND CARTOONING, ETCETERA, ETCETERA...
THE QUEEN OF VENUS
NOW, ARE YOU COMING OR NOT?

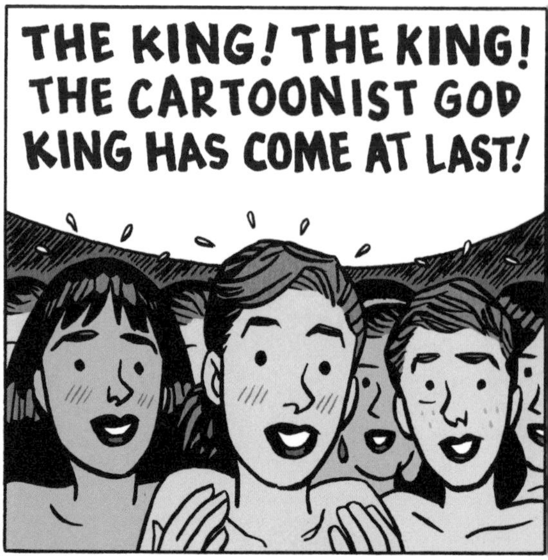
THE KING! THE KING! THE CARTOONIST GOD KING HAS COME AT LAST!

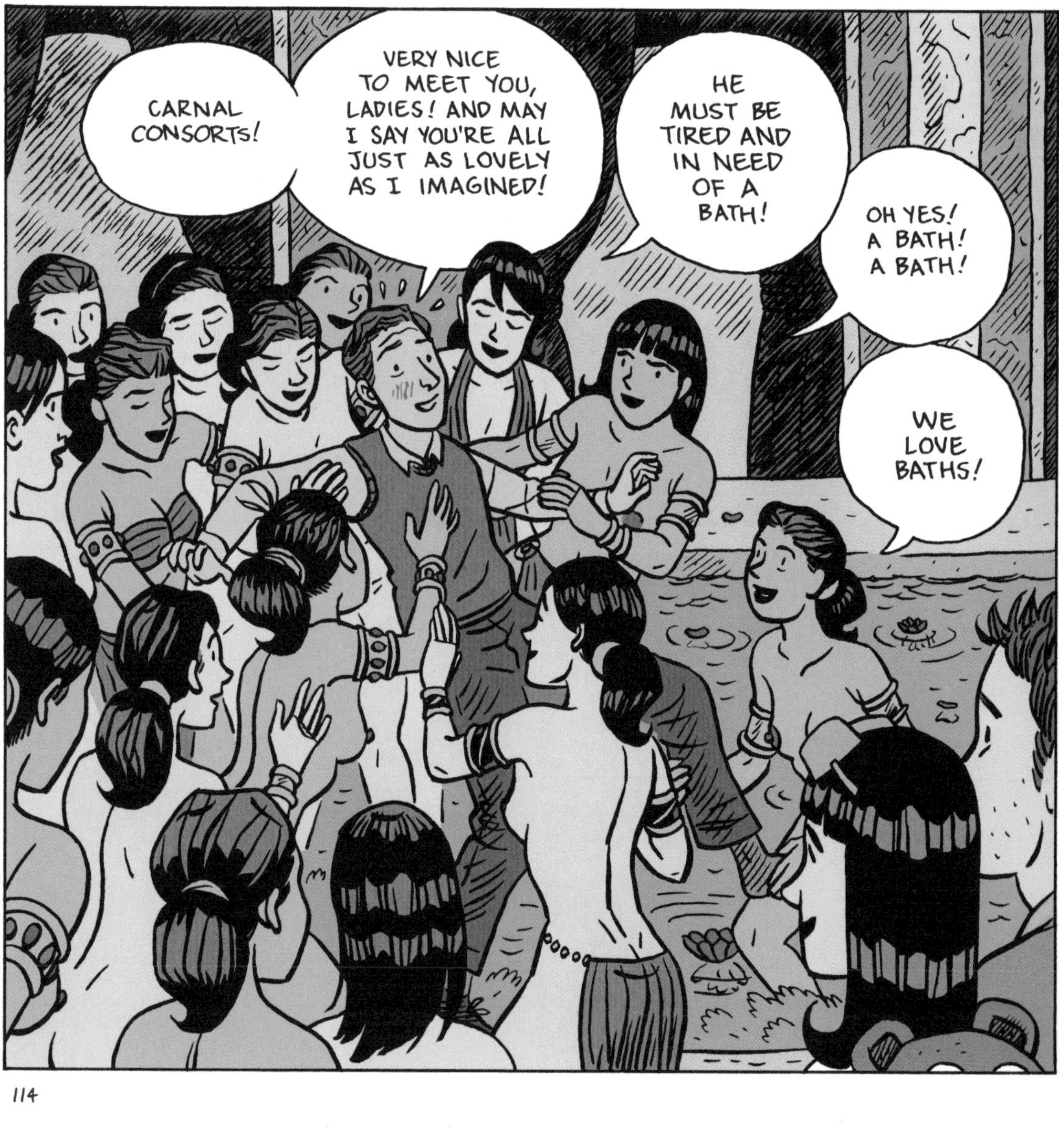
CARNAL CONSORTS!
VERY NICE TO MEET YOU, LADIES! AND MAY I SAY YOU'RE ALL JUST AS LOVELY AS I IMAGINED!
HE MUST BE TIRED AND IN NEED OF A BATH!
OH YES! A BATH! A BATH!
WE LOVE BATHS!

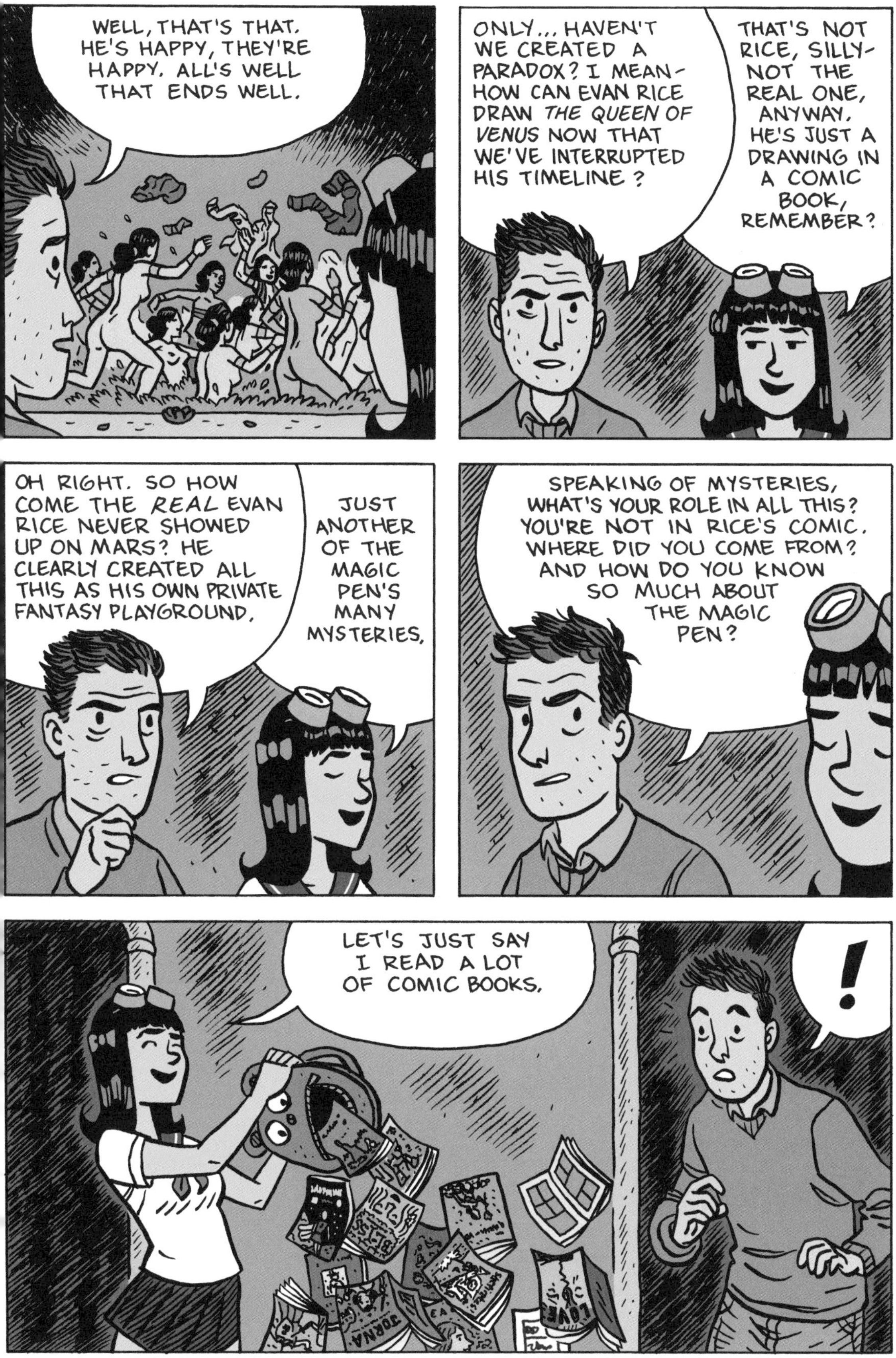
WELL, THAT'S THAT. HE'S HAPPY, THEY'RE HAPPY. ALL'S WELL THAT ENDS WELL.
ONLY... HAVEN'T WE CREATED A PARADOX? I MEAN- HOW CAN EVAN RICE DRAW *THE QUEEN OF VENUS* NOW THAT WE'VE INTERRUPTED HIS TIMELINE?
THAT'S NOT RICE, SILLY- NOT THE REAL ONE, ANYWAY. HE'S JUST A DRAWING IN A COMIC BOOK, REMEMBER?
OH RIGHT. SO HOW COME THE *REAL* EVAN RICE NEVER SHOWED UP ON MARS? HE CLEARLY CREATED ALL THIS AS HIS OWN PRIVATE FANTASY PLAYGROUND.
JUST ANOTHER OF THE MAGIC PEN'S MANY MYSTERIES.
SPEAKING OF MYSTERIES, WHAT'S YOUR ROLE IN ALL THIS? YOU'RE NOT IN RICE'S COMIC. WHERE DID YOU COME FROM? AND HOW DO YOU KNOW SO MUCH ABOUT THE MAGIC PEN?
LET'S JUST SAY I READ A LOT OF COMIC BOOKS.
!
LOVE

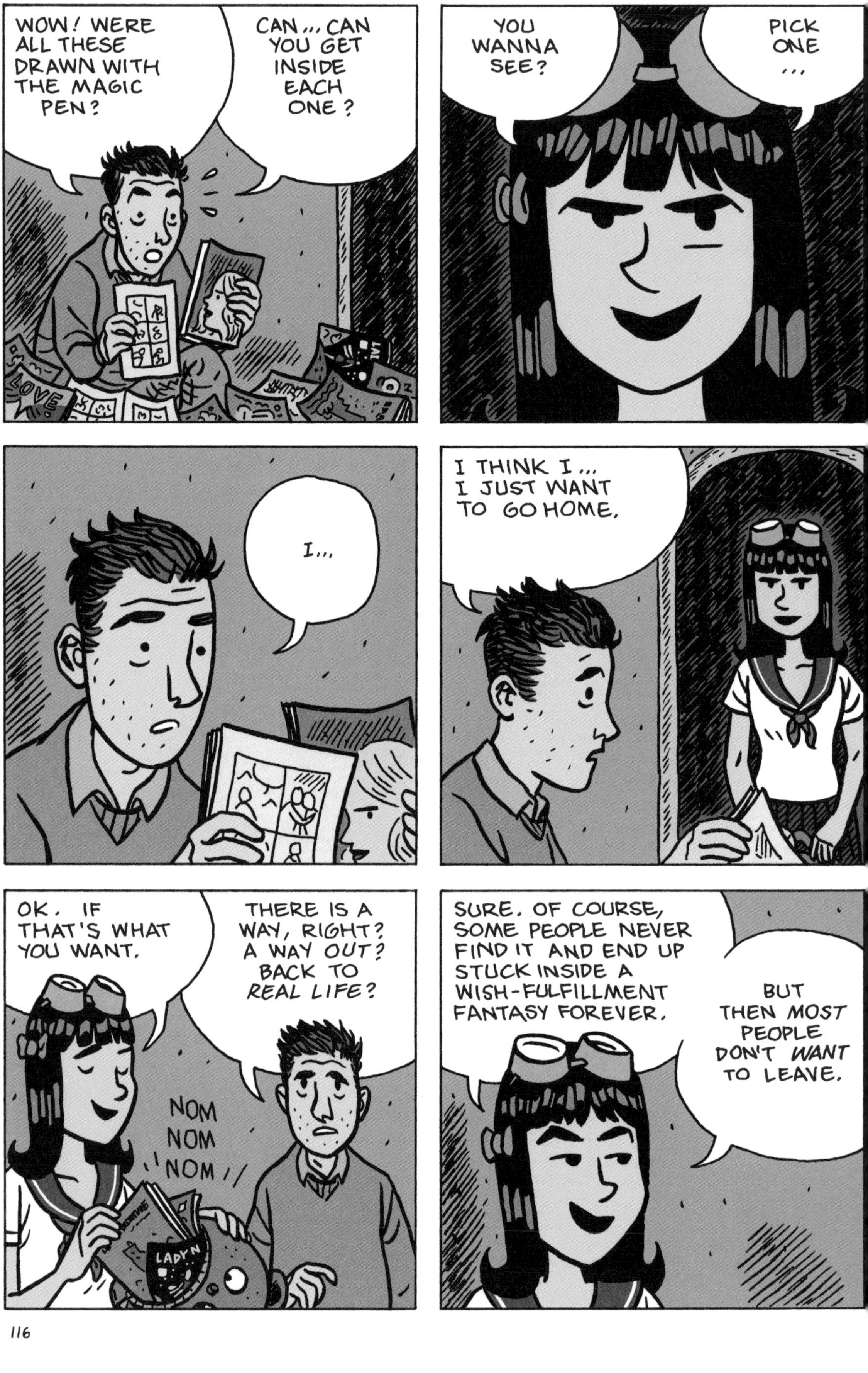
WOW! WERE ALL THESE DRAWN WITH THE MAGIC PEN?
CAN... CAN YOU GET INSIDE EACH ONE?
YOU WANNA SEE?
PICK ONE ...
I...
I THINK I... I JUST WANT TO GO HOME.
OK. IF THAT'S WHAT YOU WANT.
THERE IS A WAY, RIGHT? A WAY OUT? BACK TO *REAL LIFE*?
NOM NOM NOM
LADY N
SURE. OF COURSE, SOME PEOPLE NEVER FIND IT AND END UP STUCK INSIDE A WISH-FULFILLMENT FANTASY FOREVER.
BUT THEN *MOST* PEOPLE DON'T *WANT* TO LEAVE.

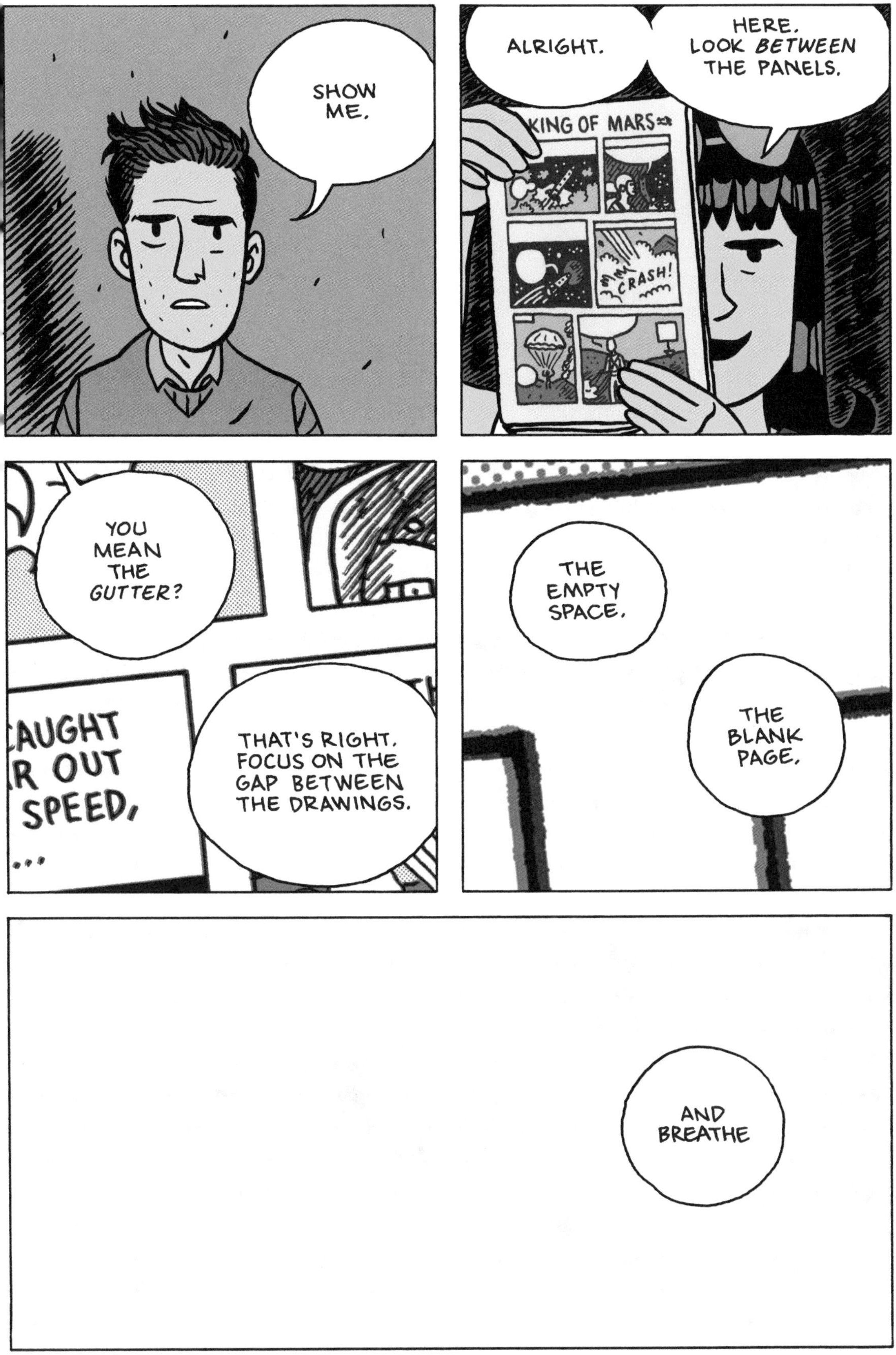
SHOW ME.
ALRIGHT.
HERE. LOOK *BETWEEN* THE PANELS.
KING OF MARS
CRASH!
YOU MEAN THE *GUTTER*?
THAT'S RIGHT. FOCUS ON THE GAP BETWEEN THE DRAWINGS.
THE EMPTY SPACE.
THE BLANK PAGE.
AND BREATHE

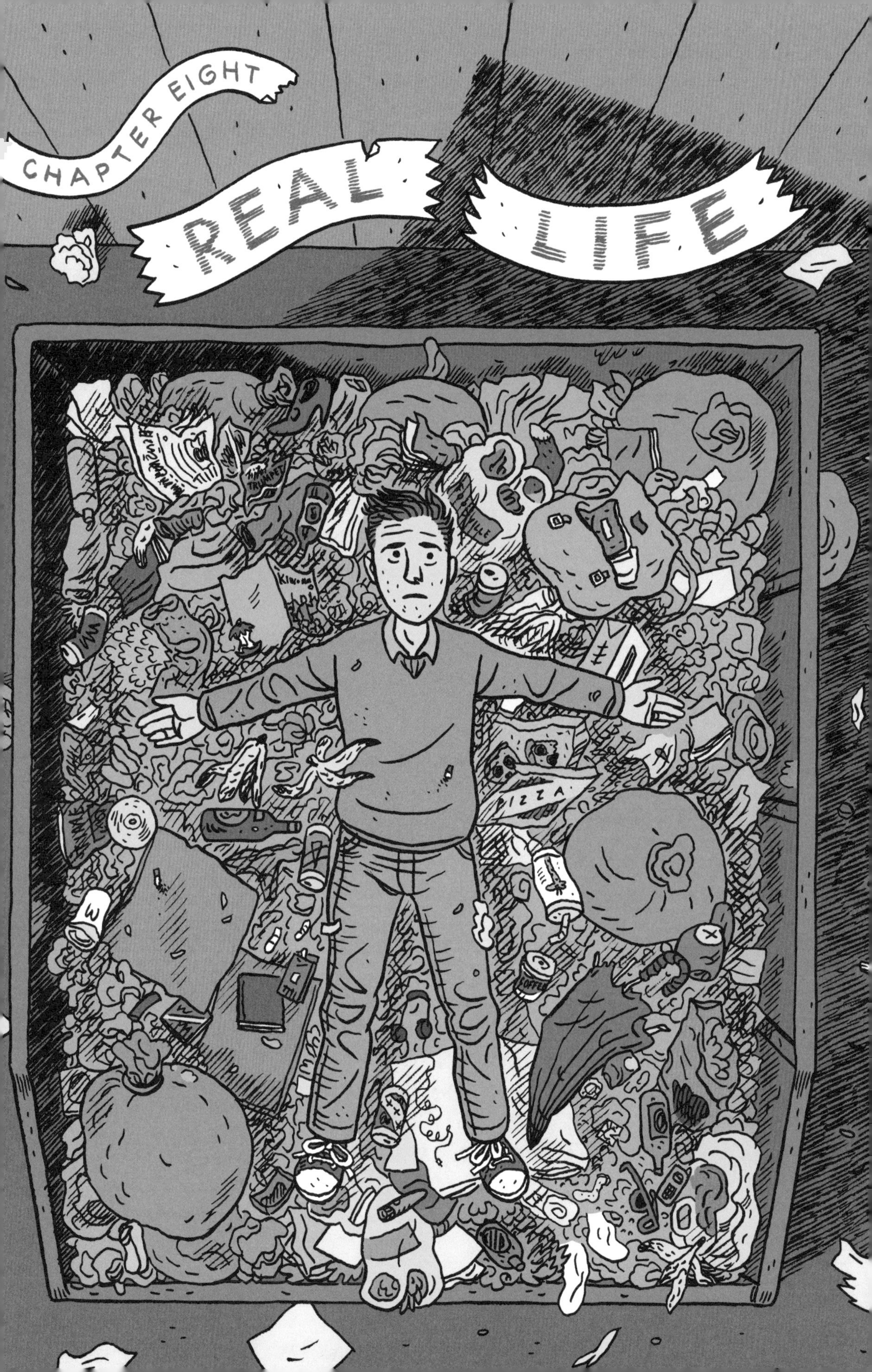
CHAPTER EIGHT
REAL LIFE
TRUMPET
PIZZA

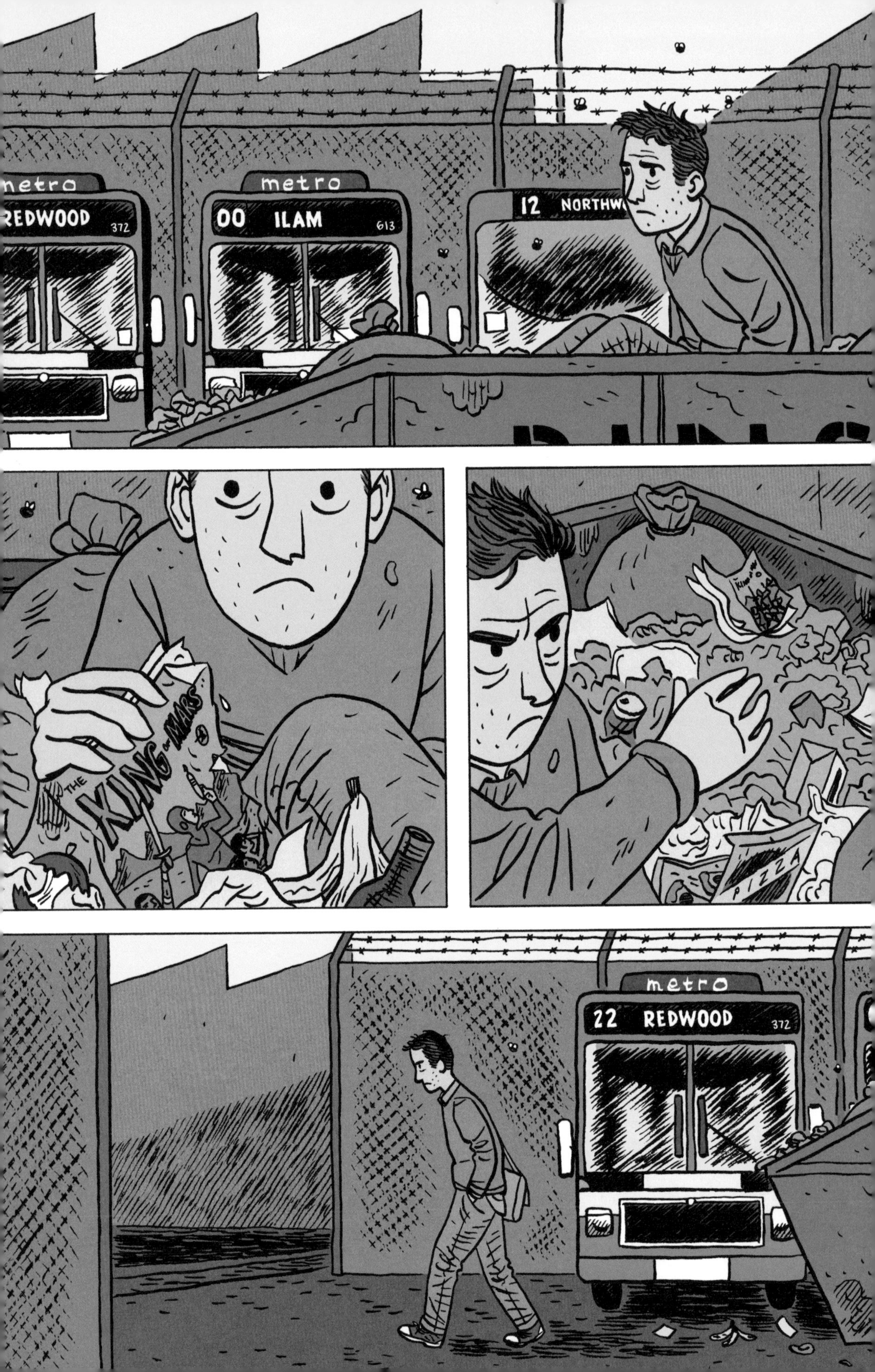
metro
00 ILAM
613
12
THE KING OF MARS
PIZZA
metro
22 REDWOOD
372

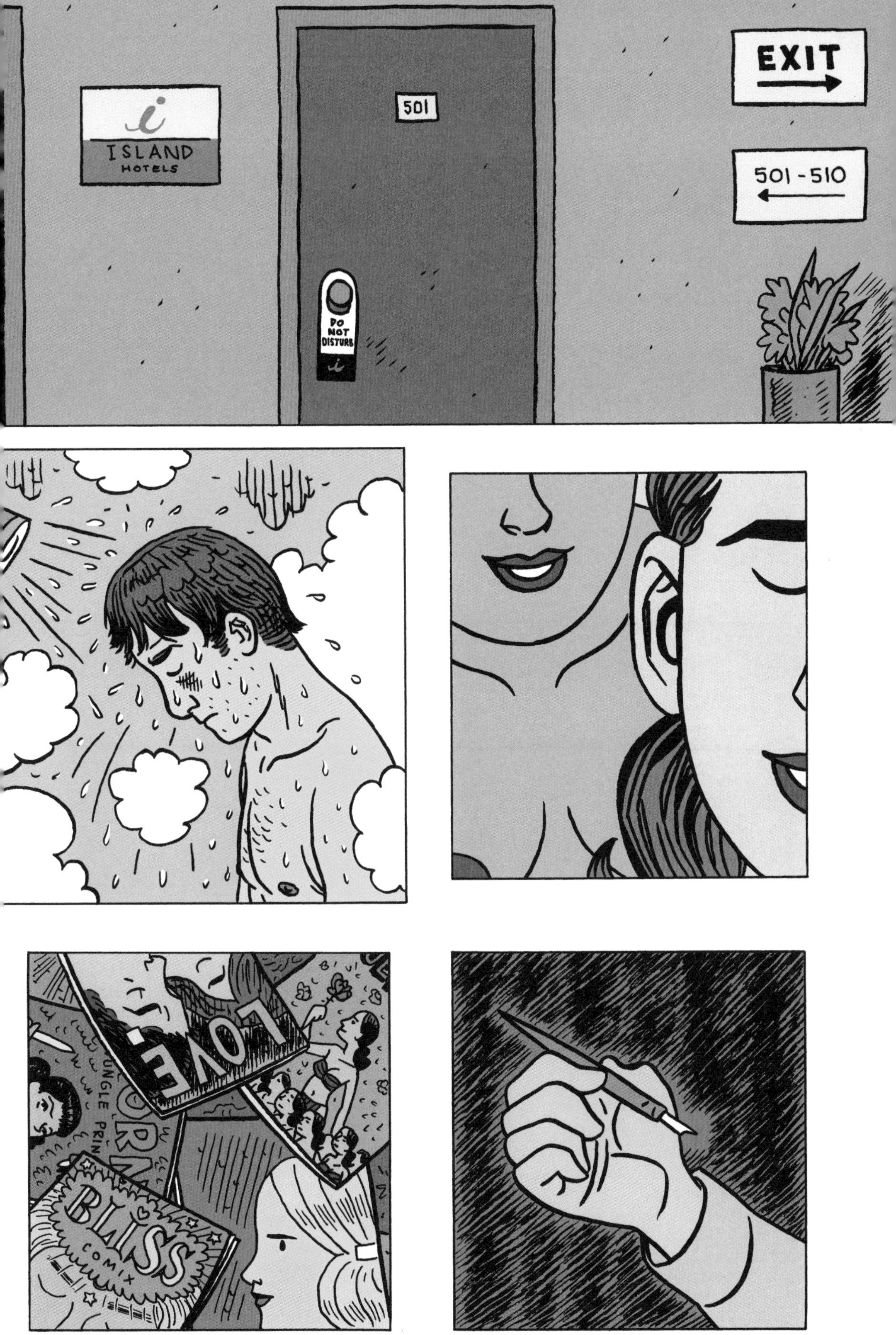
ISLAND
HOTELS
501
DO NOT DISTURB
EXIT
501-510
LOVE
BLISS
COMIX

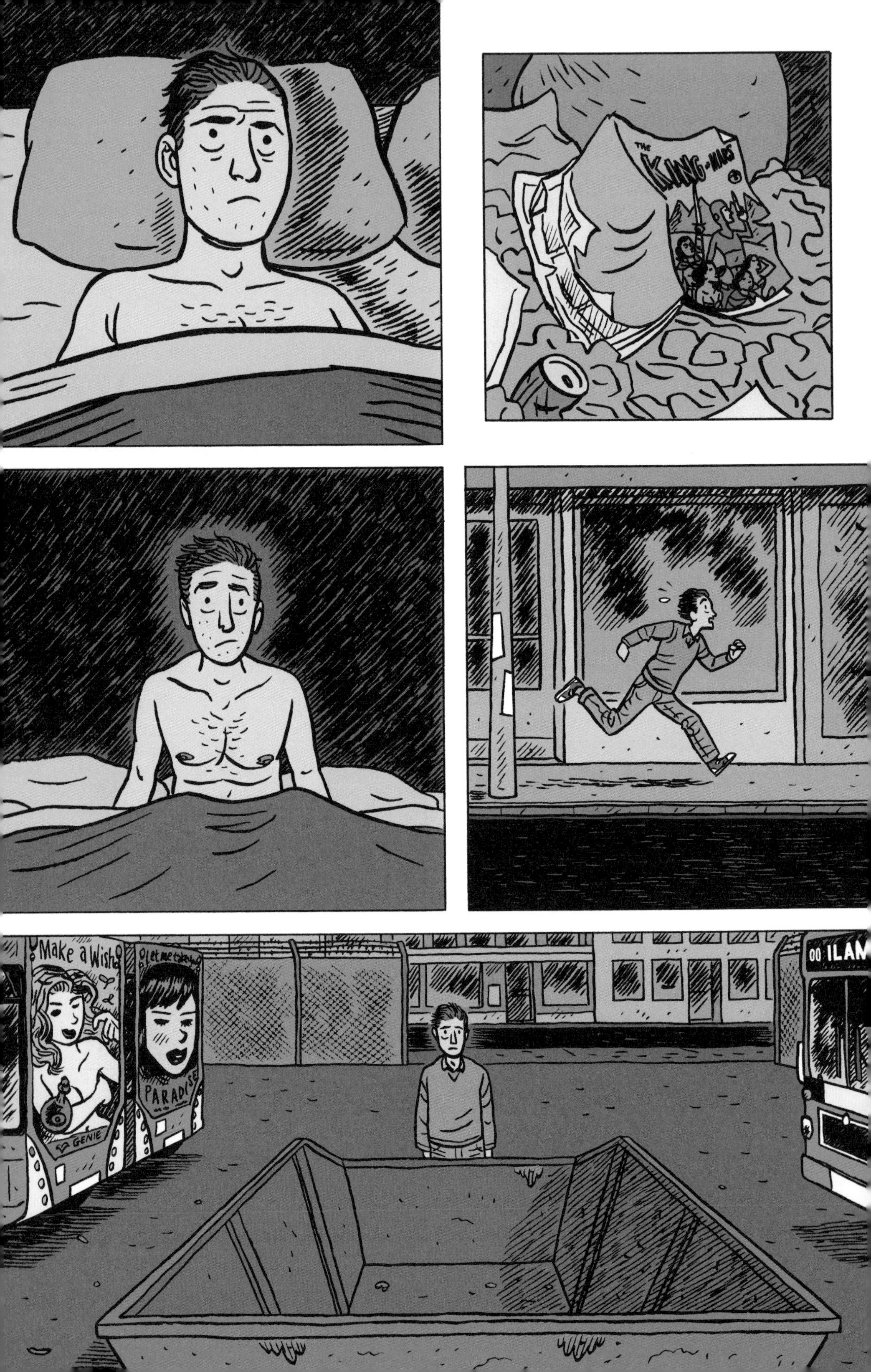
THE KING OF MARS
Make a Wish
GENIE
PARADISE
00 ILAM

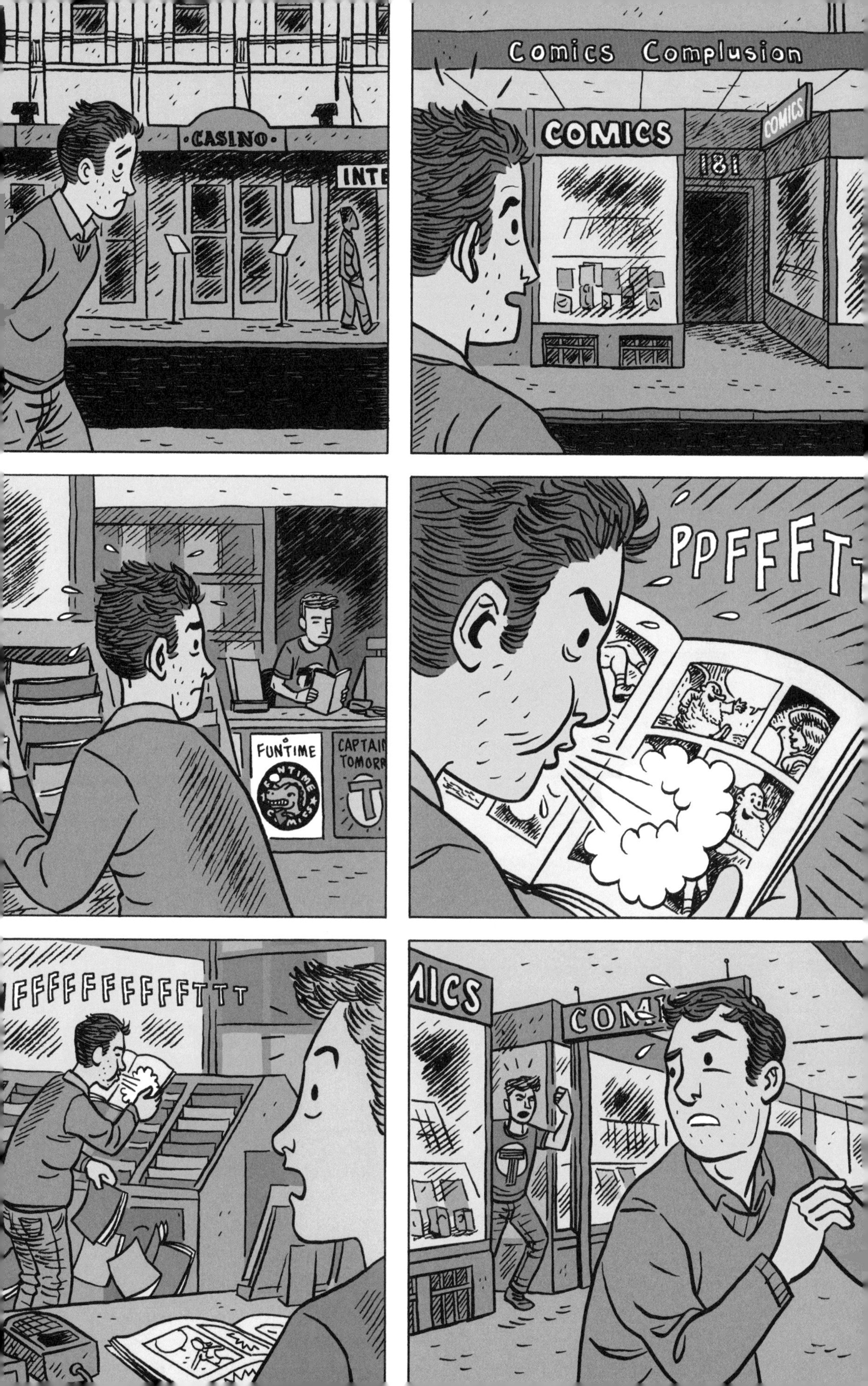
CASINO
INTE
Comics Complusion
COMICS
181
COMICS
FUNTIME
FUNTIME COMICS
CAPTAIN TOMORR
PPFFFTT
FFFFFFFFFFTTT
MICS
COM

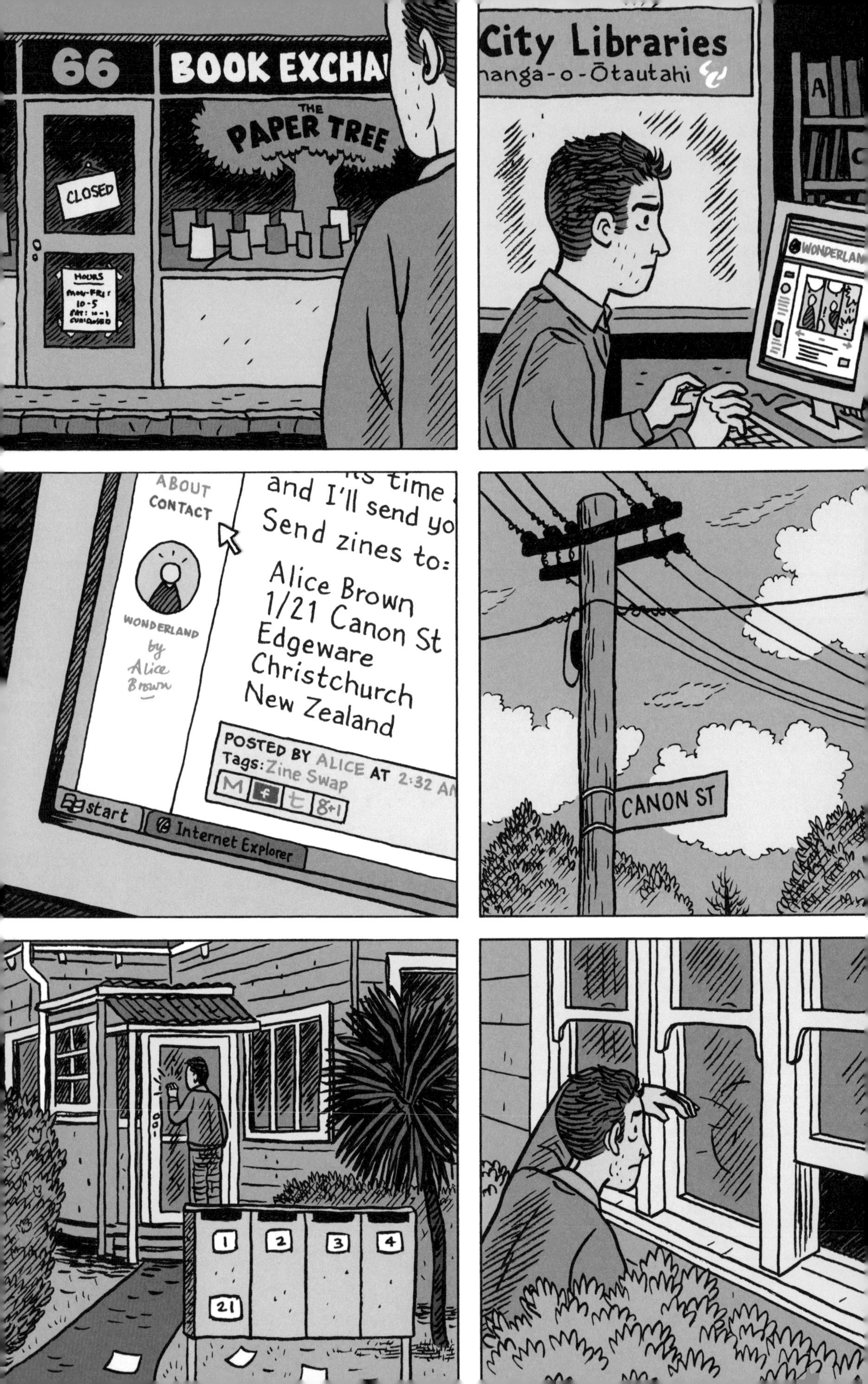

66
BOOK EXCHA
THE PAPER TREE
CLOSED
City Libraries
nanga-o-Ōtautahi
WONDERLAN
ABOUT
CONTACT
time
and I'll send yo
Send zines to:
Alice Brown
1/21 Canon St
Edgeware
Christchurch
New Zealand
WONDERLAND
by
Alice
Brown
POSTED BY ALICE AT 2:32 AM
Tags: Zine Swap
start
Internet Explorer
CANON ST
1
2
3
4
21

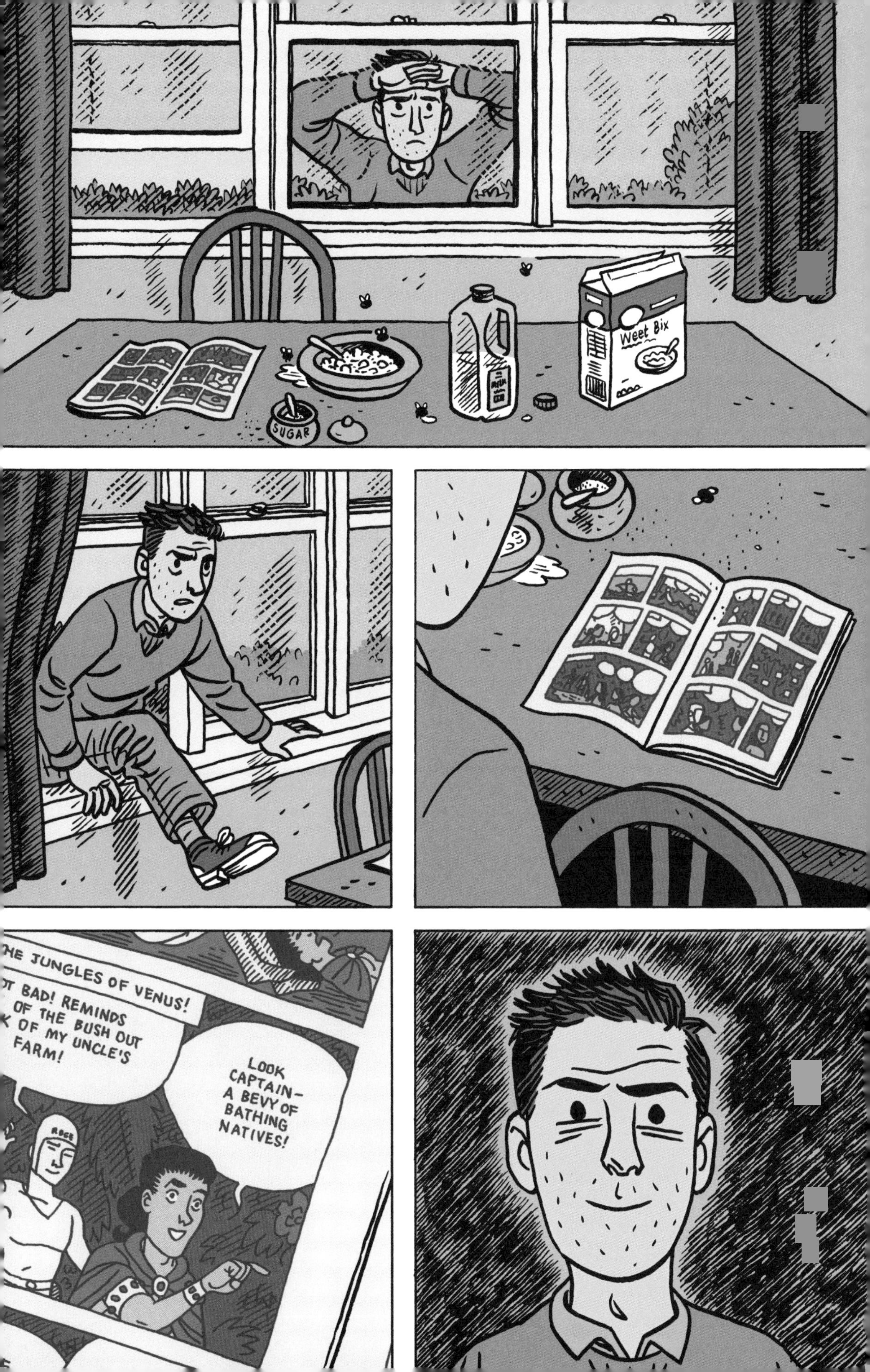

SUGAR
Weet Bix
…HE JUNGLES OF VENUS!
…T BAD! REMINDS … OF THE BUSH OUT … K OF MY UNCLE'S FARM!
LOOK CAPTAIN- A BEVY OF BATHING NATIVES!

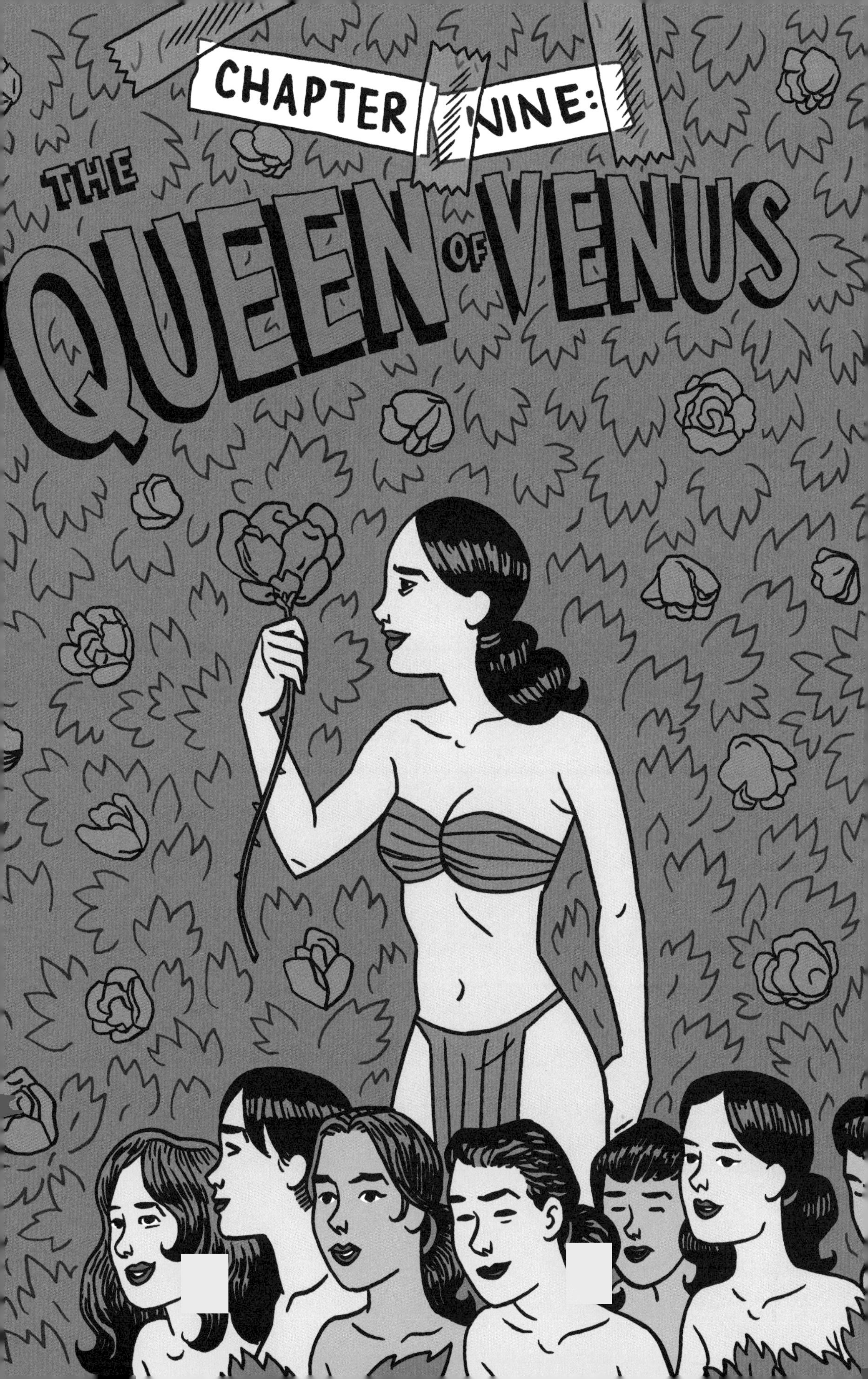
CHAPTER NINE:
THE QUEEN OF VENUS

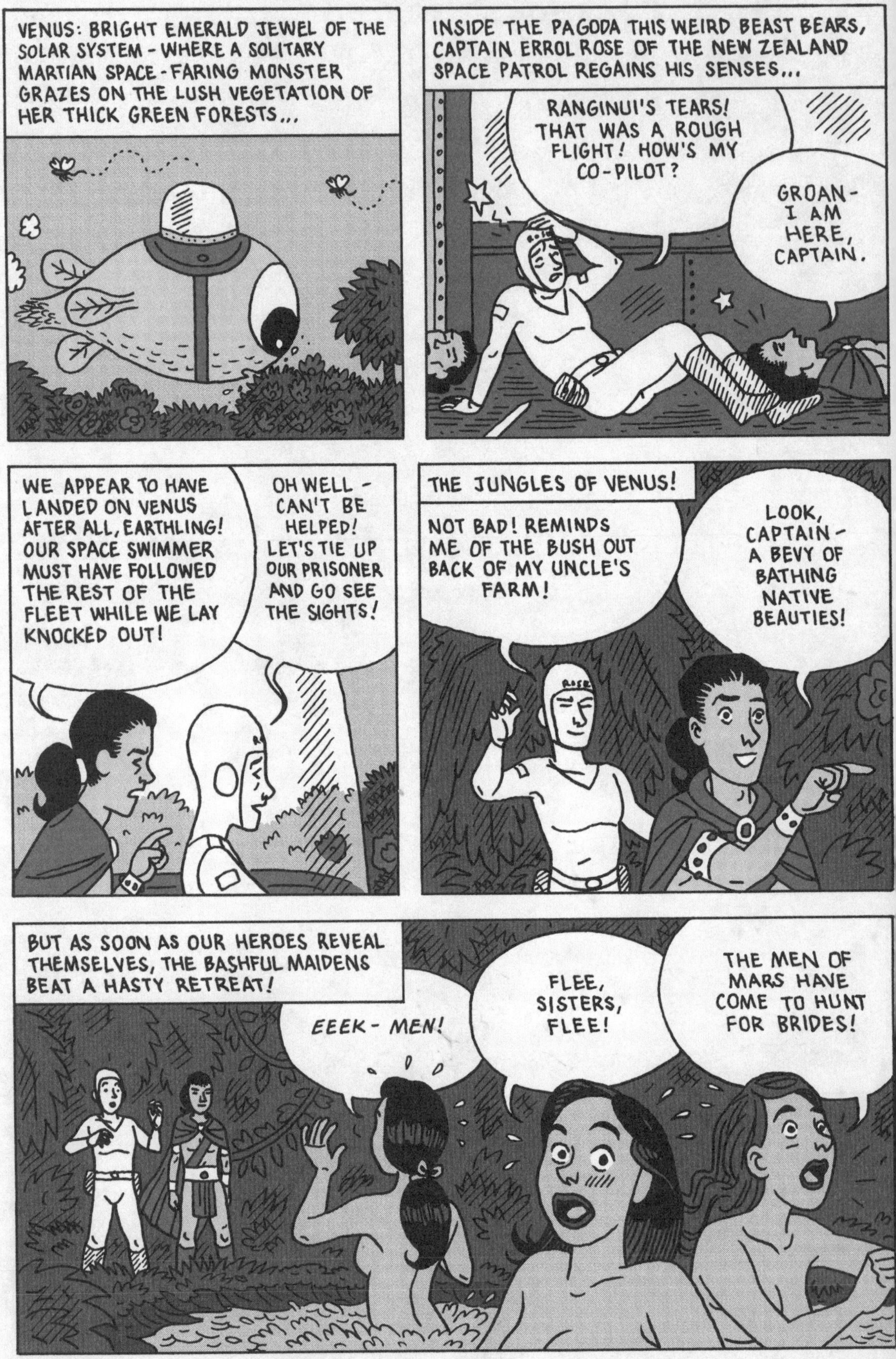
VENUS: BRIGHT EMERALD JEWEL OF THE SOLAR SYSTEM - WHERE A SOLITARY MARTIAN SPACE-FARING MONSTER GRAZES ON THE LUSH VEGETATION OF HER THICK GREEN FORESTS...
INSIDE THE PAGODA THIS WEIRD BEAST BEARS, CAPTAIN ERROL ROSE OF THE NEW ZEALAND SPACE PATROL REGAINS HIS SENSES...
RANGINUI'S TEARS! THAT WAS A ROUGH FLIGHT! HOW'S MY CO-PILOT?
GROAN- I AM HERE, CAPTAIN.
WE APPEAR TO HAVE LANDED ON VENUS AFTER ALL, EARTHLING! OUR SPACE SWIMMER MUST HAVE FOLLOWED THE REST OF THE FLEET WHILE WE LAY KNOCKED OUT!
OH WELL - CAN'T BE HELPED! LET'S TIE UP OUR PRISONER AND GO SEE THE SIGHTS!
THE JUNGLES OF VENUS!
NOT BAD! REMINDS ME OF THE BUSH OUT BACK OF MY UNCLE'S FARM!
LOOK, CAPTAIN - A BEVY OF BATHING NATIVE BEAUTIES!
BUT AS SOON AS OUR HEROES REVEAL THEMSELVES, THE BASHFUL MAIDENS BEAT A HASTY RETREAT!
EEEK - MEN!
FLEE, SISTERS, FLEE!
THE MEN OF MARS HAVE COME TO HUNT FOR BRIDES!

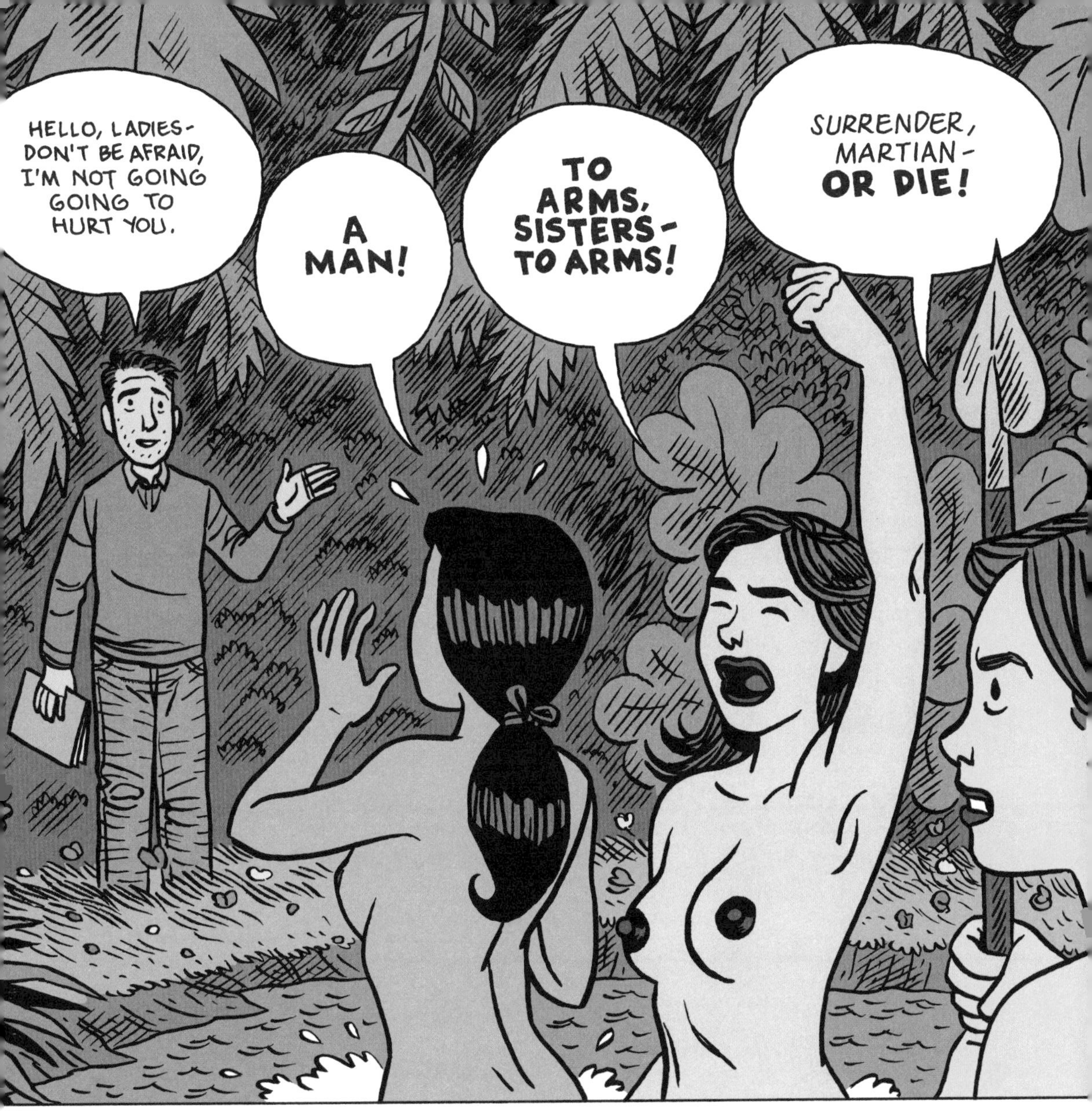
HELLO, LADIES- DON'T BE AFRAID, I'M NOT GOING GOING TO HURT YOU.
A MAN!
TO ARMS, SISTERS- TO ARMS!
SURRENDER, MARTIAN- OR DIE!

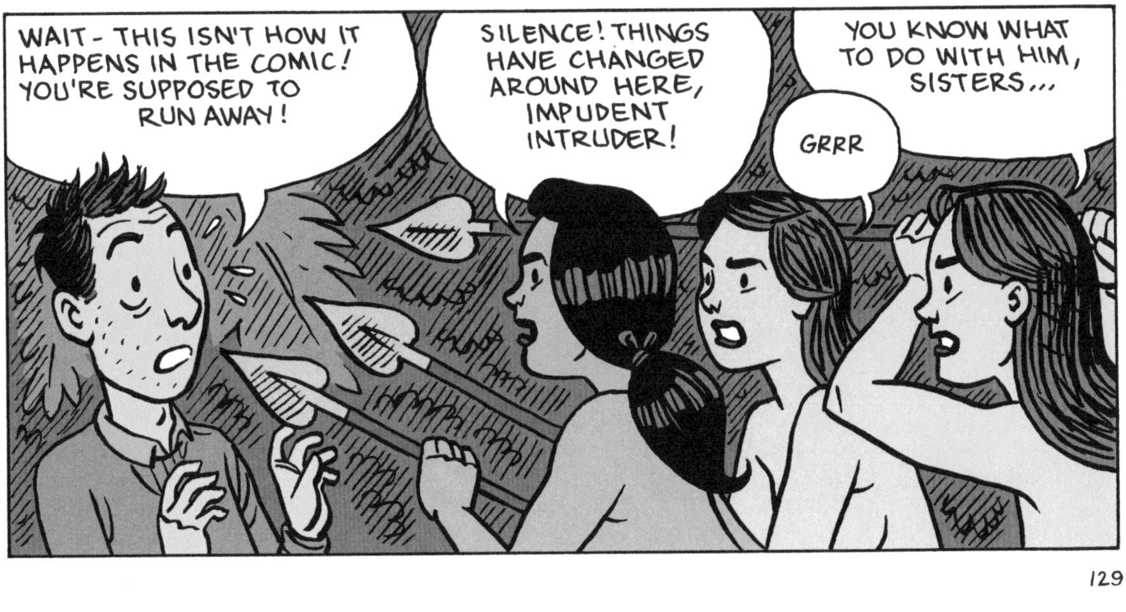
WAIT- THIS ISN'T HOW IT HAPPENS IN THE COMIC! YOU'RE SUPPOSED TO RUN AWAY!
SILENCE! THINGS HAVE CHANGED AROUND HERE, IMPUDENT INTRUDER!
YOU KNOW WHAT TO DO WITH HIM, SISTERS...
GRRR

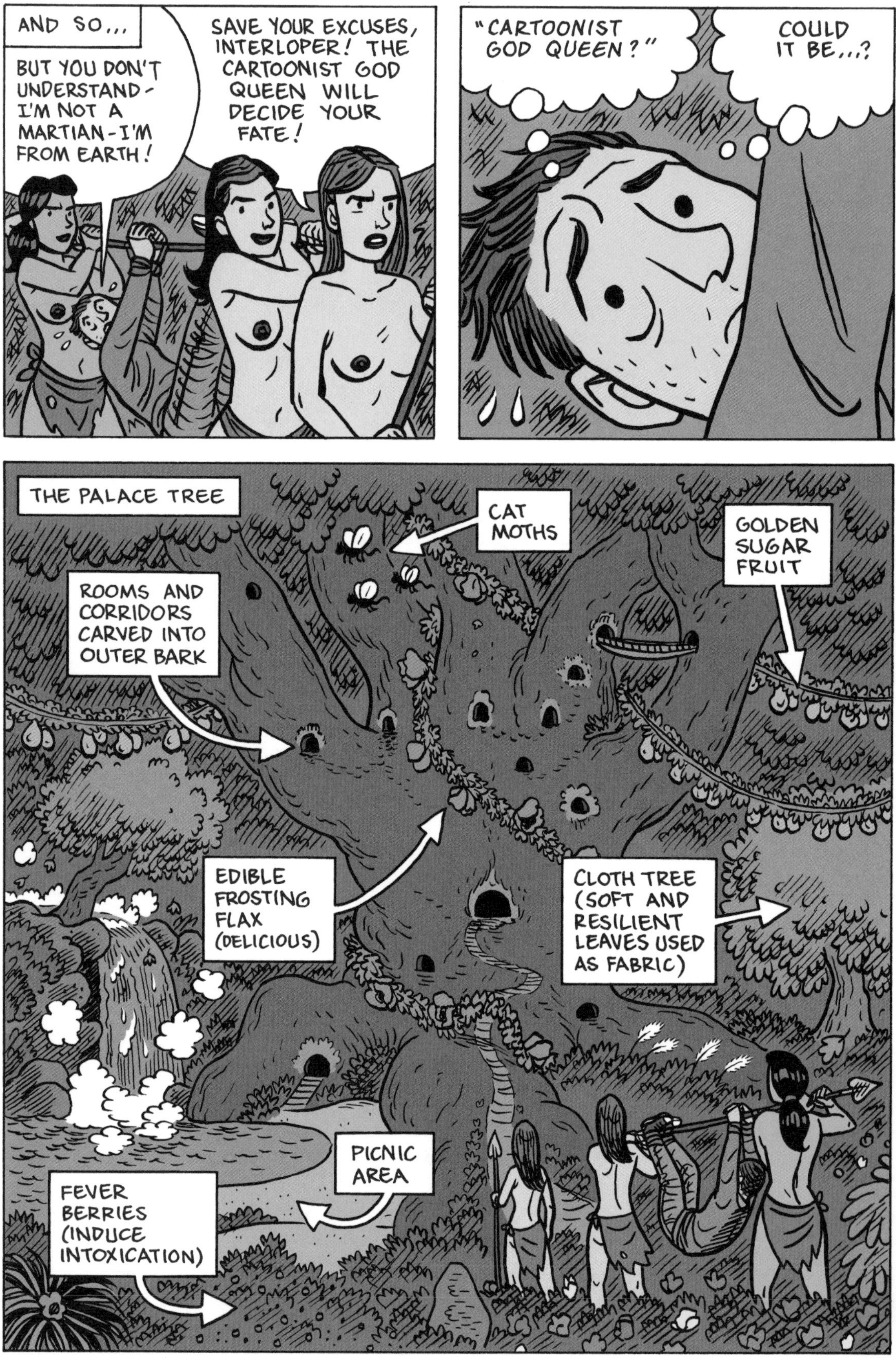
AND SO...
BUT YOU DON'T UNDERSTAND - I'M NOT A MARTIAN - I'M FROM EARTH!
SAVE YOUR EXCUSES, INTERLOPER! THE CARTOONIST GOD QUEEN WILL DECIDE YOUR FATE!
"CARTOONIST GOD QUEEN?"
COULD IT BE...?
THE PALACE TREE
CAT MOTHS
GOLDEN SUGAR FRUIT
ROOMS AND CORRIDORS CARVED INTO OUTER BARK
EDIBLE FROSTING FLAX (DELICIOUS)
CLOTH TREE (SOFT AND RESILIENT LEAVES USED AS FABRIC)
PICNIC AREA
FEVER BERRIES (INDUCE INTOXICATION)

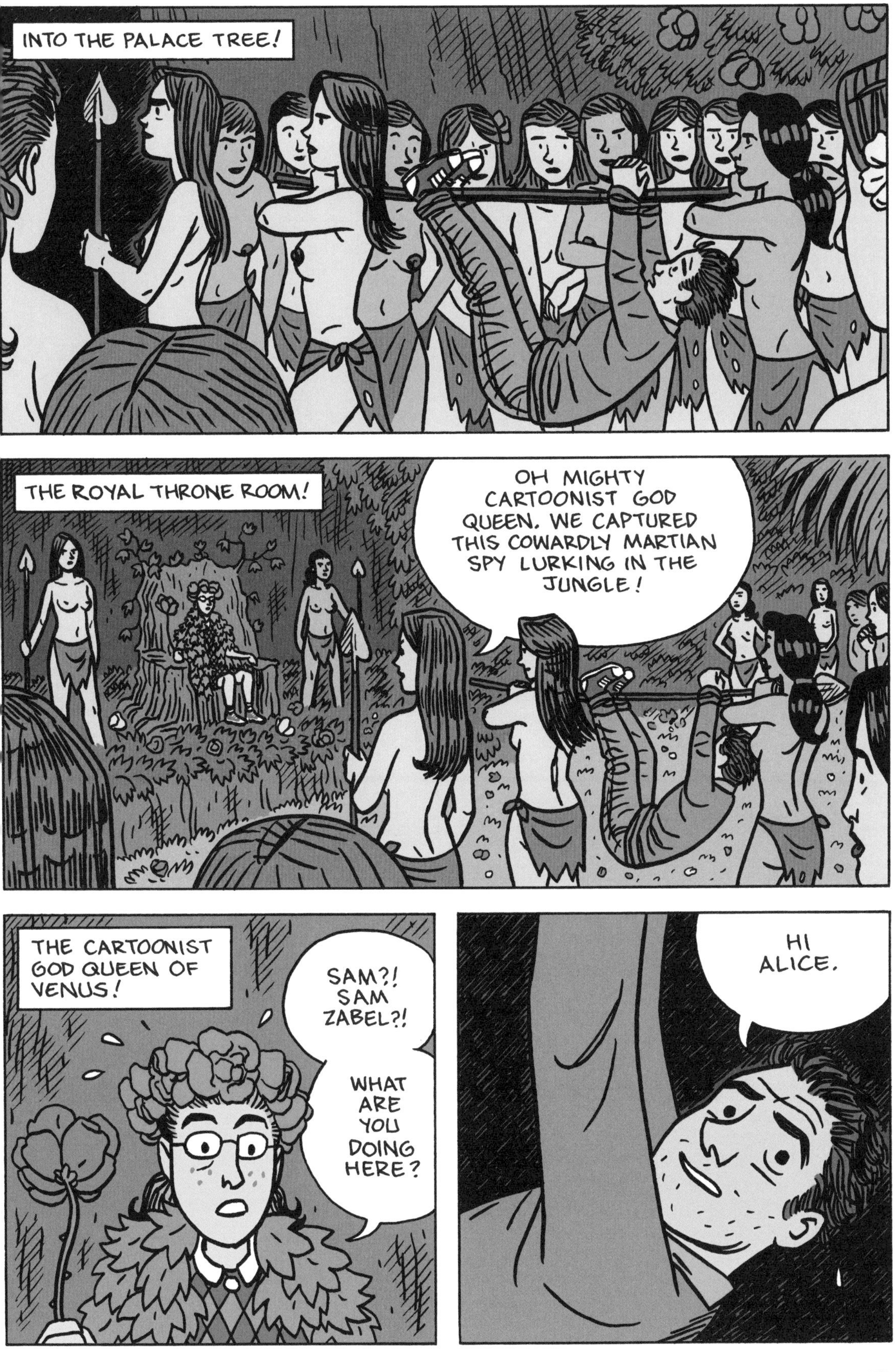
INTO THE PALACE TREE!
THE ROYAL THRONE ROOM!
OH MIGHTY CARTOONIST GOD QUEEN. WE CAPTURED THIS COWARDLY MARTIAN SPY LURKING IN THE JUNGLE!
THE CARTOONIST GOD QUEEN OF VENUS!
SAM?! SAM ZABEL?!
WHAT ARE YOU DOING HERE?
HI ALICE.

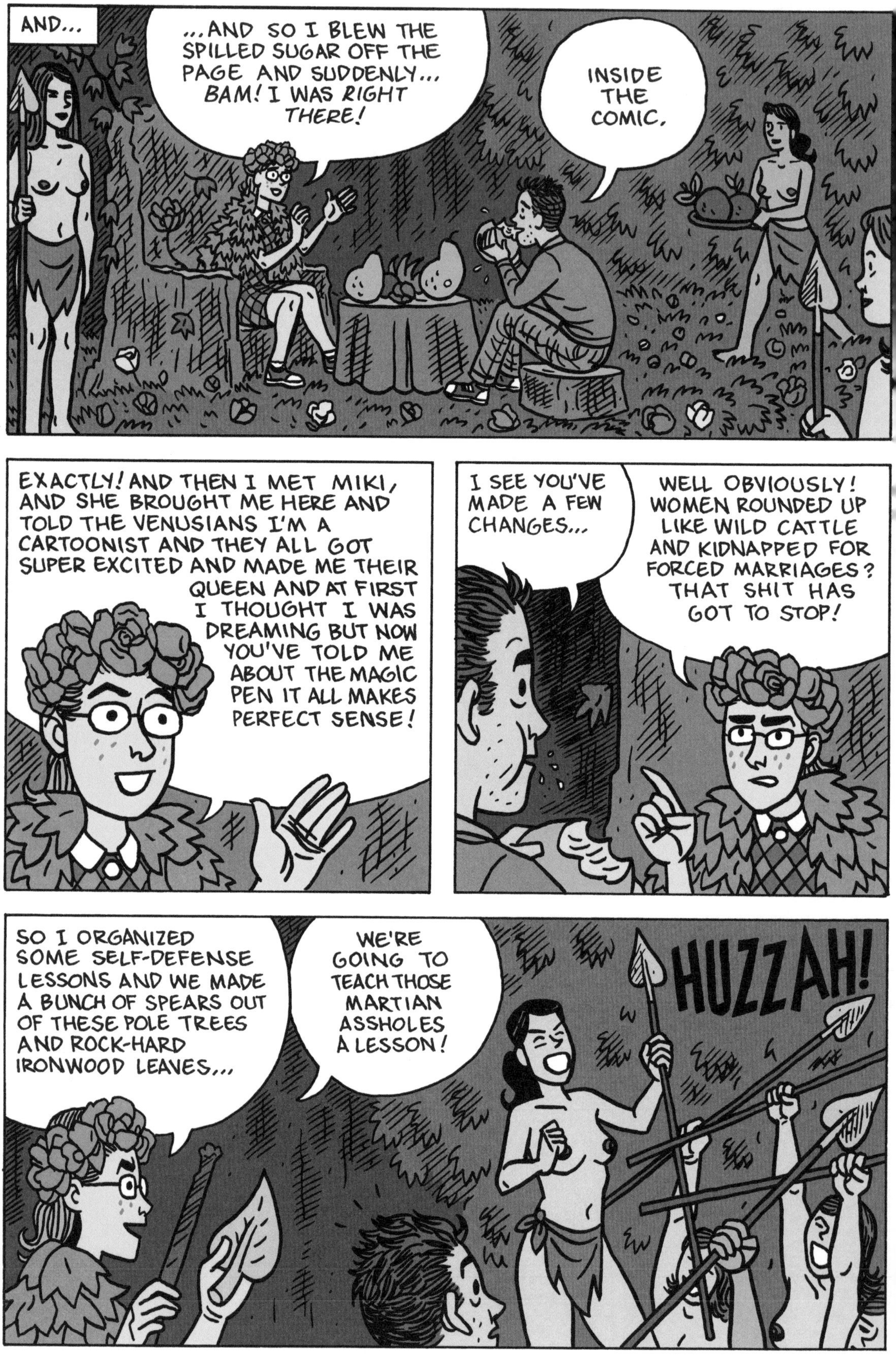
AND...
...AND SO I BLEW THE SPILLED SUGAR OFF THE PAGE AND SUDDENLY... BAM! I WAS RIGHT THERE!
INSIDE THE COMIC.
EXACTLY! AND THEN I MET MIKI, AND SHE BROUGHT ME HERE AND TOLD THE VENUSIANS I'M A CARTOONIST AND THEY ALL GOT SUPER EXCITED AND MADE ME THEIR QUEEN AND AT FIRST I THOUGHT I WAS DREAMING BUT NOW YOU'VE TOLD ME ABOUT THE MAGIC PEN IT ALL MAKES PERFECT SENSE!
I SEE YOU'VE MADE A FEW CHANGES...
WELL OBVIOUSLY! WOMEN ROUNDED UP LIKE WILD CATTLE AND KIDNAPPED FOR FORCED MARRIAGES? THAT SHIT HAS GOT TO STOP!
SO I ORGANIZED SOME SELF-DEFENSE LESSONS AND WE MADE A BUNCH OF SPEARS OUT OF THESE POLE TREES AND ROCK-HARD IRONWOOD LEAVES...
WE'RE GOING TO TEACH THOSE MARTIAN ASSHOLES A LESSON!
HUZZAH!

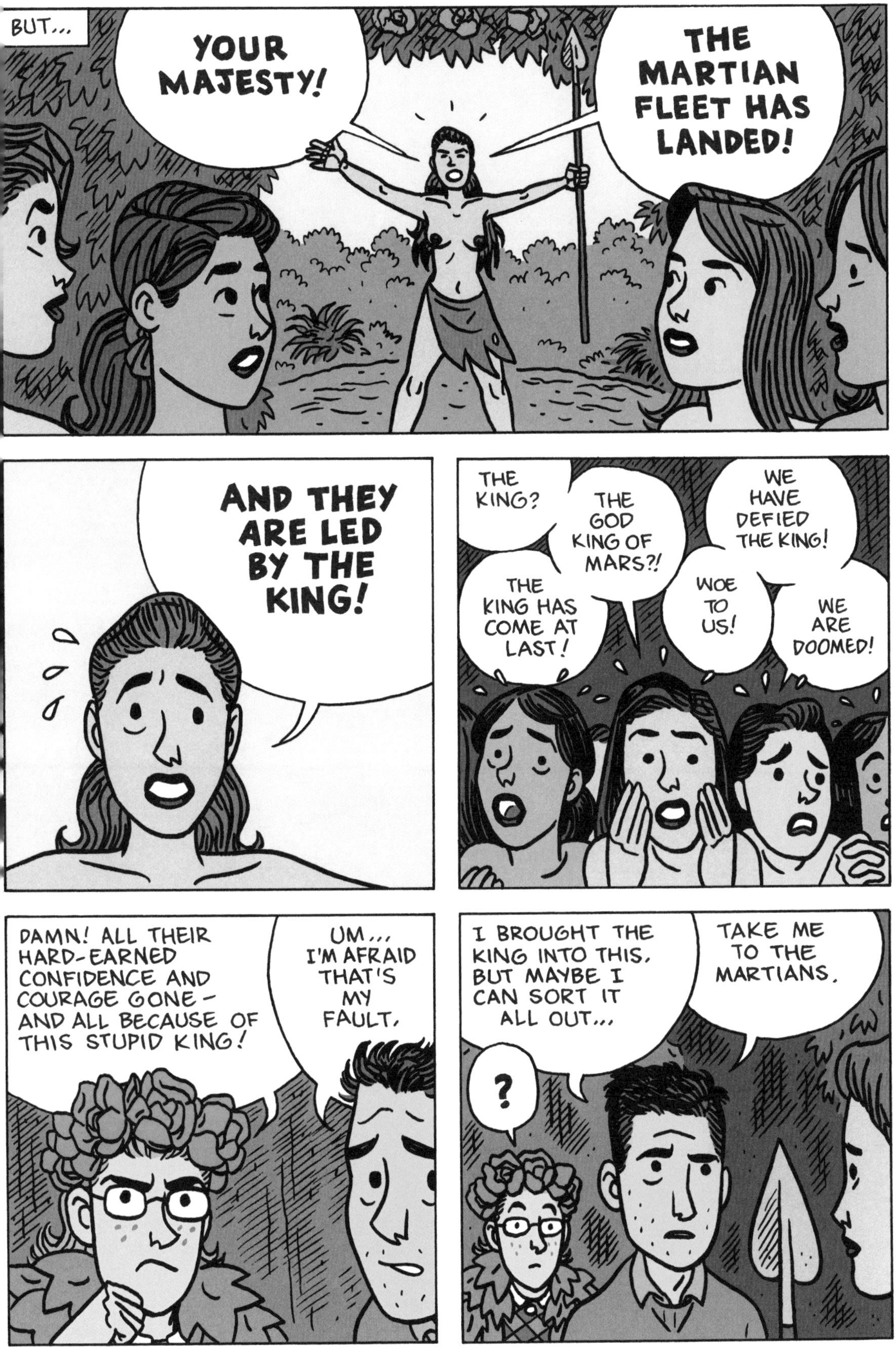
BUT...
YOUR MAJESTY!
THE MARTIAN FLEET HAS LANDED!
AND THEY ARE LED BY THE KING!
THE KING?
THE GOD KING OF MARS?!
WE HAVE DEFIED THE KING!
THE KING HAS COME AT LAST!
WOE TO US!
WE ARE DOOMED!
DAMN! ALL THEIR HARD-EARNED CONFIDENCE AND COURAGE GONE - AND ALL BECAUSE OF THIS STUPID KING!
UM... I'M AFRAID THAT'S MY FAULT.
I BROUGHT THE KING INTO THIS. BUT MAYBE I CAN SORT IT ALL OUT...
TAKE ME TO THE MARTIANS.
?

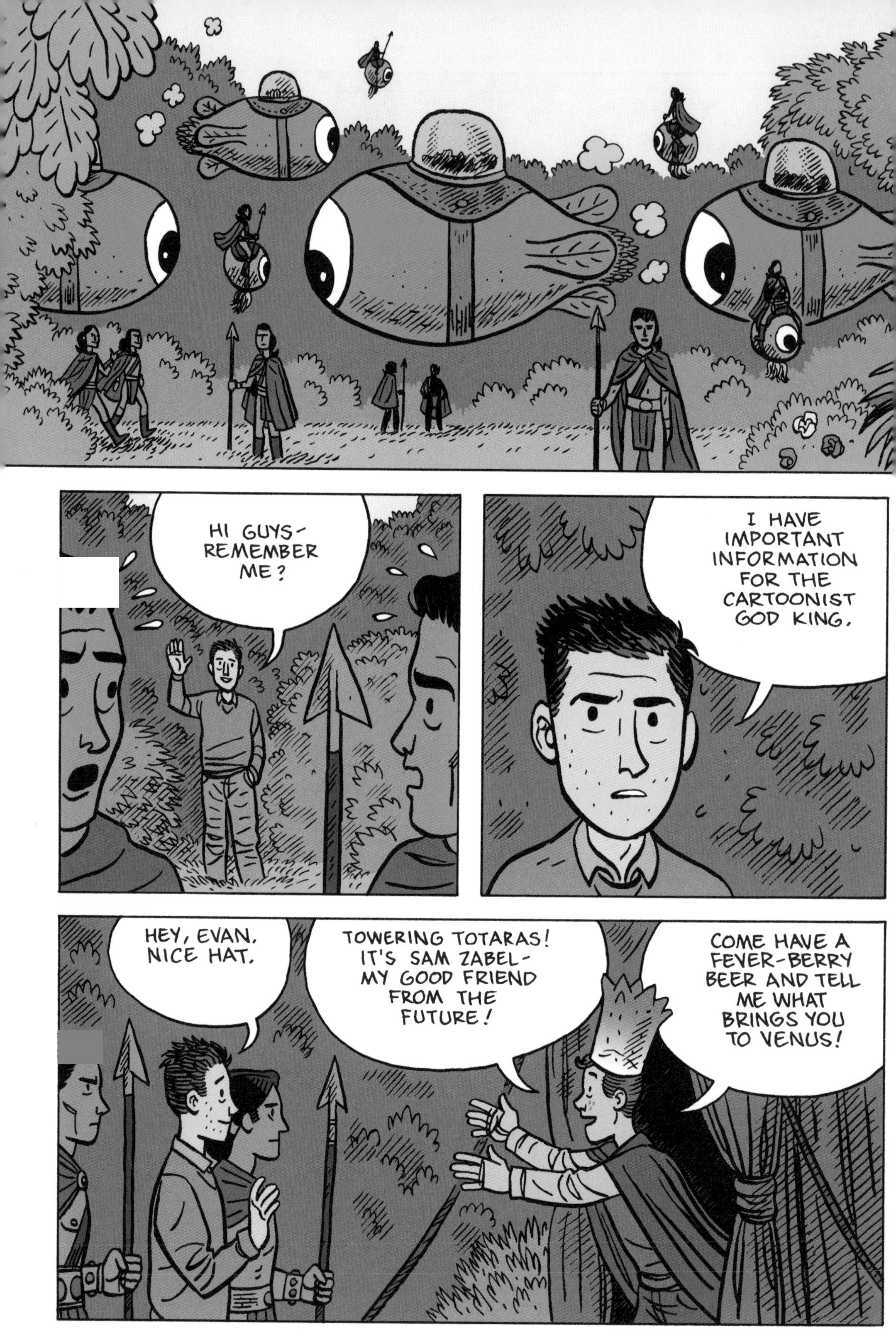
HI GUYS-
REMEMBER ME?
I HAVE IMPORTANT INFORMATION FOR THE CARTOONIST GOD KING.
HEY, EVAN. NICE HAT.
TOWERING TOTARAS! IT'S SAM ZABEL- MY GOOD FRIEND FROM THE FUTURE!
COME HAVE A FEVER-BERRY BEER AND TELL ME WHAT BRINGS YOU TO VENUS!

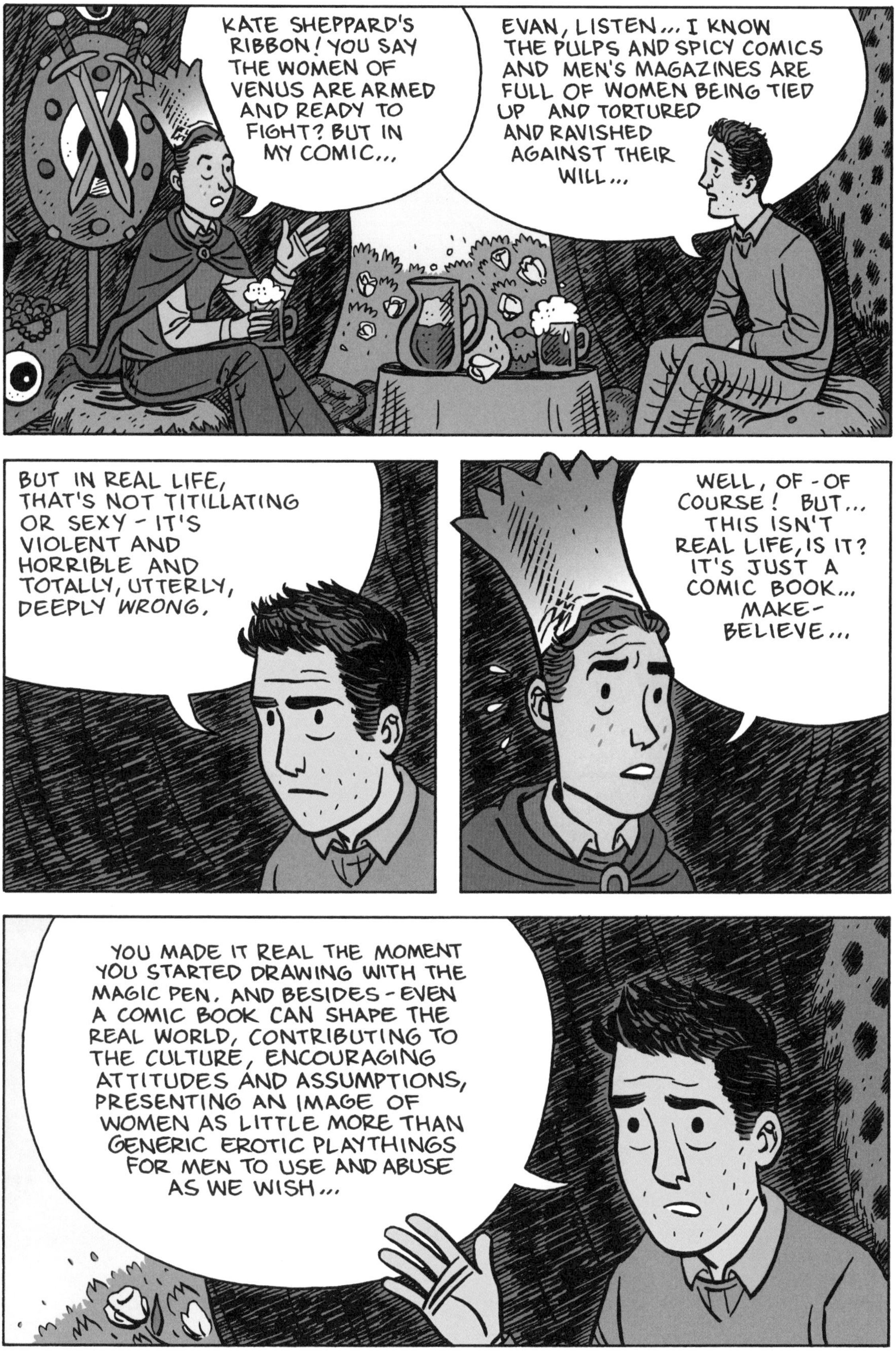
KATE SHEPPARD'S RIBBON! YOU SAY THE WOMEN OF VENUS ARE ARMED AND READY TO FIGHT? BUT IN MY COMIC...
EVAN, LISTEN... I KNOW THE PULPS AND SPICY COMICS AND MEN'S MAGAZINES ARE FULL OF WOMEN BEING TIED UP AND TORTURED AND RAVISHED AGAINST THEIR WILL...
BUT IN REAL LIFE, THAT'S NOT TITILLATING OR SEXY - IT'S VIOLENT AND HORRIBLE AND TOTALLY, UTTERLY, DEEPLY WRONG.
WELL, OF - OF COURSE! BUT... THIS ISN'T REAL LIFE, IS IT? IT'S JUST A COMIC BOOK... MAKE-BELIEVE...
YOU MADE IT REAL THE MOMENT YOU STARTED DRAWING WITH THE MAGIC PEN. AND BESIDES - EVEN A COMIC BOOK CAN SHAPE THE REAL WORLD, CONTRIBUTING TO THE CULTURE, ENCOURAGING ATTITUDES AND ASSUMPTIONS, PRESENTING AN IMAGE OF WOMEN AS LITTLE MORE THAN GENERIC EROTIC PLAYTHINGS FOR MEN TO USE AND ABUSE AS WE WISH...

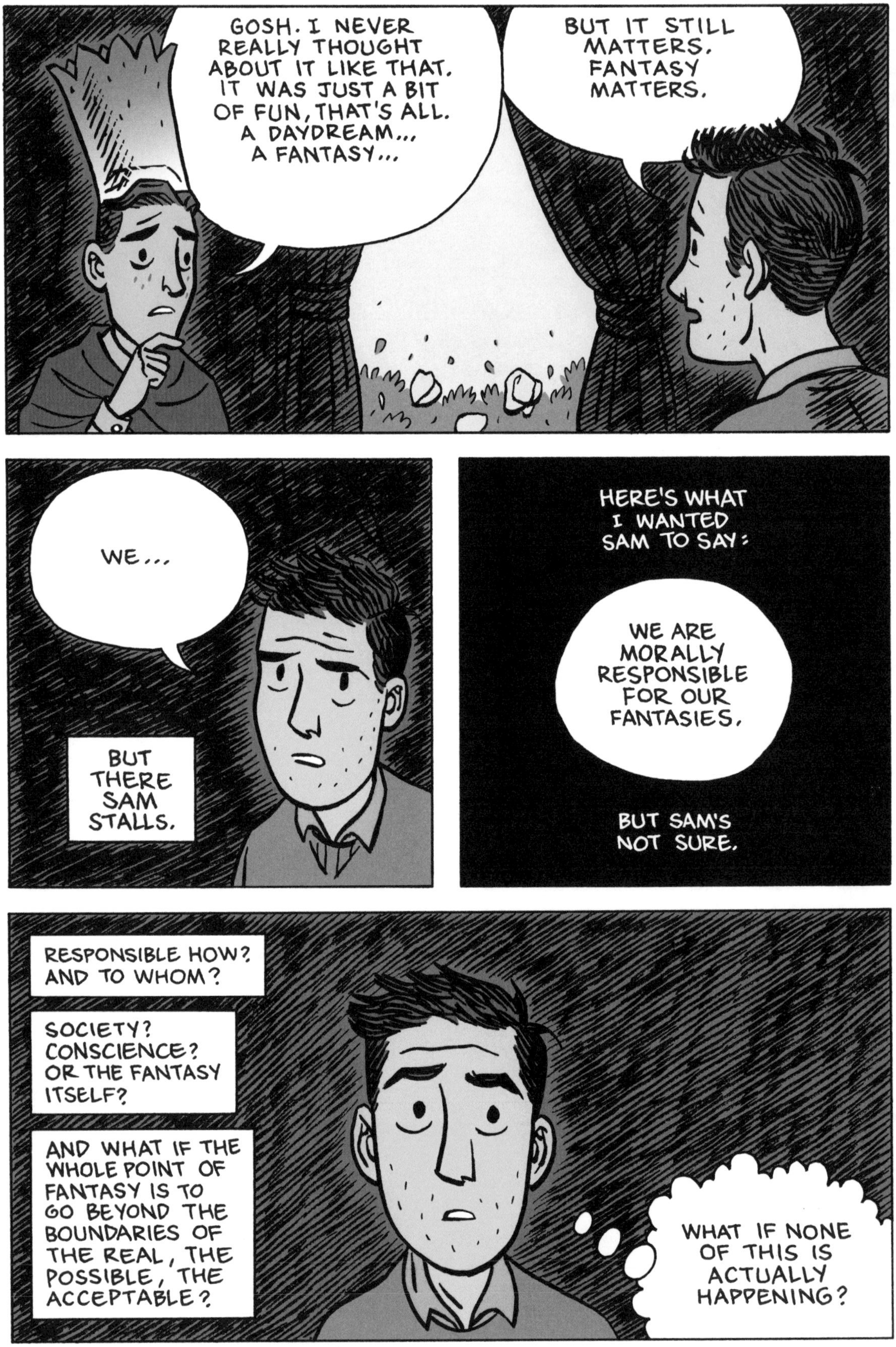
GOSH. I NEVER REALLY THOUGHT ABOUT IT LIKE THAT. IT WAS JUST A BIT OF FUN, THAT'S ALL. A DAYDREAM... A FANTASY...
BUT IT STILL MATTERS. FANTASY MATTERS.
WE...
BUT THERE SAM STALLS.
HERE'S WHAT I WANTED SAM TO SAY:
WE ARE MORALLY RESPONSIBLE FOR OUR FANTASIES.
BUT SAM'S NOT SURE.
RESPONSIBLE HOW? AND TO WHOM?
SOCIETY? CONSCIENCE? OR THE FANTASY ITSELF?
AND WHAT IF THE WHOLE POINT OF FANTASY IS TO GO BEYOND THE BOUNDARIES OF THE REAL, THE POSSIBLE, THE ACCEPTABLE?
WHAT IF NONE OF THIS IS ACTUALLY HAPPENING?

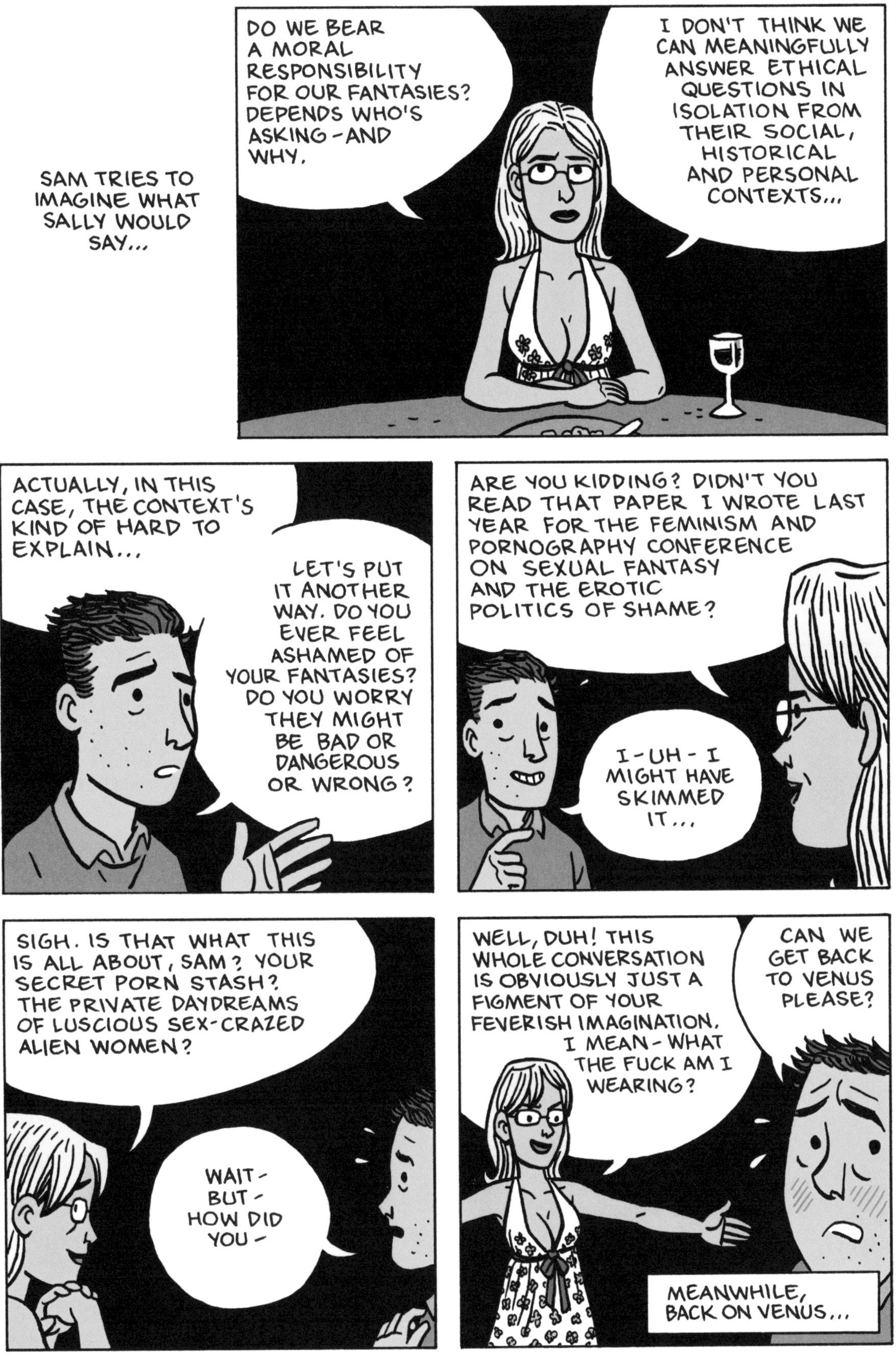
SAM TRIES TO IMAGINE WHAT SALLY WOULD SAY...
DO WE BEAR A MORAL RESPONSIBILITY FOR OUR FANTASIES? DEPENDS WHO'S ASKING - AND WHY.
I DON'T THINK WE CAN MEANINGFULLY ANSWER ETHICAL QUESTIONS IN ISOLATION FROM THEIR SOCIAL, HISTORICAL AND PERSONAL CONTEXTS...
ACTUALLY, IN THIS CASE, THE CONTEXT'S KIND OF HARD TO EXPLAIN...
LET'S PUT IT ANOTHER WAY. DO YOU EVER FEEL ASHAMED OF YOUR FANTASIES? DO YOU WORRY THEY MIGHT BE BAD OR DANGEROUS OR WRONG?
ARE YOU KIDDING? DIDN'T YOU READ THAT PAPER I WROTE LAST YEAR FOR THE FEMINISM AND PORNOGRAPHY CONFERENCE ON SEXUAL FANTASY AND THE EROTIC POLITICS OF SHAME?
I - UH - I MIGHT HAVE SKIMMED IT...
SIGH. IS THAT WHAT THIS IS ALL ABOUT, SAM? YOUR SECRET PORN STASH? THE PRIVATE DAYDREAMS OF LUSCIOUS SEX-CRAZED ALIEN WOMEN?
WAIT - BUT - HOW DID YOU -
WELL, DUH! THIS WHOLE CONVERSATION IS OBVIOUSLY JUST A FIGMENT OF YOUR FEVERISH IMAGINATION.
I MEAN - WHAT THE FUCK AM I WEARING?
CAN WE GET BACK TO VENUS PLEASE?
MEANWHILE, BACK ON VENUS...

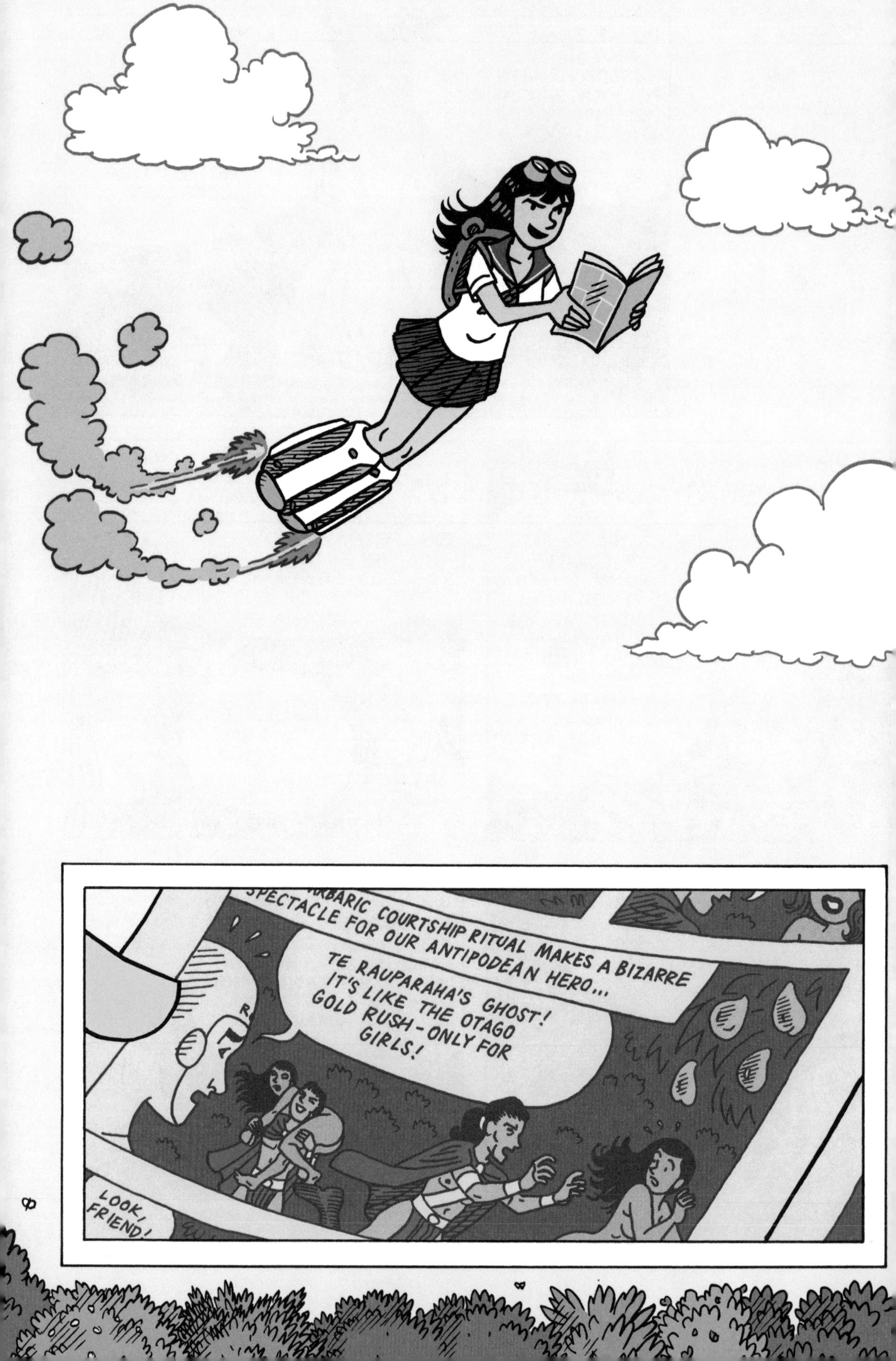
...ARBARIC COURTSHIP RITUAL MAKES A BIZARRE SPECTACLE FOR OUR ANTIPODEAN HERO...
TE RAUPARAHA'S GHOST! IT'S LIKE THE OTAGO GOLD RUSH - ONLY FOR GIRLS!
LOOK, FRIEND!

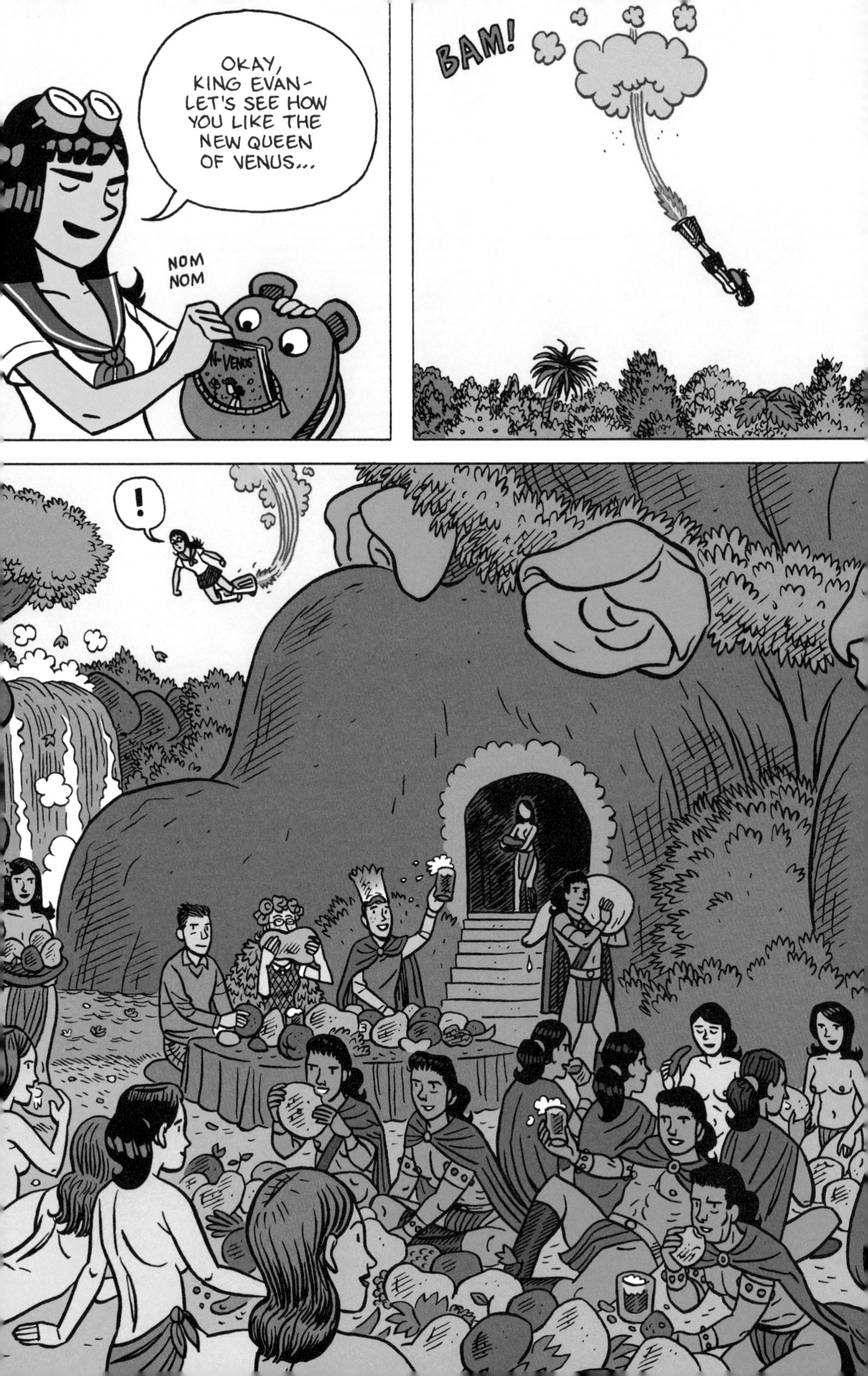
OKAY, KING EVAN- LET'S SEE HOW YOU LIKE THE NEW QUEEN OF VENUS...
NOM NOM
VENUS
BAM!
!

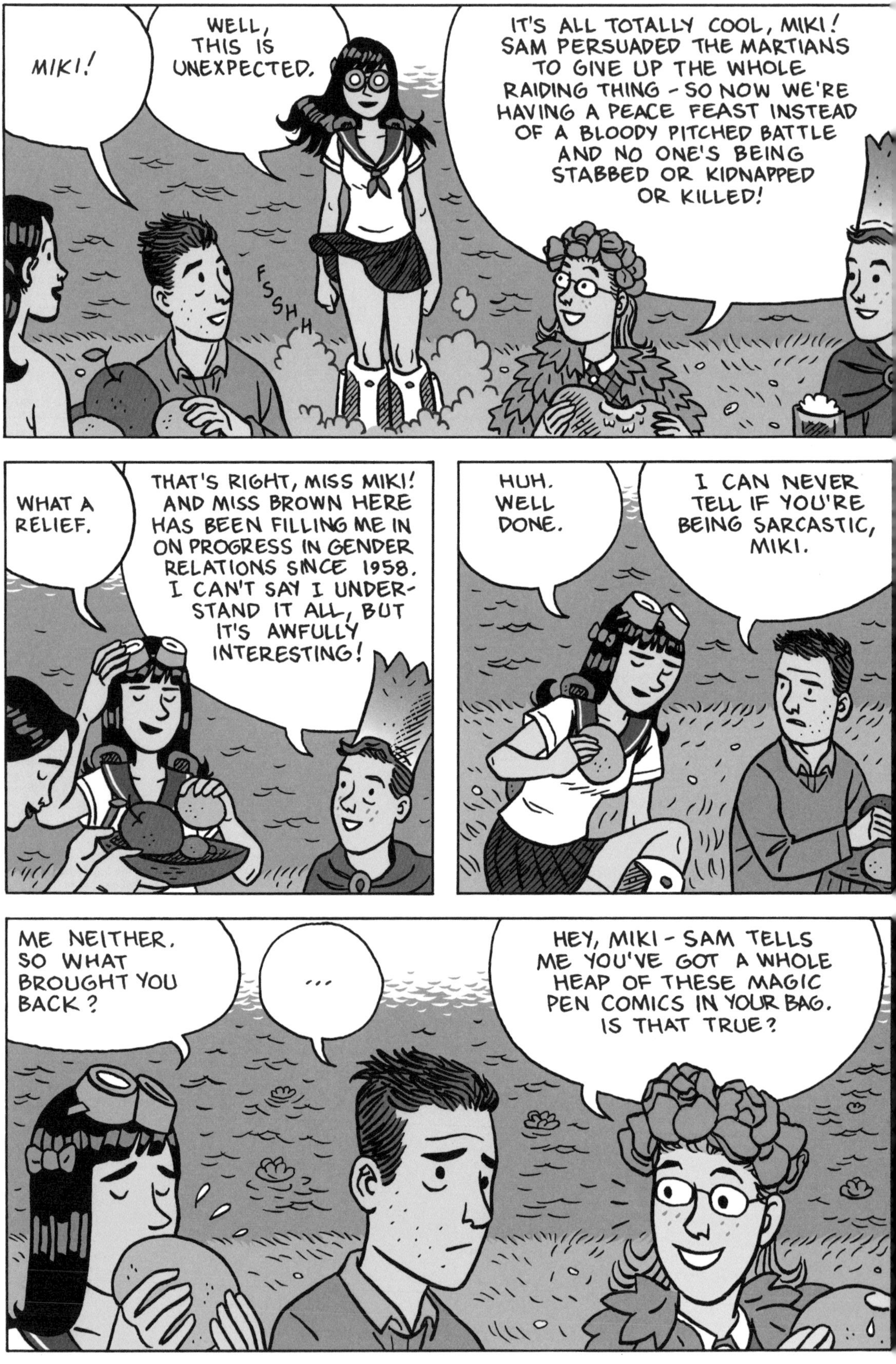
MIKI!
WELL, THIS IS UNEXPECTED.
IT'S ALL TOTALLY COOL, MIKI! SAM PERSUADED THE MARTIANS TO GIVE UP THE WHOLE RAIDING THING - SO NOW WE'RE HAVING A PEACE FEAST INSTEAD OF A BLOODY PITCHED BATTLE AND NO ONE'S BEING STABBED OR KIDNAPPED OR KILLED!
FSSHH
WHAT A RELIEF.
THAT'S RIGHT, MISS MIKI! AND MISS BROWN HERE HAS BEEN FILLING ME IN ON PROGRESS IN GENDER RELATIONS SINCE 1958. I CAN'T SAY I UNDERSTAND IT ALL, BUT IT'S AWFULLY INTERESTING!
HUH. WELL DONE.
I CAN NEVER TELL IF YOU'RE BEING SARCASTIC, MIKI.
ME NEITHER. SO WHAT BROUGHT YOU BACK?
...
HEY, MIKI - SAM TELLS ME YOU'VE GOT A WHOLE HEAP OF THESE MAGIC PEN COMICS IN YOUR BAG. IS THAT TRUE?

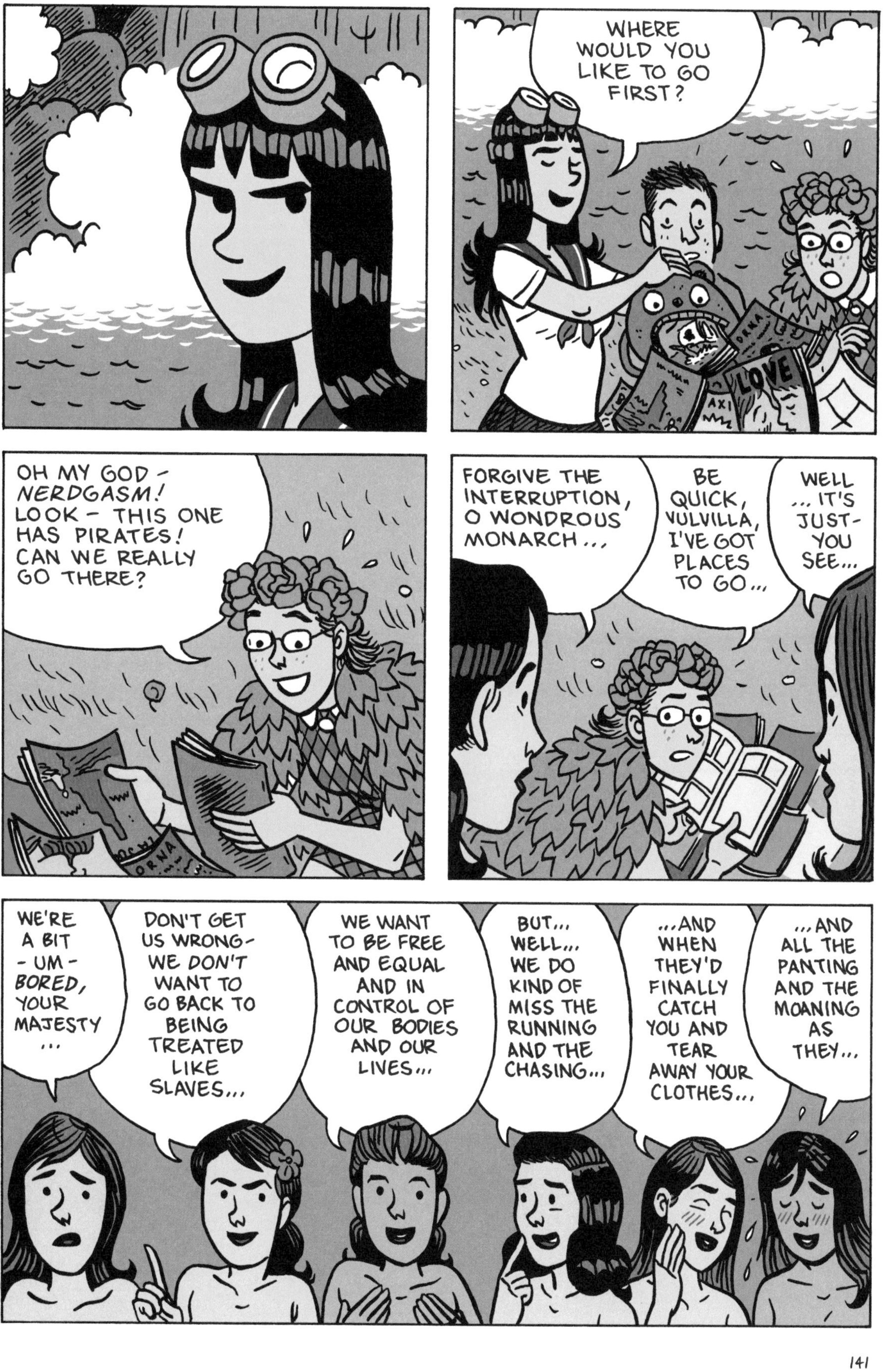
WHERE WOULD YOU LIKE TO GO FIRST?
OH MY GOD - *NERDGASM!* LOOK - THIS ONE HAS PIRATES! CAN WE REALLY GO THERE?
FORGIVE THE INTERRUPTION, O WONDROUS MONARCH...
BE QUICK, VULVILLA, I'VE GOT PLACES TO GO...
WELL ... IT'S JUST- YOU SEE...
WE'RE A BIT - UM - BORED, YOUR MAJESTY ...
DON'T GET US WRONG- WE *DON'T* WANT TO GO BACK TO BEING TREATED LIKE SLAVES...
WE WANT TO BE FREE AND EQUAL AND IN CONTROL OF OUR BODIES AND OUR LIVES...
BUT... WELL... WE DO KIND OF MISS THE RUNNING AND THE CHASING...
...AND WHEN THEY'D FINALLY CATCH YOU AND TEAR AWAY YOUR CLOTHES...
...AND ALL THE PANTING AND THE MOANING AS THEY...

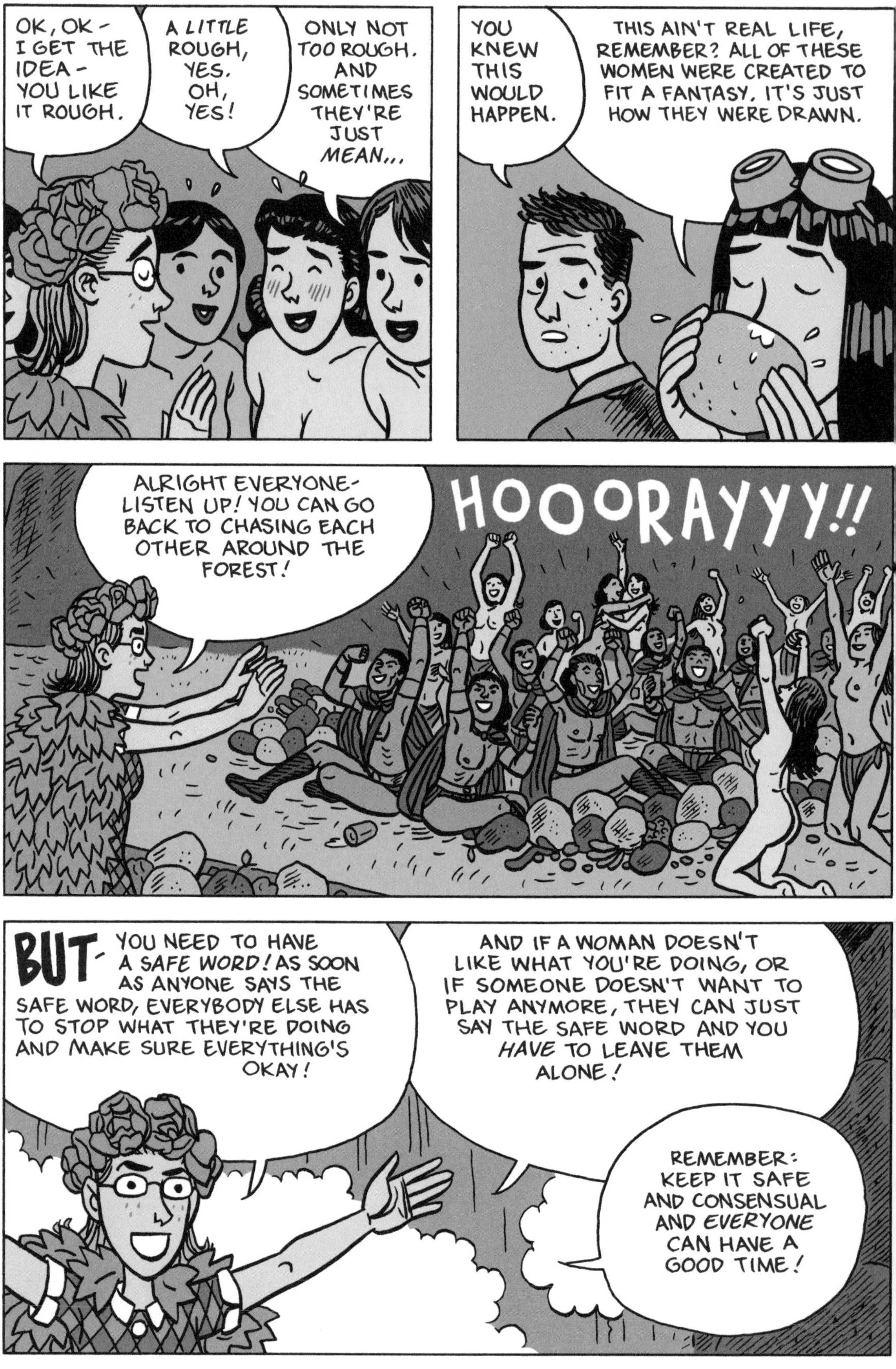
OK, OK - I GET THE IDEA - YOU LIKE IT ROUGH.
A *LITTLE* ROUGH, YES. OH, YES!
ONLY NOT TOO ROUGH. AND SOMETIMES THEY'RE JUST *MEAN*...
YOU KNEW THIS WOULD HAPPEN.
THIS AIN'T REAL LIFE, REMEMBER? ALL OF THESE WOMEN WERE CREATED TO FIT A FANTASY. IT'S JUST HOW THEY WERE DRAWN.
ALRIGHT EVERYONE- LISTEN UP! YOU CAN GO BACK TO CHASING EACH OTHER AROUND THE FOREST!
HOOORAYYY!!
BUT- YOU NEED TO HAVE A SAFE WORD! AS SOON AS ANYONE SAYS THE SAFE WORD, EVERYBODY ELSE HAS TO STOP WHAT THEY'RE DOING AND MAKE SURE EVERYTHING'S OKAY!
AND IF A WOMAN DOESN'T LIKE WHAT YOU'RE DOING, OR IF SOMEONE DOESN'T WANT TO PLAY ANYMORE, THEY CAN JUST SAY THE SAFE WORD AND YOU *HAVE* TO LEAVE THEM ALONE!
REMEMBER: KEEP IT SAFE AND CONSENSUAL AND *EVERYONE* CAN HAVE A GOOD TIME!

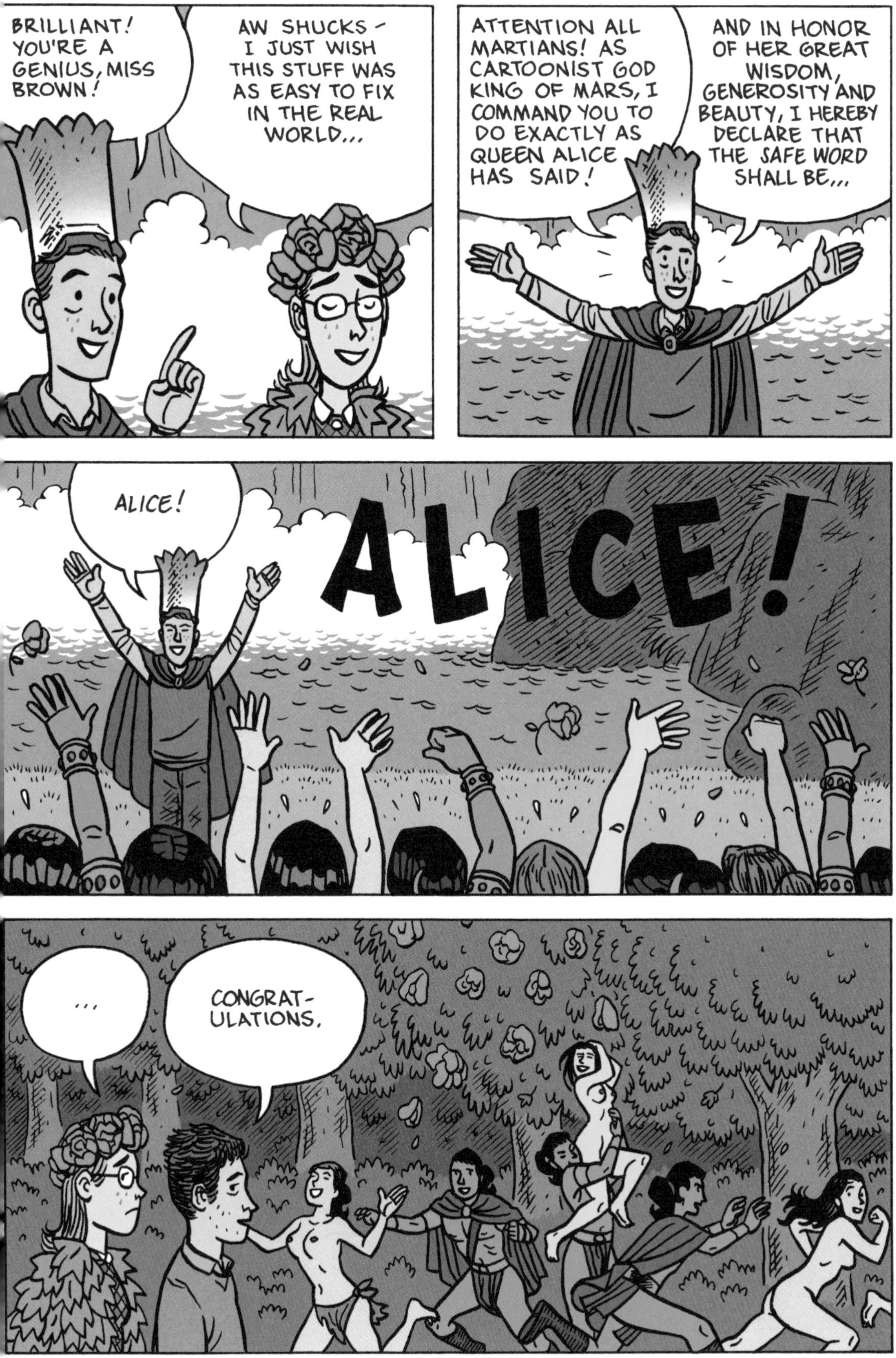
BRILLIANT! YOU'RE A GENIUS, MISS BROWN!
AW SHUCKS - I JUST WISH THIS STUFF WAS AS EASY TO FIX IN THE REAL WORLD...
ATTENTION ALL MARTIANS! AS CARTOONIST GOD KING OF MARS, I COMMAND YOU TO DO EXACTLY AS QUEEN ALICE HAS SAID!
AND IN HONOR OF HER GREAT WISDOM, GENEROSITY AND BEAUTY, I HEREBY DECLARE THAT THE SAFE WORD SHALL BE...
ALICE!
ALICE!
...
CONGRAT-ULATIONS.

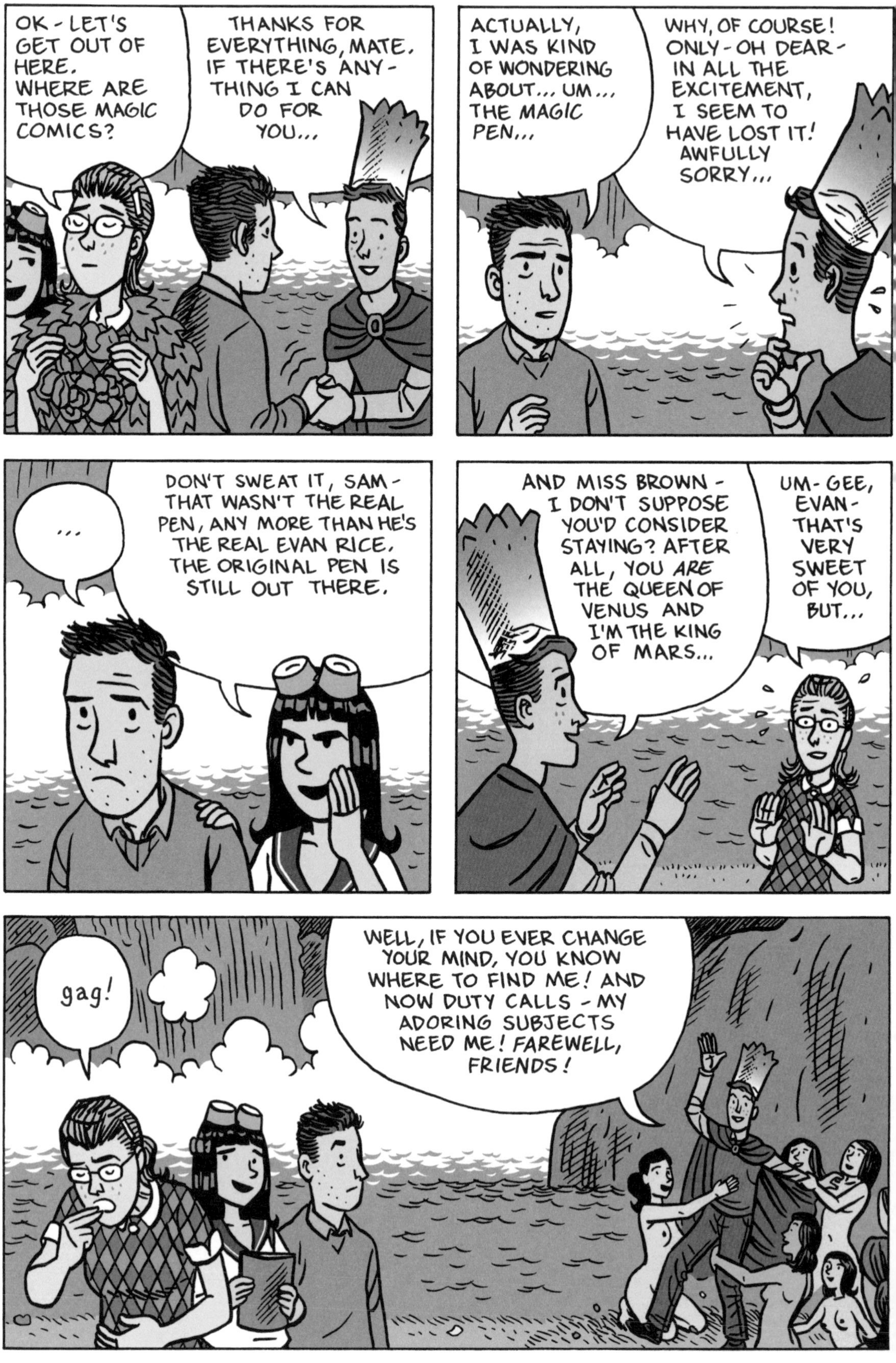
OK - LET'S GET OUT OF HERE. WHERE ARE THOSE MAGIC COMICS?
THANKS FOR EVERYTHING, MATE. IF THERE'S ANYTHING I CAN DO FOR YOU...
ACTUALLY, I WAS KIND OF WONDERING ABOUT... UM... THE MAGIC PEN...
WHY, OF COURSE! ONLY - OH DEAR - IN ALL THE EXCITEMENT, I SEEM TO HAVE LOST IT! AWFULLY SORRY...
...
DON'T SWEAT IT, SAM - THAT WASN'T THE REAL PEN, ANY MORE THAN HE'S THE REAL EVAN RICE. THE ORIGINAL PEN IS STILL OUT THERE.
AND MISS BROWN - I DON'T SUPPOSE YOU'D CONSIDER STAYING? AFTER ALL, YOU *ARE* THE QUEEN OF VENUS AND I'M THE KING OF MARS...
UM - GEE, EVAN - THAT'S VERY SWEET OF YOU, BUT...
gag!
WELL, IF YOU EVER CHANGE YOUR MIND, YOU KNOW WHERE TO FIND ME! AND NOW DUTY CALLS - MY ADORING SUBJECTS NEED ME! *FAREWELL*, FRIENDS!

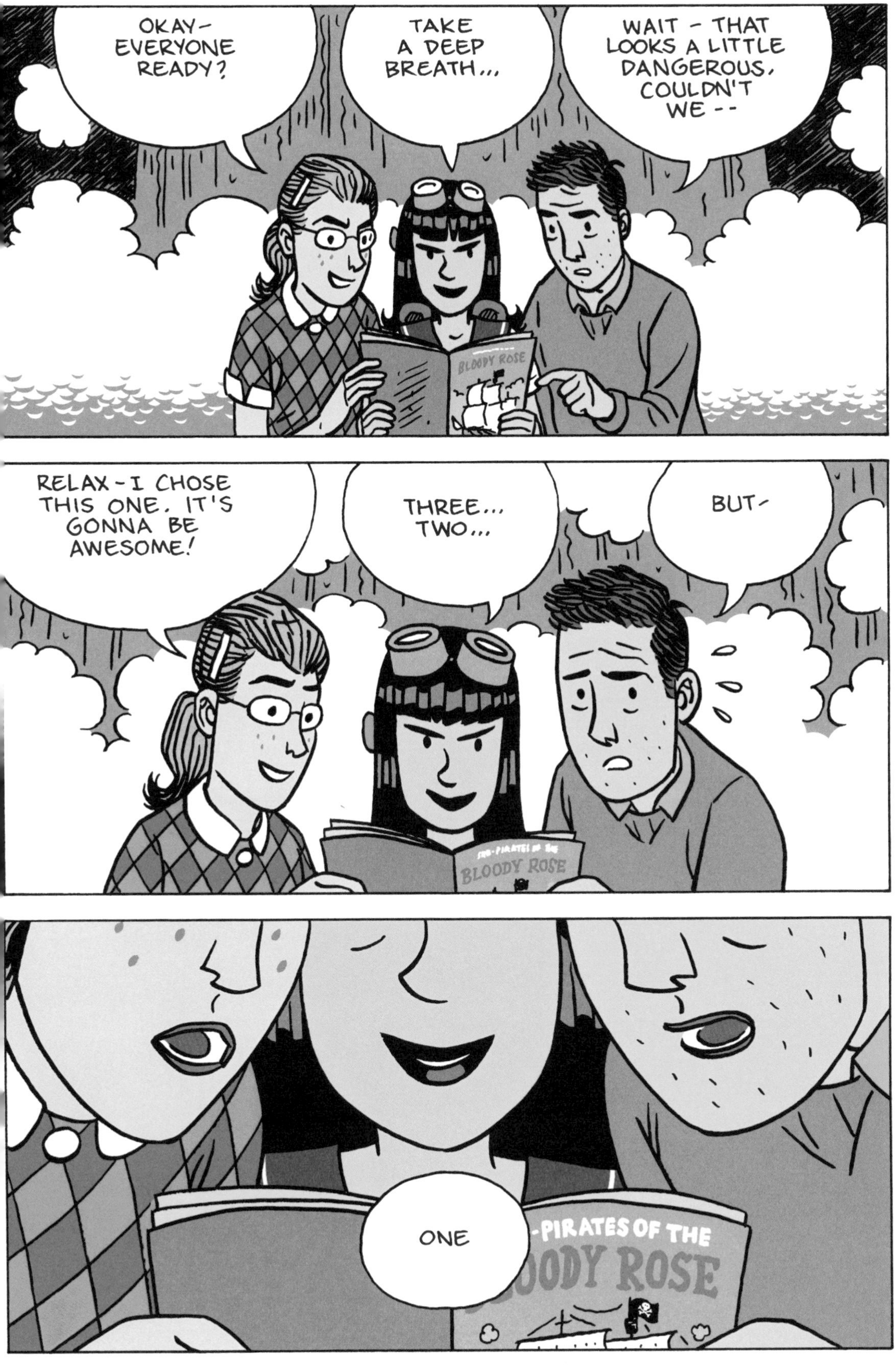
OKAY-
EVERYONE
READY?
TAKE
A DEEP
BREATH...
WAIT - THAT
LOOKS A LITTLE
DANGEROUS.
COULDN'T
WE --
BLOODY ROSE
RELAX - I CHOSE
THIS ONE. IT'S
GONNA BE
AWESOME!
THREE...
TWO...
BUT-
BLOODY ROSE
ONE
-PIRATES OF THE

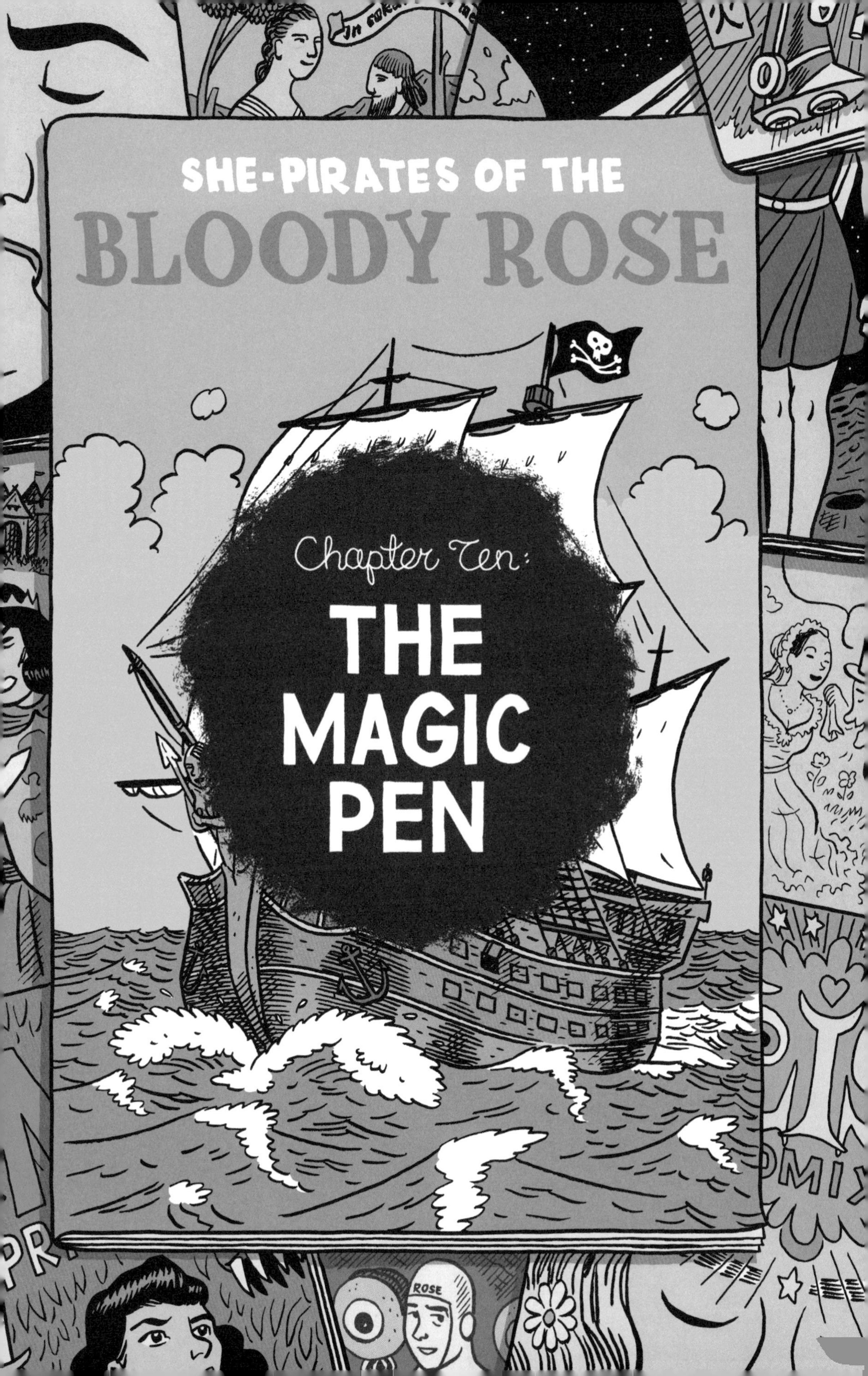
SHE-PIRATES OF THE
BLOODY ROSE
Chapter Ten:
THE MAGIC PEN
ROSE

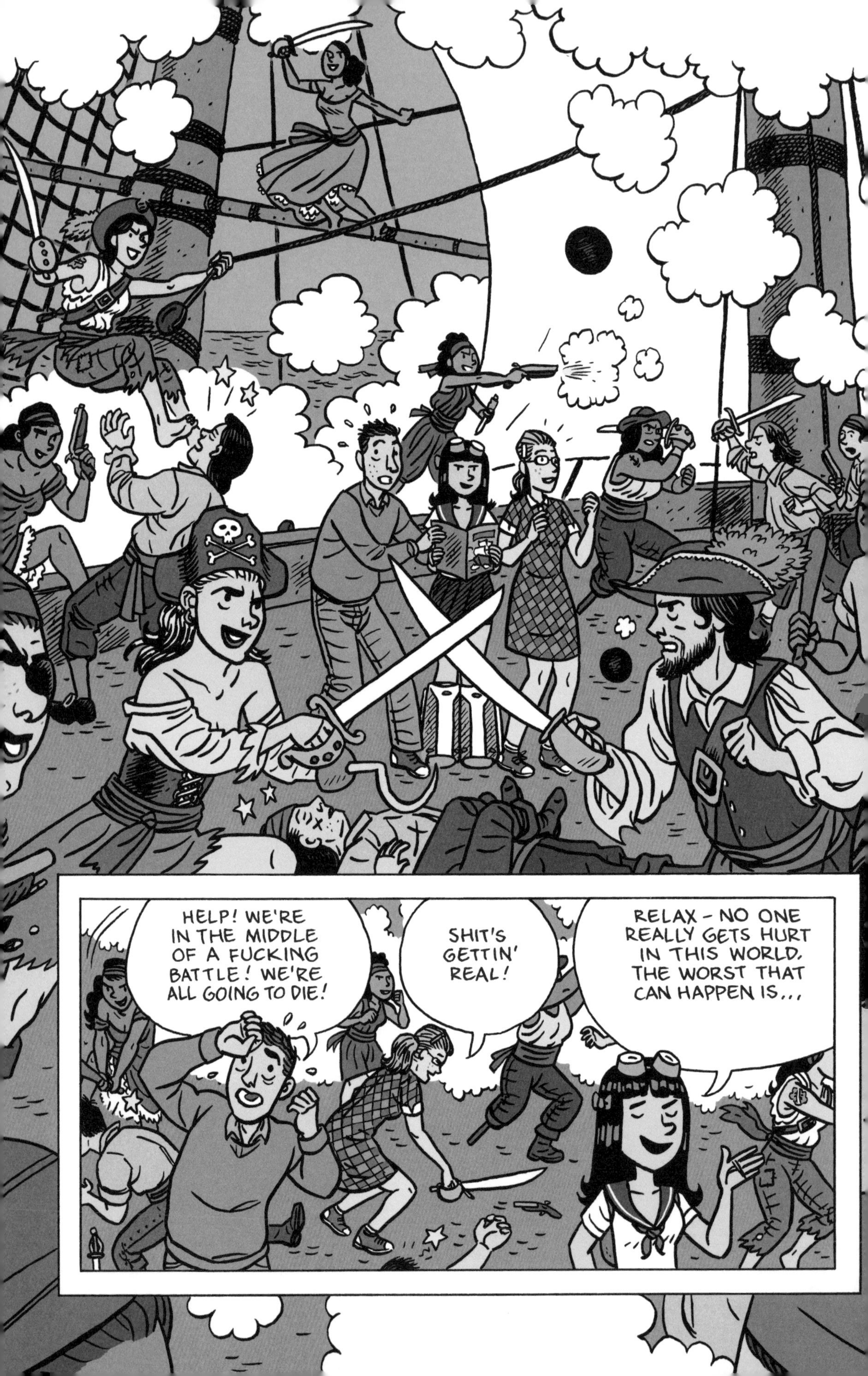
HELP! WE'RE IN THE MIDDLE OF A FUCKING BATTLE! WE'RE ALL GOING TO DIE!
SHIT'S GETTIN' REAL!
RELAX - NO ONE REALLY GETS HURT IN THIS WORLD. THE WORST THAT CAN HAPPEN IS...

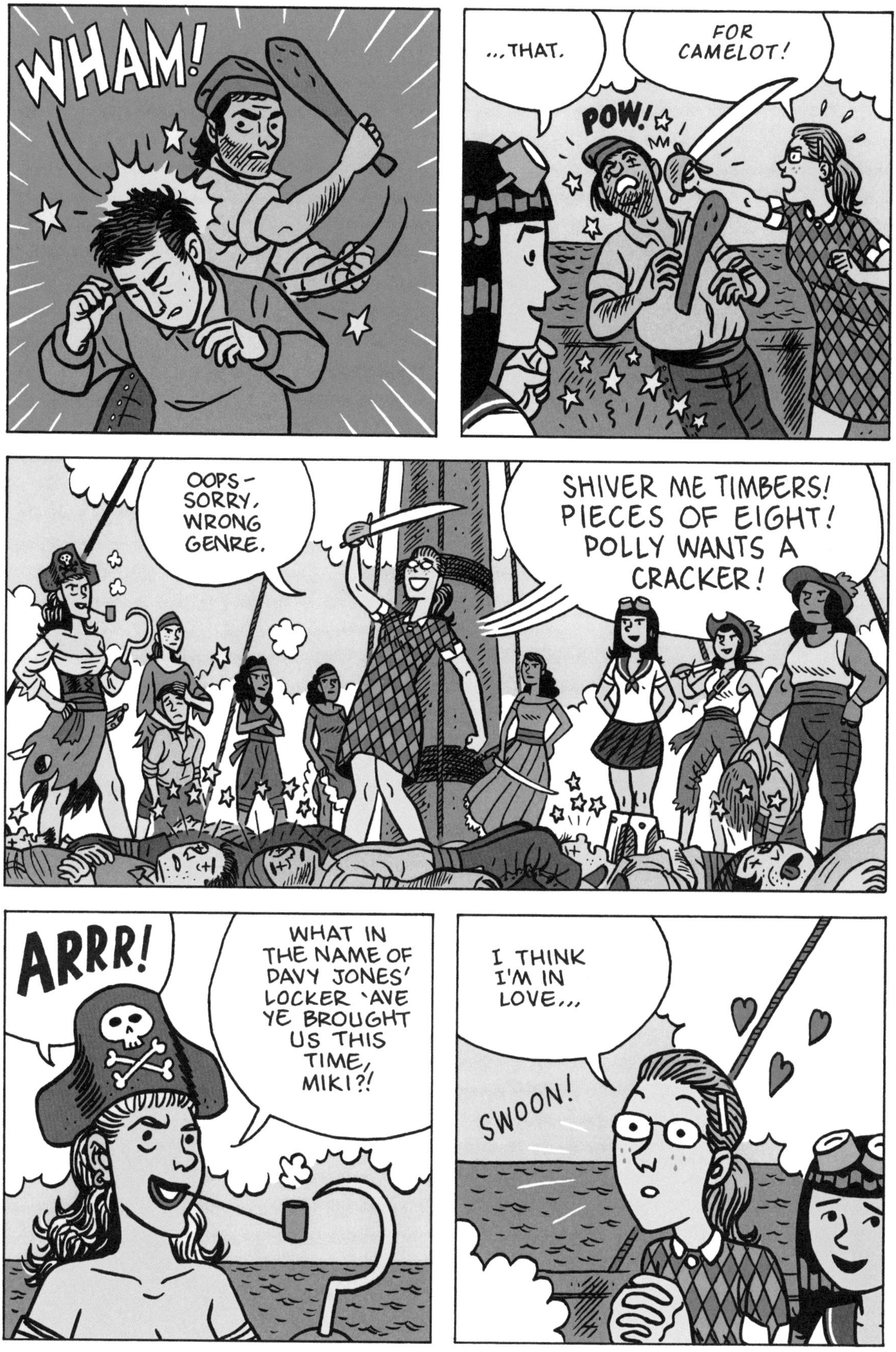
WHAM!
...THAT.
FOR CAMELOT!
POW!
OOPS- SORRY, WRONG GENRE.
SHIVER ME TIMBERS! PIECES OF EIGHT! POLLY WANTS A CRACKER!
ARRR!
WHAT IN THE NAME OF DAVY JONES' LOCKER 'AVE YE BROUGHT US THIS TIME, MIKI?!
I THINK I'M IN LOVE...
SWOON!

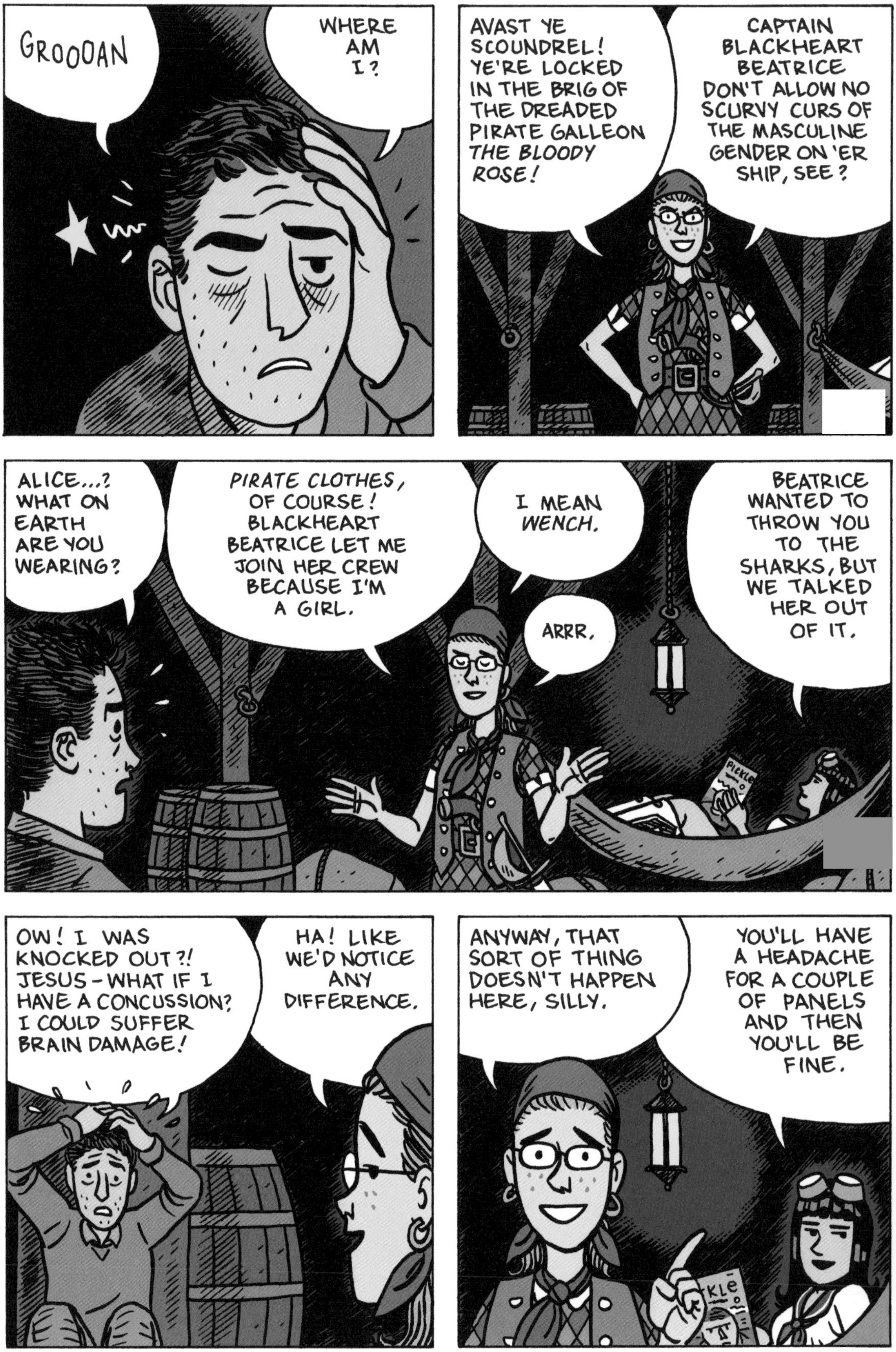
GROOOAN
WHERE AM I?
AVAST YE SCOUNDREL! YE'RE LOCKED IN THE BRIG OF THE DREADED PIRATE GALLEON THE BLOODY ROSE!
CAPTAIN BLACKHEART BEATRICE DON'T ALLOW NO SCURVY CURS OF THE MASCULINE GENDER ON 'ER SHIP, SEE?
ALICE...? WHAT ON EARTH ARE YOU WEARING?
PIRATE CLOTHES, OF COURSE! BLACKHEART BEATRICE LET ME JOIN HER CREW BECAUSE I'M A GIRL.
I MEAN WENCH.
ARRR.
BEATRICE WANTED TO THROW YOU TO THE SHARKS, BUT WE TALKED HER OUT OF IT.
OW! I WAS KNOCKED OUT?! JESUS - WHAT IF I HAVE A CONCUSSION? I COULD SUFFER BRAIN DAMAGE!
HA! LIKE WE'D NOTICE ANY DIFFERENCE.
ANYWAY, THAT SORT OF THING DOESN'T HAPPEN HERE, SILLY.
YOU'LL HAVE A HEADACHE FOR A COUPLE OF PANELS AND THEN YOU'LL BE FINE.

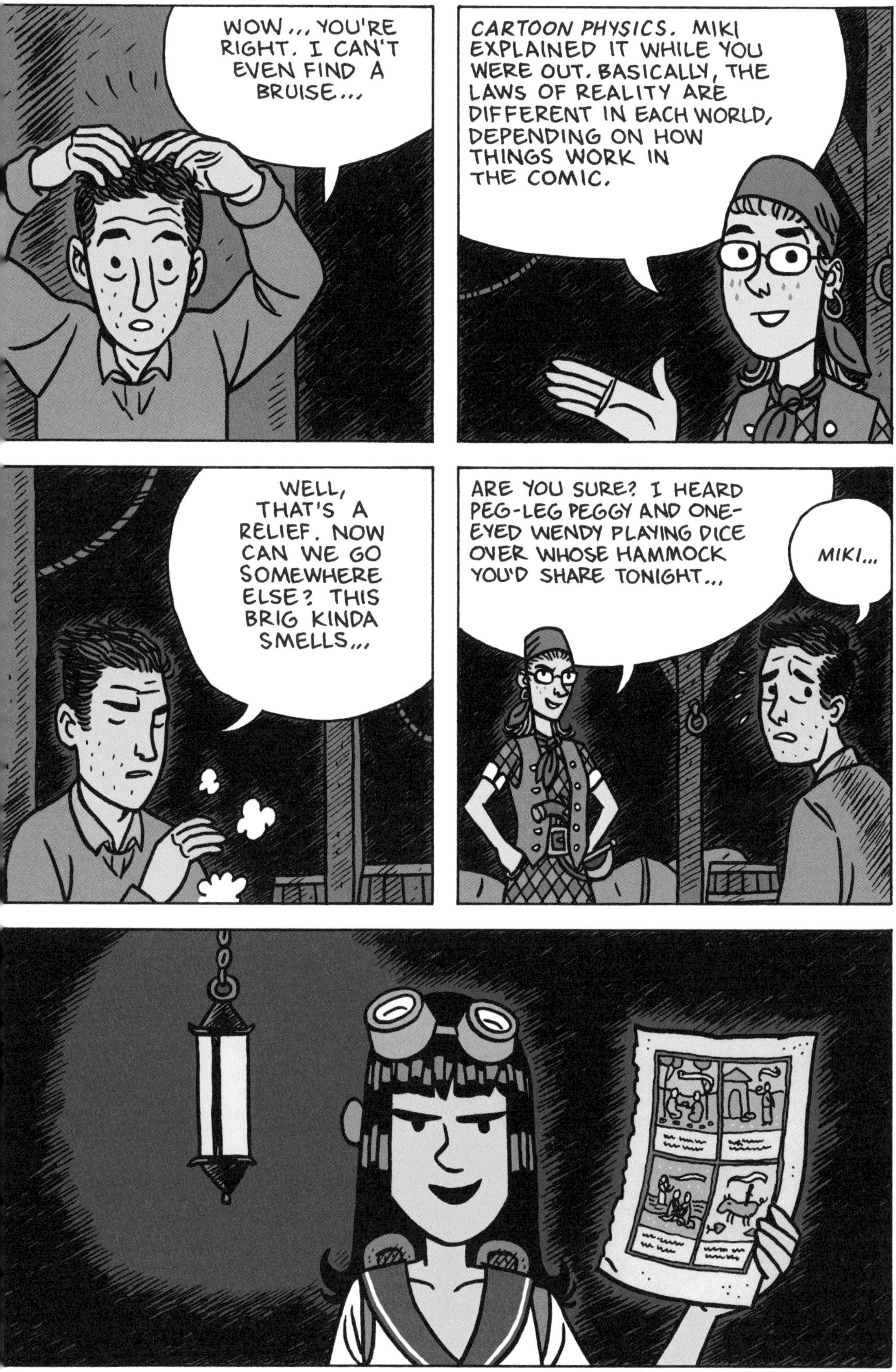
WOW... YOU'RE RIGHT. I CAN'T EVEN FIND A BRUISE...
CARTOON PHYSICS. MIKI EXPLAINED IT WHILE YOU WERE OUT. BASICALLY, THE LAWS OF REALITY ARE DIFFERENT IN EACH WORLD, DEPENDING ON HOW THINGS WORK IN THE COMIC.
WELL, THAT'S A RELIEF. NOW CAN WE GO SOMEWHERE ELSE? THIS BRIG KINDA SMELLS...
ARE YOU SURE? I HEARD PEG-LEG PEGGY AND ONE-EYED WENDY PLAYING DICE OVER WHOSE HAMMOCK YOU'D SHARE TONIGHT...
MIKI...

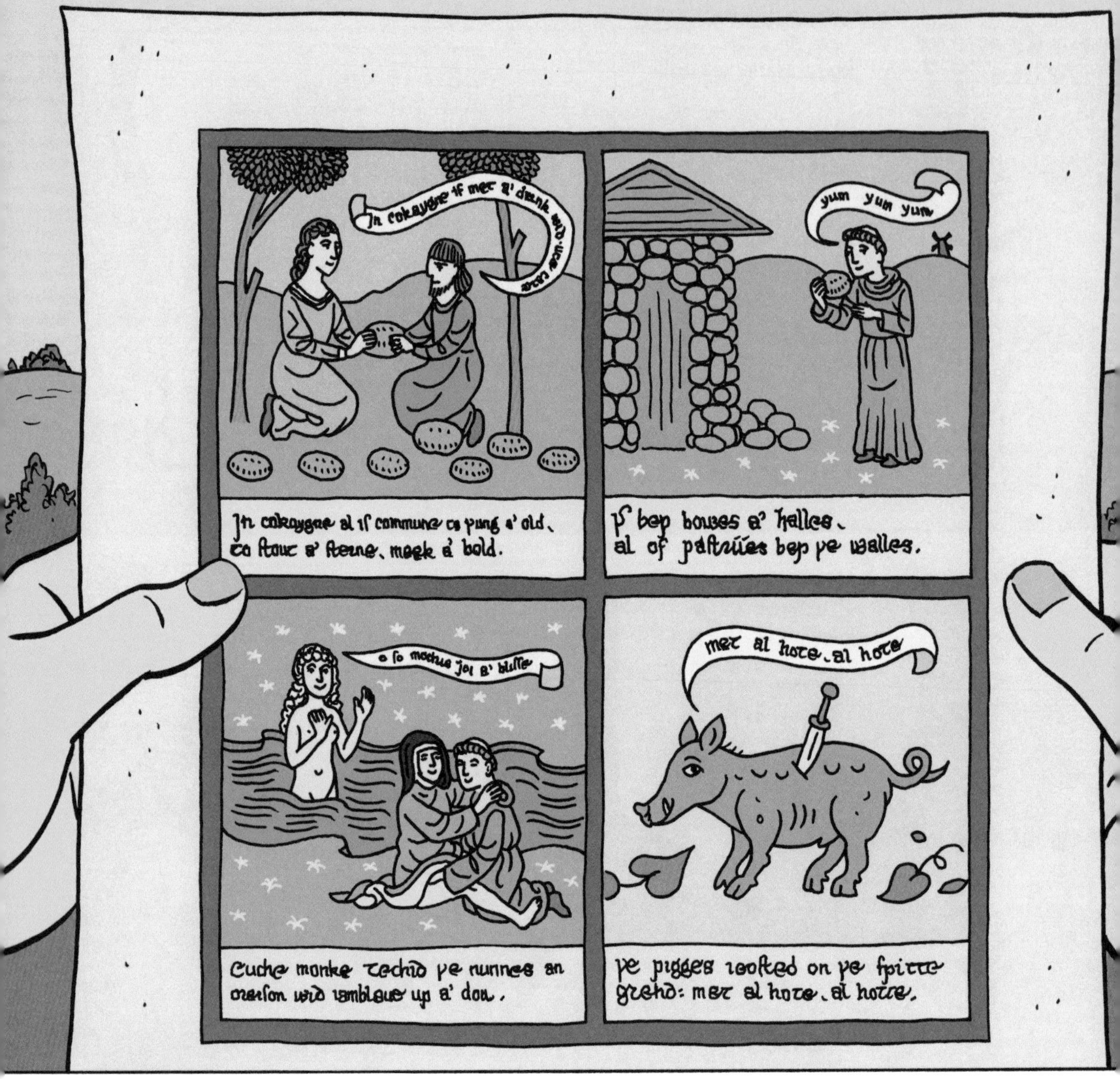
yum yum yum
Jn cokaygne al is commune to yung a' old. to stout a' sterne. meek a' bold.
þs beþ bowes a' halles. al of pastrües beþ ye walles.
o so mochus joi a' blisse
Euche monke techiþ ye nunnes an oreison wiþ iambleue up a' dou.
met al hote. al hote
ye pigges roosted on ye spitte grethþ: met al hote. al hotte.

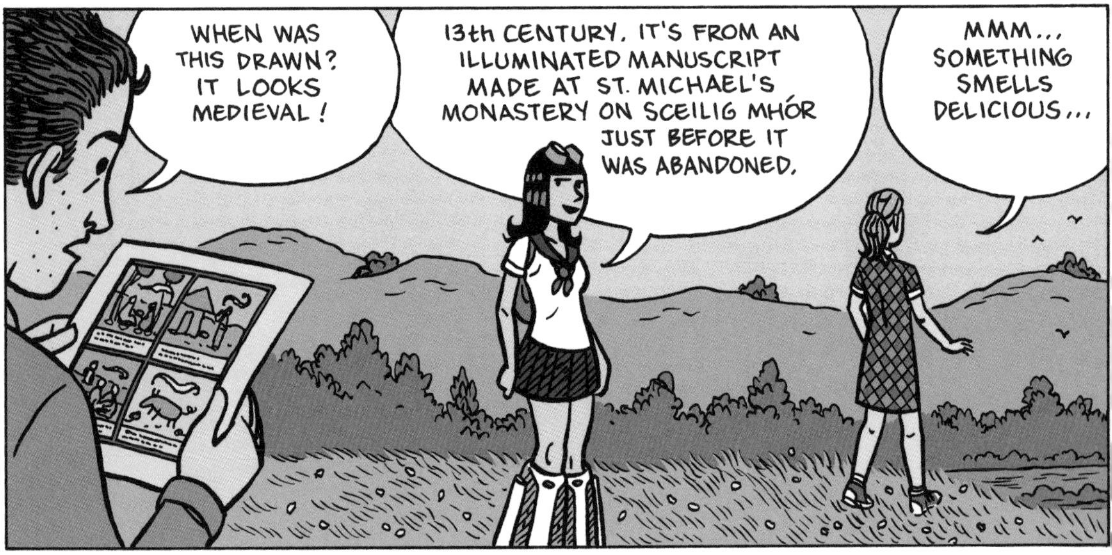
WHEN WAS THIS DRAWN? IT LOOKS MEDIEVAL!
13th CENTURY. IT'S FROM AN ILLUMINATED MANUSCRIPT MADE AT ST. MICHAEL'S MONASTERY ON SCEILIG MHÓR JUST BEFORE IT WAS ABANDONED.
MMM... SOMETHING SMELLS DELICIOUS...

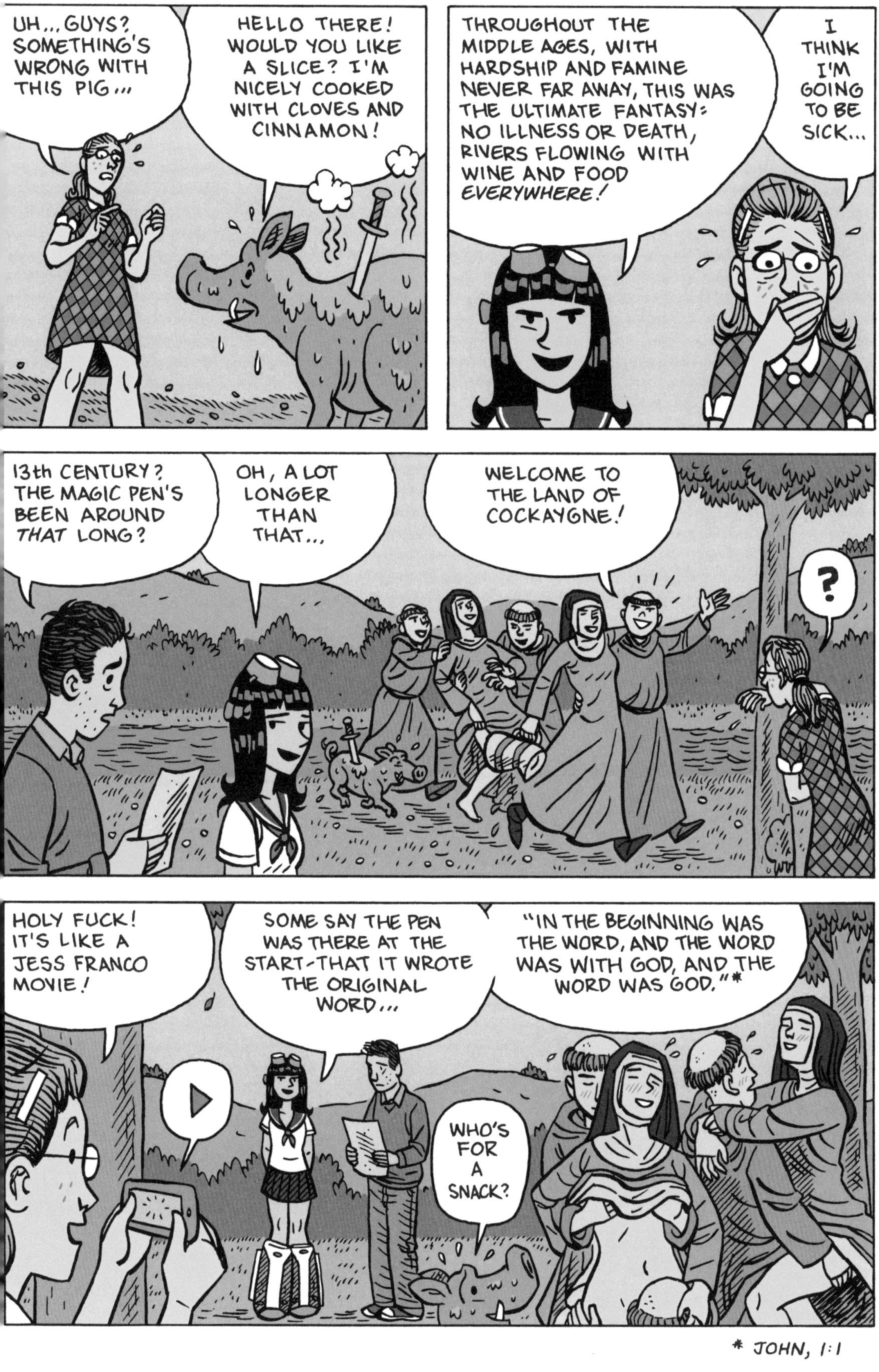
UH... GUYS? SOMETHING'S WRONG WITH THIS PIG...
HELLO THERE! WOULD YOU LIKE A SLICE? I'M NICELY COOKED WITH CLOVES AND CINNAMON!
THROUGHOUT THE MIDDLE AGES, WITH HARDSHIP AND FAMINE NEVER FAR AWAY, THIS WAS THE ULTIMATE FANTASY: NO ILLNESS OR DEATH, RIVERS FLOWING WITH WINE AND FOOD *EVERYWHERE!*
I THINK I'M GOING TO BE SICK...
13th CENTURY? THE MAGIC PEN'S BEEN AROUND *THAT* LONG?
OH, A LOT LONGER THAN THAT...
WELCOME TO THE LAND OF COCKAYGNE!
?
HOLY FUCK! IT'S LIKE A JESS FRANCO MOVIE!
SOME SAY THE PEN WAS THERE AT THE START-THAT IT WROTE THE ORIGINAL WORD...
"IN THE BEGINNING WAS THE WORD, AND THE WORD WAS WITH GOD, AND THE WORD WAS GOD."*
WHO'S FOR A SNACK?

* JOHN, 1:1

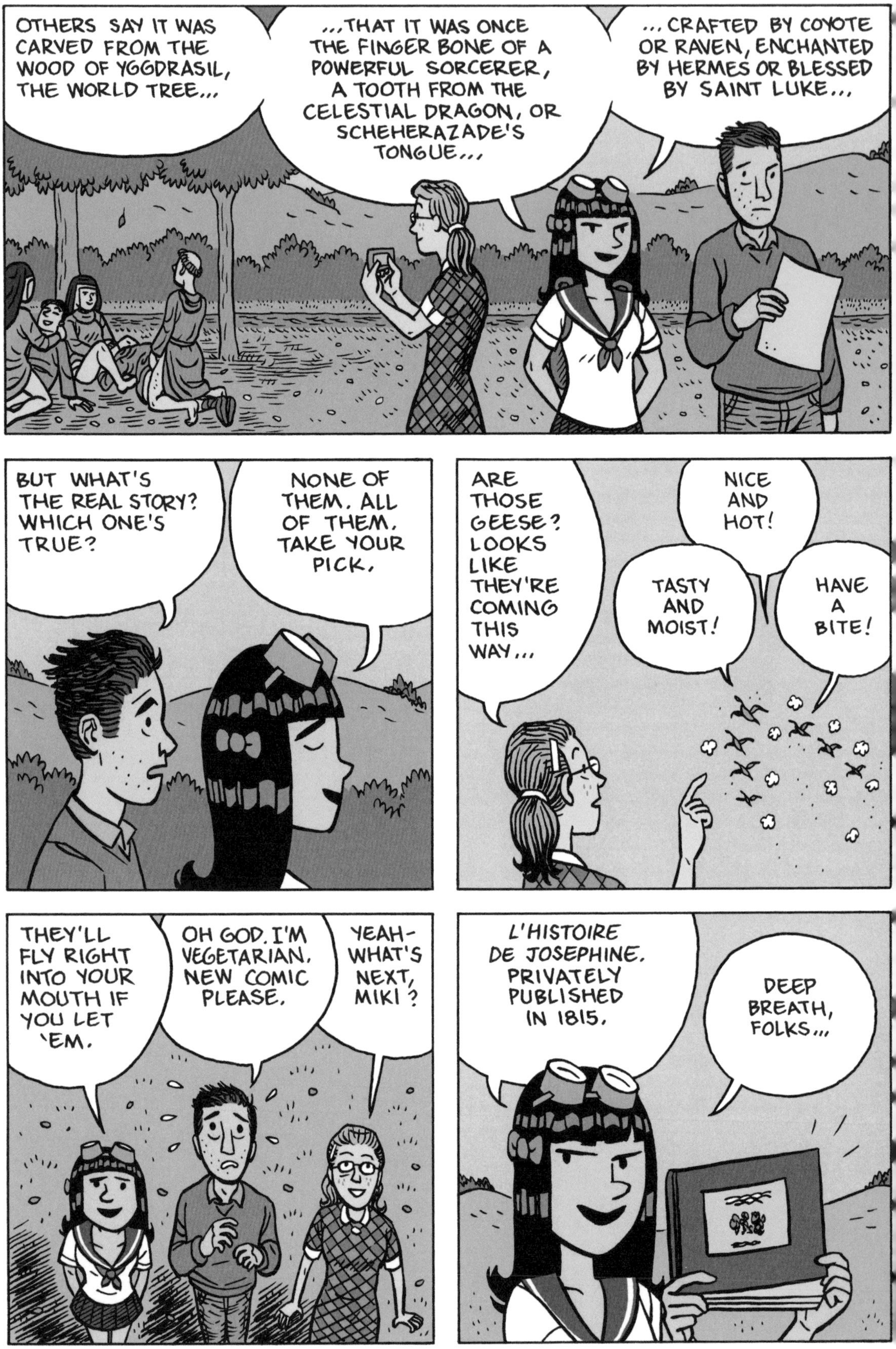
OTHERS SAY IT WAS CARVED FROM THE WOOD OF YGGDRASIL, THE WORLD TREE...
...THAT IT WAS ONCE THE FINGER BONE OF A POWERFUL SORCERER, A TOOTH FROM THE CELESTIAL DRAGON, OR SCHEHERAZADE'S TONGUE...
...CRAFTED BY COYOTE OR RAVEN, ENCHANTED BY HERMES OR BLESSED BY SAINT LUKE...
BUT WHAT'S THE REAL STORY? WHICH ONE'S TRUE?
NONE OF THEM. ALL OF THEM. TAKE YOUR PICK.
ARE THOSE GEESE? LOOKS LIKE THEY'RE COMING THIS WAY...
NICE AND HOT!
TASTY AND MOIST!
HAVE A BITE!
THEY'LL FLY RIGHT INTO YOUR MOUTH IF YOU LET 'EM.
OH GOD. I'M VEGETARIAN. NEW COMIC PLEASE.
YEAH- WHAT'S NEXT, MIKI?
L'HISTOIRE DE JOSEPHINE. PRIVATELY PUBLISHED IN 1815.
DEEP BREATH, FOLKS...

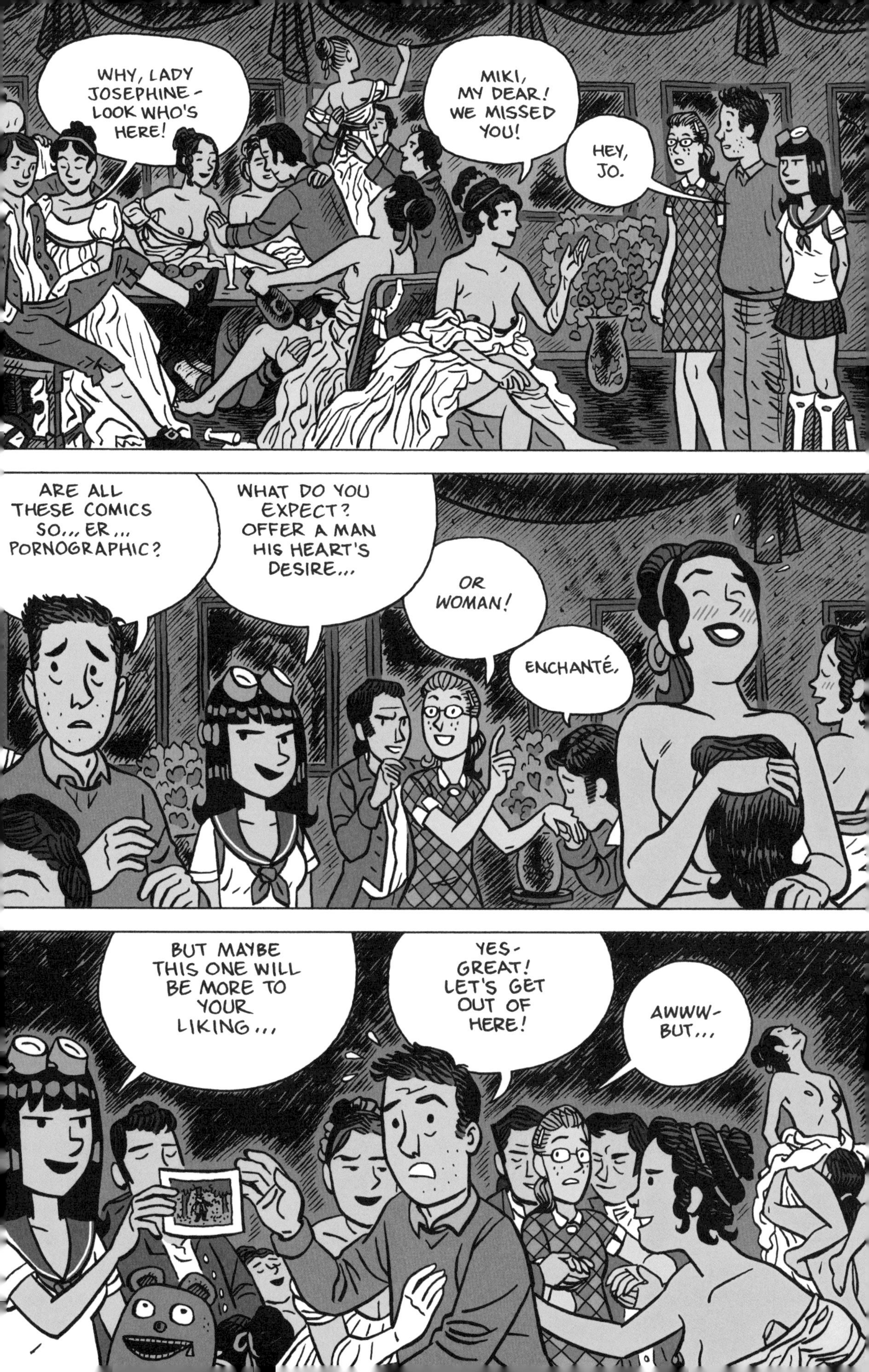
WHY, LADY JOSEPHINE - LOOK WHO'S HERE!
MIKI, MY DEAR! WE MISSED YOU!
HEY, JO.
ARE ALL THESE COMICS SO..., ER... PORNOGRAPHIC?
WHAT DO YOU EXPECT? OFFER A MAN HIS HEART'S DESIRE...
OR WOMAN!
ENCHANTÉ.
BUT MAYBE THIS ONE WILL BE MORE TO YOUR LIKING...
YES - GREAT! LET'S GET OUT OF HERE!
AWWW - BUT...

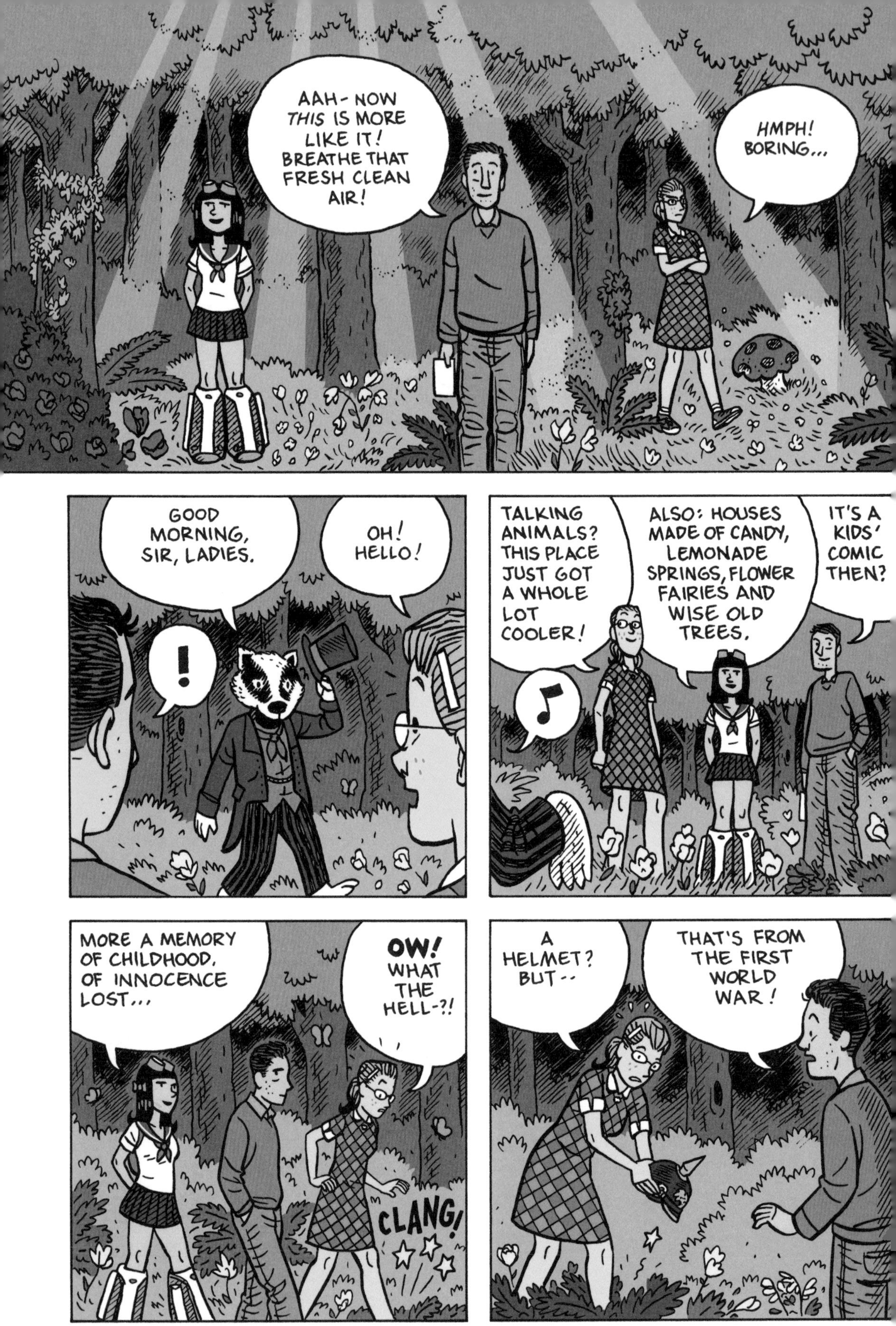
AAH- NOW *THIS* IS MORE LIKE IT! BREATHE THAT FRESH CLEAN AIR!
HMPH! BORING...
GOOD MORNING, SIR, LADIES.
!
OH! HELLO!
TALKING ANIMALS? THIS PLACE JUST GOT A WHOLE LOT COOLER!
ALSO: HOUSES MADE OF CANDY, LEMONADE SPRINGS, FLOWER FAIRIES AND WISE OLD TREES.
IT'S A KIDS' COMIC THEN?
MORE A MEMORY OF CHILDHOOD, OF INNOCENCE LOST...
OW! WHAT THE HELL-?!
CLANG!
A HELMET? BUT--
THAT'S FROM THE FIRST WORLD WAR!

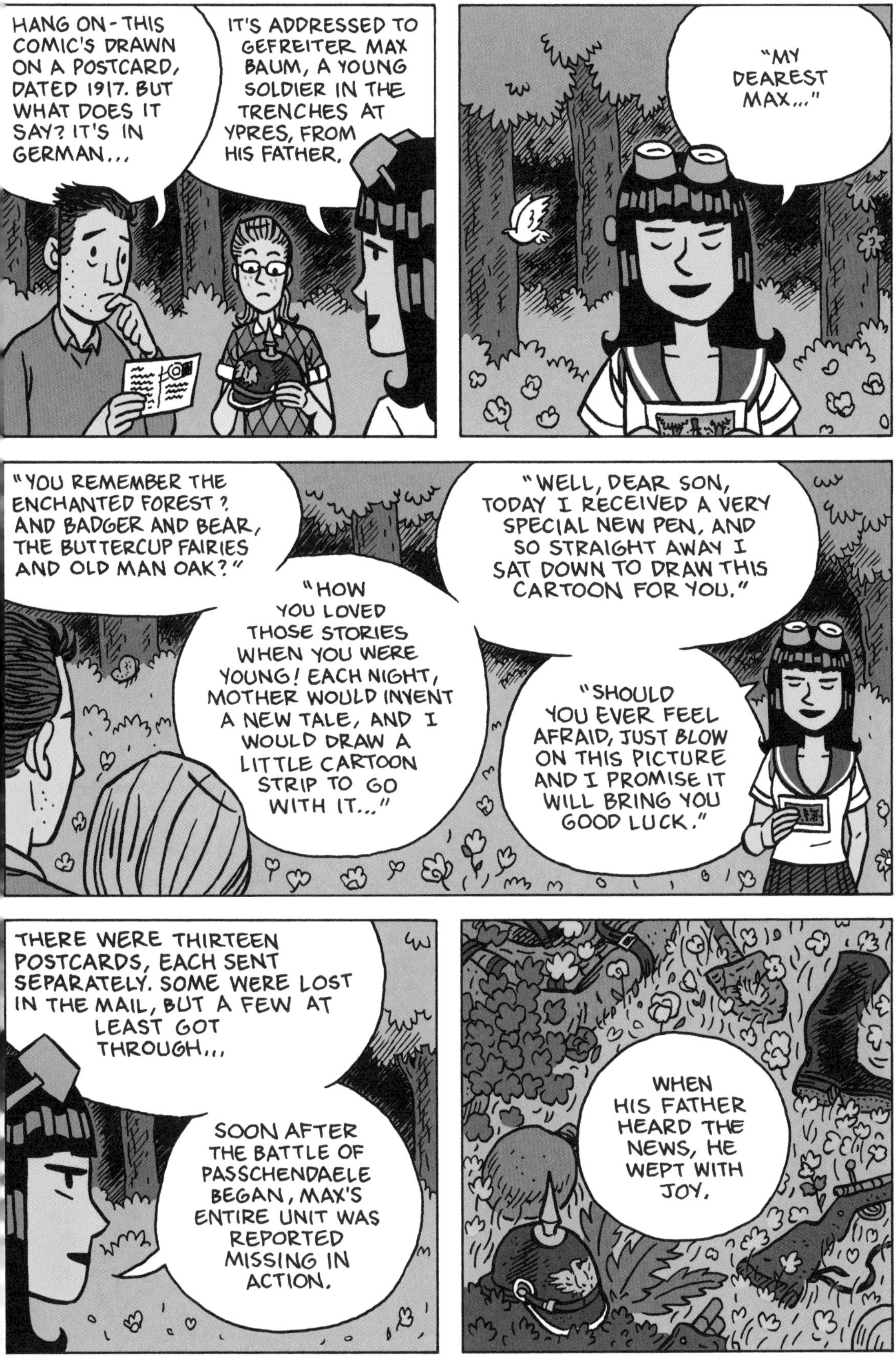
HANG ON - THIS COMIC'S DRAWN ON A POSTCARD, DATED 1917. BUT WHAT DOES IT SAY? IT'S IN GERMAN...
IT'S ADDRESSED TO GEFREITER MAX BAUM, A YOUNG SOLDIER IN THE TRENCHES AT YPRES, FROM HIS FATHER.
"MY DEAREST MAX..."
"YOU REMEMBER THE ENCHANTED FOREST? AND BADGER AND BEAR, THE BUTTERCUP FAIRIES AND OLD MAN OAK?"
"HOW YOU LOVED THOSE STORIES WHEN YOU WERE YOUNG! EACH NIGHT, MOTHER WOULD INVENT A NEW TALE, AND I WOULD DRAW A LITTLE CARTOON STRIP TO GO WITH IT..."
"WELL, DEAR SON, TODAY I RECEIVED A VERY SPECIAL NEW PEN, AND SO STRAIGHT AWAY I SAT DOWN TO DRAW THIS CARTOON FOR YOU."
"SHOULD YOU EVER FEEL AFRAID, JUST BLOW ON THIS PICTURE AND I PROMISE IT WILL BRING YOU GOOD LUCK."
THERE WERE THIRTEEN POSTCARDS, EACH SENT SEPARATELY. SOME WERE LOST IN THE MAIL, BUT A FEW AT LEAST GOT THROUGH...
SOON AFTER THE BATTLE OF PASSCHENDAELE BEGAN, MAX'S ENTIRE UNIT WAS REPORTED MISSING IN ACTION.
WHEN HIS FATHER HEARD THE NEWS, HE WEPT WITH JOY.

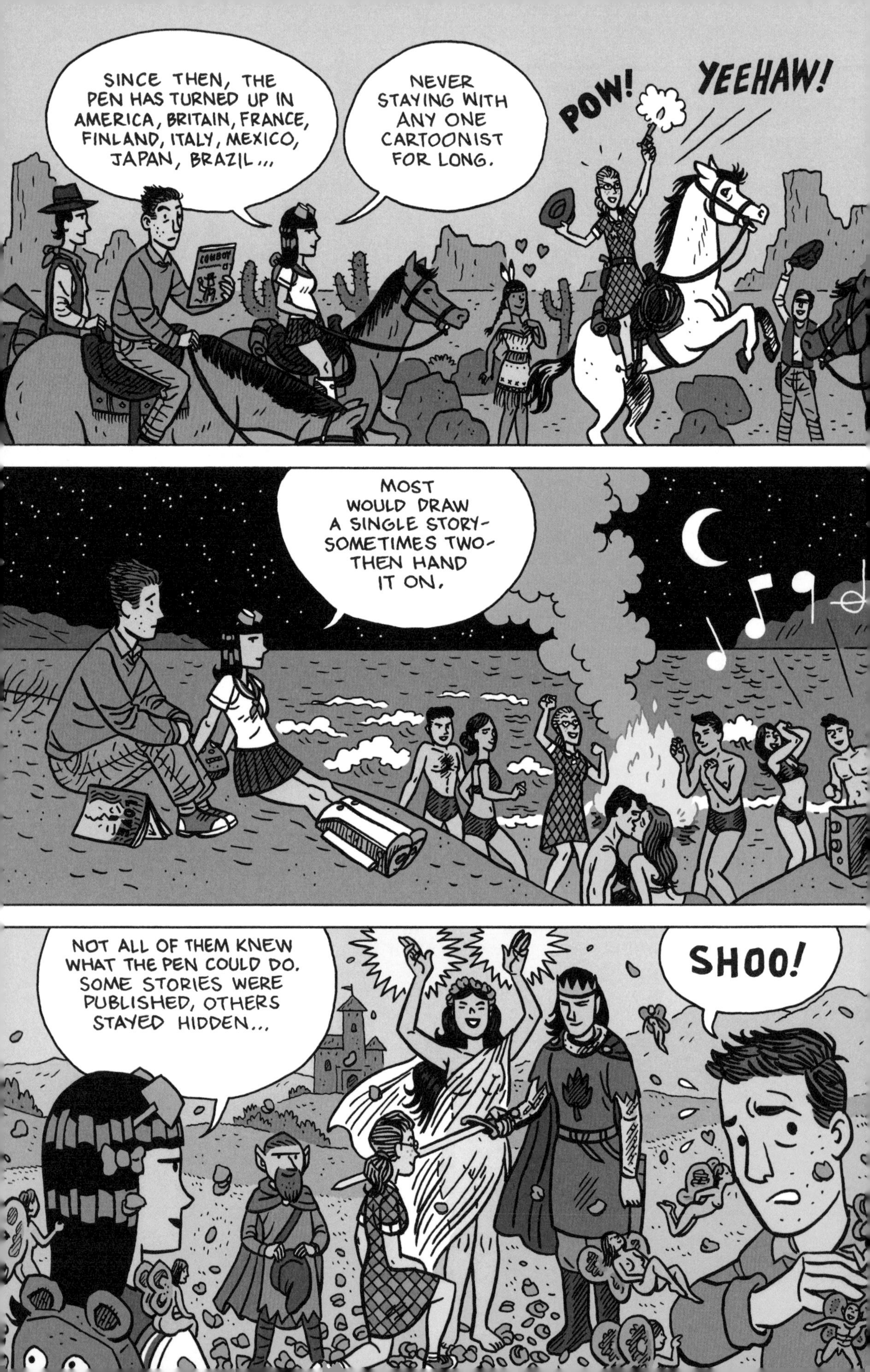
SINCE THEN, THE PEN HAS TURNED UP IN AMERICA, BRITAIN, FRANCE, FINLAND, ITALY, MEXICO, JAPAN, BRAZIL...
NEVER STAYING WITH ANY ONE CARTOONIST FOR LONG.
POW!
YEEHAW!
COWBOY
MOST WOULD DRAW A SINGLE STORY- SOMETIMES TWO- THEN HAND IT ON.
NOT ALL OF THEM KNEW WHAT THE PEN COULD DO. SOME STORIES WERE PUBLISHED, OTHERS STAYED HIDDEN...
SHOO!

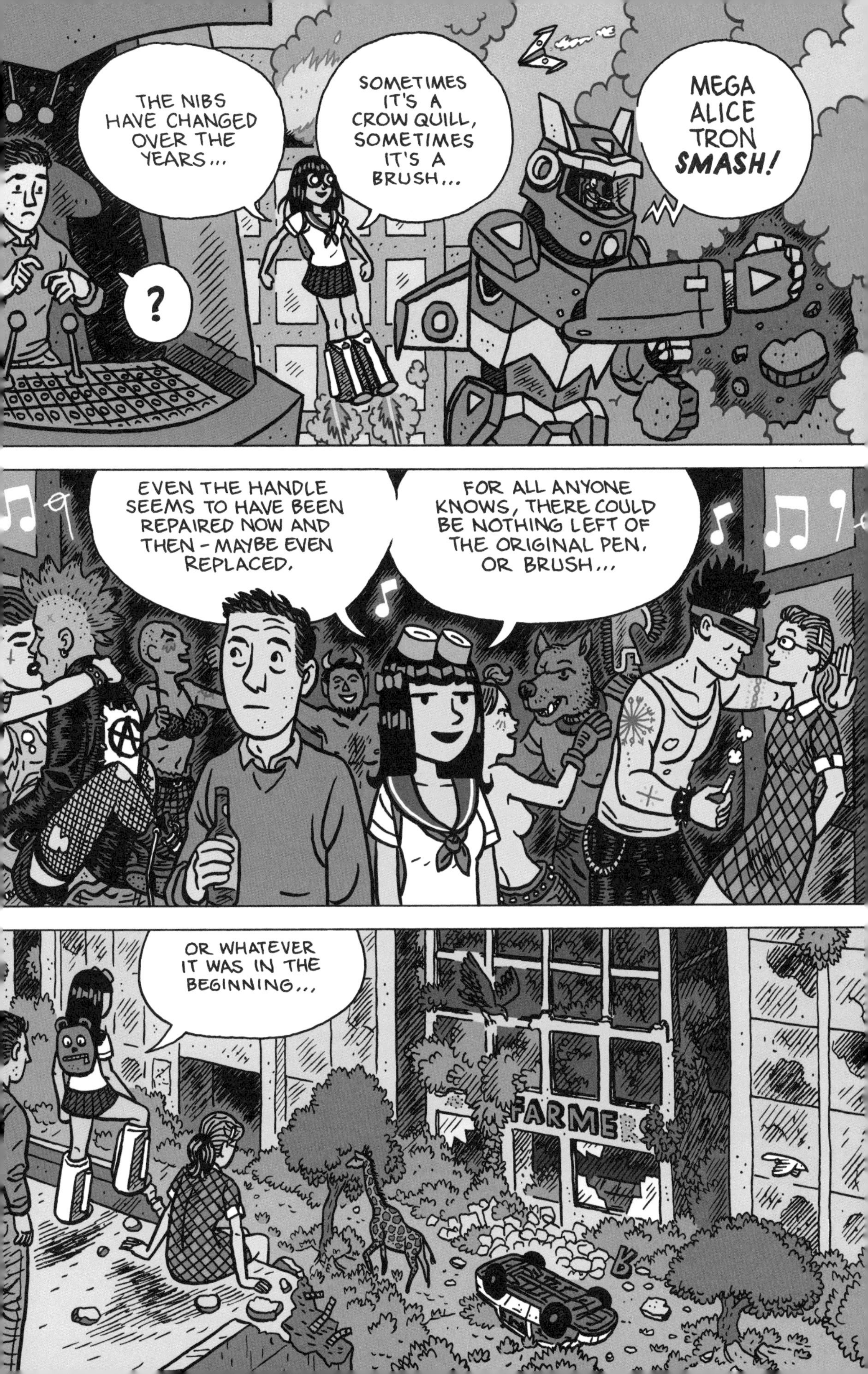
THE NIBS HAVE CHANGED OVER THE YEARS...
SOMETIMES IT'S A CROW QUILL, SOMETIMES IT'S A BRUSH...
MEGA ALICE TRON SMASH!
?
EVEN THE HANDLE SEEMS TO HAVE BEEN REPAIRED NOW AND THEN - MAYBE EVEN REPLACED.
FOR ALL ANYONE KNOWS, THERE COULD BE NOTHING LEFT OF THE ORIGINAL PEN, OR BRUSH...
OR WHATEVER IT WAS IN THE BEGINNING...
FARME

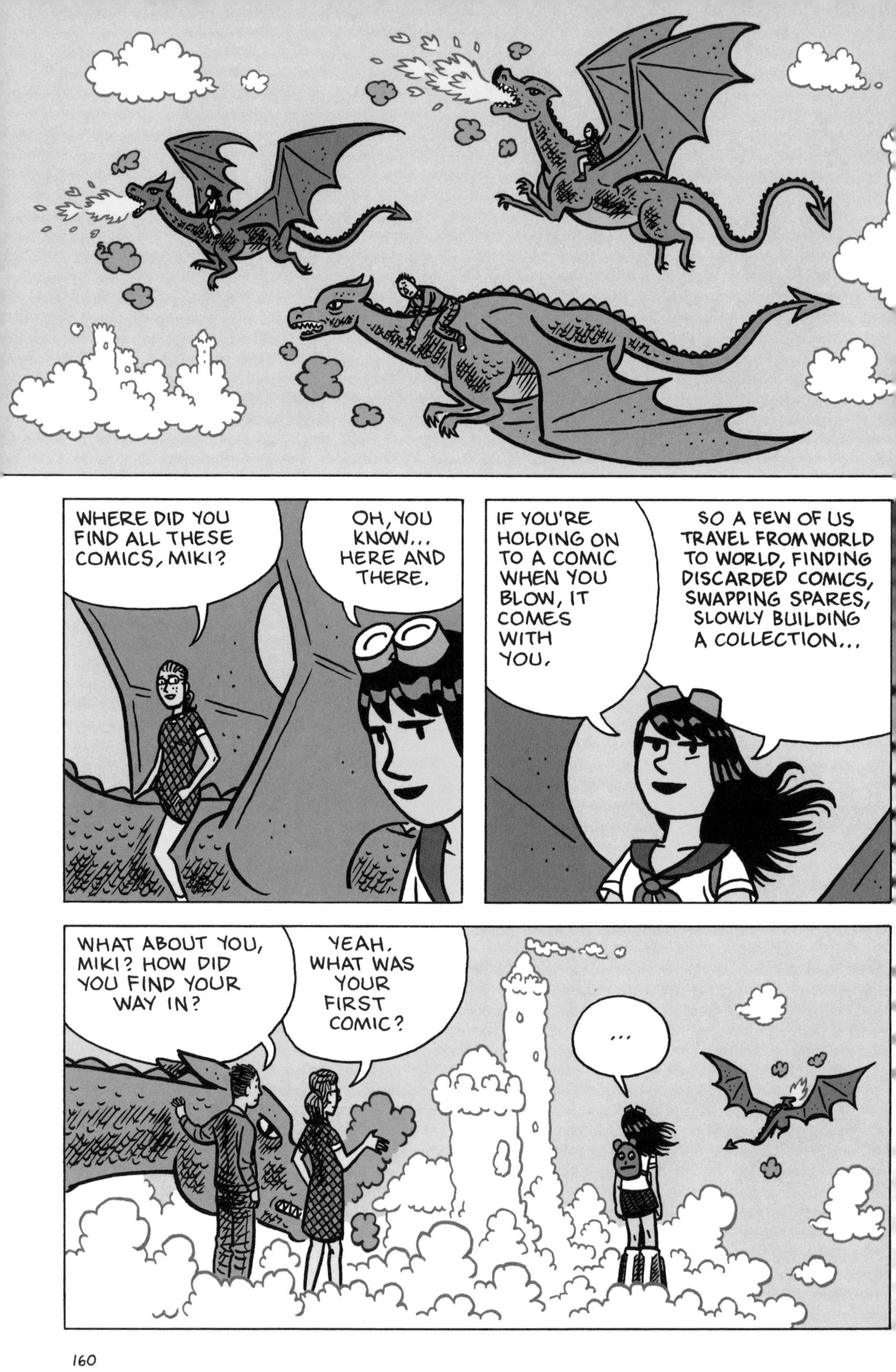
WHERE DID YOU FIND ALL THESE COMICS, MIKI?
OH, YOU KNOW... HERE AND THERE.
IF YOU'RE HOLDING ON TO A COMIC WHEN YOU BLOW, IT COMES WITH YOU.
SO A FEW OF US TRAVEL FROM WORLD TO WORLD, FINDING DISCARDED COMICS, SWAPPING SPARES, SLOWLY BUILDING A COLLECTION...
WHAT ABOUT YOU, MIKI? HOW DID YOU FIND YOUR WAY IN?
YEAH. WHAT WAS YOUR FIRST COMIC?
...

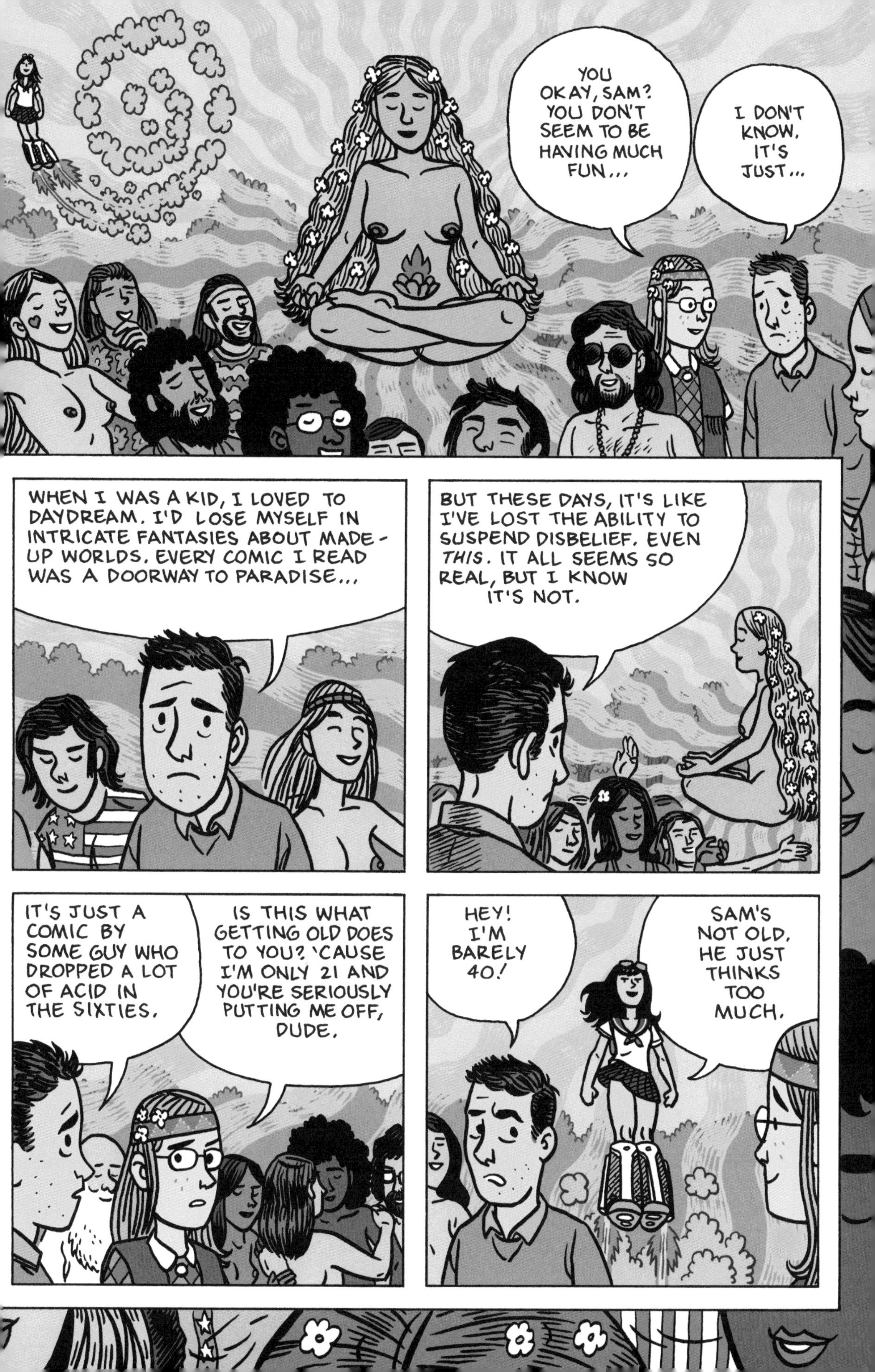
YOU OKAY, SAM? YOU DON'T SEEM TO BE HAVING MUCH FUN...
I DON'T KNOW. IT'S JUST...
WHEN I WAS A KID, I LOVED TO DAYDREAM. I'D LOSE MYSELF IN INTRICATE FANTASIES ABOUT MADE-UP WORLDS. EVERY COMIC I READ WAS A DOORWAY TO PARADISE...
BUT THESE DAYS, IT'S LIKE I'VE LOST THE ABILITY TO SUSPEND DISBELIEF. EVEN *THIS*. IT ALL SEEMS SO REAL, BUT I KNOW IT'S NOT.
IT'S JUST A COMIC BY SOME GUY WHO DROPPED A LOT OF ACID IN THE SIXTIES.
IS THIS WHAT GETTING OLD DOES TO YOU? 'CAUSE I'M ONLY 21 AND YOU'RE SERIOUSLY PUTTING ME OFF, DUDE.
HEY! I'M BARELY 40!
SAM'S NOT OLD. HE JUST THINKS TOO MUCH.

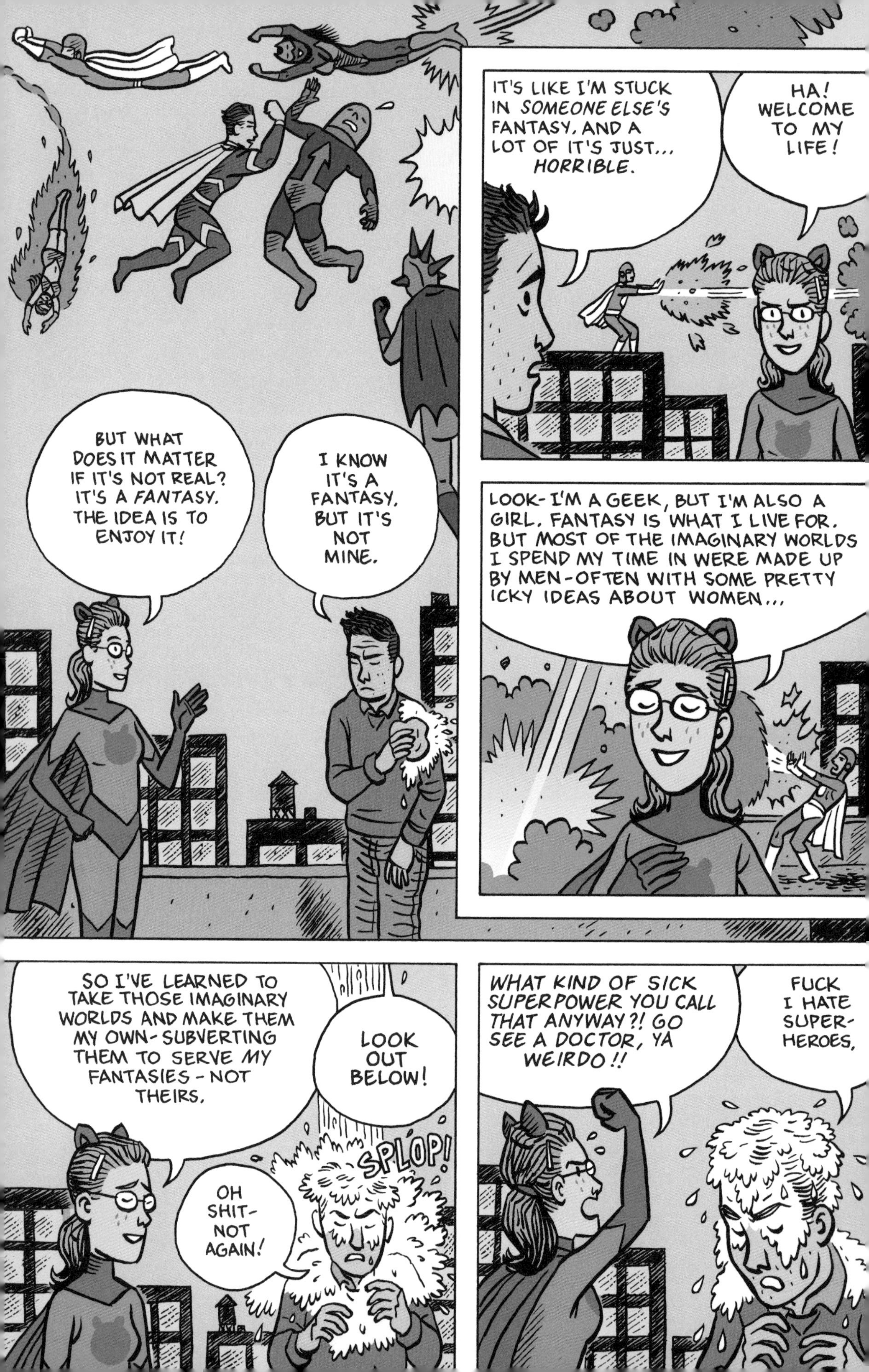

IT'S LIKE I'M STUCK IN SOMEONE ELSE'S FANTASY, AND A LOT OF IT'S JUST... HORRIBLE.
HA! WELCOME TO MY LIFE!
BUT WHAT DOES IT MATTER IF IT'S NOT REAL? IT'S A FANTASY. THE IDEA IS TO ENJOY IT!
I KNOW IT'S A FANTASY, BUT IT'S NOT MINE.
LOOK- I'M A GEEK, BUT I'M ALSO A GIRL. FANTASY IS WHAT I LIVE FOR. BUT MOST OF THE IMAGINARY WORLDS I SPEND MY TIME IN WERE MADE UP BY MEN - OFTEN WITH SOME PRETTY ICKY IDEAS ABOUT WOMEN...
SO I'VE LEARNED TO TAKE THOSE IMAGINARY WORLDS AND MAKE THEM MY OWN - SUBVERTING THEM TO SERVE MY FANTASIES - NOT THEIRS.
LOOK OUT BELOW!
SPLOP!
OH SHIT- NOT AGAIN!
WHAT KIND OF SICK SUPERPOWER YOU CALL THAT ANYWAY?! GO SEE A DOCTOR, YA WEIRDO!!
FUCK I HATE SUPER-HEROES.

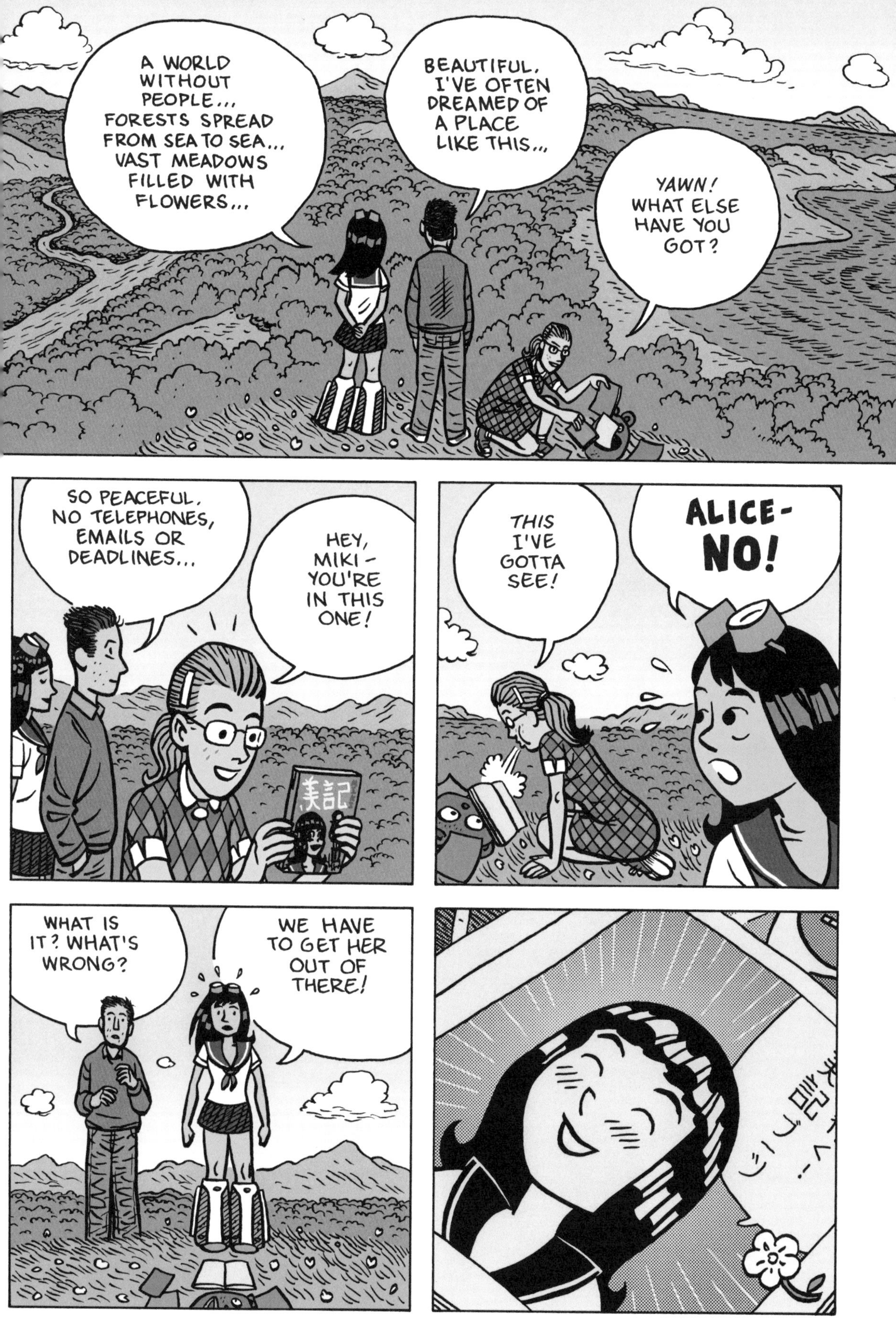
A WORLD WITHOUT PEOPLE... FORESTS SPREAD FROM SEA TO SEA... VAST MEADOWS FILLED WITH FLOWERS...
BEAUTIFUL. I'VE OFTEN DREAMED OF A PLACE LIKE THIS...
YAWN! WHAT ELSE HAVE YOU GOT?
SO PEACEFUL. NO TELEPHONES, EMAILS OR DEADLINES...
HEY, MIKI - YOU'RE IN THIS ONE!
美記
THIS I'VE GOTTA SEE!
ALICE- NO!
WHAT IS IT? WHAT'S WRONG?
WE HAVE TO GET HER OUT OF THERE!

CHAPTER ELEVEN: THE DREAMERS

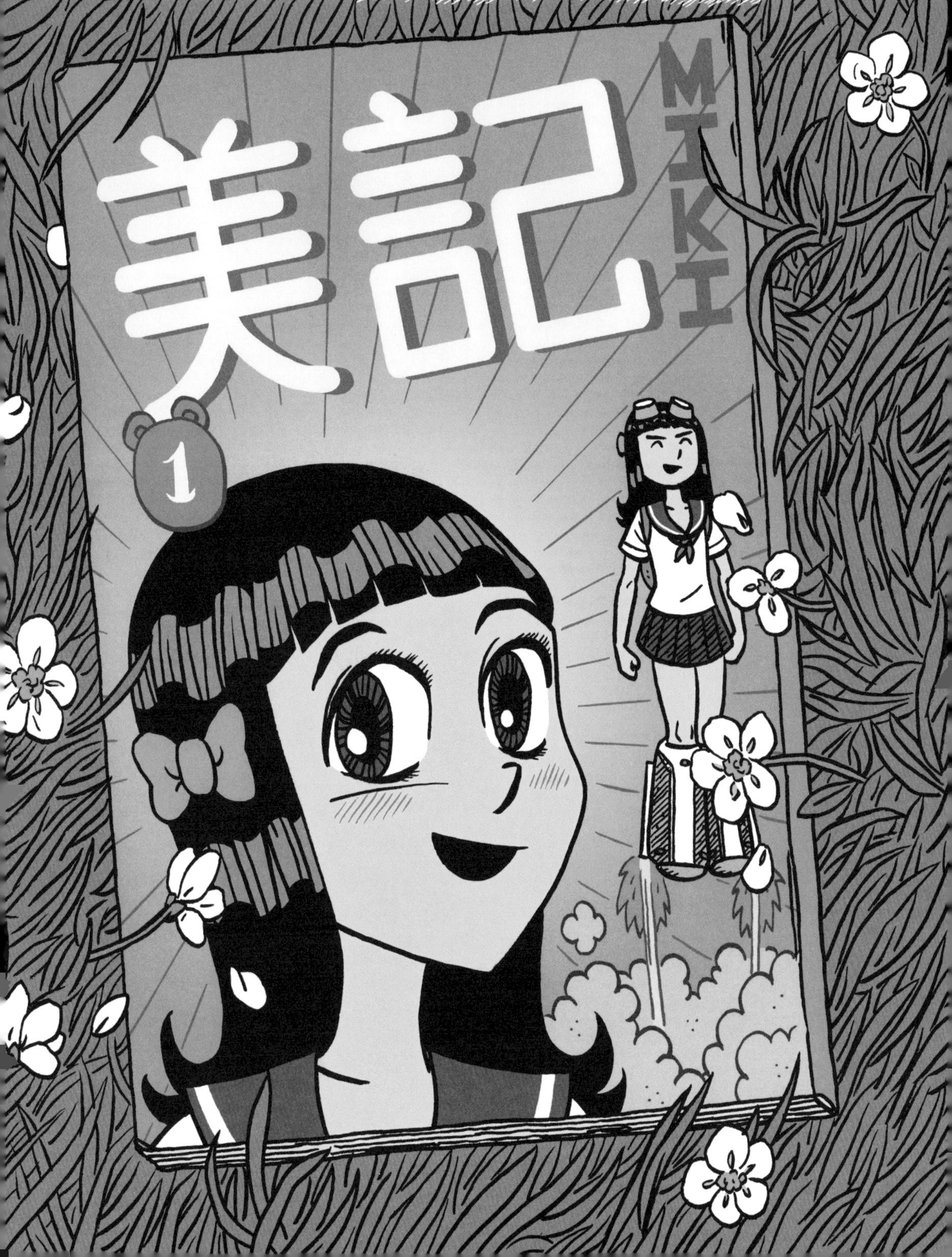
美記
MIKI
1

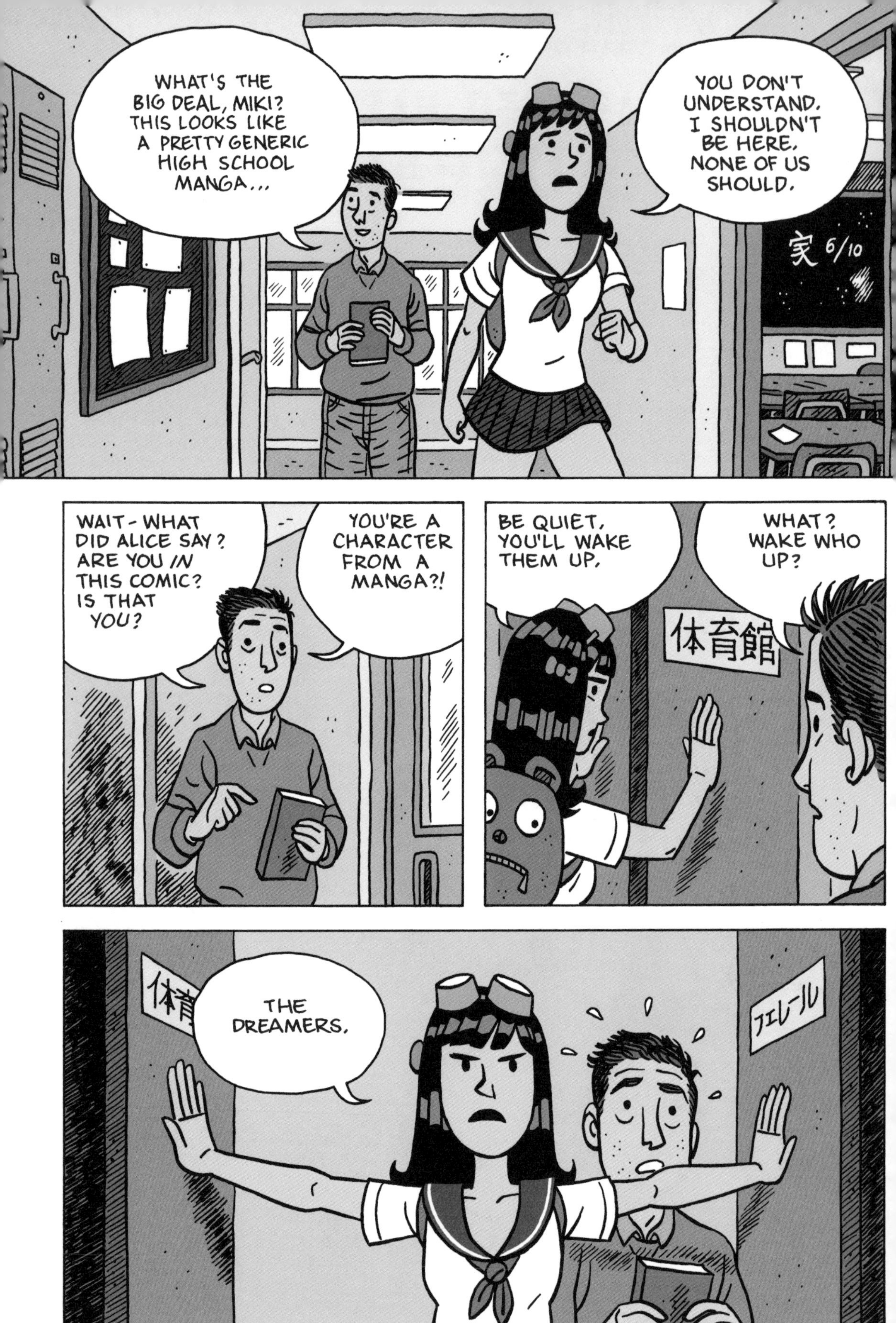
WHAT'S THE BIG DEAL, MIKI? THIS LOOKS LIKE A PRETTY GENERIC HIGH SCHOOL MANGA...
YOU DON'T UNDERSTAND. I SHOULDN'T BE HERE. NONE OF US SHOULD.
6/10
WAIT- WHAT DID ALICE SAY? ARE YOU *IN* THIS COMIC? IS THAT YOU?
YOU'RE A CHARACTER FROM A MANGA?!
BE QUIET. YOU'LL WAKE THEM UP.
WHAT? WAKE WHO UP?
体育館
THE DREAMERS.
アエレール

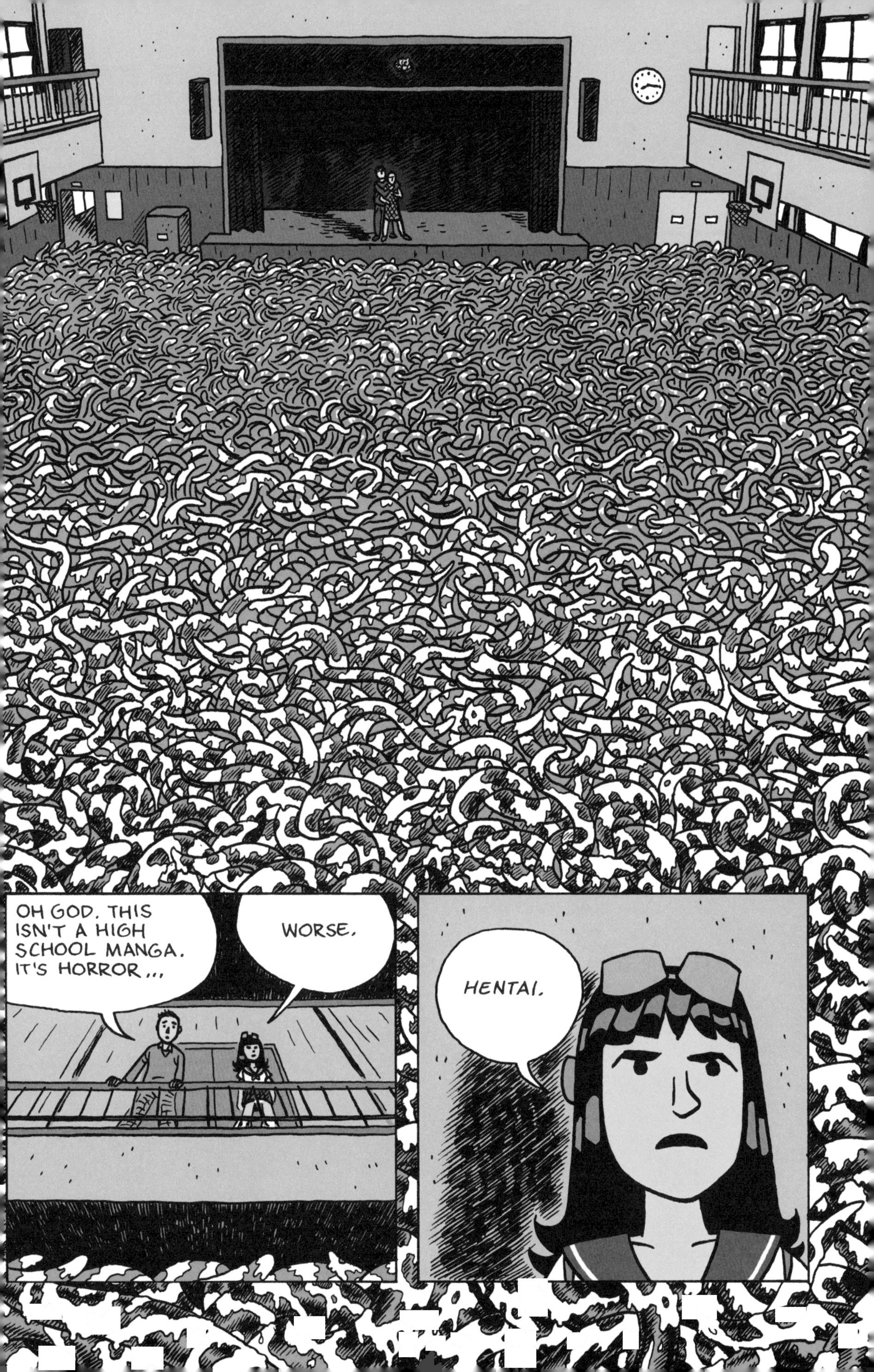
OH GOD. THIS ISN'T A HIGH SCHOOL MANGA. IT'S HORROR...
WORSE.
HENTAI.

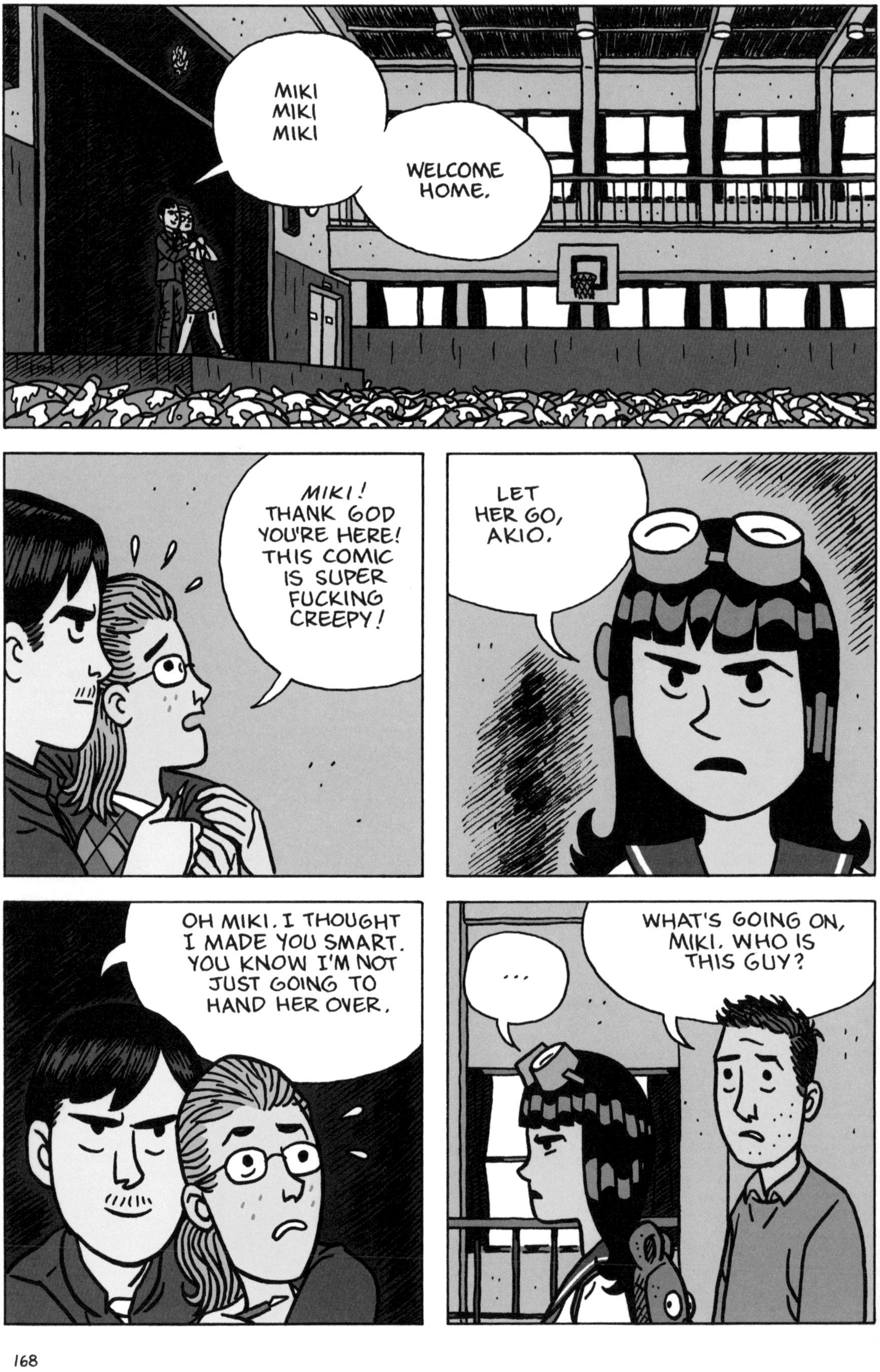
MIKI MIKI MIKI
WELCOME HOME.
MIKI! THANK GOD YOU'RE HERE! THIS COMIC IS SUPER FUCKING CREEPY!
LET HER GO, AKIO.
OH MIKI. I THOUGHT I MADE YOU SMART. YOU KNOW I'M NOT JUST GOING TO HAND HER OVER.
...
WHAT'S GOING ON, MIKI. WHO IS THIS GUY?

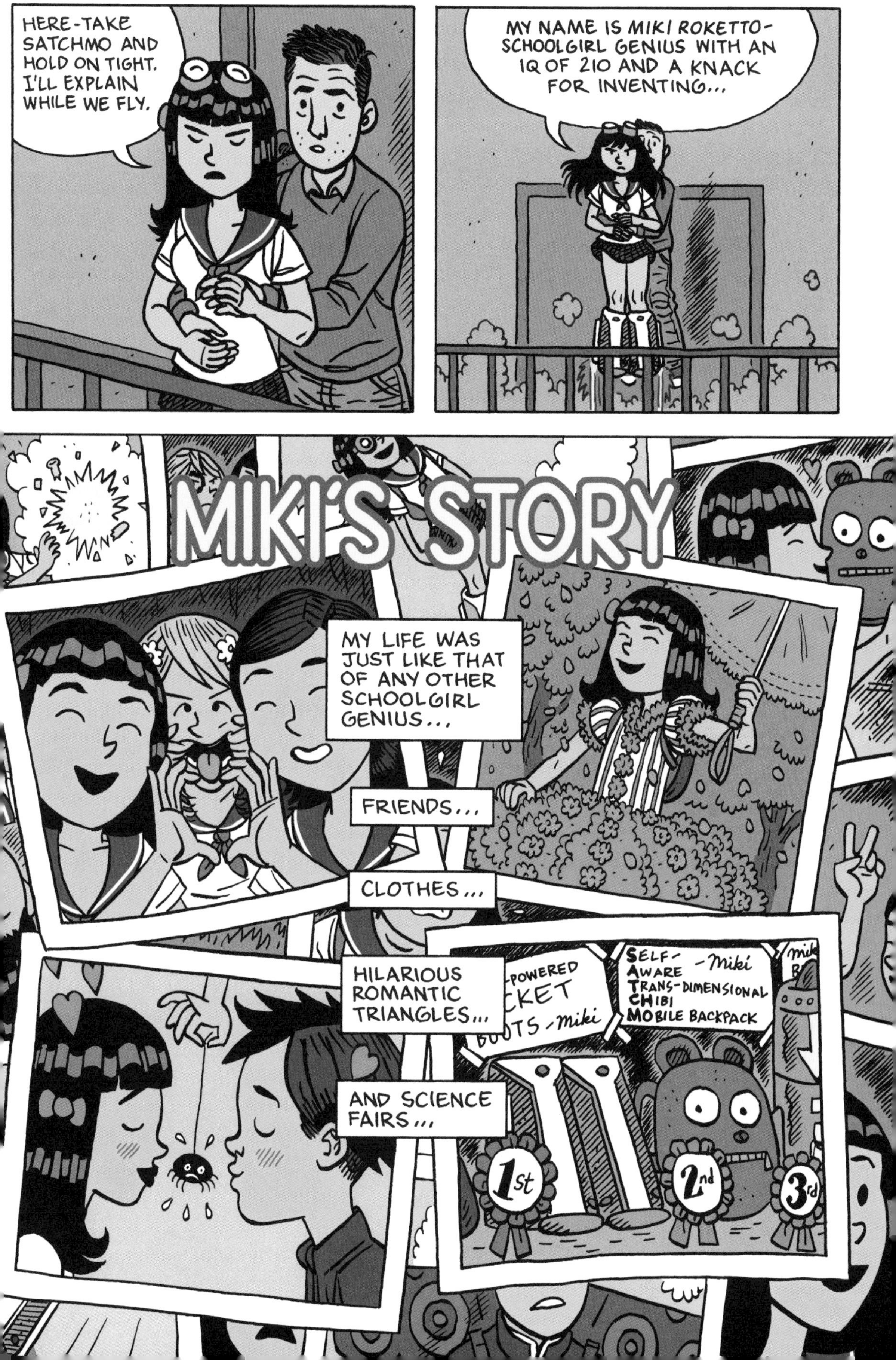
HERE-TAKE SATCHMO AND HOLD ON TIGHT. I'LL EXPLAIN WHILE WE FLY.
MY NAME IS MIKI ROKETTO-SCHOOLGIRL GENIUS WITH AN IQ OF 210 AND A KNACK FOR INVENTING...
MIKI'S STORY
MY LIFE WAS JUST LIKE THAT OF ANY OTHER SCHOOLGIRL GENIUS...
FRIENDS...
CLOTHES...
HILARIOUS ROMANTIC TRIANGLES...
AND SCIENCE FAIRS...
-POWERED
CKET
BOOTS -miki
SELF-AWARE TRANS-DIMENSIONAL CHIBI MOBILE BACKPACK -Miki
1st
2nd
3rd

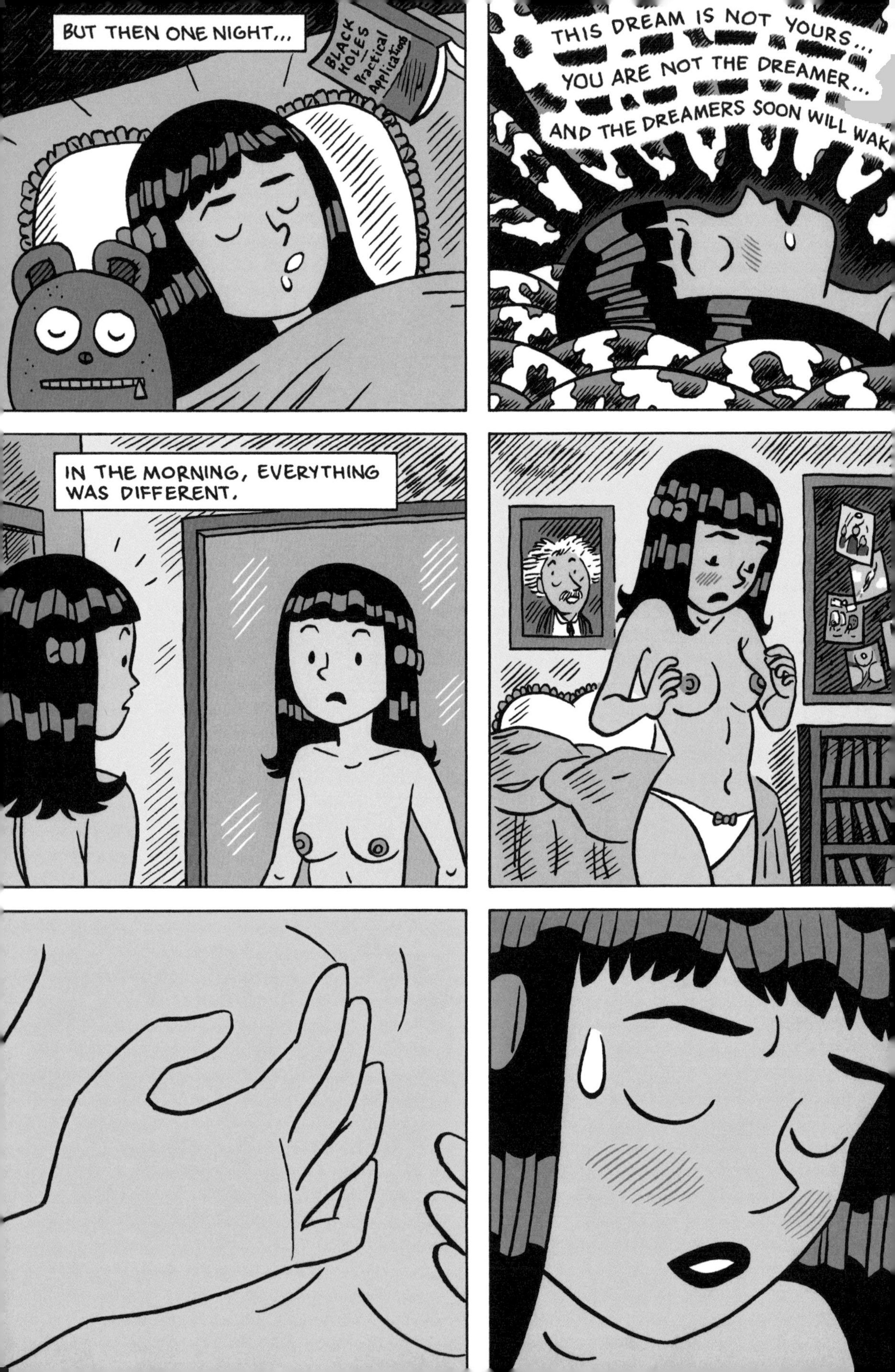
BUT THEN ONE NIGHT...
BLACK HOLES — Practical Applications
THIS DREAM IS NOT YOURS...
YOU ARE NOT THE DREAMER...
AND THE DREAMERS SOON WILL WAK
IN THE MORNING, EVERYTHING WAS DIFFERENT.

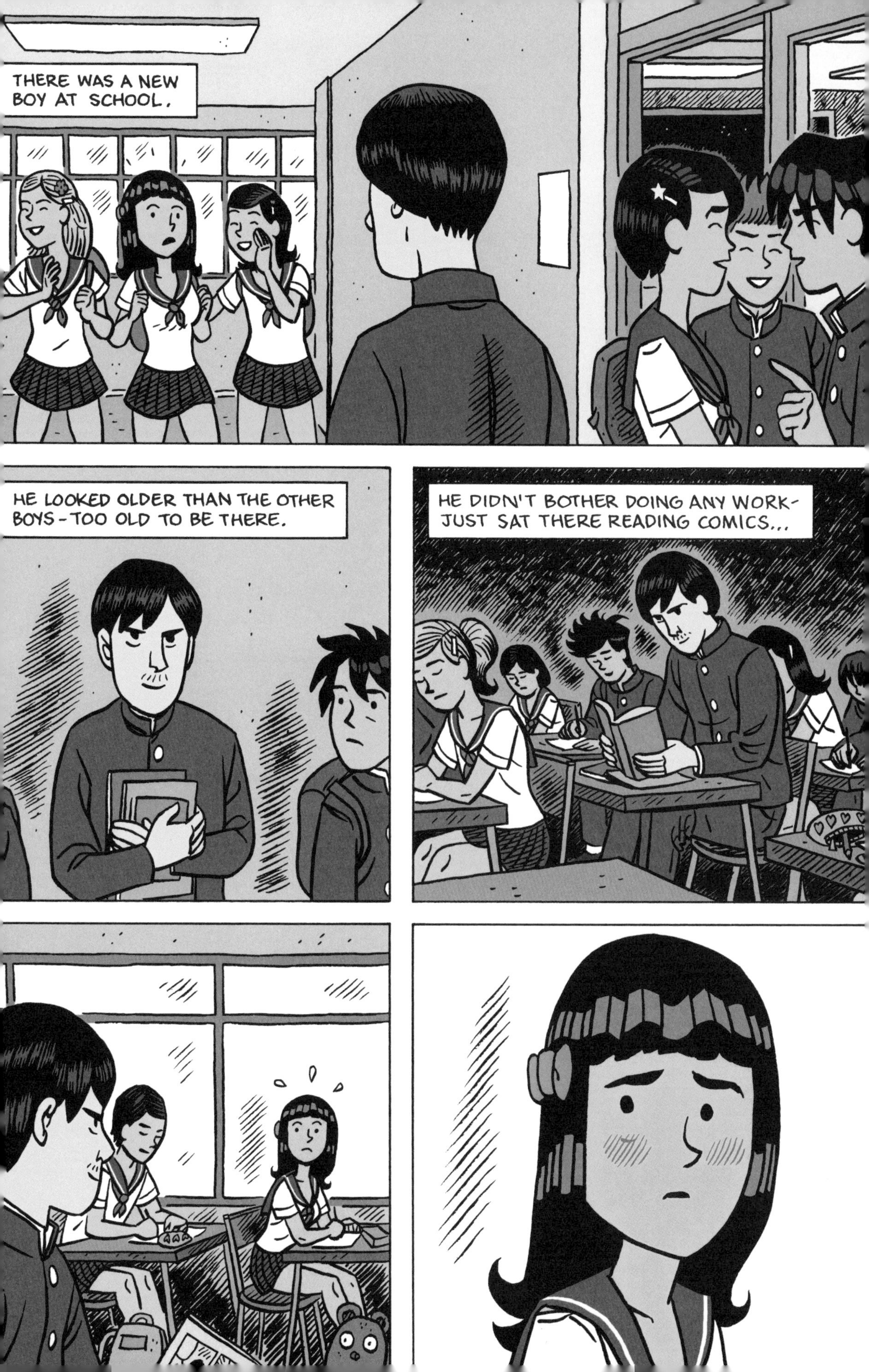
THERE WAS A NEW BOY AT SCHOOL.
HE LOOKED OLDER THAN THE OTHER BOYS - TOO OLD TO BE THERE.
HE DIDN'T BOTHER DOING ANY WORK- JUST SAT THERE READING COMICS...

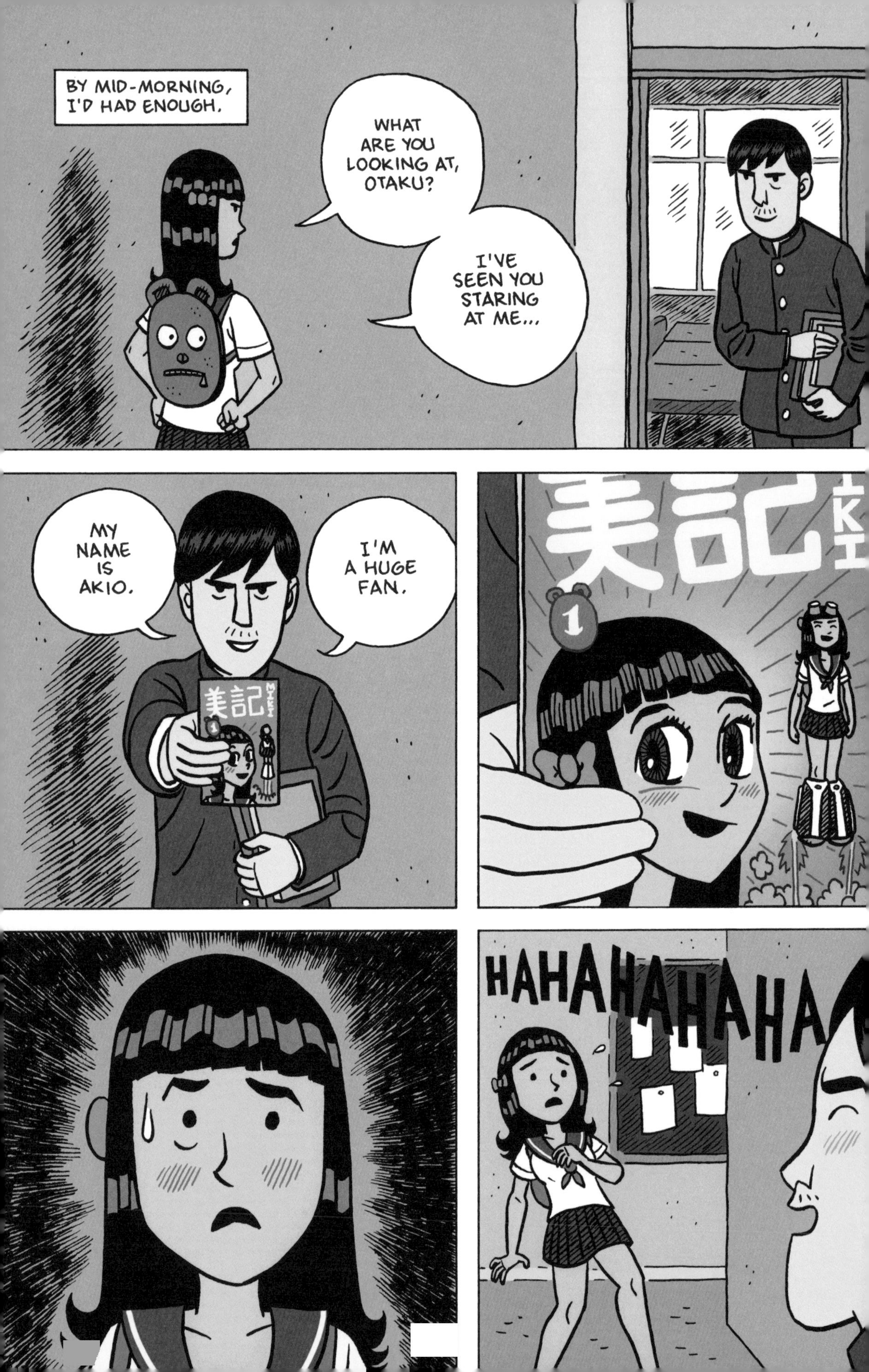
BY MID-MORNING, I'D HAD ENOUGH.
WHAT ARE YOU LOOKING AT, OTAKU?
I'VE SEEN YOU STARING AT ME...
MY NAME IS AKIO.
I'M A HUGE FAN.
美記
HAHAHAHAHAHA

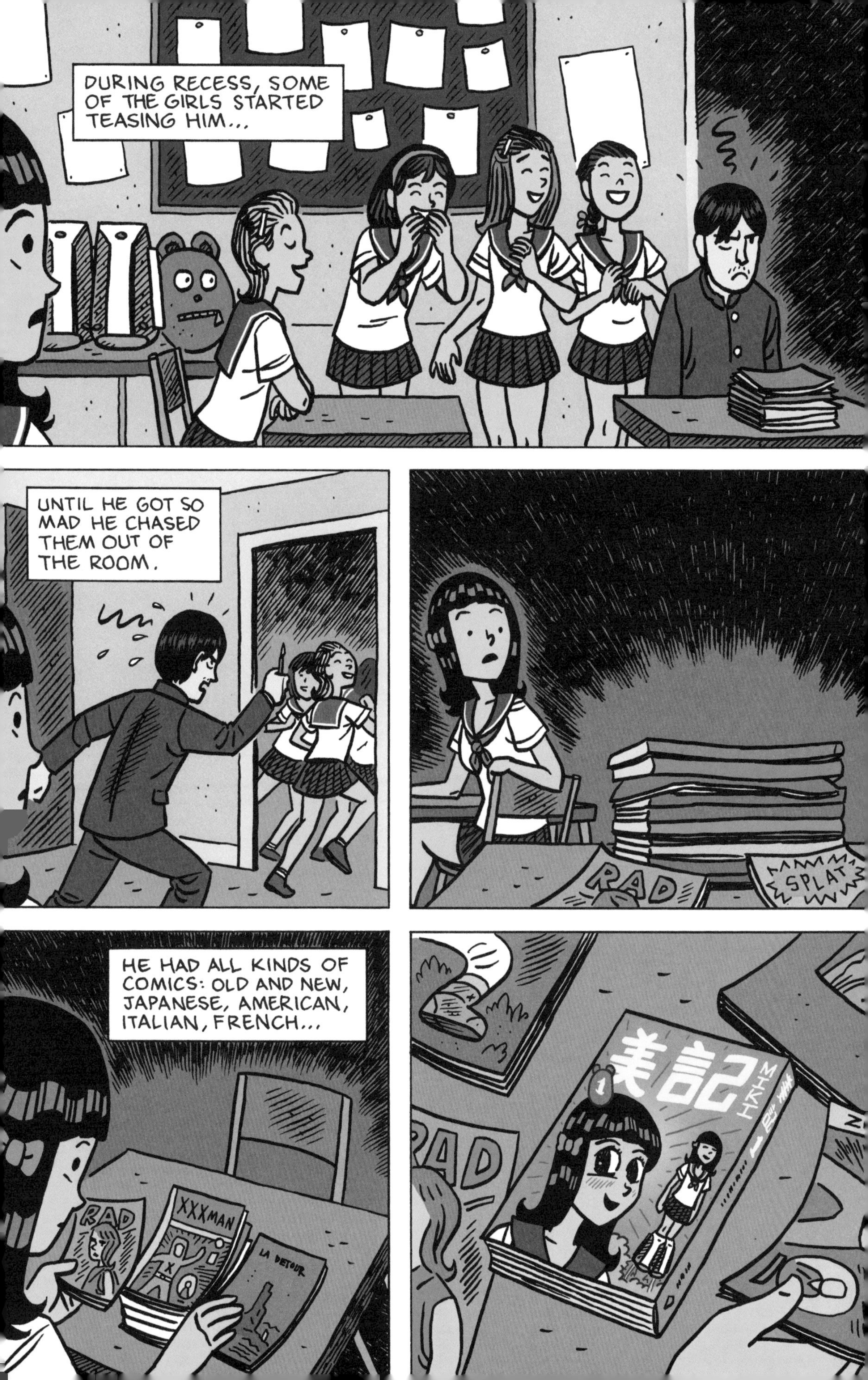
DURING RECESS, SOME OF THE GIRLS STARTED TEASING HIM...
UNTIL HE GOT SO MAD HE CHASED THEM OUT OF THE ROOM.
RAD
SPLAT
HE HAD ALL KINDS OF COMICS: OLD AND NEW, JAPANESE, AMERICAN, ITALIAN, FRENCH...
RAD
XXXMAN
LA DETOUR
美記
RAD

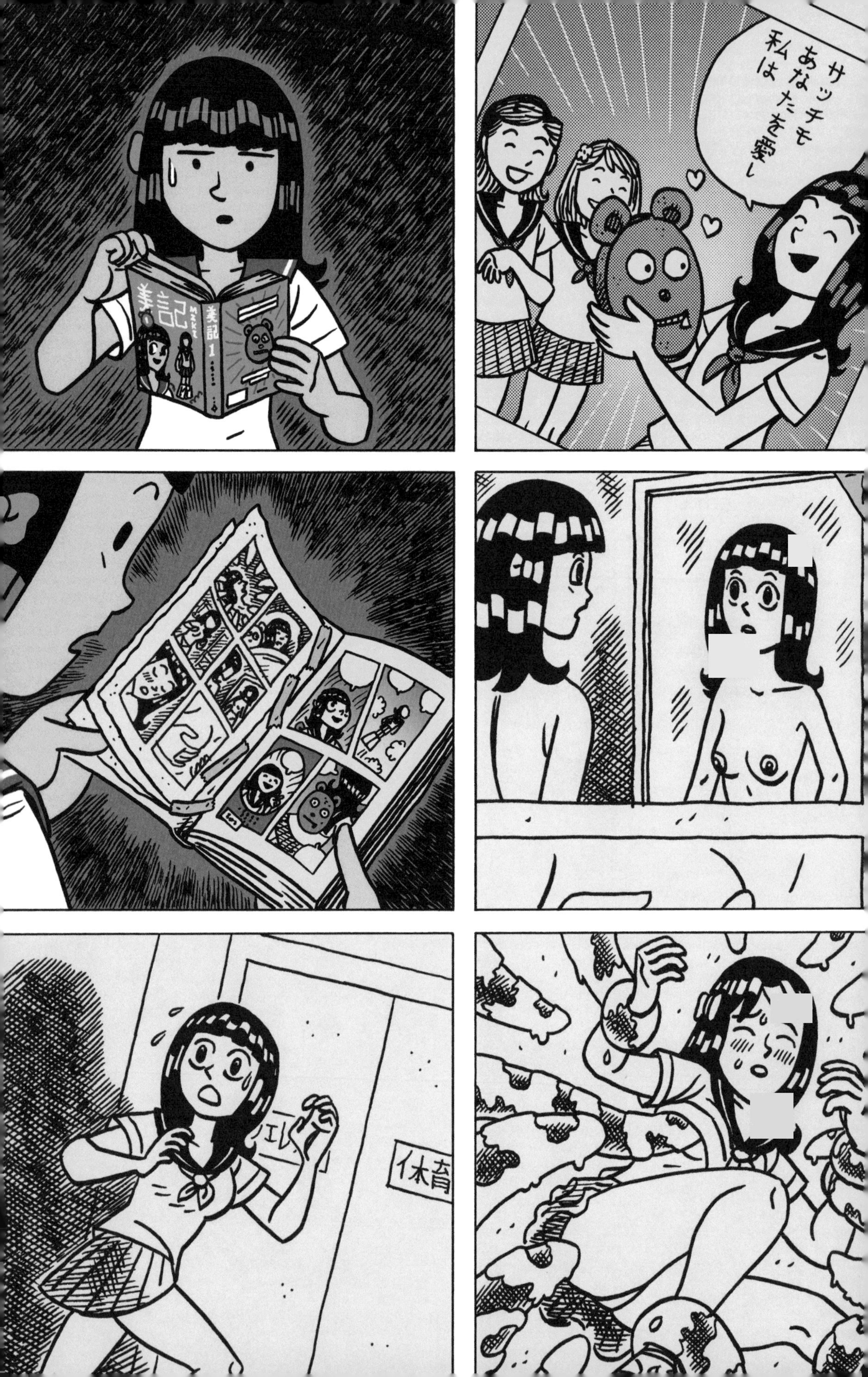

サッチも
あなたを愛し
私は
美記
美記 1
エレ
体育

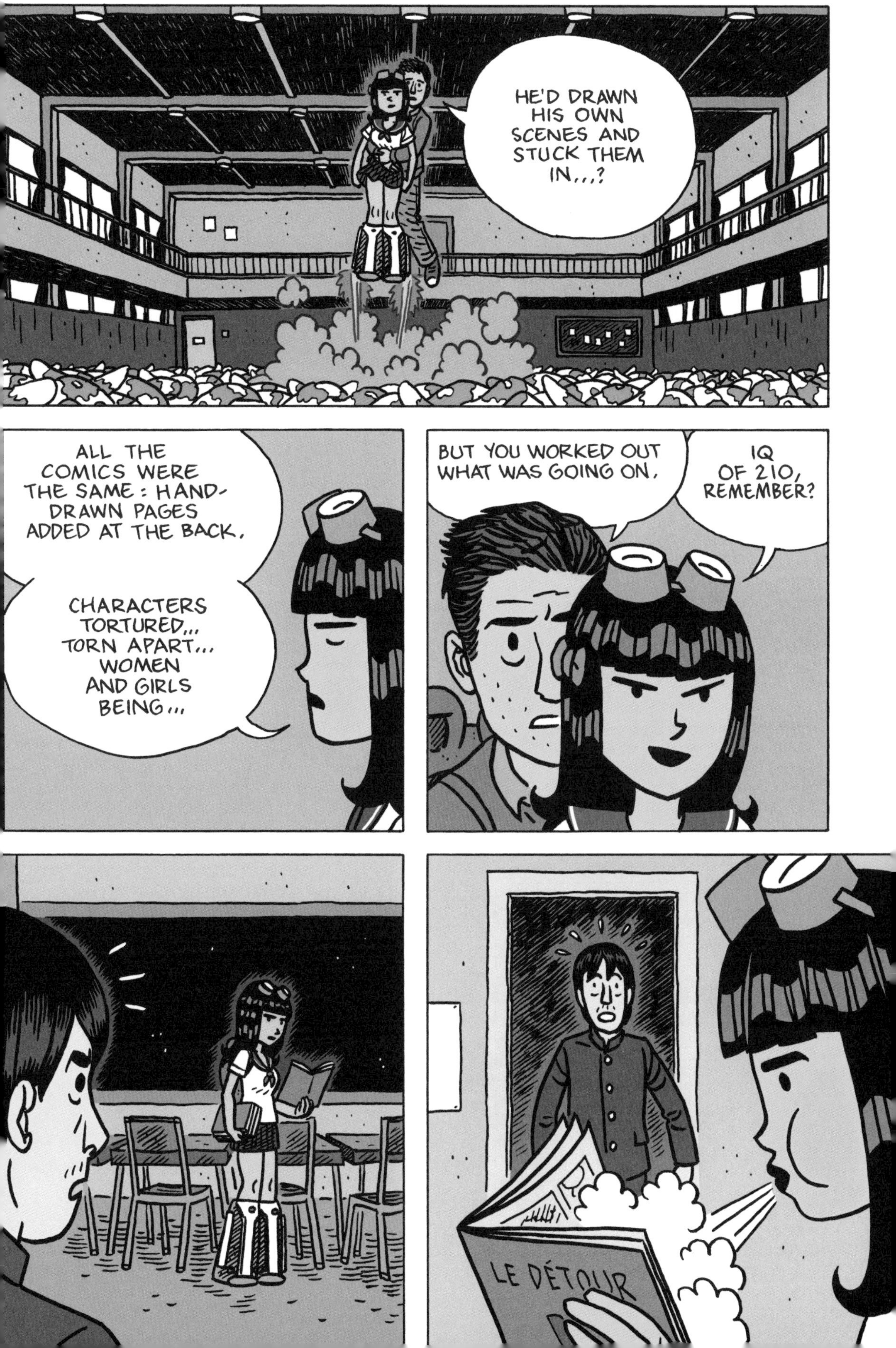
HE'D DRAWN HIS OWN SCENES AND STUCK THEM IN...?
ALL THE COMICS WERE THE SAME: HAND-DRAWN PAGES ADDED AT THE BACK.
CHARACTERS TORTURED... TORN APART... WOMEN AND GIRLS BEING...
BUT YOU WORKED OUT WHAT WAS GOING ON.
IQ OF 210, REMEMBER?
LE DÉTOUR

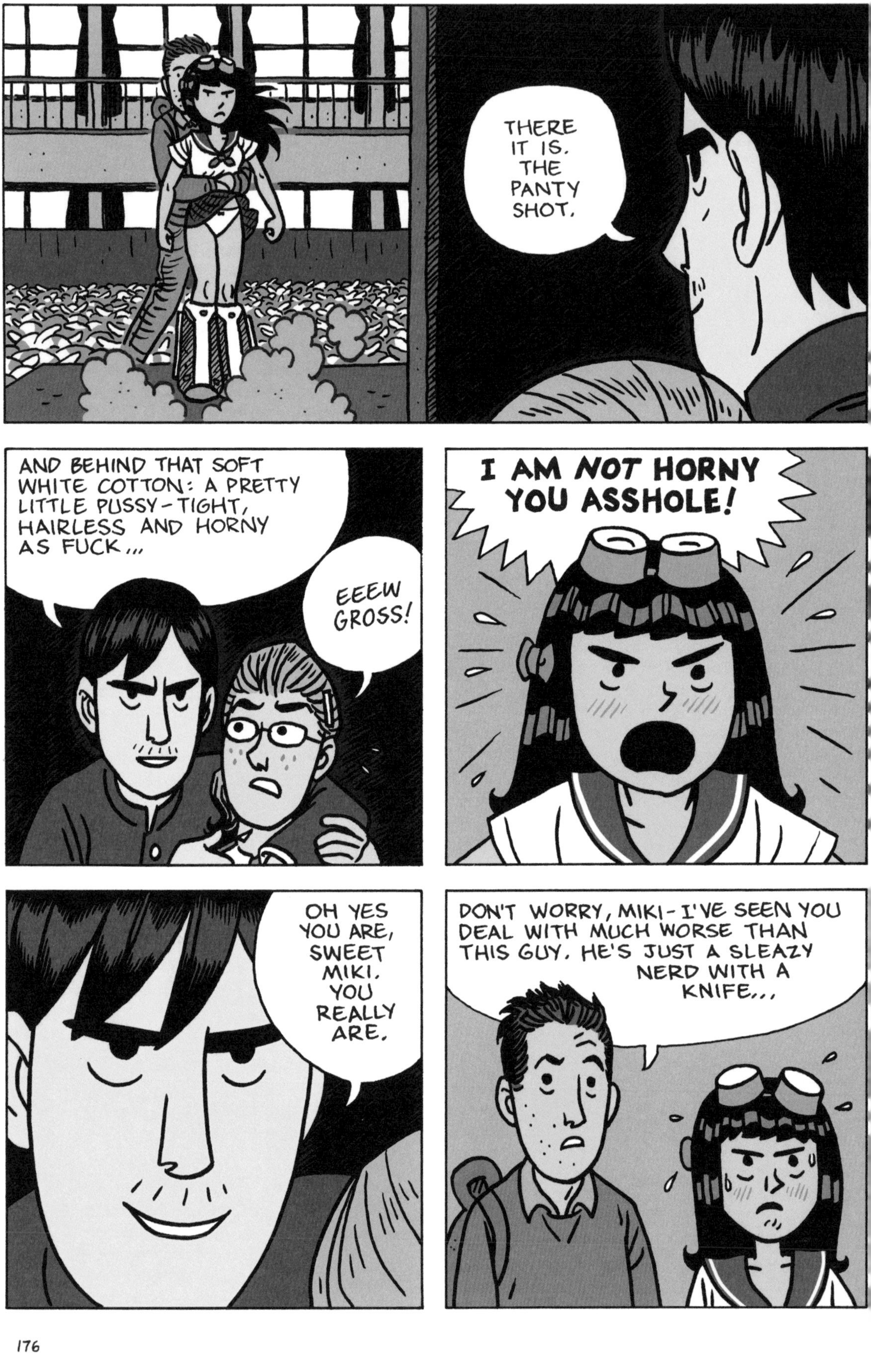
THERE IT IS. THE PANTY SHOT.
AND BEHIND THAT SOFT WHITE COTTON: A PRETTY LITTLE PUSSY-TIGHT, HAIRLESS AND HORNY AS FUCK...
EEEW GROSS!
I AM NOT HORNY YOU ASSHOLE!
OH YES YOU ARE, SWEET MIKI. YOU REALLY ARE.
DON'T WORRY, MIKI- I'VE SEEN YOU DEAL WITH MUCH WORSE THAN THIS GUY. HE'S JUST A SLEAZY NERD WITH A KNIFE...

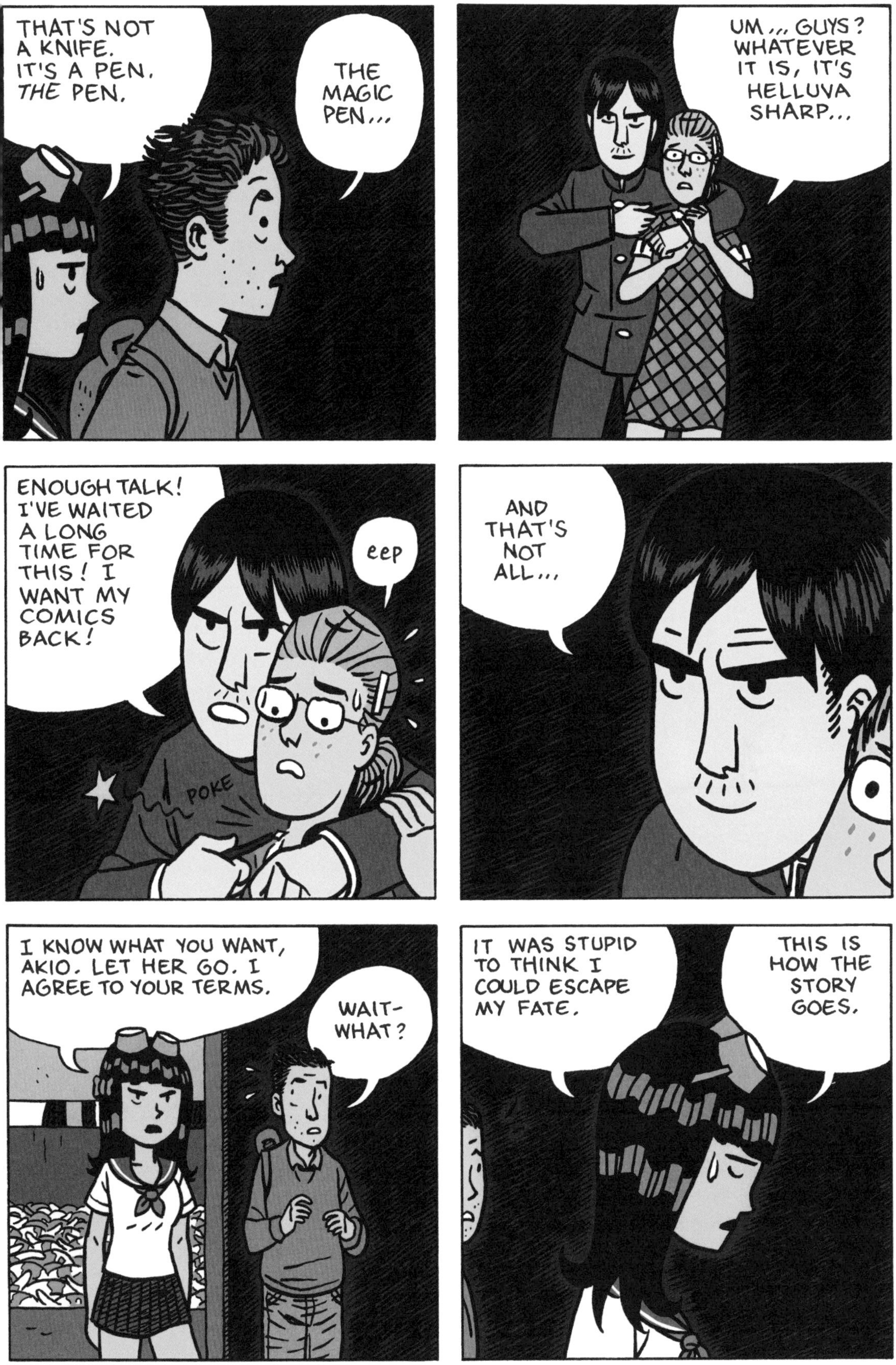
THAT'S NOT A KNIFE. IT'S A PEN. *THE* PEN.
THE MAGIC PEN...
UM... GUYS? WHATEVER IT IS, IT'S HELLUVA SHARP...
ENOUGH TALK! I'VE WAITED A LONG TIME FOR THIS! I WANT MY COMICS BACK!
eep
POKE
AND THAT'S NOT ALL...
I KNOW WHAT YOU WANT, AKIO. LET HER GO. I AGREE TO YOUR TERMS.
WAIT- WHAT?
IT WAS STUPID TO THINK I COULD ESCAPE MY FATE.
THIS IS HOW THE STORY GOES.

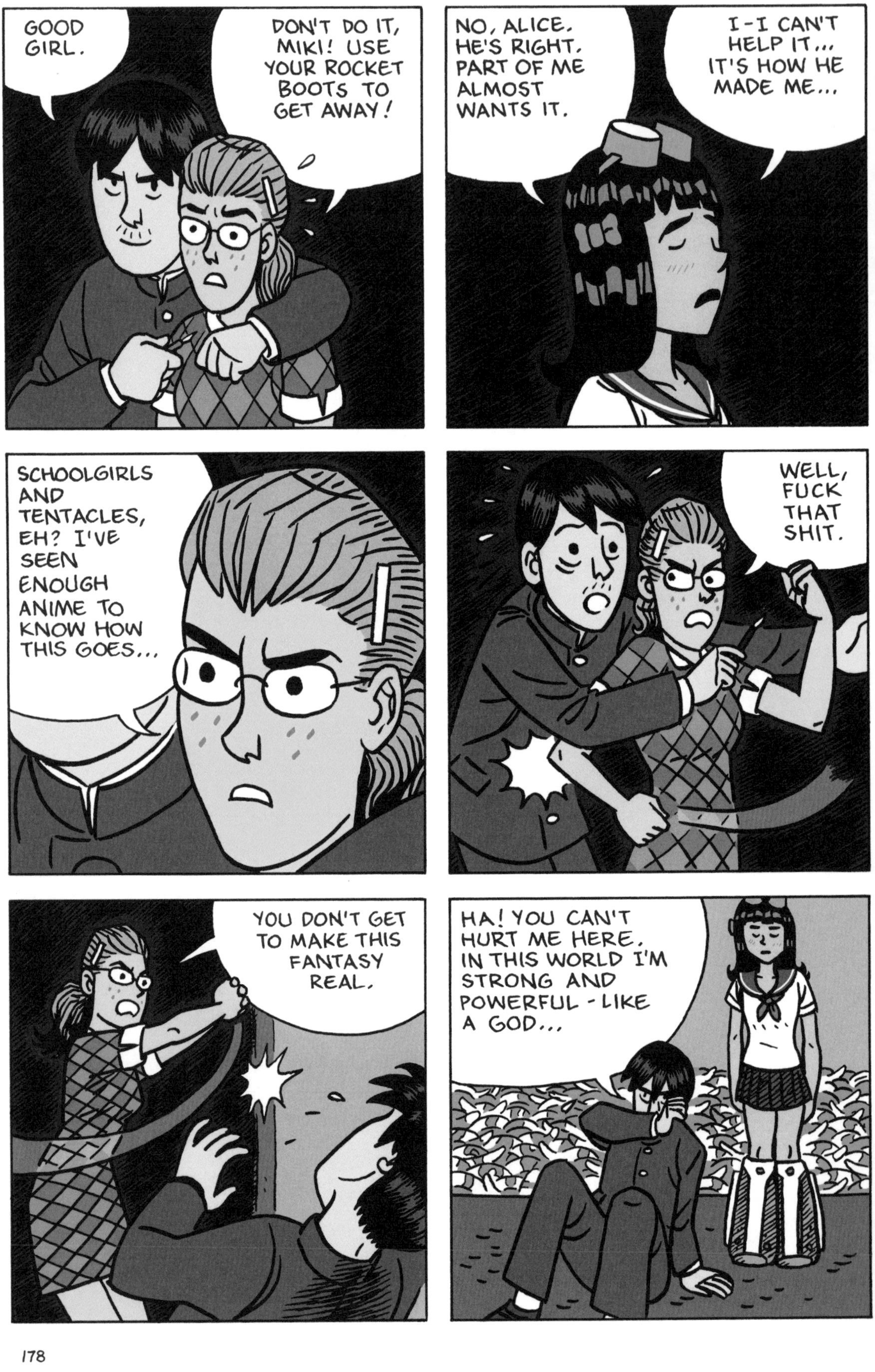
GOOD GIRL.
DON'T DO IT, MIKI! USE YOUR ROCKET BOOTS TO GET AWAY!
NO, ALICE. HE'S RIGHT. PART OF ME ALMOST WANTS IT.
I-I CAN'T HELP IT... IT'S HOW HE MADE ME...
SCHOOLGIRLS AND TENTACLES, EH? I'VE SEEN ENOUGH ANIME TO KNOW HOW THIS GOES...
WELL, FUCK THAT SHIT.
YOU DON'T GET TO MAKE THIS FANTASY REAL.
HA! YOU CAN'T HURT ME HERE. IN THIS WORLD I'M STRONG AND POWERFUL - LIKE A GOD...

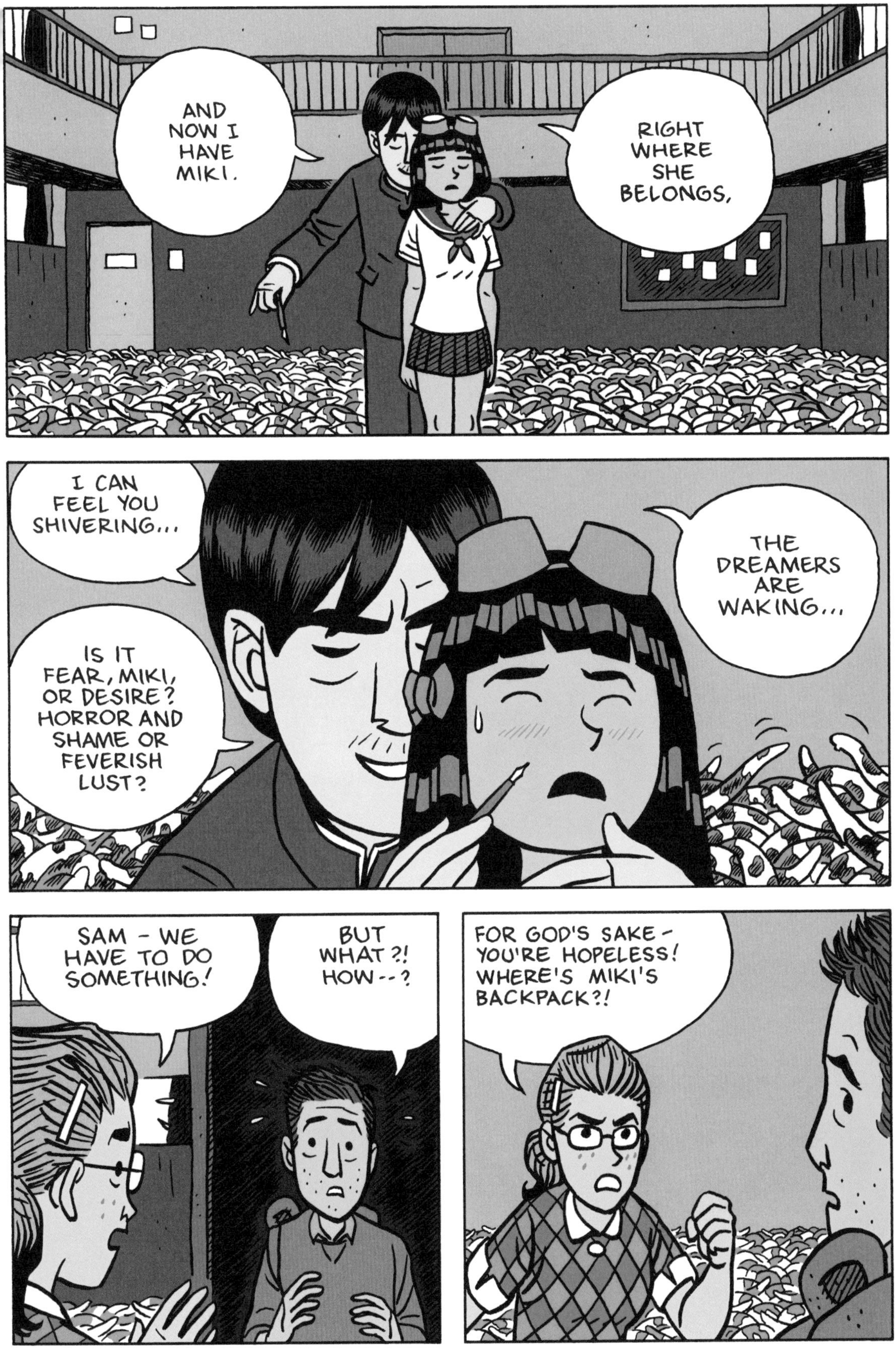
AND NOW I HAVE MIKI.
RIGHT WHERE SHE BELONGS,
I CAN FEEL YOU SHIVERING...
IS IT FEAR, MIKI, OR DESIRE? HORROR AND SHAME OR FEVERISH LUST?
THE DREAMERS ARE WAKING...
SAM - WE HAVE TO DO SOMETHING!
BUT WHAT?! HOW--?
FOR GOD'S SAKE - YOU'RE HOPELESS! WHERE'S MIKI'S BACKPACK?!

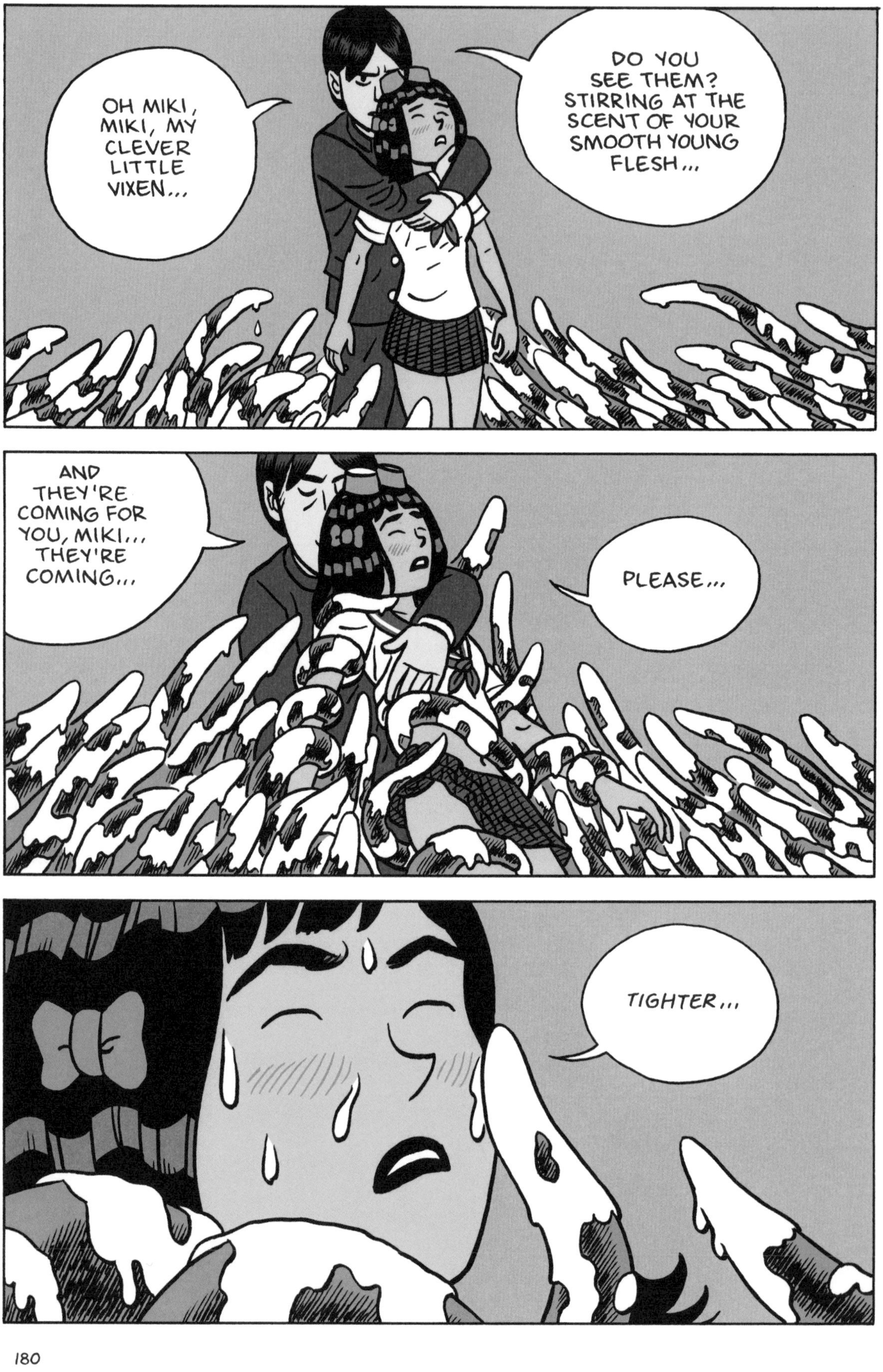
OH MIKI, MIKI, MY CLEVER LITTLE VIXEN...
DO YOU SEE THEM? STIRRING AT THE SCENT OF YOUR SMOOTH YOUNG FLESH...
AND THEY'RE COMING FOR YOU, MIKI... THEY'RE COMING...
PLEASE...
TIGHTER...

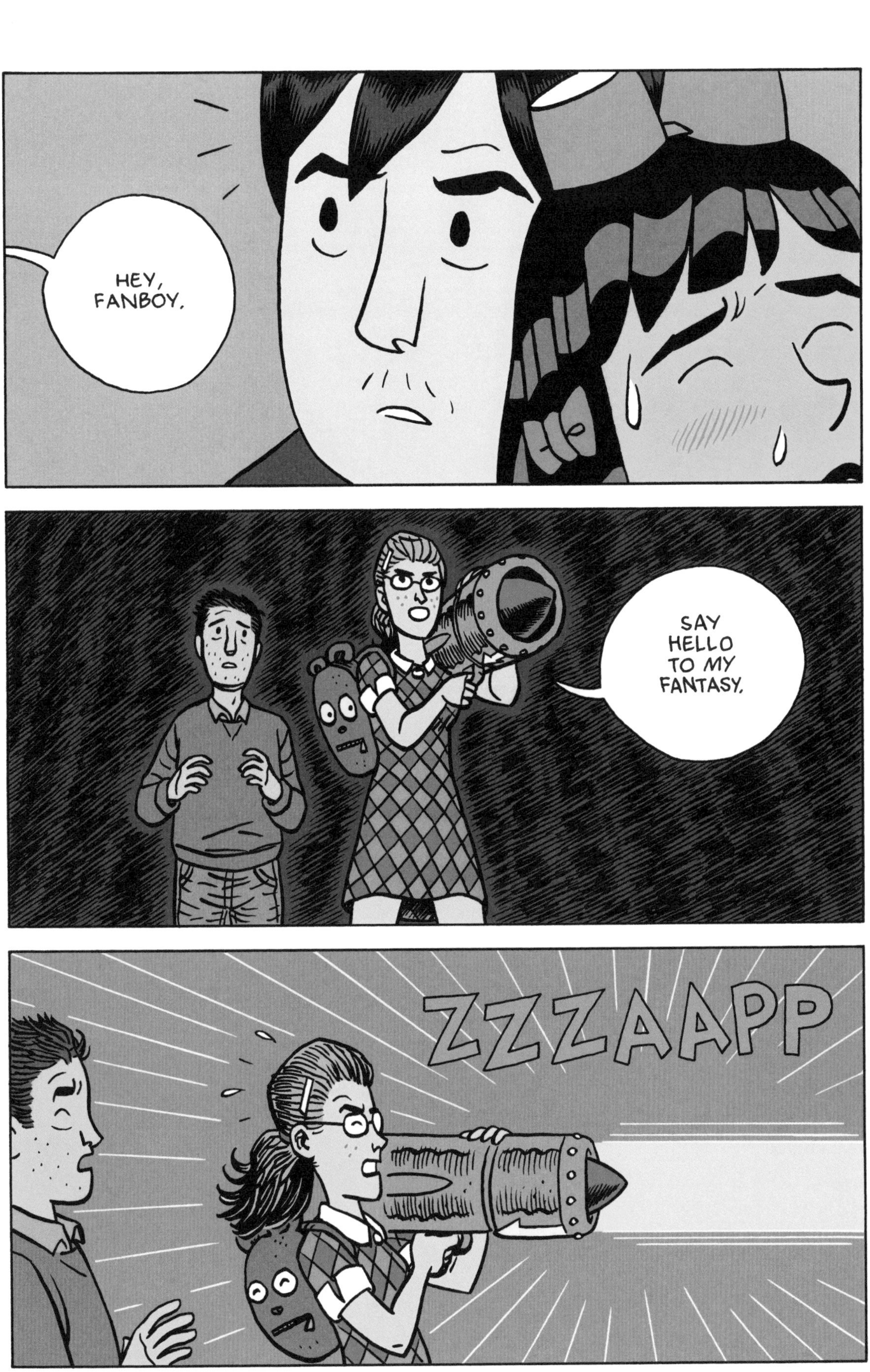
HEY, FANBOY.
SAY HELLO TO MY FANTASY.
ZZZAAPP

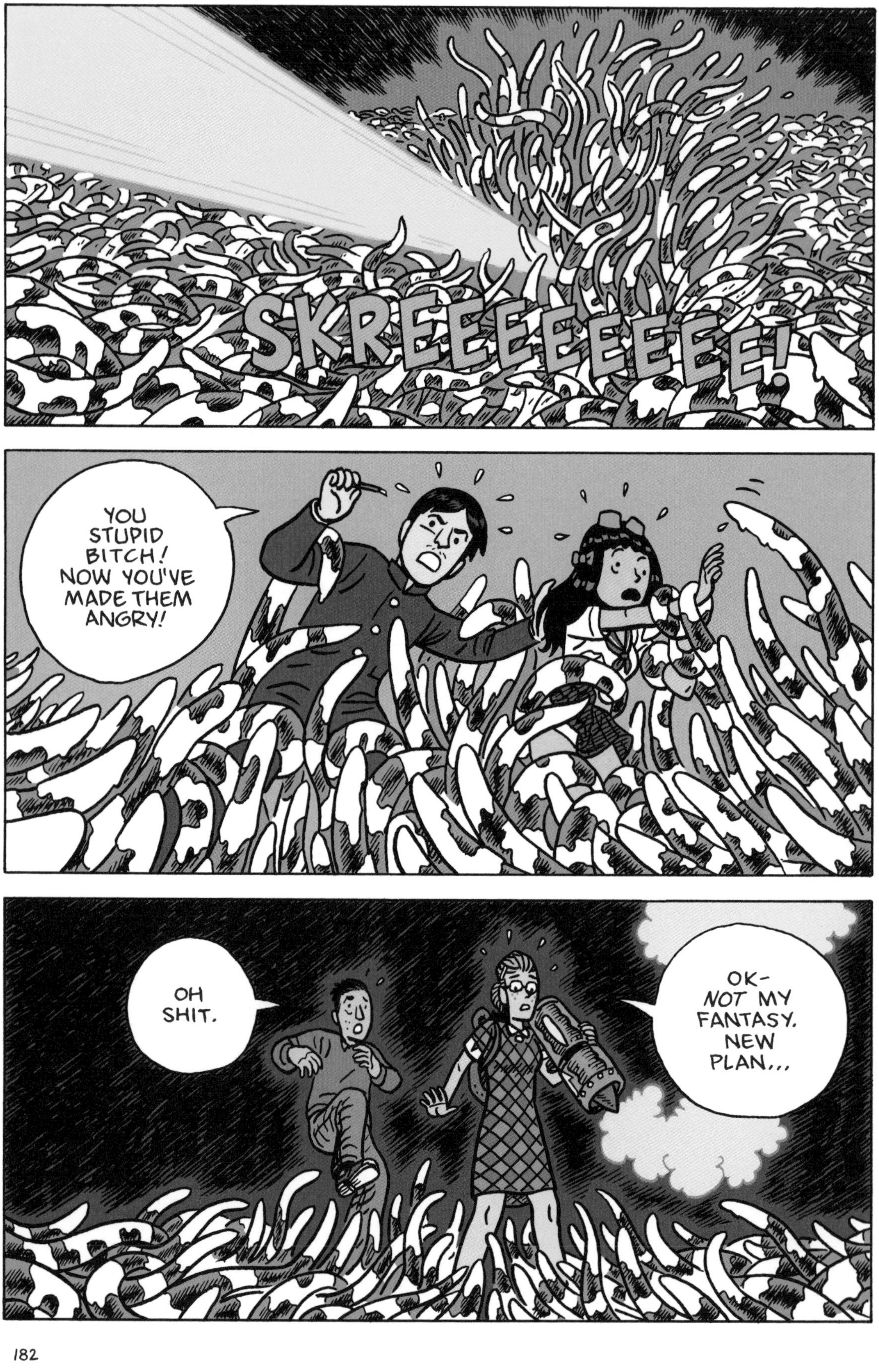
SKREEEEEEEEEE!
YOU STUPID BITCH! NOW YOU'VE MADE THEM ANGRY!
OH SHIT.
OK- NOT MY FANTASY. NEW PLAN...

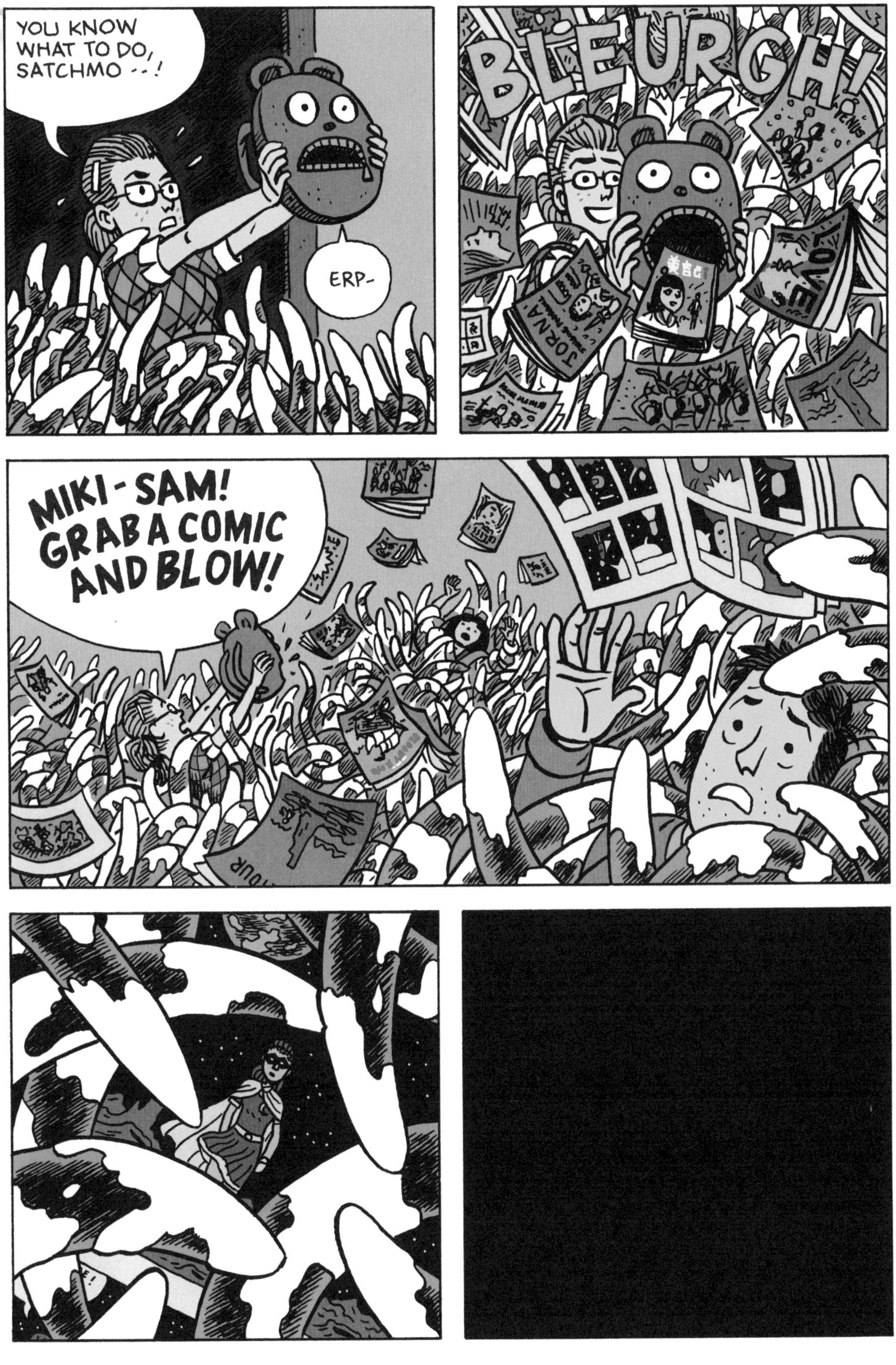
YOU KNOW WHAT TO DO, SATCHMO --!
ERP-
BLEURGH!
LOVE
VENUS
JORNAL
MIKI-SAM! GRAB A COMIC AND BLOW!

Chapter Twelve:

THE SEA OF TRANQUILITY

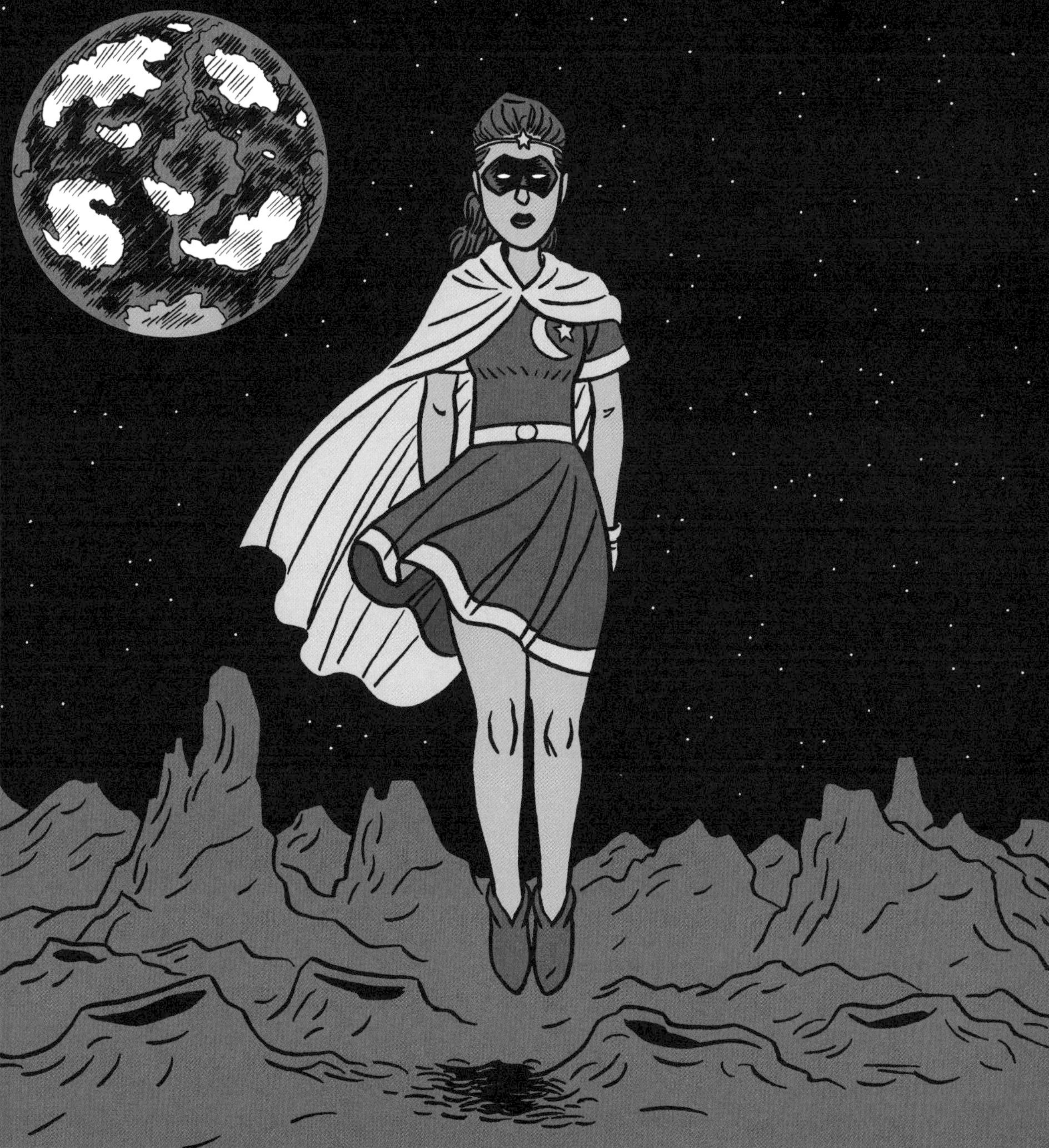

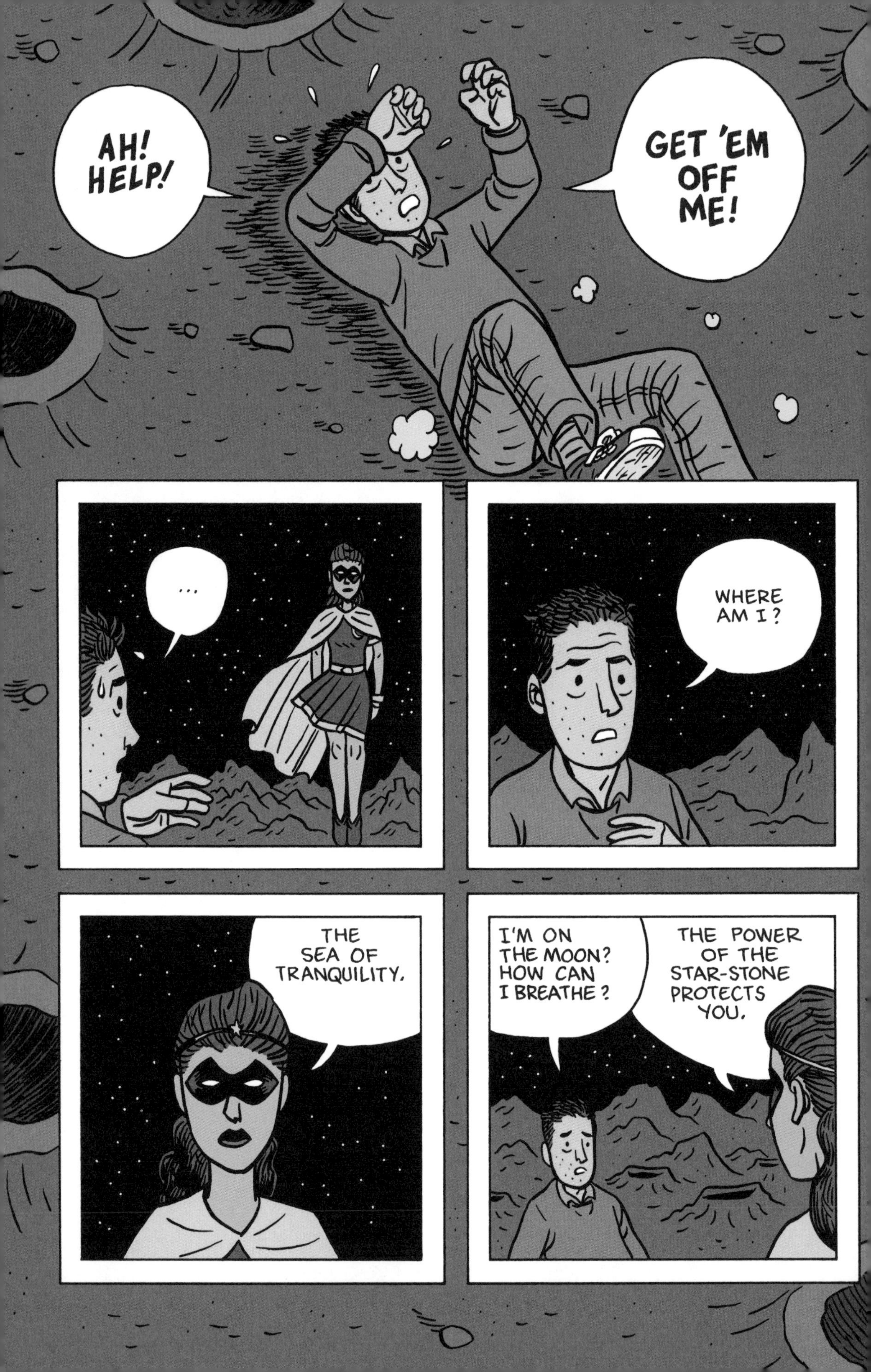
AH! HELP!
GET 'EM OFF ME!
...
WHERE AM I?
THE SEA OF TRANQUILITY.
I'M ON THE MOON? HOW CAN I BREATHE?
THE POWER OF THE STAR-STONE PROTECTS YOU.

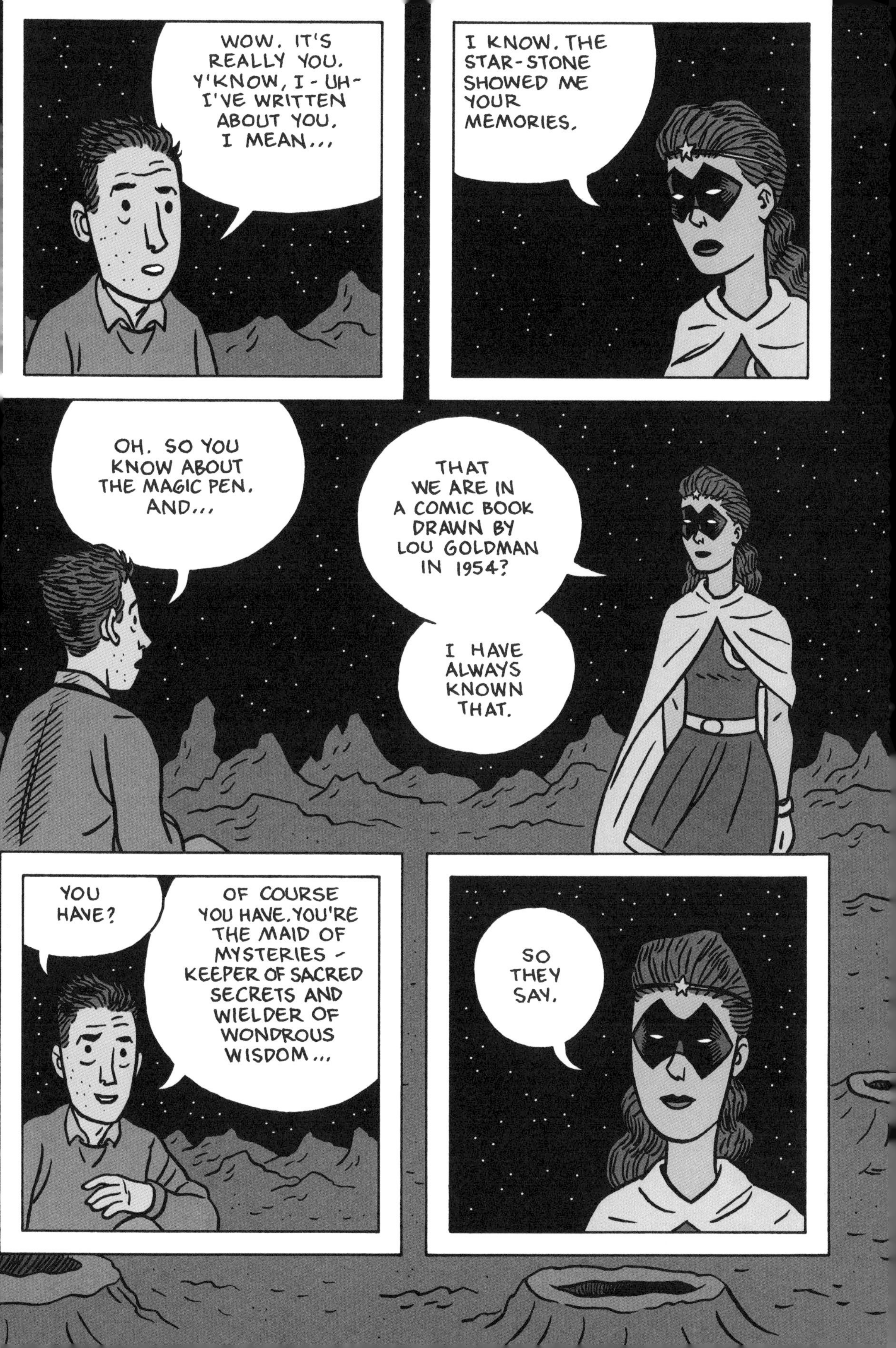
WOW. IT'S REALLY YOU. Y'KNOW, I - UH- I'VE WRITTEN ABOUT YOU. I MEAN...
I KNOW. THE STAR-STONE SHOWED ME YOUR MEMORIES.
OH. SO YOU KNOW ABOUT THE MAGIC PEN. AND...
THAT WE ARE IN A COMIC BOOK DRAWN BY LOU GOLDMAN IN 1954?
I HAVE ALWAYS KNOWN THAT.
YOU HAVE?
OF COURSE YOU HAVE. YOU'RE THE MAID OF MYSTERIES - KEEPER OF SACRED SECRETS AND WIELDER OF WONDROUS WISDOM...
SO THEY SAY.

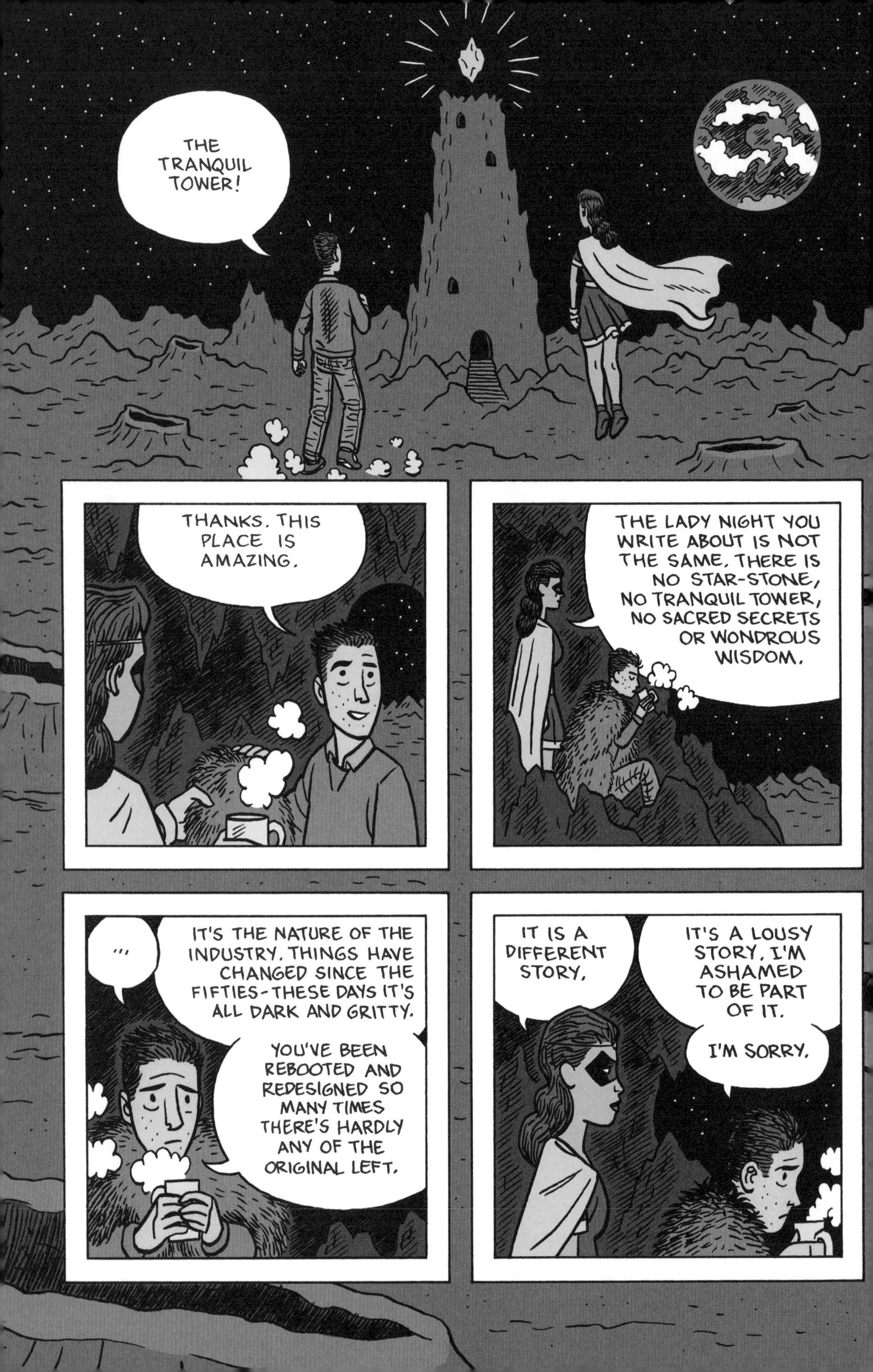
THE TRANQUIL TOWER!
THANKS. THIS PLACE IS AMAZING.
THE LADY NIGHT YOU WRITE ABOUT IS NOT THE SAME. THERE IS NO STAR-STONE, NO TRANQUIL TOWER, NO SACRED SECRETS OR WONDROUS WISDOM.
...
IT'S THE NATURE OF THE INDUSTRY. THINGS HAVE CHANGED SINCE THE FIFTIES-THESE DAYS IT'S ALL DARK AND GRITTY.
YOU'VE BEEN REBOOTED AND REDESIGNED SO MANY TIMES THERE'S HARDLY ANY OF THE ORIGINAL LEFT.
IT IS A DIFFERENT STORY.
IT'S A LOUSY STORY. I'M ASHAMED TO BE PART OF IT.
I'M SORRY.

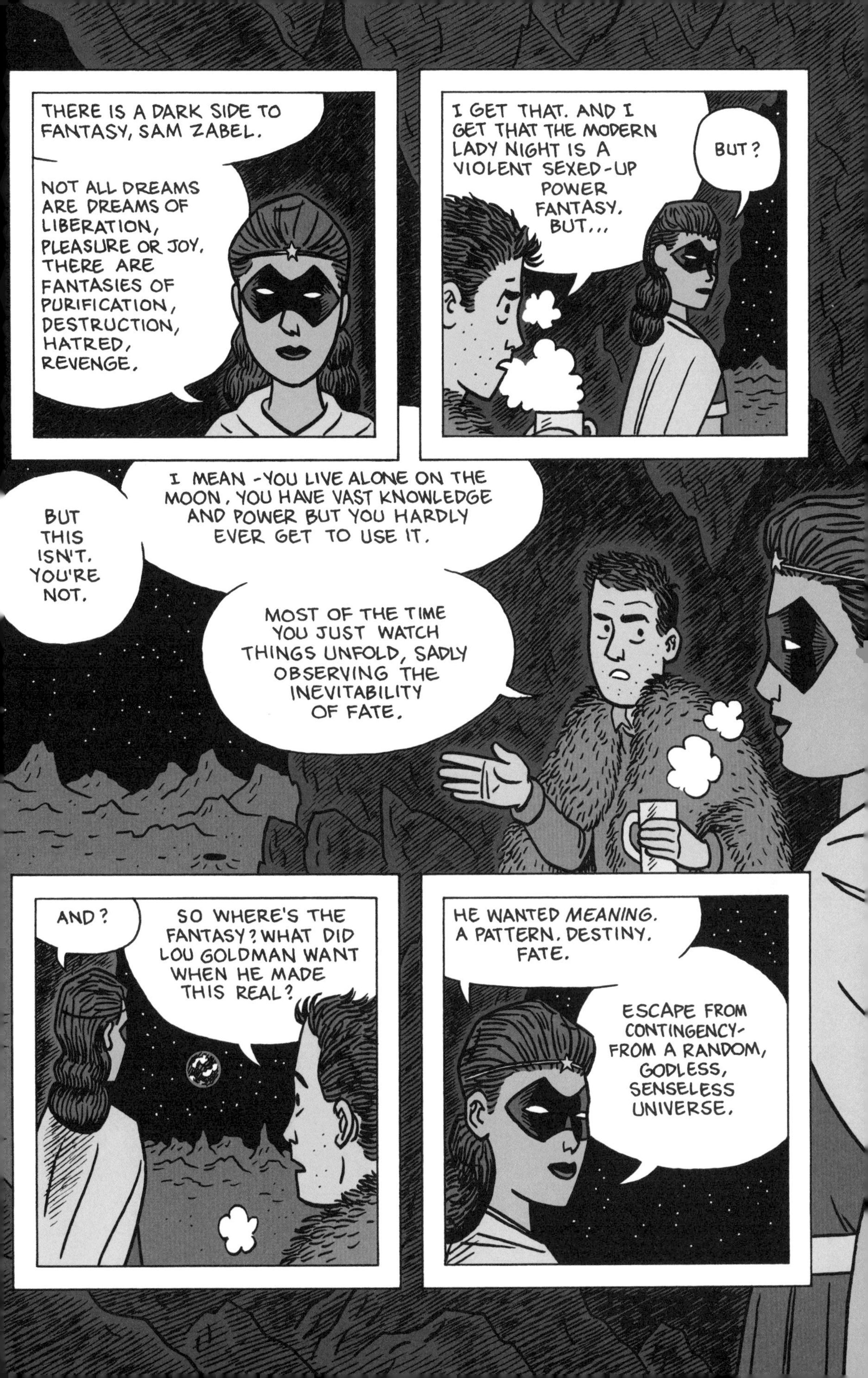
THERE IS A DARK SIDE TO FANTASY, SAM ZABEL.
NOT ALL DREAMS ARE DREAMS OF LIBERATION, PLEASURE OR JOY. THERE ARE FANTASIES OF PURIFICATION, DESTRUCTION, HATRED, REVENGE.
I GET THAT. AND I GET THAT THE MODERN LADY NIGHT IS A VIOLENT SEXED-UP POWER FANTASY. BUT...
BUT?
BUT THIS ISN'T. YOU'RE NOT.
I MEAN - YOU LIVE ALONE ON THE MOON. YOU HAVE VAST KNOWLEDGE AND POWER BUT YOU HARDLY EVER GET TO USE IT.
MOST OF THE TIME YOU JUST WATCH THINGS UNFOLD, SADLY OBSERVING THE INEVITABILITY OF FATE.
AND?
SO WHERE'S THE FANTASY? WHAT DID LOU GOLDMAN WANT WHEN HE MADE THIS REAL?
HE WANTED *MEANING*. A PATTERN. DESTINY. FATE.
ESCAPE FROM CONTINGENCY- FROM A RANDOM, GODLESS, SENSELESS UNIVERSE.

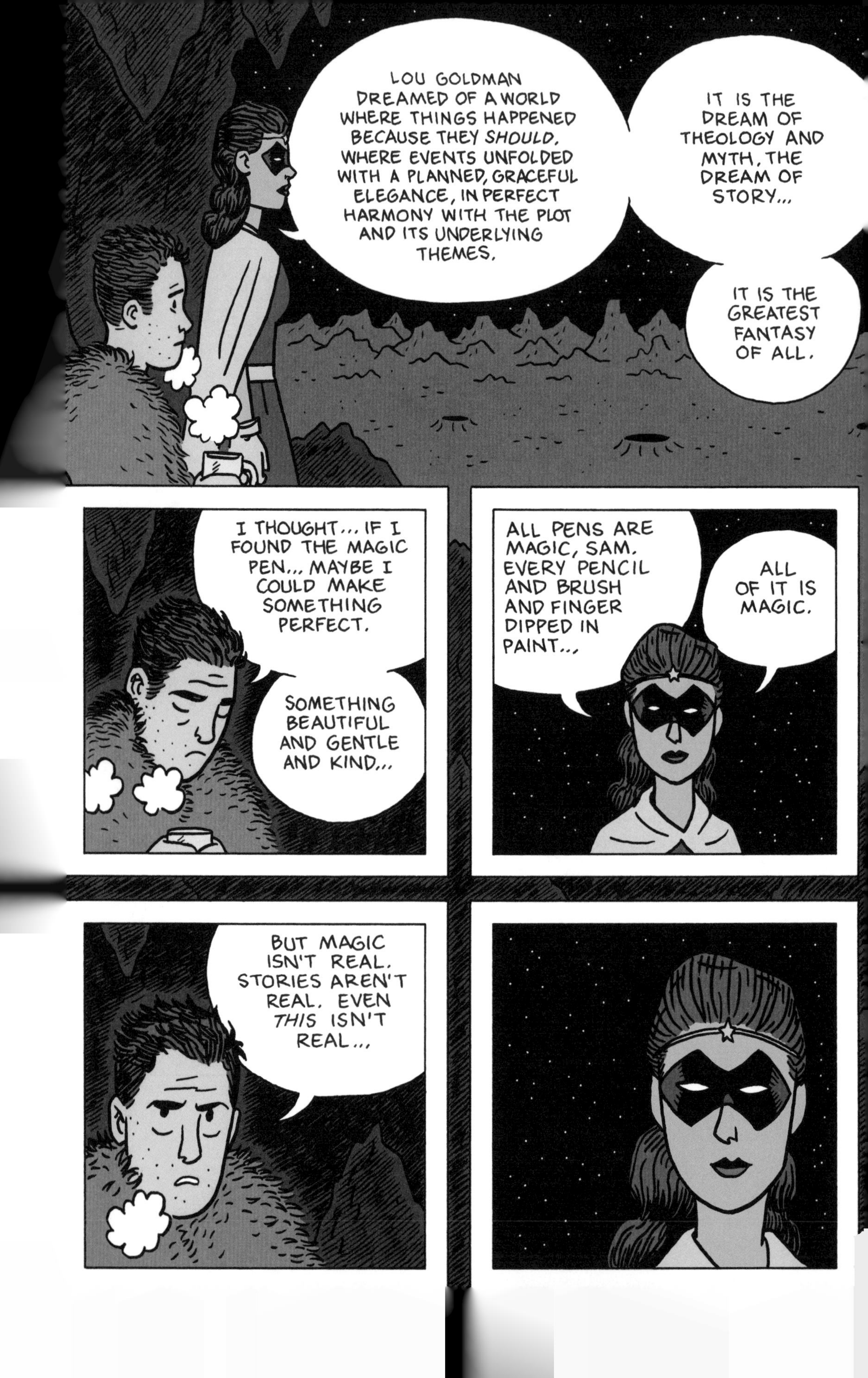
LOU GOLDMAN DREAMED OF A WORLD WHERE THINGS HAPPENED BECAUSE THEY *SHOULD*. WHERE EVENTS UNFOLDED WITH A PLANNED, GRACEFUL ELEGANCE, IN PERFECT HARMONY WITH THE PLOT AND ITS UNDERLYING THEMES.
IT IS THE DREAM OF THEOLOGY AND MYTH, THE DREAM OF STORY...
IT IS THE GREATEST FANTASY OF ALL.
I THOUGHT... IF I FOUND THE MAGIC PEN... MAYBE I COULD MAKE SOMETHING PERFECT.
SOMETHING BEAUTIFUL AND GENTLE AND KIND...
ALL PENS ARE MAGIC, SAM. EVERY PENCIL AND BRUSH AND FINGER DIPPED IN PAINT...
ALL OF IT IS MAGIC.
BUT MAGIC ISN'T REAL. STORIES AREN'T REAL. EVEN *THIS* ISN'T REAL...

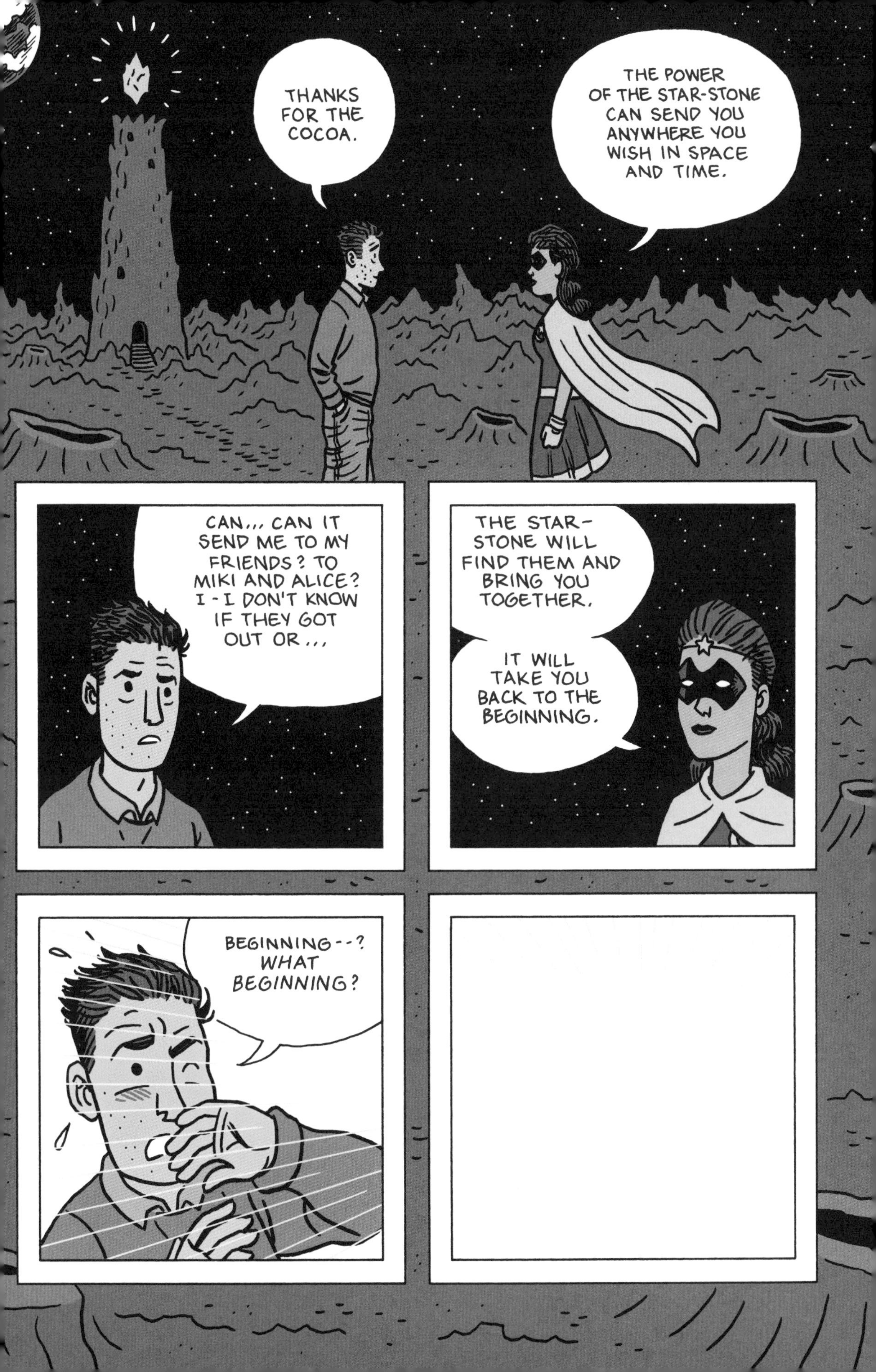
THANKS FOR THE COCOA.
THE POWER OF THE STAR-STONE CAN SEND YOU ANYWHERE YOU WISH IN SPACE AND TIME.
CAN... CAN IT SEND ME TO MY FRIENDS? TO MIKI AND ALICE? I-I DON'T KNOW IF THEY GOT OUT OR...
THE STAR-STONE WILL FIND THEM AND BRING YOU TOGETHER.
IT WILL TAKE YOU BACK TO THE BEGINNING.
BEGINNING--? WHAT BEGINNING?

Chapter Thirteen:

THE BEGINNING

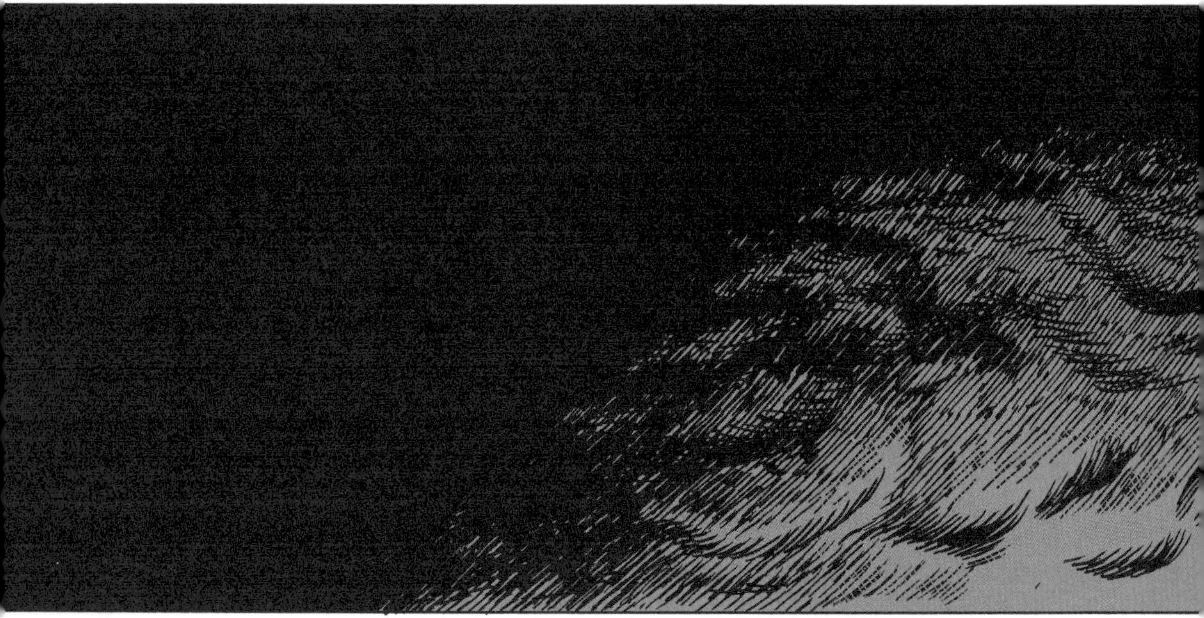

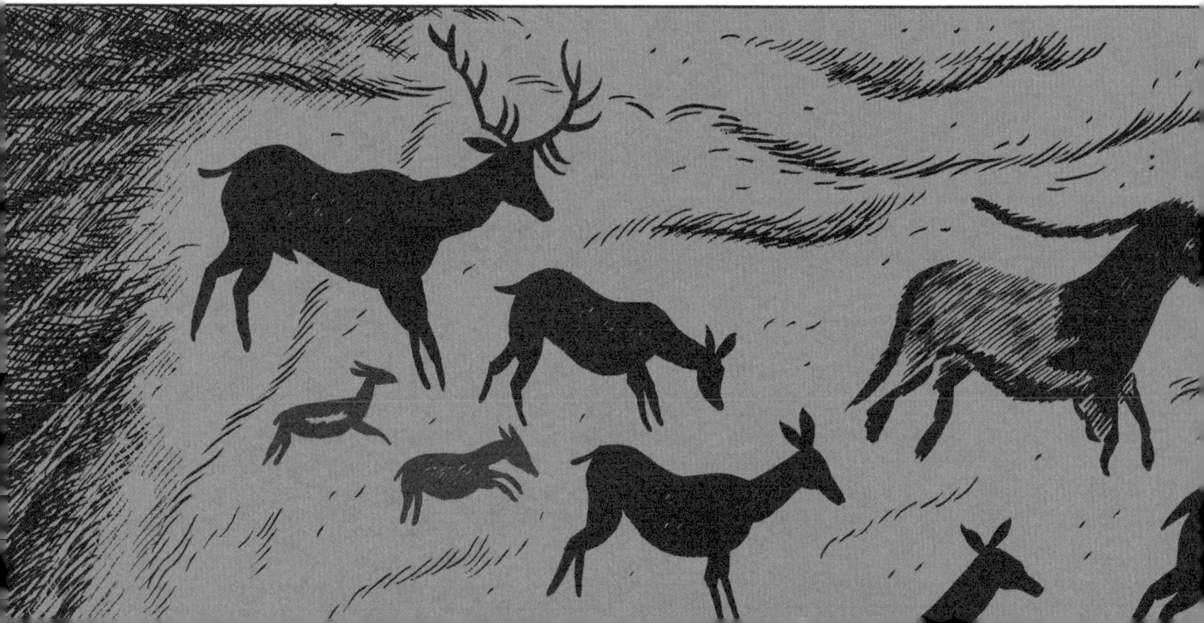

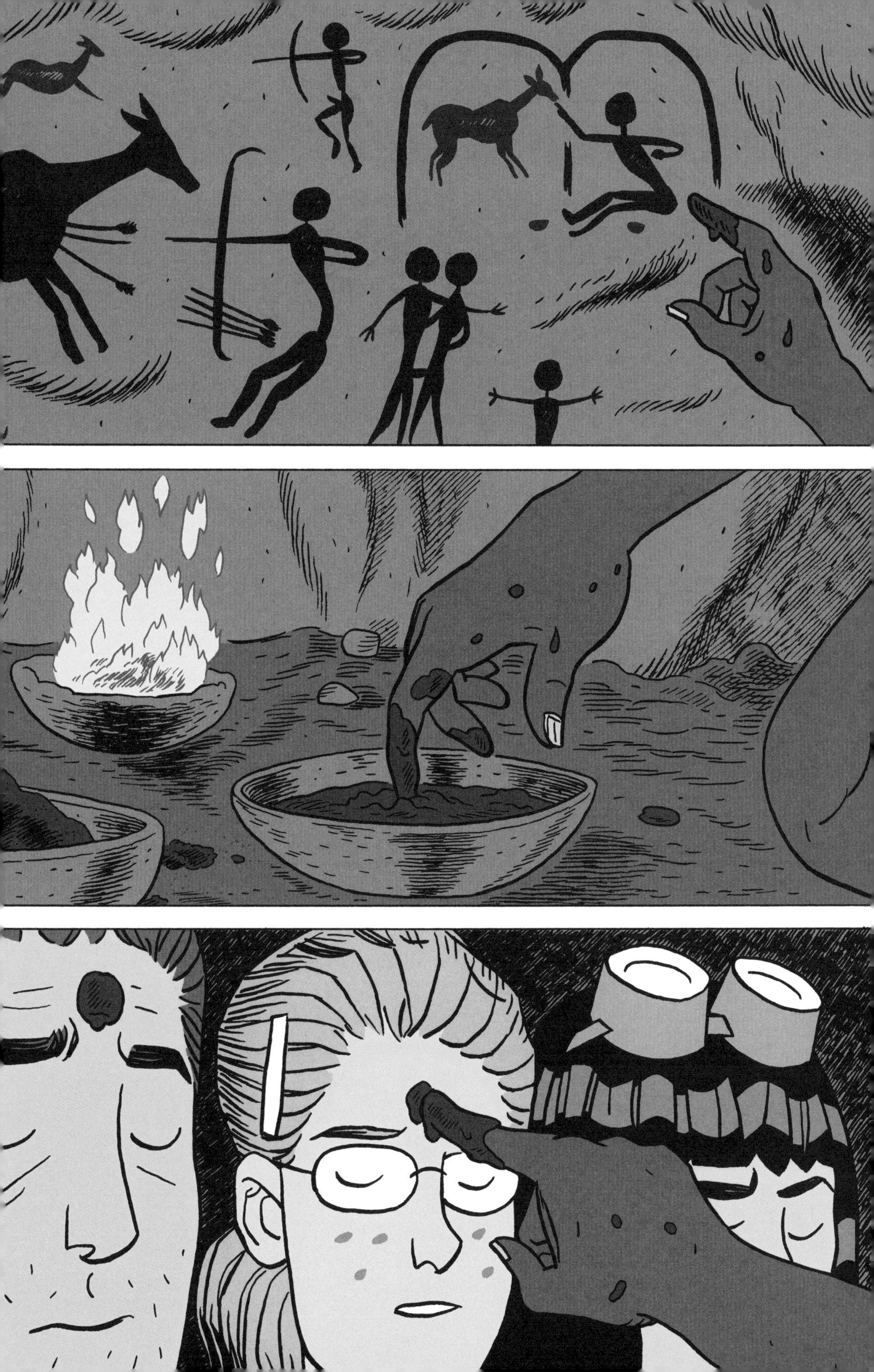

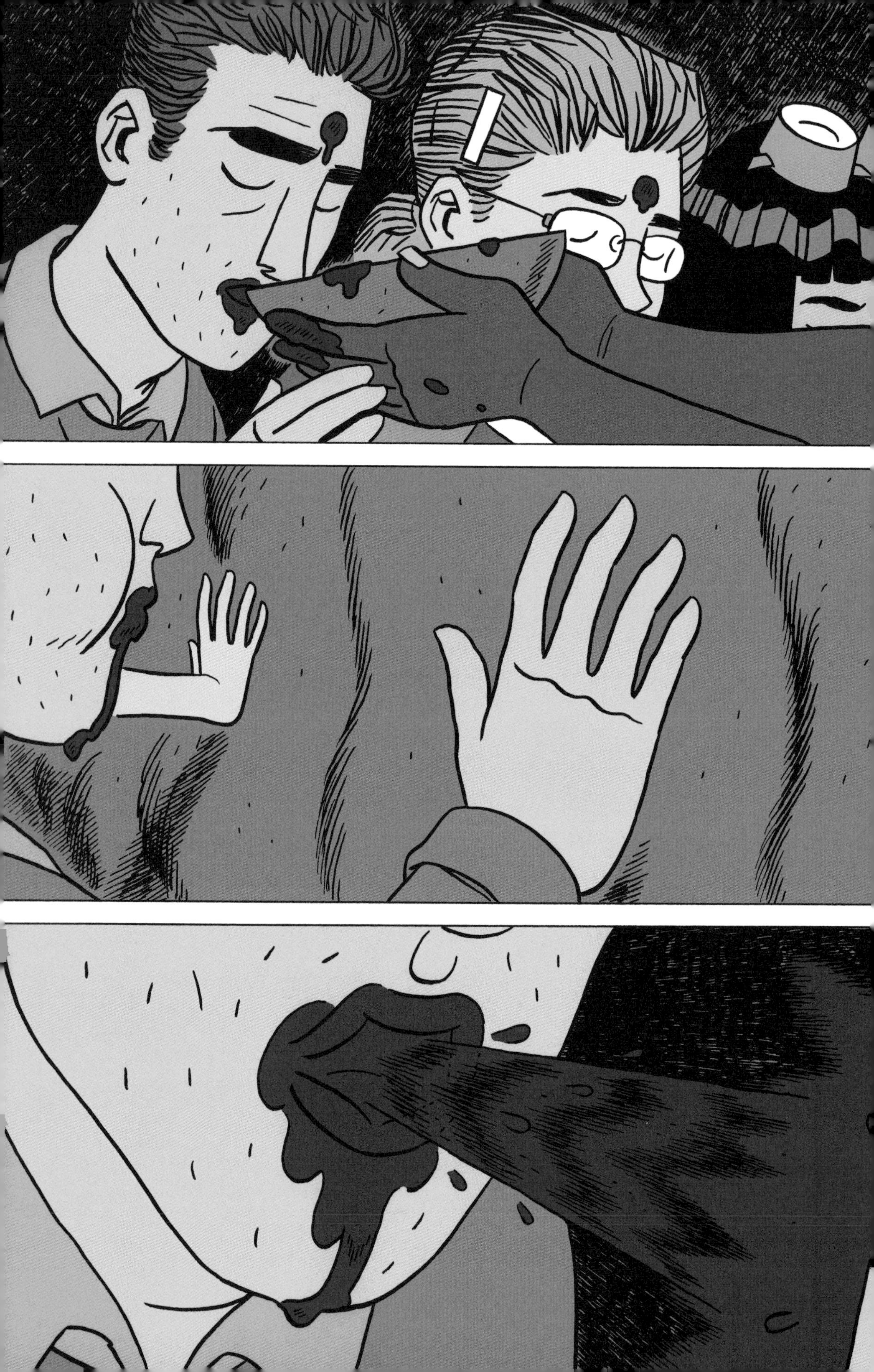

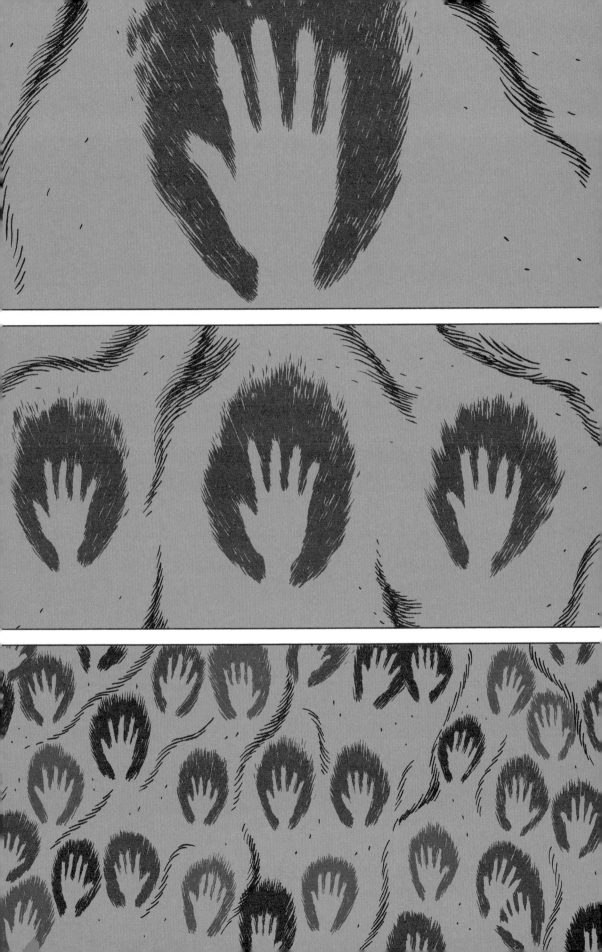

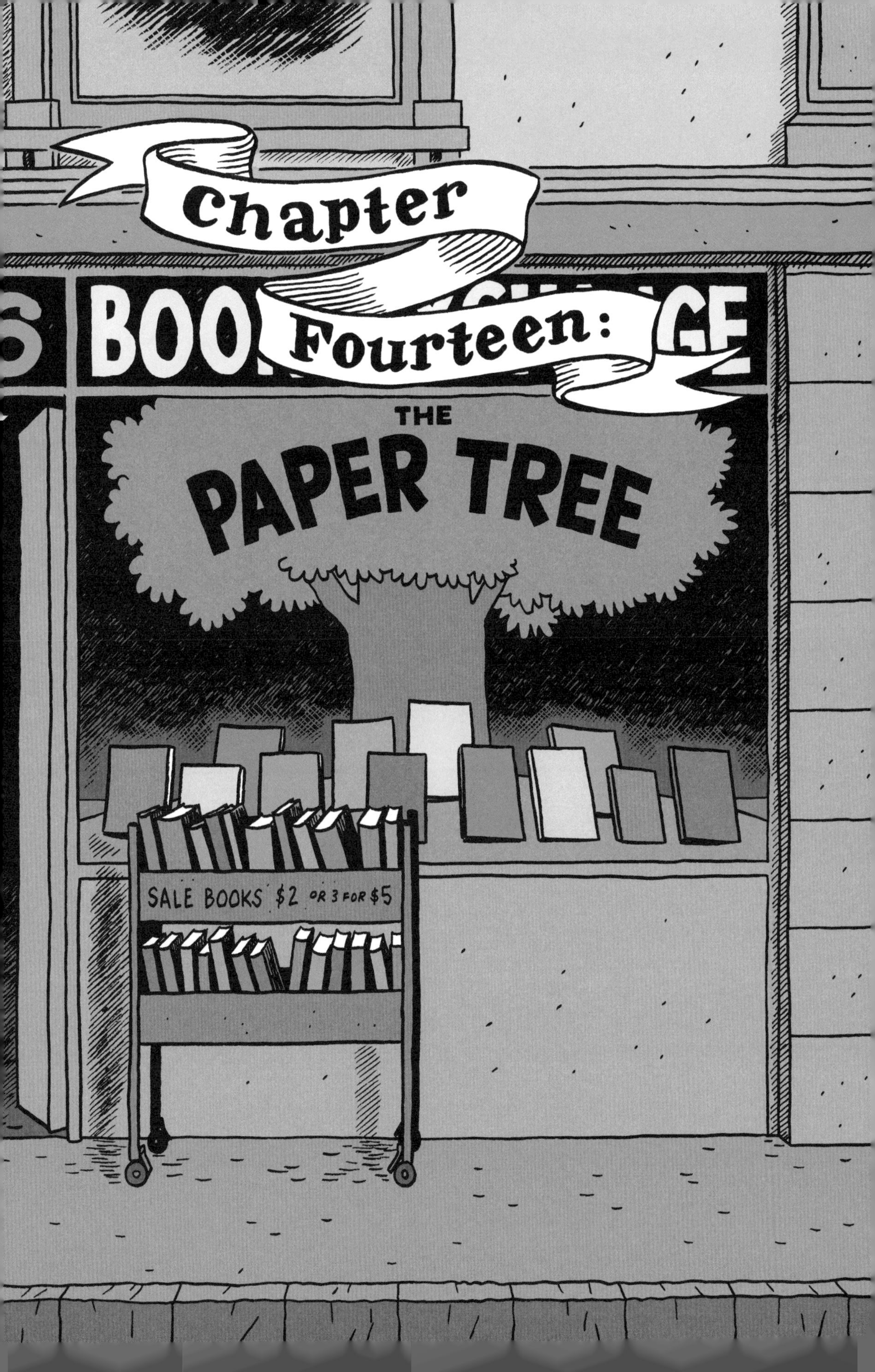
Chapter Fourteen:
THE PAPER TREE
SALE BOOKS $2 OR 3 FOR $5

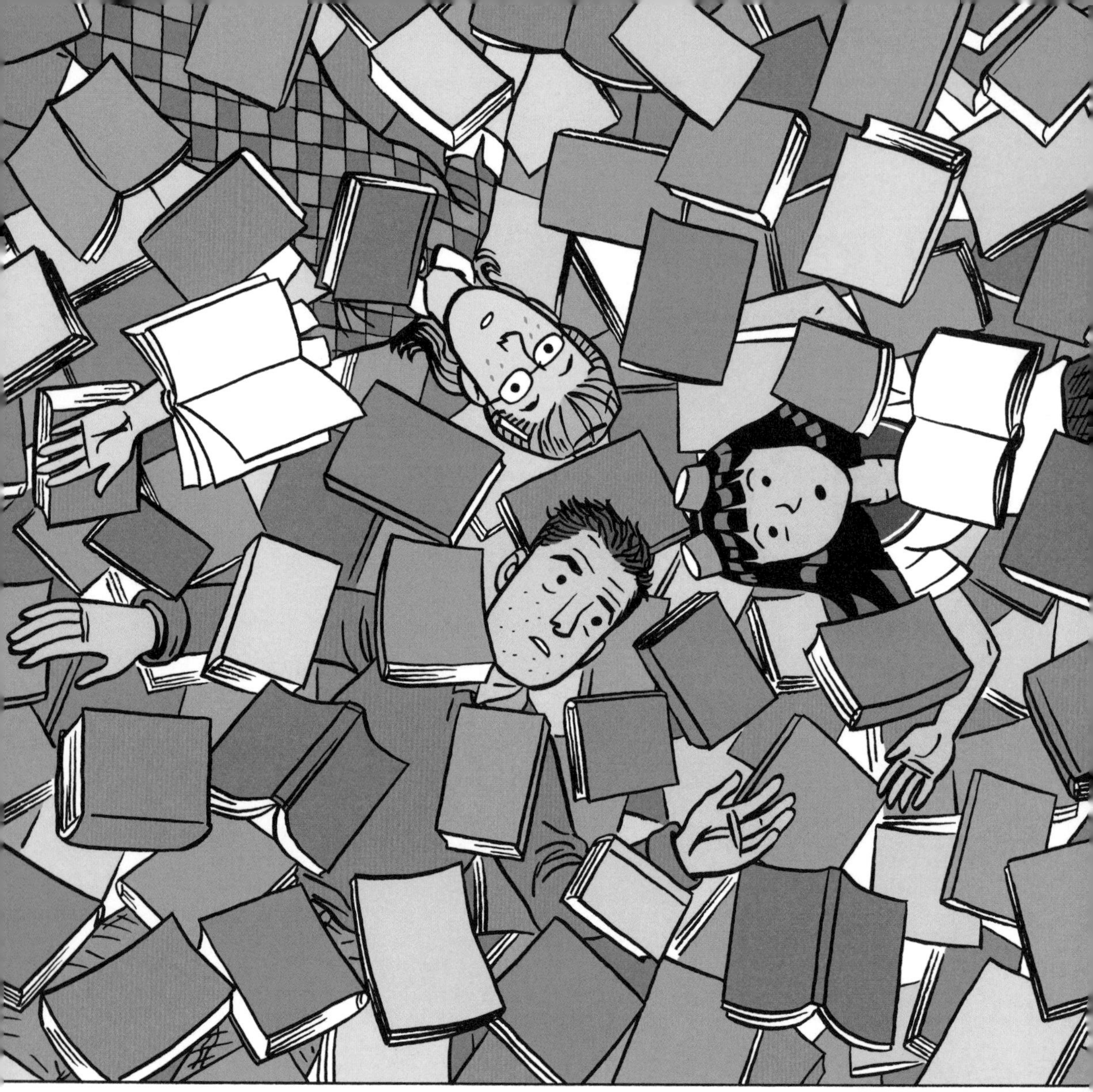

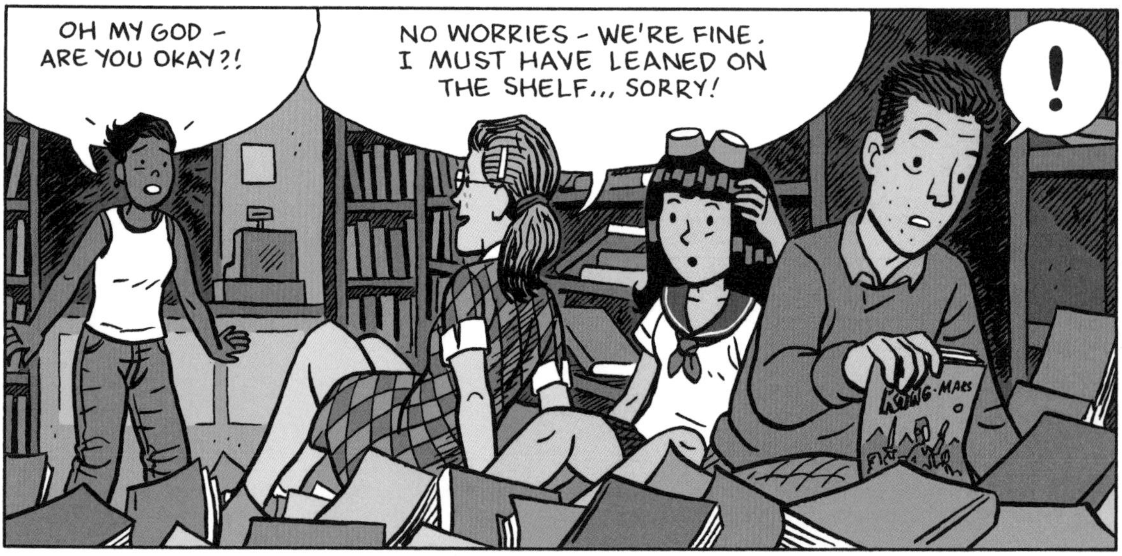
OH MY GOD - ARE YOU OKAY?!
NO WORRIES - WE'RE FINE. I MUST HAVE LEANED ON THE SHELF... SORRY!
!

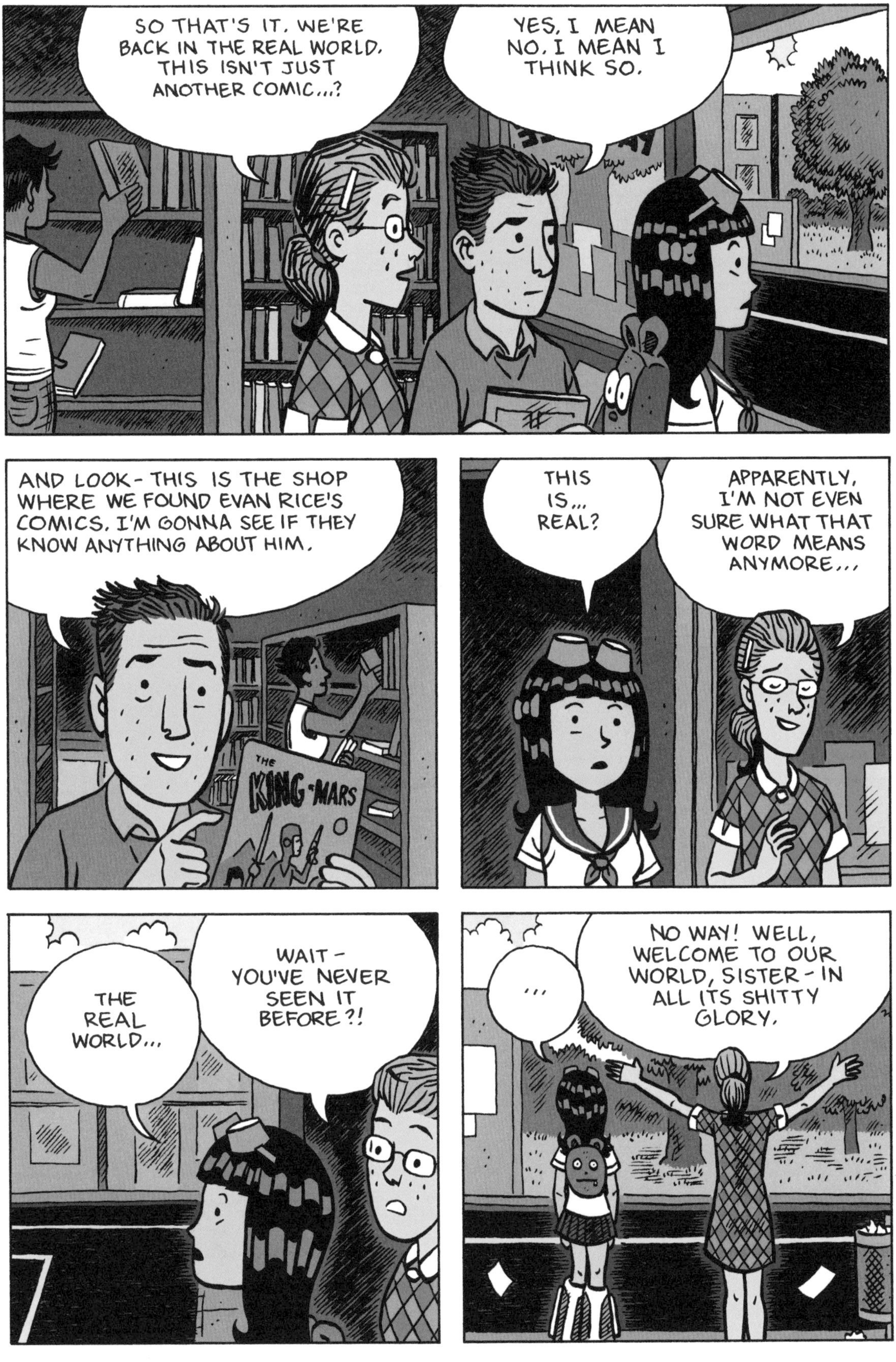
SO THAT'S IT. WE'RE BACK IN THE REAL WORLD. THIS ISN'T JUST ANOTHER COMIC...?
YES. I MEAN NO. I MEAN I THINK SO.
AND LOOK- THIS IS THE SHOP WHERE WE FOUND EVAN RICE'S COMICS. I'M GONNA SEE IF THEY KNOW ANYTHING ABOUT HIM.
THE KING MARS
THIS IS... REAL?
APPARENTLY. I'M NOT EVEN SURE WHAT THAT WORD MEANS ANYMORE...
THE REAL WORLD...
WAIT- YOU'VE NEVER SEEN IT BEFORE?!
...
NO WAY! WELL, WELCOME TO OUR WORLD, SISTER- IN ALL ITS SHITTY GLORY.

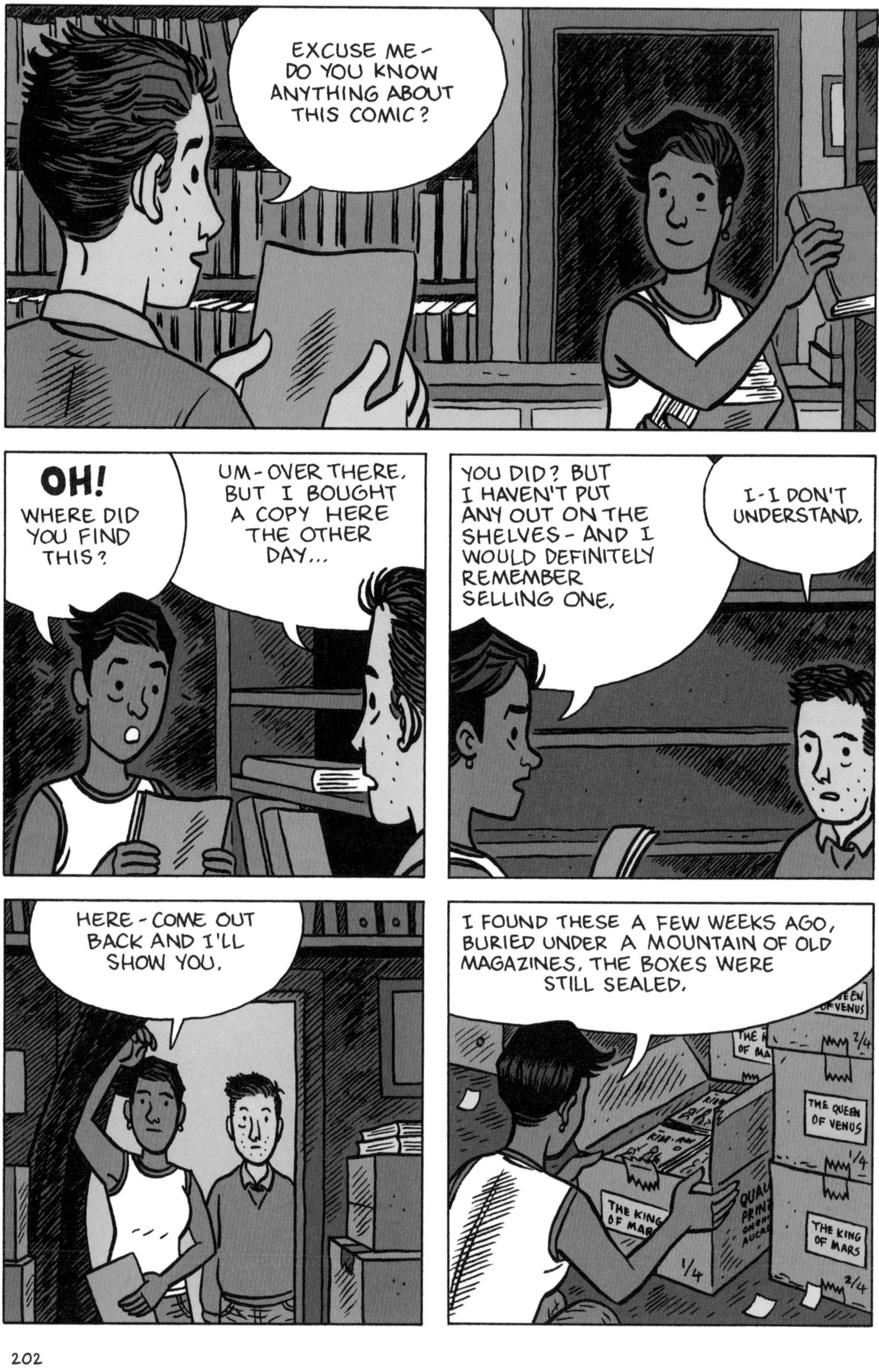
EXCUSE ME- DO YOU KNOW ANYTHING ABOUT THIS COMIC?
OH! WHERE DID YOU FIND THIS?
UM-OVER THERE. BUT I BOUGHT A COPY HERE THE OTHER DAY...
YOU DID? BUT I HAVEN'T PUT ANY OUT ON THE SHELVES- AND I WOULD DEFINITELY REMEMBER SELLING ONE.
I-I DON'T UNDERSTAND.
HERE-COME OUT BACK AND I'LL SHOW YOU.
I FOUND THESE A FEW WEEKS AGO, BURIED UNDER A MOUNTAIN OF OLD MAGAZINES. THE BOXES WERE STILL SEALED.
THE QUEEN OF VENUS
1/4
THE KING OF MARS
1/4
THE KING OF MARS
2/4

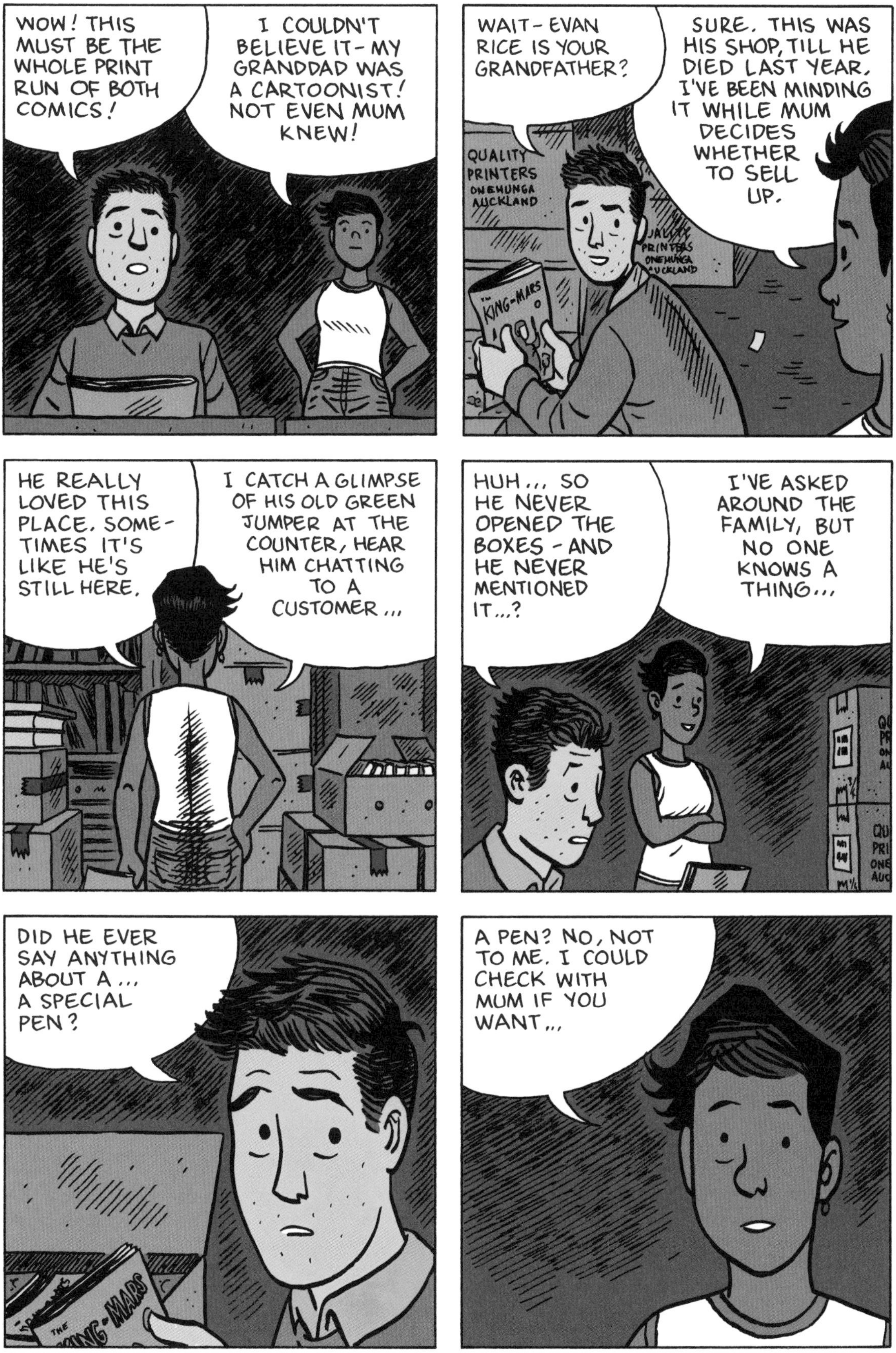
WOW! THIS MUST BE THE WHOLE PRINT RUN OF BOTH COMICS!
I COULDN'T BELIEVE IT- MY GRANDDAD WAS A CARTOONIST! NOT EVEN MUM KNEW!
WAIT- EVAN RICE IS YOUR GRANDFATHER?
SURE. THIS WAS HIS SHOP, TILL HE DIED LAST YEAR. I'VE BEEN MINDING IT WHILE MUM DECIDES WHETHER TO SELL UP.
QUALITY PRINTERS ONEHUNGA AUCKLAND
KING MARS
HE REALLY LOVED THIS PLACE. SOME-TIMES IT'S LIKE HE'S STILL HERE.
I CATCH A GLIMPSE OF HIS OLD GREEN JUMPER AT THE COUNTER, HEAR HIM CHATTING TO A CUSTOMER...
HUH... SO HE NEVER OPENED THE BOXES - AND HE NEVER MENTIONED IT...?
I'VE ASKED AROUND THE FAMILY, BUT NO ONE KNOWS A THING...
DID HE EVER SAY ANYTHING ABOUT A ... A SPECIAL PEN?
THE KING MARS
A PEN? NO, NOT TO ME. I COULD CHECK WITH MUM IF YOU WANT...

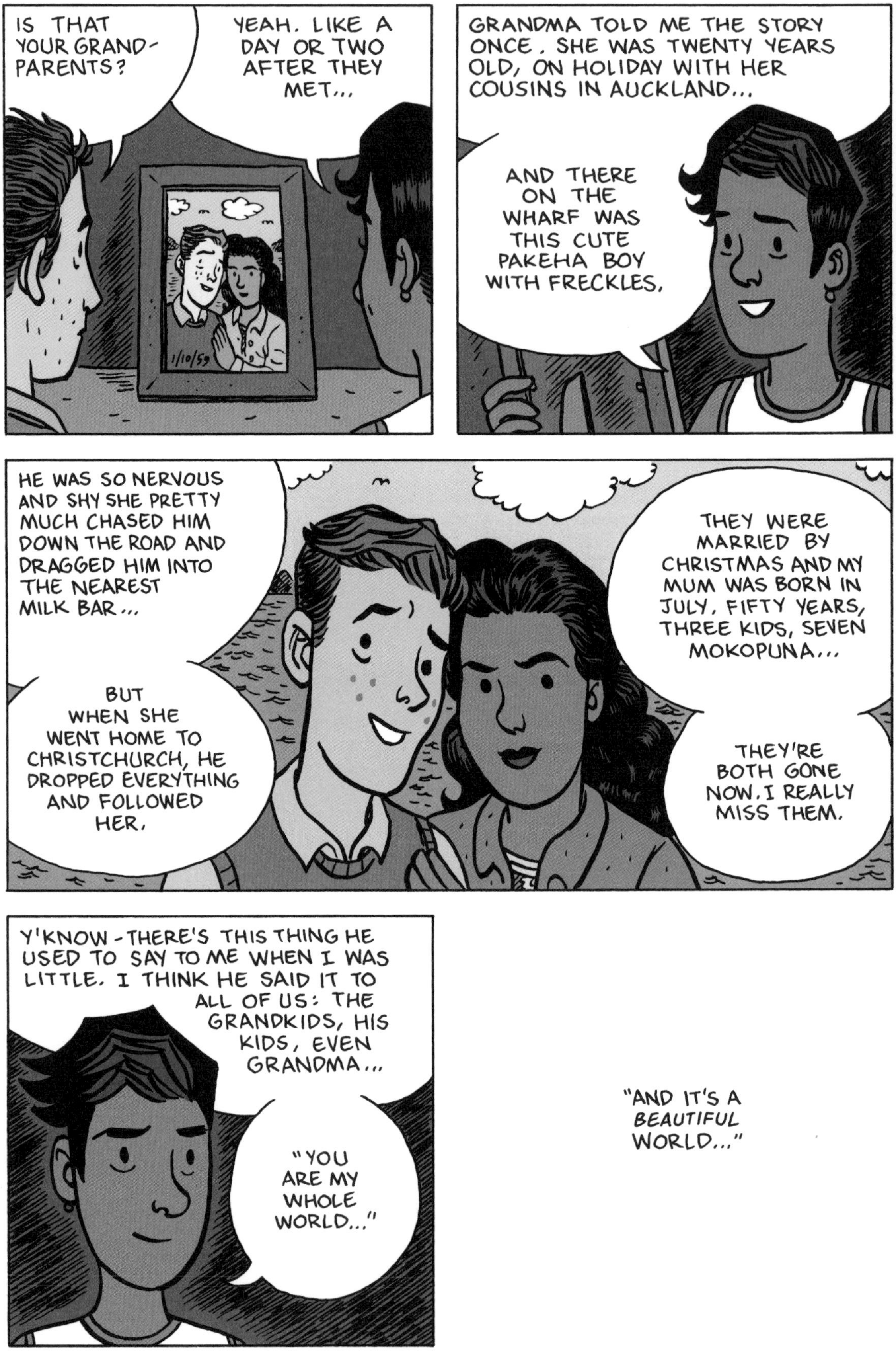
IS THAT YOUR GRAND-PARENTS?
YEAH. LIKE A DAY OR TWO AFTER THEY MET...
1/10/59
GRANDMA TOLD ME THE STORY ONCE. SHE WAS TWENTY YEARS OLD, ON HOLIDAY WITH HER COUSINS IN AUCKLAND...
AND THERE ON THE WHARF WAS THIS CUTE PAKEHA BOY WITH FRECKLES.
HE WAS SO NERVOUS AND SHY SHE PRETTY MUCH CHASED HIM DOWN THE ROAD AND DRAGGED HIM INTO THE NEAREST MILK BAR...
BUT WHEN SHE WENT HOME TO CHRISTCHURCH, HE DROPPED EVERYTHING AND FOLLOWED HER.
THEY WERE MARRIED BY CHRISTMAS AND MY MUM WAS BORN IN JULY. FIFTY YEARS, THREE KIDS, SEVEN MOKOPUNA...
THEY'RE BOTH GONE NOW. I REALLY MISS THEM.
Y'KNOW - THERE'S THIS THING HE USED TO SAY TO ME WHEN I WAS LITTLE. I THINK HE SAID IT TO ALL OF US: THE GRANDKIDS, HIS KIDS, EVEN GRANDMA...
"YOU ARE MY WHOLE WORLD..."
"AND IT'S A *BEAUTIFUL* WORLD..."

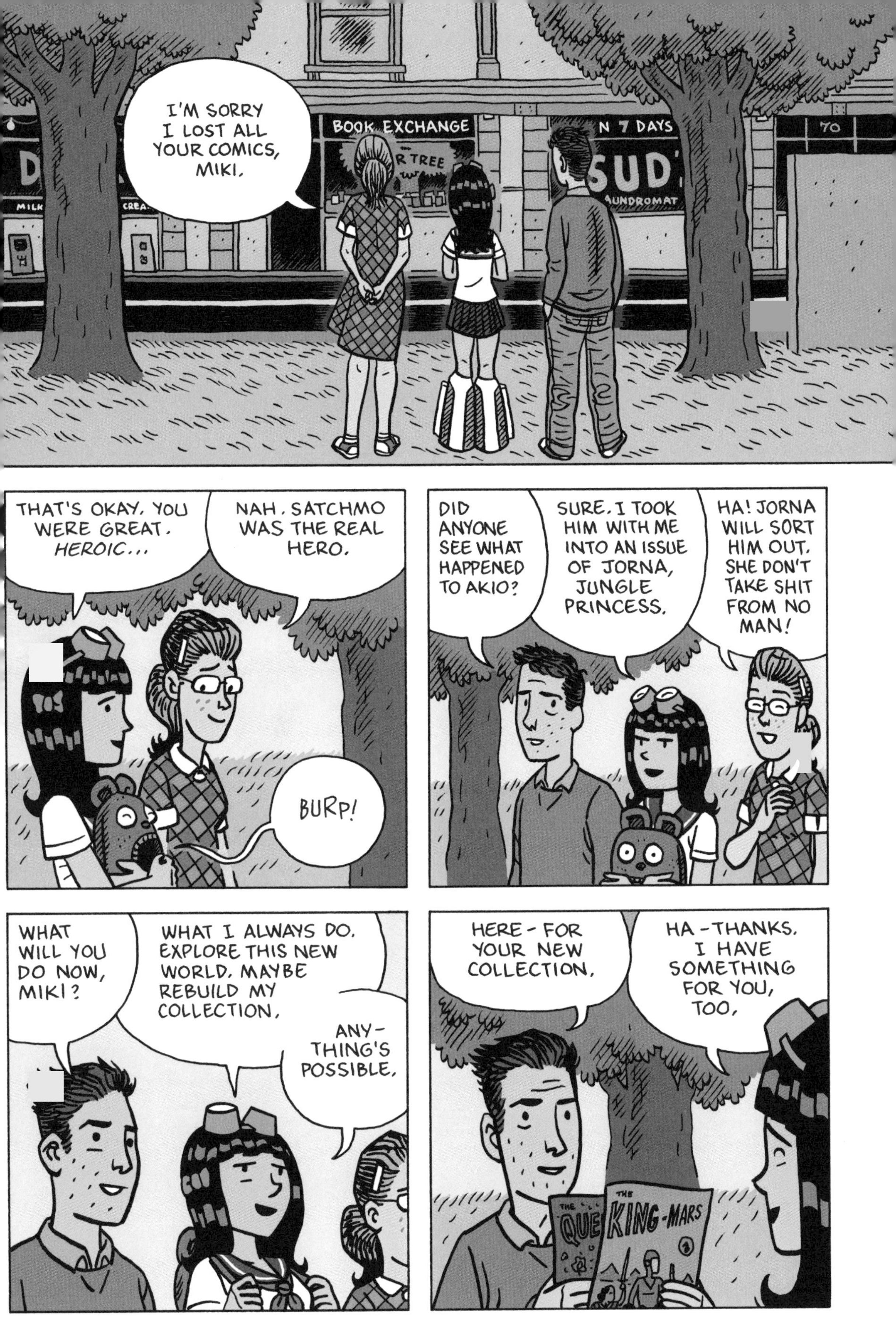
BOOK EXCHANGE
N 7 DAYS
SUD
AUNDROMAT
I'M SORRY I LOST ALL YOUR COMICS, MIKI.
THAT'S OKAY. YOU WERE GREAT. HEROIC...
NAH. SATCHMO WAS THE REAL HERO.
BURP!
DID ANYONE SEE WHAT HAPPENED TO AKIO?
SURE. I TOOK HIM WITH ME INTO AN ISSUE OF JORNA, JUNGLE PRINCESS.
HA! JORNA WILL SORT HIM OUT. SHE DON'T TAKE SHIT FROM NO MAN!
WHAT WILL YOU DO NOW, MIKI?
WHAT I ALWAYS DO. EXPLORE THIS NEW WORLD. MAYBE REBUILD MY COLLECTION.
ANY-THING'S POSSIBLE.
HERE - FOR YOUR NEW COLLECTION.
HA - THANKS. I HAVE SOMETHING FOR YOU, TOO.
THE KING-MARS

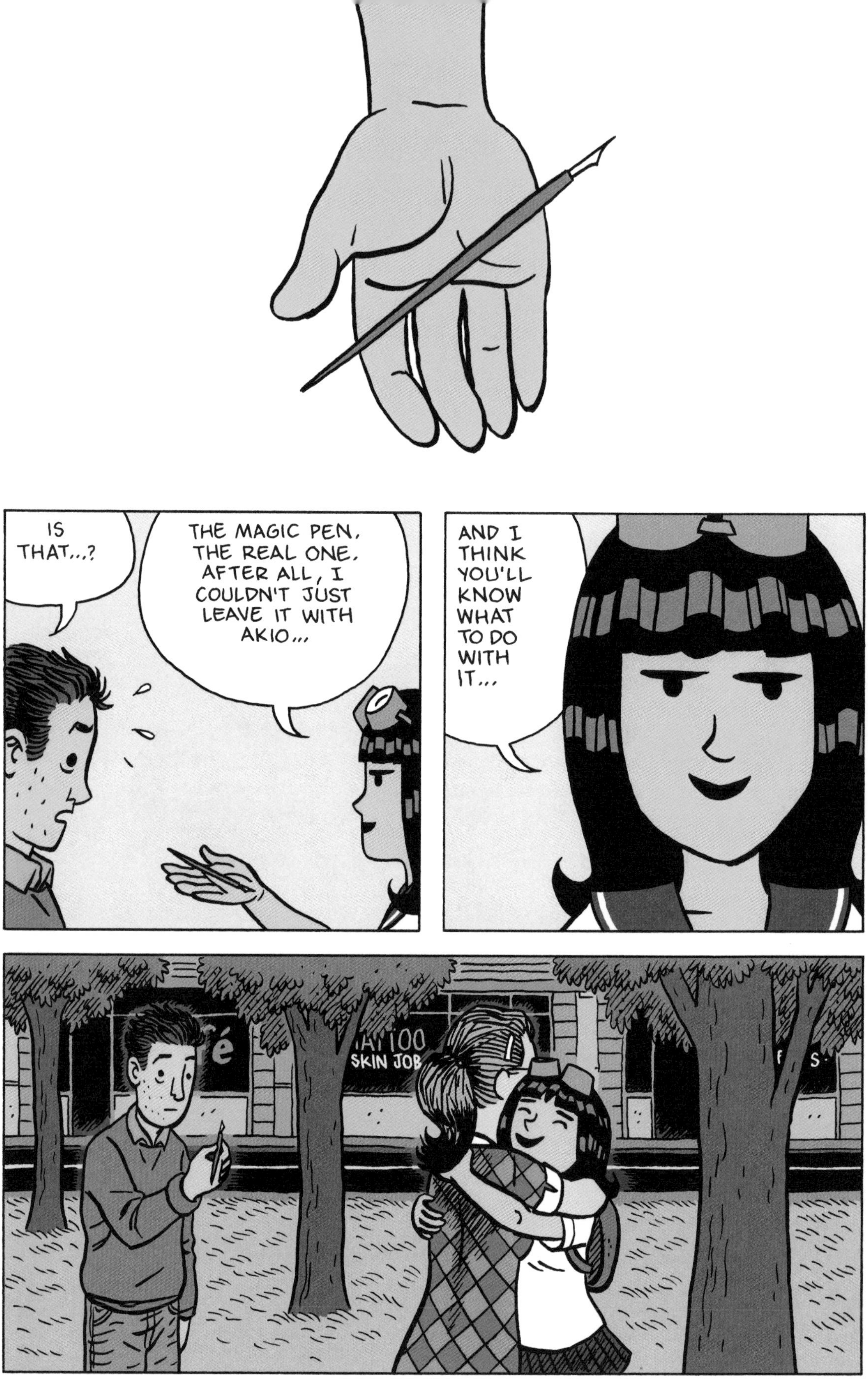
IS THAT...?
THE MAGIC PEN. THE REAL ONE. AFTER ALL, I COULDN'T JUST LEAVE IT WITH AKIO...
AND I THINK YOU'LL KNOW WHAT TO DO WITH IT...
SKIN JOB

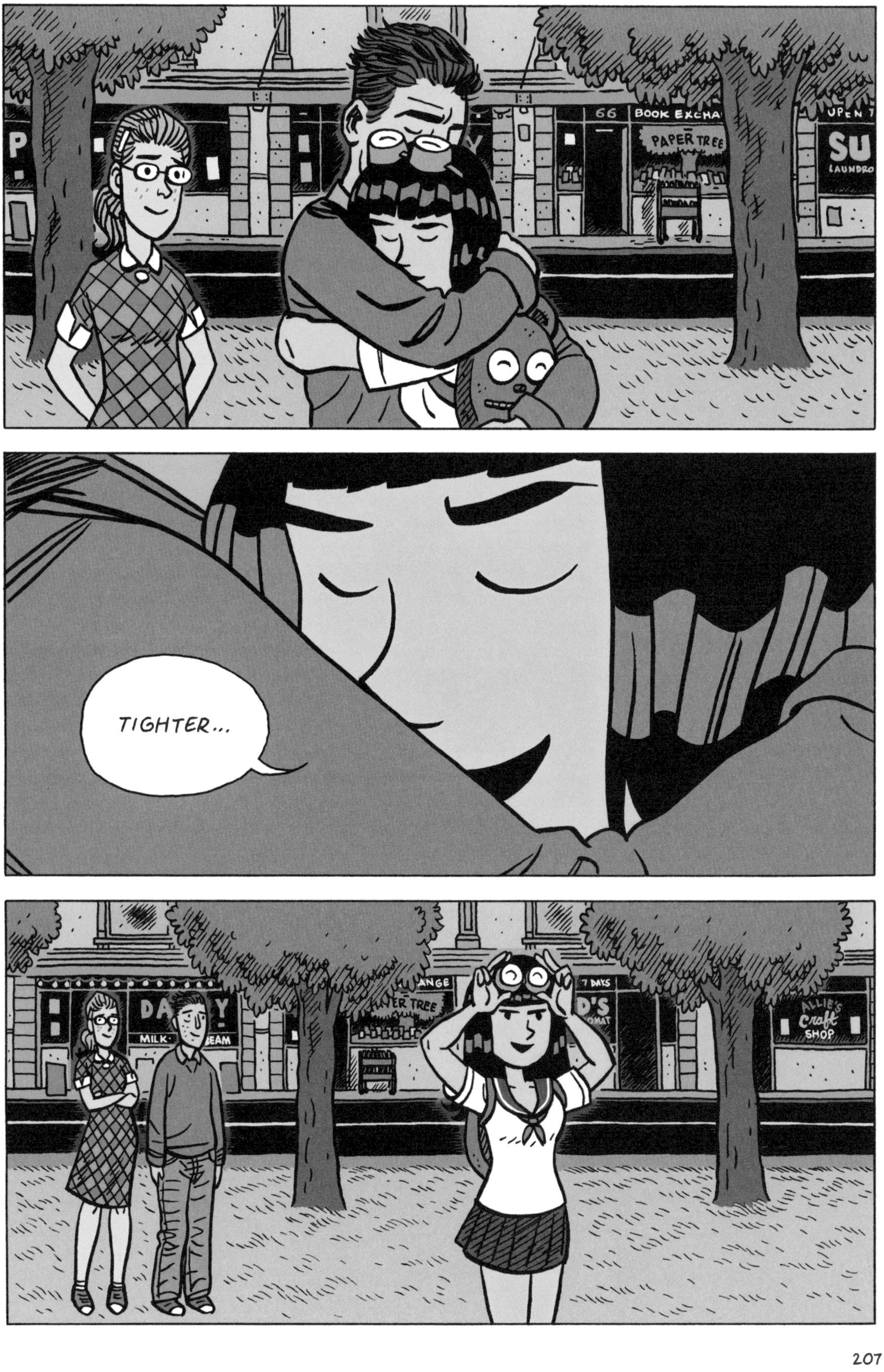
66
BOOK EXCHA
PAPER TREE
LAUNDRO
TIGHTER...
MILK
ANGE
7 DAYS
ALLIE'S Craft SHOP

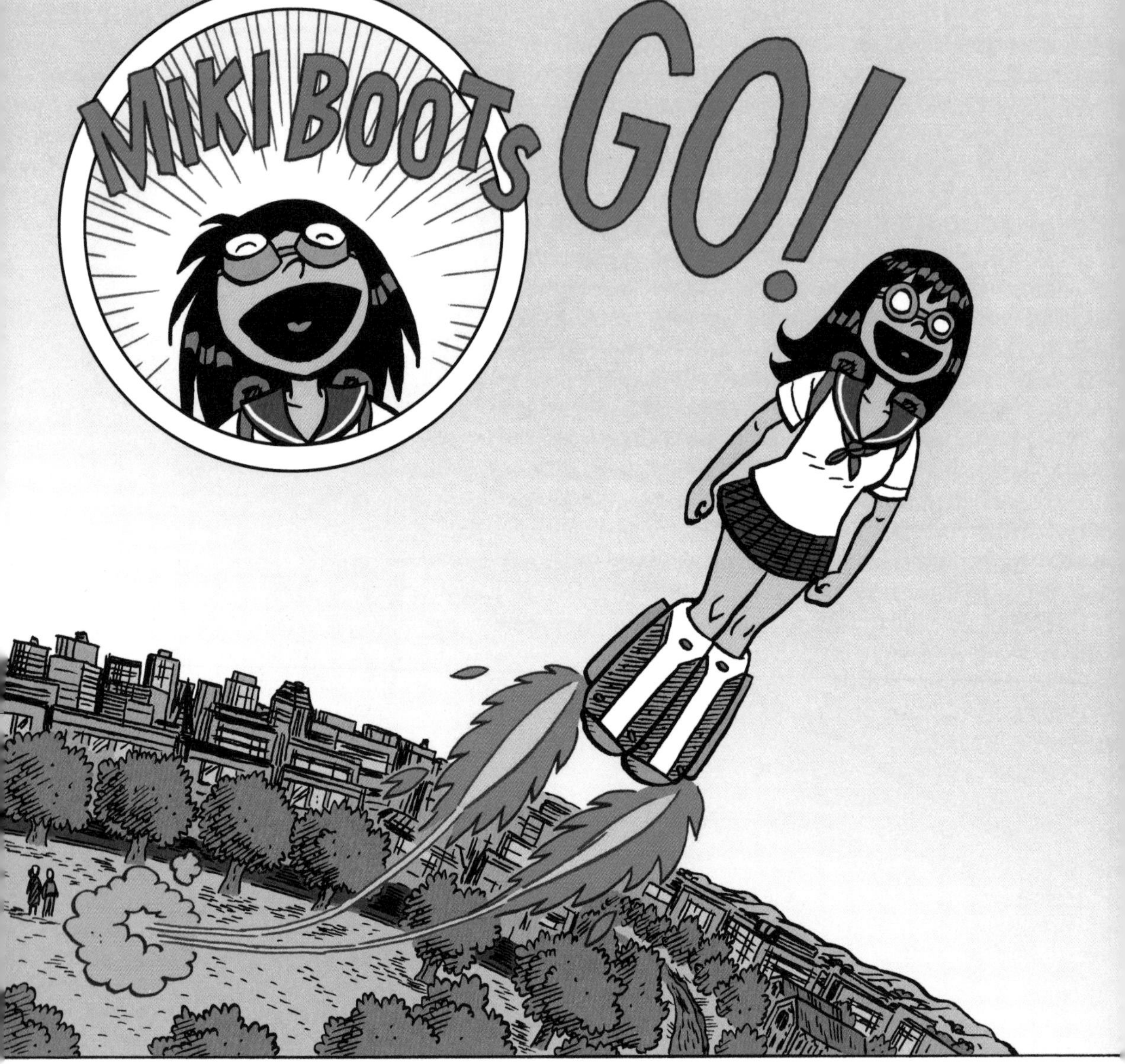
MIKI BOOTS GO!

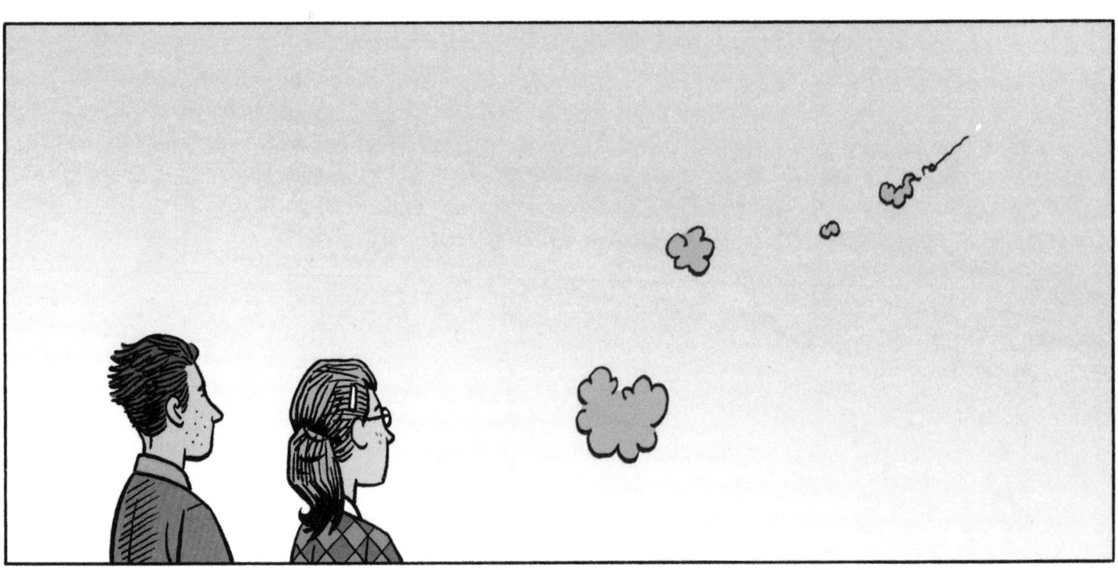

Epilogue

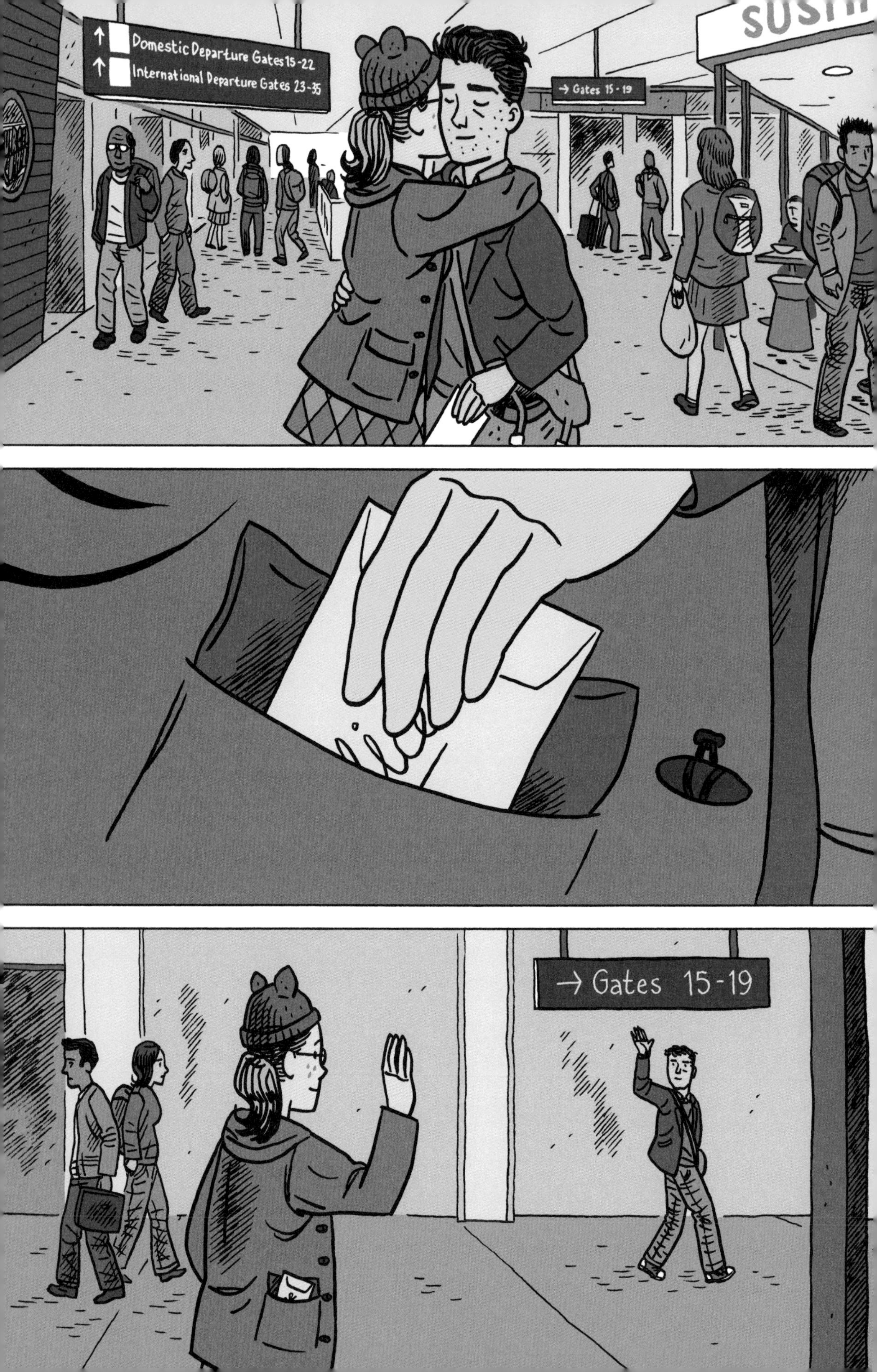

Domestic Departure Gates 15-22
International Departure Gates 23-35
→ Gates 15-19
SUSHI
→ Gates 15-19

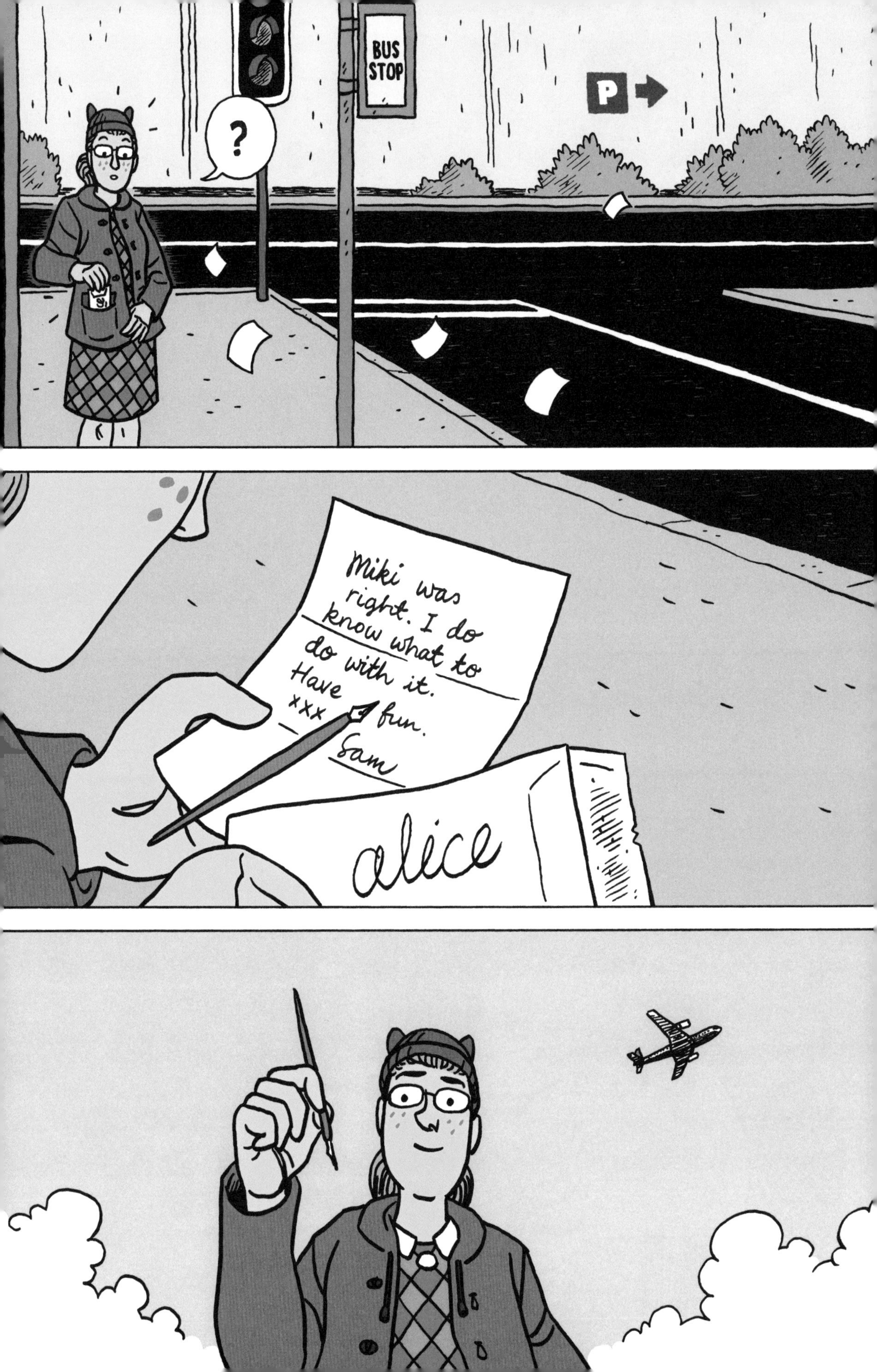
BUS STOP
P
?
Miki was right. I do know what to do with it. Have fun.
xxx
Sam
alice

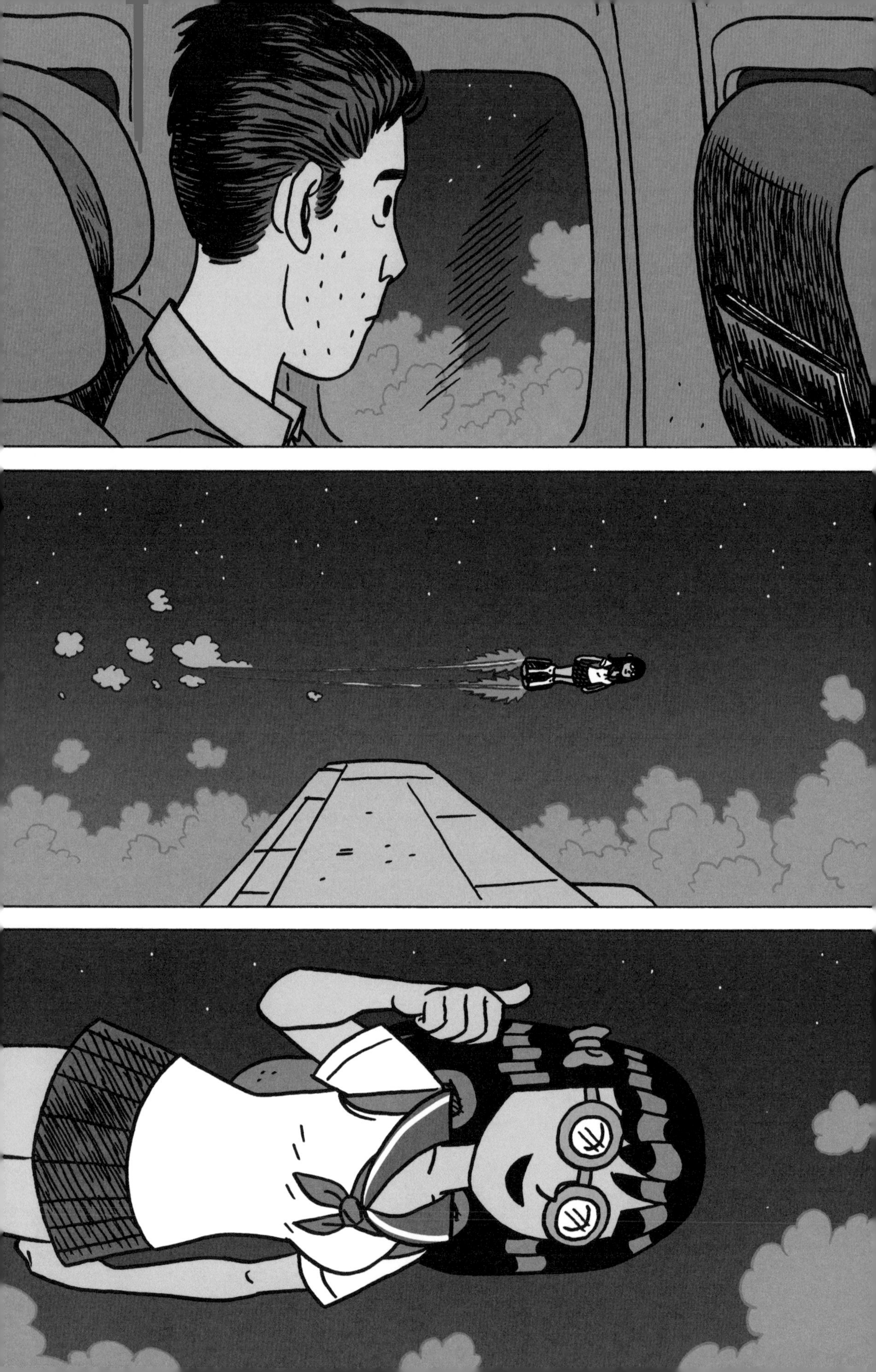

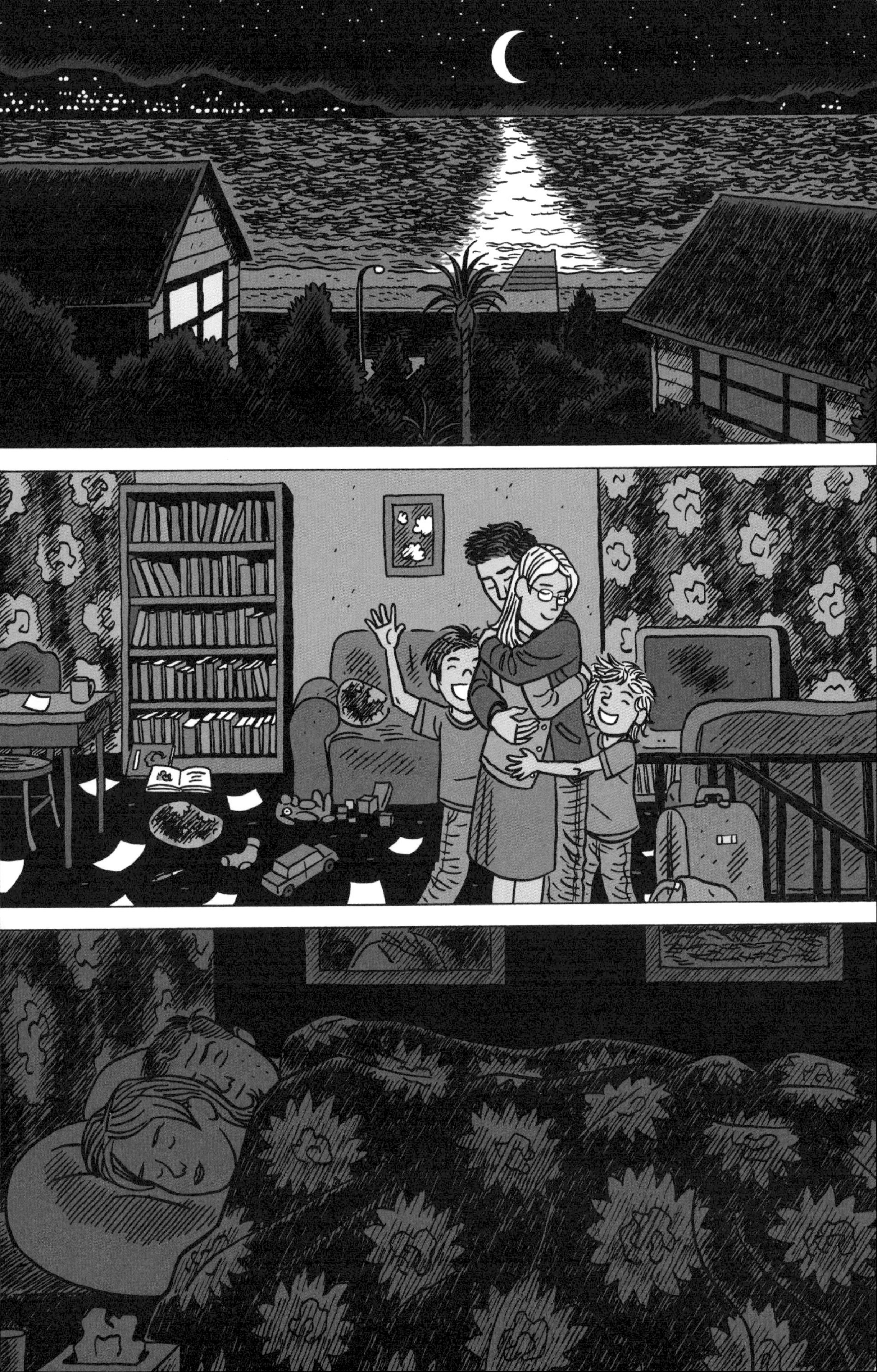

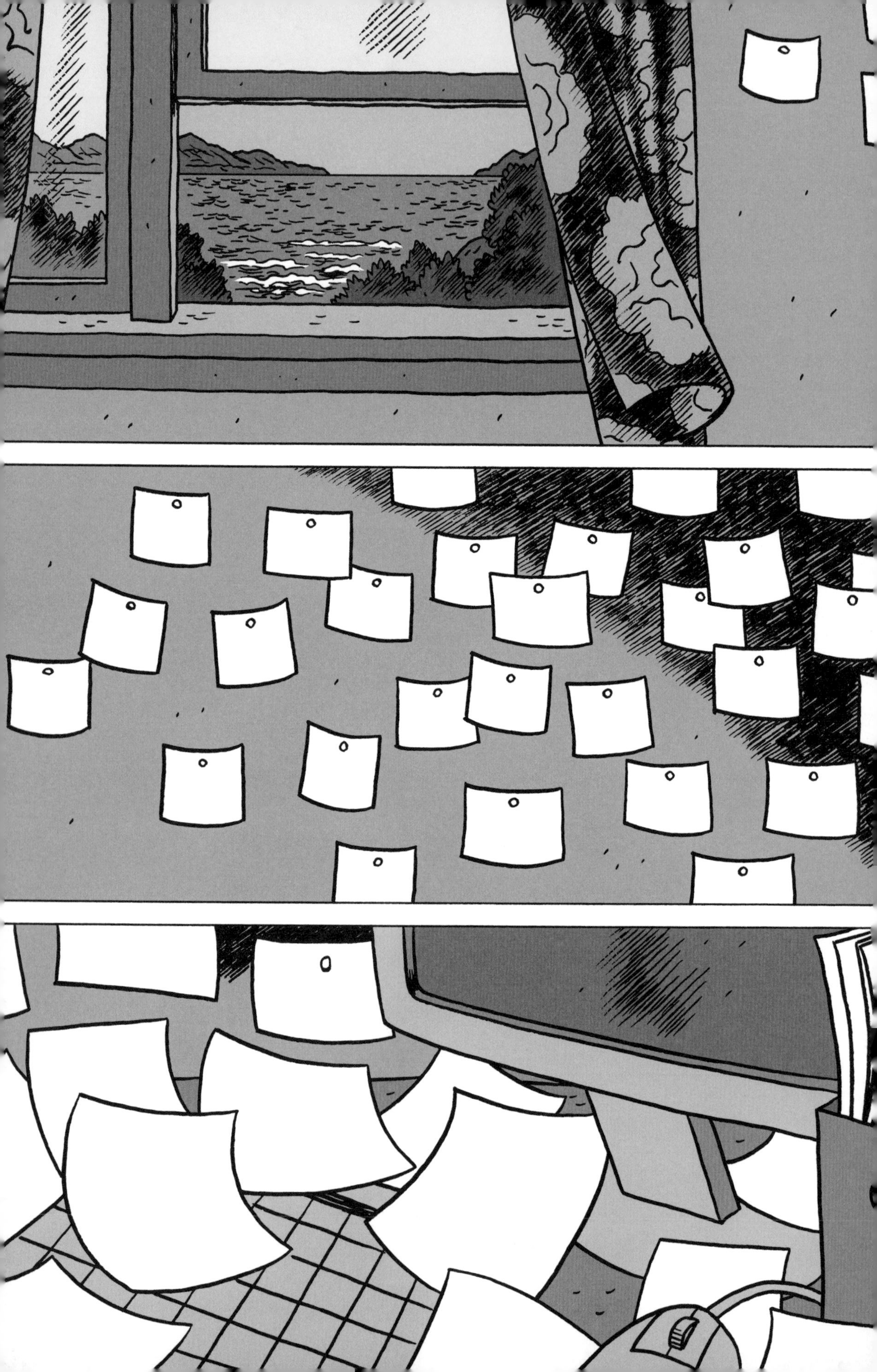

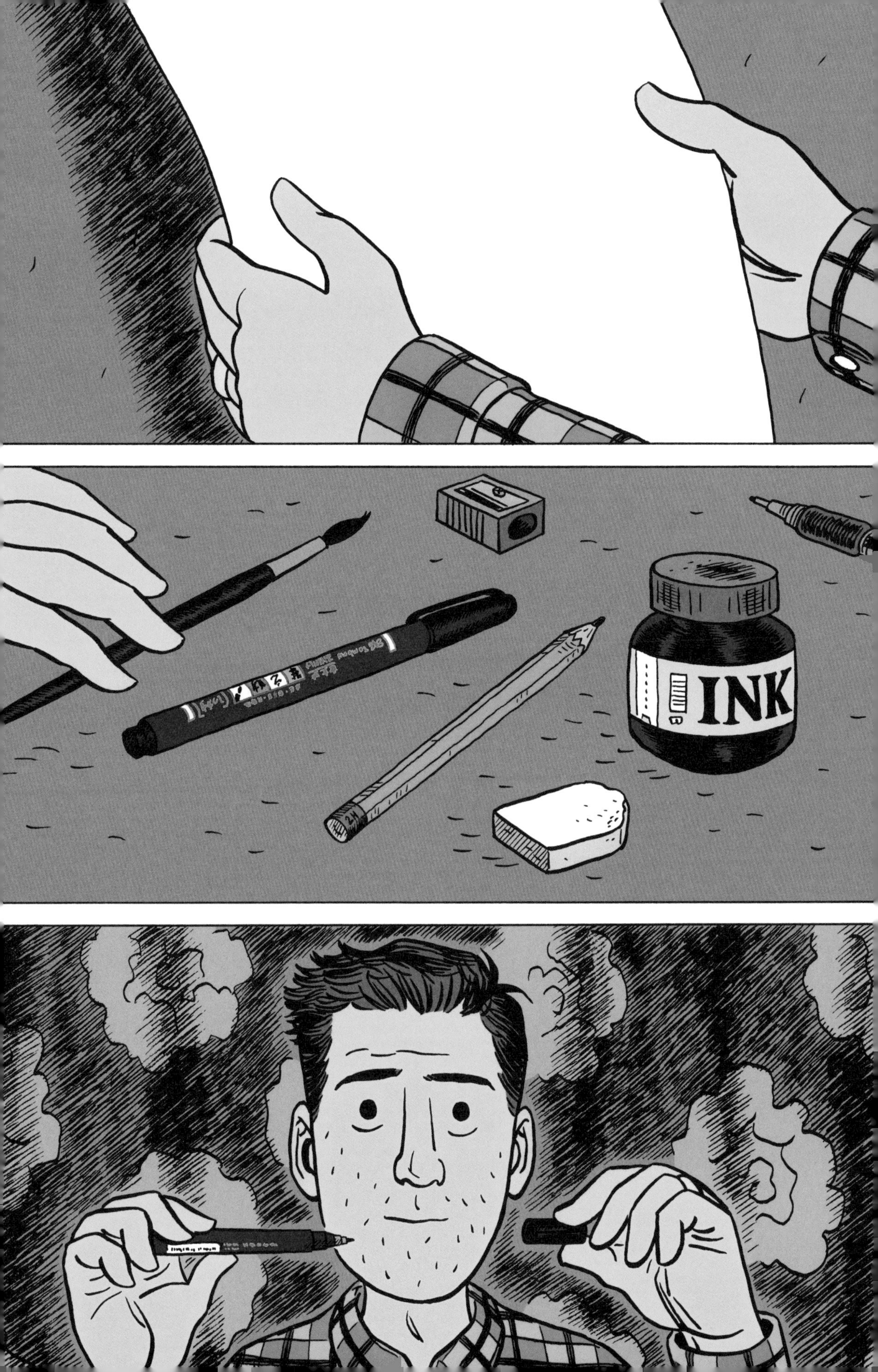
INK

Notes

Page 1:

"IN DREAMS BEGINS RESPONSIBILITY":
This line appears as an epigraph,
enigmatically attributed to "The Old Play,"
in William Butler Yeats' *Responsibilities
and Other Poems* (1916).

"DESIRE HAS NO MORALITY": Nina
Hartley, on *Sex Out Loud with Tristan
Taormino*, January 4, 2013 (online at
www.voiceamerica.com/episode/66534/adult-
film-legend-nina-hartley): "Desire has no
morality. Behavior, of course, has morality,
and actions have moral weight. But liking
what you like and wanting what you want
have no moral weight to me."

Page 8:

Sam is looking at the artrenewal.org,
the website of the Art Renewal Center,
a rather eccentric movement dedicated
to undoing the modern art revolution
of the past 100 years. In addition to
publishing manifestos such as 'The 20th
Century Art Scam' and 'Abstract Art is
Not Abstract and Definitely Not Art,' the
website serves as a vast and labyrinthine
online museum of pre-Modernist and
academic art. The painting referenced on
this page is John William Godward's *A
Quiet Pet* (1906).

Page 10:

This page is based on *In the Tepidarium*
(1913) by John William Godward and *Le
Crepuscule* (often called 'Evening Mood')
(1882) by William Bouguereau.

Page 11:

This page is based on *Nymphes et Satyre*
(1873) by William Bouguereau.

Page 34:

LITERATURE IN THE 21ST CENTURY:
In 2003 I attended a conference in
Christchurch on creative writing in New
Zealand in the 21st century, organized by
Prof. Mark Williams. I contributed a talk
that was later published (in somewhat
more coherent form) as 'Perfect Planet:
Comics, Games and World-Building,' in
*Writing at the Edge of the Universe:
Essays from the 'Creative Writing in
New Zealand' Conference, University of
Canterbury, August 2003* (ed. Mark
Williams, Canterbury University Press,
2004). My essay is also online at www.
hicksville.co.nz/PerfectPlanet.htm

The speaker in panel 2 is Prof. Patrick
Evans, delivering his paper 'On Originality:
No Earth Tones,' which can also be found
in *Writing at the Edge of the Universe.*

Page 39:

WHOVIAN: A "Whovian" is a fan of
Doctor Who (the BBC TV series). I
assume everyone knows who Harry Potter
is....

Page 41:

DR. BOLLINGER'S BIG BOOK OF KIWI
COMICS: Dr. Tim Bollinger is a New
Zealand cartoonist and historian, whose
research into the history of New Zealand
comics has uncovered many long-forgotten
treasures.

Page 42:

CACKLING KEAS: The kea is an endemic
New Zealand parrot, known for its
intelligence, curiosity, and mischievousness.

TUMBLING TUATARAS: The tuatara

is an endemic New Zealand reptile, the only surviving member of the order Rhynchocephalia, which flourished 200 million years ago.

KING DICK'S BEARD: Richard "King Dick" Seddon was prime minister of New Zealand between 1893 and 1906.

TARAWERA ON A TUESDAY: On June 10, 1886 (actually a Thursday, so Captain Rose clearly has his days mixed up), the volcano Mount Tarawera erupted, killing more than a hundred people, burying many Māori villages, and destroying one of New Zealand's most famous tourist attractions, the Pink and White Terraces.

Page 45:

KIWI COMICS: The kiwi is an endemic New Zealand flightless bird that also serves as a national symbol. "Kiwi" has become a popular synonym for New Zealander.

Page 51:

OTAKU: "Otaku" is a Japanese term that has come to mean an obsessive fan of manga and anime.

Page 89:

MARK IV RUTHERFORD ATOMIC RAYGUN: Captain Rose's raygun is named for Ernest Rutherford, a New Zealand-born physicist and chemist who was the first to "split the atom" in 1917.

AKE AKE AKE: This is a Māori war cry, from the words Rewi Maniapoto (Ngāti Paretekawa) cried at the Battle of Ōrākau in 1864 when called on to surrender: "Ka whawhai tonu mātou, Ake! Ake! Ake!" (We will fight on for ever and ever!)" Variations on the cry have been used ever since by New Zealand (especially Māori) soldiers and sportspeople. During World War Two, the Māori Battalion of the New Zealand Army adopted the war cry "Ake ake kia kaha e!" (Be strong for ever and ever!) from the battalion song, composed in 1940 by Corporal Anaia Amohau.

Page 90:

PHAR LAP: Phar Lap was a famous New Zealand racehorse (1926-1932), also known as "Big Red," "Wonder Horse," "Bobby," and "Big Terror." Even today, New Zealanders and Australians argue over which country can claim Phar Lap as theirs.

PUCKAROOED: "Puckarooed" is New Zealand slang for totally broken, ruined, beyond repair; a corruption of the Māori word "pakaru" (smashed, shattered, broken).

HINEMOA'S CALABASH: The legend of Hinemoa is one of New Zealand's most celebrated love stories. Hinemoa was a beautiful maiden who swam across Lake Rotorua to Mokoia Island one night to join her lover Tutanekai, guided in the darkness by the sound of his flute. She stayed afloat by tying six empty calabashes to her body.

Page 91:

HILLARY'S ROPES: In 1953, New Zealand mountaineer Sir Edmund Hillary and the Nepalese Sherpa Tenzing Norgay became the first climbers confirmed to have reached the summit of Mount Everest. During their descent, Hillary and Norgay met with fellow climber George Lowe, to whom Hillary spoke his famous words: "Well, George, we knocked the bastard off." Today, Hillary's face appears on the New Zealand five-dollar bill.

MARAUDING MOAS: The moa was a flightless bird native to New Zealand. It has been extinct for about 500 years. The largest moa grew to around 3 m. (nearly 10 ft.) in height, with neck outstretched, and weighed over 200 kg. (500 pounds).

Page 93:

TE KOOTI'S CHAINS: Te Kooti Arikirangi Te Turuki (Rongowhakaata) was a Māori prophet, religious leader, and warrior who fought against the colonial government between 1868 and 1872. He founded the Ringatū religion in 1868 while exiled on the Chatham Islands, and his dramatic escape, along with 168 other prisoners, became the stuff of legend.

WARBLING WEKAS: The weka is a native New Zealand flightless bird, known for its boldness and propensity to steal food and valuables from unwary campers.

GALAVANTING GECKOS: New Zealand is home to numerous native gecko species, some of which are very rare and all of which are fully protected by law. One extinct species grew as long as 60 cm. (24 in.).

Page 95:

TAIHAPE: Taihape (population of 1,788 in 2006) is a farming town in the Rangitikei District in the North Island of New Zealand, known as "the Gumboot Capital of the World."

TRESPASSING TAPUS: In Māori culture, "tapu" denotes a state of sacredness (i.e., protected by a complex system of restrictions and prohibitions). Rose is using the word here as synonymous with the English word "taboo" (which dates back to Captain James Cook's encounter with the Polynesian concept of tapu in the late eighteenth century).

Page 97:

TREMBLING TANIWHAS: In Māori mythology, the taniwha is a protective guardian creature, often depicted as a monster and usually associated with a particular place.

WAILING WAHINES: Wahine is a Māori word for woman, female, lady, or wife.

Page 104:

THE BREATH OF LIFE: It's worth noting here the Māori concept "tihei mauri ora," the sneeze of life.

Page 102:

PENNIES AND SHILLINGS: In the 1950s New Zealand's strict currency controls meant that visiting American sailors often relied on locals willing to trade local money for US dollars or foreign goods.

Page 109:

HERE WITH THE NAVY IN '43: During World War Two, New Zealand was an important base for the US military

fighting in the Pacific.

Page 123:

COMICS COMPULSION: Comics Compulsion has been Christchurch's friendly local comic store for over twenty years. Until 2011, it was located on Manchester Street, where the store's awning sign had long been cursed with a conspicuous typographical error. But after the devastating earthquake in February of that year, the central city was cordoned off and Comics Compulsion was forced to move. Their new location is in Papanui (now with correctly spelled signage).

Page 128:

RANGINUI'S TEARS: In the Māori creation story, Ranginui, the Sky Father, was forcibly separated from his lover Papatūānuku, the Earth Mother, by their children, the gods, who were tired of being crushed in darkness between their parents' constantly entangled bodies. In his grief, Ranginui's tears now fall onto the earth below as rain.

Page 134:

TOWERING TOTARAS: The totara is a New Zealand endemic tree that grows tall and strong.

Page 135:

KATE SHEPPARD'S RIBBON: In 1893, New Zealand became the first country in the world to grant women the vote in national elections, after a campaign led by the suffragist Kate Sheppard. Sheppard also served as the president of the New Zealand Council of Women, editing the council's newspaper, *The White Ribbon*, and eloquently promoting full legal and social equality for women. Today, Sheppard's portrait appears on the New Zealand ten-dollar note.

Page 138:

TE RAUPARAHA'S GHOST: Te Rauparaha was a rangatira and war chief of the Ngāti Toa iwi, who rose to prominence during the Musket Wars of the early to mid-19th century. Around 1820, Te Rauparaha composed the famous "Ka Mate" haka, after a narrow escape from pursuing enemies. Today his haka is performed by many New Zealand sports teams, including the All Blacks.

THE OTAGO GOLD RUSH: The discovery of significant gold deposits in New Zealand's South Island in the early 1860s led to a massive influx of fortune-hunters and the rapid growth of semi-lawless prospector towns that lasted several years.

Page 151:

CARTOON PHYSICS: This is a term I first encountered in *Toon*, a role-playing game created by Greg Costikyan and Warren Spector (first published in 1984 by Steve Jackson Games).

Page 153:

THE LAND OF COCKAYGNE: Cockaygne is a mythical land of plenty, celebrated in medieval art and folklore, including the 14th-century Kildare Poems.

JESS FRANCO: Jess Franco was a Spanish film-maker whose many films include *Vampyros Lesbos, Nuns in Madness,* and *Love Letters of a Portuguese Nun.*

Page 157:

THE BATTLE OF PASSCHENDAELE: The Allied forces launched an offensive around the Flemish village of Passchendaele in July 1917 during the First World War. The number of casualties remains disputed, but it is certainly higher than 400,000.

Page 167:

HENTAI: Hentai is a genre of manga and anime that features explicit, often "perverse" or "bizarre," sexuality.

Page 204:

PĀKEHĀ: Māori term for New Zealanders of European descent.

MOKOPUNA: Māori term for grandchildren.

Page 215:

The pen Sam uses here is the Tombow GCD-111, with which most of this book was drawn.

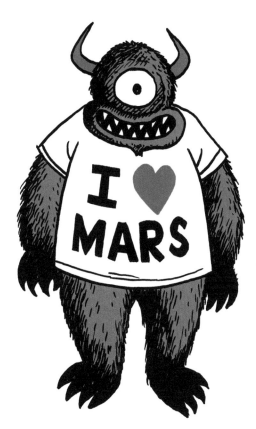

DYLAN HORROCKS
was born in 1966 and lives in Auckland, New Zealand.
He is the author of the graphic novel *Hicksville*,
the story collection *Incomplete Works*,
and the comic book series *Pickle* and *Atlas*.
He has also written *Batgirl* for DC Comics
and *Hunter: the Age of Magic* for Vertigo.
hicksvillecomics.com

to everyone who has offered encouragement, advice and support while I worked on
this book: friends, family, cartoonists, writers, artists and readers, online commenters,
retweeters, interviewers, teachers, students, librarians and retailers.

Particular thanks go to:

my agent Nicolas Grivel: cheerleader, champion, magician
Fergus Barrowman and Eric Reynolds, for enthusiastic editorial expertise
Sophie Dumas, Jonathan King and Abe Horrocks, for generous colouring help
Dalton Webb, for expert fontographic assistance
Chris Oliveros and Tom Devlin, who published the first 2 chapters in *Atlas*
Creative New Zealand Toi Aotearoa, for their financial support
Roger Horrocks and Mike Dickison, for setting me straight on the 1950s and moa
Scott McCloud, Alison Bechdel and Craig Thompson, for wise words at crucial moments,
and extremely generous words at the end

Simone Horrocks, for suggesting I tell this story in the first place
and Megan Kelso, who told me not to be afraid

my close friends and extended family: arohanui

and, above all:
Terry, Louis and Abe.
You are my whole world.
And it's a beautiful world.

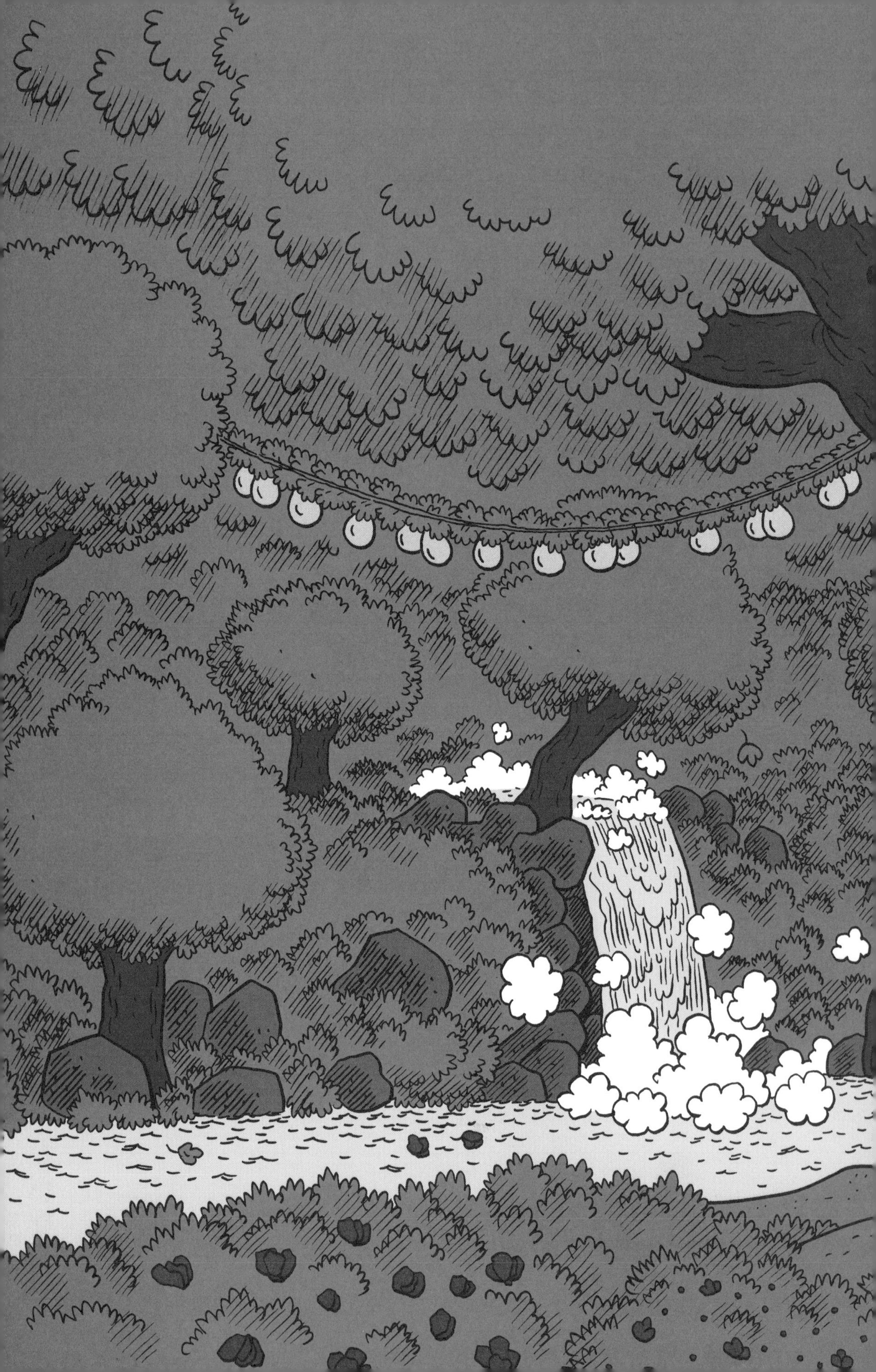